JN446850

# Collaborative Governance in East Asia

## Evolution Towards Multi-stakeholder Partnerships

Edited by

Sook Jong Lee
Rosa Minhyo Cho
Hyung Jun Park
Sung Min Park

Daeyoung Moonhwasa Publishing Company
Gyeonggi-do, Republic of Korea

# Collaborative Governance in East Asia

## Evolution Towards Multi-stakeholder Partnerships

Edited by

Sook Jong Lee
Rosa Minhyo Cho
Hyung Jun Park
Sung Min Park

Copyright © 2020 by Sook Jong Lee, Rosa Minhyo Cho,
Hyung Jun Park, and Sung Min Park
All rights reserved.
No part of this book may be reproduced without the
permission of the authors and the publisher.

**ISBN** 978-89-7644-765-4
**Published by** Choon Hwan Lim
Daeyoung Moonhwasa Publishing Co.
307ho Wooshin Plaza, 70 Juhwa-ro, Ilsanseo-gu, Goyang-si,
Gyeonggi-do, Korea, 10387
**TEL** (031) 913-3062, (031) 914-3884~5
**FAX** (031) 913-3839
Hompage http://www.dymbook.co.kr
**Published on July 10, 2020**

***Price*** **KRW 25,000**

This work was supported by the Ministry of Education of the Republic of Korea and the National Research Foundation of Korea (NRF-2016S1A3A2924832)

# Acknowledgements

In public administration and public policy studies, collaborative governance has become a buzzword as complex, modern social problems demand greater cooperative efforts and collective intelligence from both public and private sector stakeholders. Despite the rise in research on collaborative governance, however, there has been a dearth of related studies on East Asian countries. This book aims to fill this gap and inspire comparative studies that attempt to understand how the region is coping with the increasing challenges of managing social problems.

The role of government in public governance has been recognized as a strong one in East Asia due to the state-led development of many countries in the region and the historical legacy of meritocratic bureaucracy intervening in social issues. However, several contributing factors have weakened the effectiveness of top-down rational planning and policy implementation, especially that of central governments, over the last few decades. First, contemporary social problems and public issues are often poorly predicted and diagnosed by bureaucracies. Natural disasters and pandemic diseases are good examples. The current COVID-19 pandemic has changed our lives dramatically, revealing which countries have the resiliency and effective public-private cooperation necessary to win the fight against this deadly virus. The second factor is the limited resources and authority of central governments. Most public programs related to the environment, transportation, and education are locally implemented. Central governments are too far removed to grasp the issues of local communities, while local governments have better information and resources that they can mobilize. Power devolution from central to local governments is an ongoing process in East Asia as the principle of subsidiarity gains wider acceptance. The third is the increasing demand for citizen participation in the public policy process. Increasing awareness of citizen rights in governing a country are driving more people to express their opinions, organize their interests, and demand representation in the policy decision-making process. Democratization is certainly contributing to this awareness and increased digital connectivity aids people to participate. Many public programs face difficulty in the implementation phase if civil society organizations or local resident groups are not properly consulted. Many governments have provided participatory mechanisms to allow policy input from citizens in order to improve policy effectiveness and legitimacy.

The demand for public-private collaboration tends to be higher in places with a greater number of social conflicts. In this sense, conflict and collaboration are two sides of the same coin in governance studies. In order to understand social conflict and develop a dynamic and resilient collaboration model, several scholars at Sungkyunkwan University's Graduate School of Governance launched a series of research papers with funding from the National Research Foundation of South Korea. This research network quickly expanded to include fourteen professors and post-doctoral researchers from eight universities. In order to understand how citizens view social problems, take action to resolve them, and rate their government conflict management systems, the East Asia Collaboration Center (EACC) inside Sungkyunkwan University conducted surveys in 2018 and 2019 in the five East Asian countries of Indonesia, Japan, South Korea, Taiwan, and Thailand. Two chapters of this book are dedicated to analyzing this survey data. This book itself is also part of the Center's collective research efforts. We invited several East Asian scholars working on collaborative governance in East Asia to contribute to this book. The initial workshop to facilitate our collaboration was held on Jeju Island in South Korea from August 21 to 23 in 2019. We invited more scholars from the network of the Asian Association for Public Administration to contribute, and ultimately were able to include eleven chapters written by scholars from China, Indonesia, Japan, the Philippines, South Korea, Taiwan, and Thailand in this book.

The chapters are divided into three parts for the sake of convenience as they address some overlapping problems. In Part I, Lee and Kim's chapter reveals the interesting finding that people who have participated in public conflict resolution attempts with their government are discouraged from participating in similar future attempts. Further study is needed into why engaging with the government to solve social conflict has such a negative impact on the willingness of the public to participate in conflict resolution. Ugaddan, Yang, and Park find that people who feel positively about their government's conflict management methods are also less likely to perceive that they are in conflict with the government. They also find that trust in government has a significant moderating effect on this relationship. Yoo and Cho's chapter compares the deliberative polling that was introduced in Japan and South Korea on nuclear energy policy. They argue that while both polls were meant to encourage citizen participation in reducing the number of nuclear power plants, they had different, limited impacts as they lacked the legal grounds necessary for enforcement.

Part II contains examples of collaborative governance at the local government level. Brillantes Jr. and Ruiz introduce several successful cases of local government programs in the Philippines. They identify leadership, public participation, multisectoral cooperation, media and information dissemination, and support from international institutions as the major factors supporting innovative collaborative governance. Situating the collaborative governance framework on the relations between local governments and residents, Kikuchi's chapter examines a new waste management system that resulted from improved collaboration between the two. He argues that new policy tools such as evidence-based policy making, which helps the public make informed decisions, and randomized control trials, which allow for more effective evaluation of policy impacts, are contributing to the collaborative participation of community residents in recycling programs run by local governments. The chapter by Lee, Cho, and Park analyzes the Korean energy policy making interaction between central government ministries, local governments, public enterprises, and civil society leaders. They argue that energy governance among these multiple stakeholders has evolved from a hierarchical form to a participatory form that provides more space for local governments and civil society leaders. Nonetheless, they point out that policy coordination among ministries and trust building between public and private stakeholders necessary for successful collaborative governance are still lacking. The chapter by Sun, Lin, and Phan offers an interesting analysis of how the views individuals hold towards democracy affect their attitudes regarding a local placemaking program in Taiwan. They identify five democratic subjectivities using a Q methodology.

Part Ⅲ addresses inter-governmental or inter-agency collaborative governance. The two chapters on Chinese collaborative governance both focus on the cooperation patterns of local governments through the lens of collective action theory. The chapter by Wu, Liu, Chen, and Qin examines the collaborative governance mechanisms to prevent and control air pollution in the Yangtze River Delta. They highlight both the structural mechanism of gathering the relevant actors and providing a platform for information sharing, decision-making, implementation, and evaluation as well as the procedural mechanism of determining tasks, formulating specific programs, promoting policy implementation, and ensuring the effectiveness of each policy. They argue that China needs to further develop its procedural mechanism by building trust between local governments. Suo, Kan, Ma, and Chen analyze the bilateral agreements of eight provincial governments in the Pan Pearl River Delta region, dividing them into four groups using the two criteria of willingness to cooperate and risk of cooperation. They find that many local governments view cooperation with other local governments as risky, even as the majority intend to cooperate. Prasojo and Abubakar examine collaborative governance among the law enforcement agencies of Indonesia in prosecuting corruption. Comparing the strategies of cooperation, competition, conflict, non-use of cooperation, and the absence of relationship, they find that non-use of cooperation is the dominant relationship type, and conclude that this is due to the institutional design which maximizes each agency's authority to combat corruption. Kamolvej and Luangprapat's chapter on Thailand, on the other hand, describes more cooperative inter-agency risk management collaboration in combating a tsunami, flooding, and COVID-19. However, despite the active response of the three administrative layers of central, provincial, and local government to disasters under the focal agency of Disaster Prevention and Mitigation, agency coordination and adherence to international standards still leave much to be desired for the successful management of disaster risks.

Publishing a book is always a time-consuming endeavor that requires the effort of many. Thanks to the cooperation from our colleagues at Sungkyunkwan University and our other valued contributors, however, we were able to publish this volume in the space of a year. We would like to thank the National Research Foundation (NRF-2016S1A3A2924832) for funding this project and the hard-working support staff at EACC. Dr. Joo Young Lee deserves a great deal of credit for collecting manuscripts and handling administrative issues with contributors. My final thanks goes to the Korean publisher Daeyoung Moonhwasa and Prof. Sung Min Park, who played the invaluable role as our bridge to the publisher and offered so much wonderful advice in the final stages of publication.

On behalf of contributors,
Sook Jong Lee
Seoul, Korea, May 2020

# Contents

## Part 2. Government-Citizen Collaboration in a Public Program

Part 1

# Cross-national Comparison of Citizen Views on Social Conflicts and Conflict Management System

- Factors Affecting the Collaborative Participation of Citizens in Public Conflict
  : The Paradox of Participation
- Towards a Collaborative Governance
  : Exploring Consequences of Conflict Resolution Initiatives in Asia
- Comparative Analysis of the Nuclear Energy Policy Process in South Korea and Japan
  : Focusing on Citizen Participation Systems Enhancing Coexistence

1

# Factors Affecting the Collaborative Participation of Citizens in Public Conflict: The Paradox of Participation

Sook Jong Lee and Bomi Kim

## Introduction

Over the last two decades, social conflicts surrounding public issues and policies have emerged powerfully across East Asia. Democratization of the region has left many governments facing the difficulty of carrying out the conventionally accepted "Decide-Announce-Defend (DAD)" rules. People are growing more aware of their right to defend and protect their interests and expect their governments to be responsive to their demands. The increasing level of public conflict has led to the introduction of institutional mechanisms by governments to manage clashes that arise, not only for the cause of democratic responsiveness but also to reduce the economic costs that public conflicts incur.

Engaging and motivating conflicting stakeholders to forge cooperation and reach binding decisions for joint action are crucial elements in designing collaborative governance. Emerson et al. (2011, 6) maintain that collaborative dynamics consist of three interactive components, i.e., principled engagement, shared motivation, and capacity for joint action. When these components interact, collaborative actions or the steps taken in order to implement the shared purpose of the "collaborative governance regime" is sustained. Most conflict-management mechanisms, however, are limited to certain kinds of communication and co-ordination between government and nongovernmental actors or resident groups, especially when constructing public facilities. With this narrow approach, the broader and more complex social conflicts developing in many East Asian countries are difficult to manage, let alone to resolve for good. The literature on collaborative governance has been developed primarily from the experiences of advanced Western democracies, the American experience in particular, where civil society and the private sector are more independent and resourceful. Accordingly, it has focused on how to more effectively design collaborative interactions without being overly concerned with the participatory capacity and social trust of individual citizens. In East Asian countries, the initial engagement of people in cooperative collective actions is a primary challenge, while designing a more effective participatory process remains secondary. The popular collaboration model of Ansell and Gash (2008) has included the power-resource-knowledge asymmetries and the initial trust level as preconditions to inducing people to participate in any collaborative action. In East Asia, where the level of democratization differs and government capacities and willingness to institutionalize participatory mechanisms are weaker, we need to approach collaborative governance from the perspective of bottom-up citizen participation.

This chapter takes the position that collaborative governance mechanisms are embedded in broader participatory actions. Without understanding public attitudes toward participation, government efforts to engage citizens in managing social conflicts will be to no avail. Accordingly, the study of collaborative governance in East Asia is better approached from the perspective of understanding the conditions under which people recognize government as a reliable and trustworthy cooperative partner.

The five East Asian countries dealt with in this paper have different religions. South Korea and Taiwan share a Confucian culture with Christian influence, while Thailand has a strong Buddhist culture, and Indonesia has a secular Islamic culture. Japan adheres to a mixture of Shintoism and Buddhism.

Their democratic politics also quite different. Japan is a prominent representative democracy that has long been led by the powerful Liberal Democratic Party. South Korea and Taiwan are dynamic democracies, where two major parties compete amidst expanding political polarization. Indonesia is the world's largest Islamic democracy, where coalition government is the norm because of the multi-ethnic system. Thailand has been unstable in comparison to these countries, suffering frequent military coups in the past, and remains problematic even with the recent recovery of popular elections. The country's rank in the Freedom House and Economist Intelligence Unit democracy indices is much lower than that of the other four countries. Despite this diversity, it is worthwhile to examine how people in these countries view their society's conflicts and what choices they make to voice their opinions. We analyze survey data from the five countries of Indonesia, Japan, South Korea, Taiwan, and Thailand using a multi-nominal logistic regression to identify the influential factors that induce people to cooperate with the government in the task of public governance. Surveys were carried out in March of 2018; only the Indonesia survey was conducted in January 2019. Through this analysis, we hope to suggest better alternatives for building collaborative governance in East Asia.

## Theoretical Debates and Research Framework

### Social Conflicts and Public Conflicts

Conflict has been defined differently across academic disciplines. For psychologists, conflict is an individual's psychological state which arises in the process of making a choice (Whittaker, 1966). In a conflict situation, a party can take one of the four strategies of contending, yielding, problem solving, or avoiding. Needless to say, from this perspective, conflict management is about finding solutions that are acceptable to both sides. Pruitt and Rubin (1986) have delineated the famous social conflict stages of escalation, stalemate, and settlement. Sociologists tend to view conflict as a struggle between the organizations, classes, or different strata of a given society. Dahrendorf (1958, 1962) posits the view that conflict is present in all societies and functions positively by making social change possible. Economists approach conflict as a struggle that emerges in the process of distributing scarce resources to individuals and groups (Abcarian & Palmer, 1974). In public policy studies, Moore (1996) maintains that everyone has an orientation towards conflict such that conflict is normal and necessary to the task of achieving any result in a public decision-making process. Constructing his model of the "Circle of Conflict", he defines the six main sources of conflict as values, relationships, interests, data, structure, and language.

Public conflict is a specific form of social conflict where government is involved as an important stakeholder. Typically, public conflicts occur surrounding government decisions regarding the environment, labor, education, regional development, and public facility programs. Walton and Dutton (1969) argue that public conflict arises because of interdependence, asymmetric power, the reward system, and asymmetric common goods. Public conflict primarily comprises intergovernmental or public-private conflict. Government itself can be a source of conflict through the decisions it makes that affect the everyday lives of its people. For example, the construction of an unpopular public facility in a community by a government may give rise to "not in my backyard" (NIMBY) opposition. Public conflict of this sort is more commonly found in countries where the government has stronger power than markets in deciding where to install facilities or how to allocate resources. Government can also take a neutral mediator role between confrontational private actors to reduce social cost. This role can be more difficult when a government does not have the legal authority or resources to induce negotiation between conflicting parties.

In this way, government becomes a key party in starting or intervening in emerging social conflicts. In East Asia, where government has strong authority in managing and allocating public goods and resources vis-à-vis markets and civil society, public conflict is essentially understood as government business vs. private individuals and social groups. For this reason, government is pushed to respond to social conflict and develop mechanisms to manage it. As the current public policy process tends to suffer from delays or stalemates, governments are more motivated to reduce social and economic costs arising from public conflict.

## Citizen Participation in Social Conflicts

The existing studies suggest three methods for resolving public conflict: changing the perceptions and attitudes of participants, providing appropriate economic rewards, and institutionalizing a participatory and consensual system (Lah and Park, 2004; Ha and Lee, 2007; Kim J. K., 2010; Kim S. I., 2011). Most Korean scholars emphasize the existence of citizen participation in order to reduce the public conflict that occurs in the conventional top-down policymaking and implementation process (Hong & Kim, 2008; Jeong, 2012). In the governance structure where government has asymmetrically strong power vis-à-vis civil society, government should attempt to create or reform a conflict management system to have a more inclusive perspective. How government views citizen and resident groups determines the government's position in involving and taking them on as collaborative partners (Yang, 2005). For this purpose, understanding the incentives and attitudes of citizens has become critical in forging collaborative public governance. In particular, forecasting the behaviors of citizens in times of conflict is important in the rational management of conflict. Conflict resolution constitutes taking an action that tries to move to an acceptable equilibrium point for citizens to engage in a transaction with a public party. Whether citizens willingly adopt this kind of transactional contract provides an indicator to predict the behaviors of citizens in future public conflicts. Accordingly, understanding whether citizens agree to participate in a conflict resolution process and how they view the role of the government are important elements for setting up collaborative governance (Ka, 2016).

## Research Framework

This study is based on the premise that the participatory attitude of citizens influences their willingness to engage in collaborative action when facing a conflict with the government. We focus on the three personal factors of political efficacy, government trust, and previous participatory experiences as the factors that can influence the participatory activities of citizens, and the two institutional factors of conflict management tools and the overall political system.

#### *Political Efficacy*

Political efficacy is the degree to which individuals feel that their actions can influence the political process (Campbell & Miller, 1954). If internal political efficacy means that individuals understand politics and have the knowledge and skills to participate, external political efficacy is when individuals believe that they can rely on their government or politicians to respond to their demands.

Political efficacy has been studied as an important factor influencing citizen participation. People with a higher degree of political efficacy are more likely to participate in efforts to resolve public problems since they believe they can impact politics or government decisions. Finkel (1985) found that while political efficacy makes people more likely to vote and participate in election campaigns, it does not strongly affect community participation. Political efficacy empowers individuals to actively cooperate with or oppose government decisions. Digital platforms provide individuals who otherwise would be detached from public affairs a channel through which to connect on a personal level. For example, Papacharissi (2010, 164) argues that social media sites like Twitter connect the personal in the private sphere to the political, and the self to the polity and society. Many governments try to use digital communication tools to encourage people to participate in collaborative governance. At the same time, citizens who obtain political efficacy by means of digitally coalesced communication participate in protests to express their anger. Gerbaudo (2018) also recognizes social media as gathering spaces where those who are usually underrepresented and lonely can coalesce and rally as a unified voice of the people. Social media caught on because people do not trust mainstream media and have grown tired of listening to experts tell them what to do. Citizens with political efficacy require an easily accessible institutional mechanism through which to express their opinions and demands. Otherwise, dangerous cynicism and eruptive protests are likely to threaten political stability.

### *Government Trust*

Trust in government is the belief that government operates according to normative expectations. Studying the late 1960s, Miller (1974) found that the widespread discontent prevalent in the US grew out of widespread dissatisfaction with the policy alternatives. He added that policy alternatives more acceptable to the total population will be exceedingly difficult to discover in the future owing to the existing degree of issue polarization. The economic difficulties faced by many governments these days tend to undermine the public trust in government. This lack of public confidence in the ability of democratic governments to manage the economy contributes to the decline of people's trust in democracy as a political system (Foa and Mounk, 2017; Fukuyama et al., 2015). Fortunately, the *Government at a Glance 2019* (OECD, 2019) report indicates that public trust in many OECD governments has recovered to the pre-crisis levels of 2007 due to increased social expenditures and efforts to engage citizens in public governance. Better economic performance, however, does not necessarily lead to a rise in government trust. The political polarization and the accompanying decline of trust in government which has occurred over the past several decades in the US has more to do with the ideological social divide than a declining economy (Levitsky and Ziblatt, 2018).

Government trust also correlates with political participation (Rothstein, 2001; Verba & Almond, 1963; Easton, 1965). Interacting with other factors, government trust works in two opposite ways. Trust in government encourages people to cooperate with government to respond to social problems. Rothstein (2001) finds that active participants in labor unions or political parties had greater trust in government. But empirical studies have not clearly validated whether people with greater levels of social participation or social trust have more government trust. In contrast, Kasse (1999) and Muller (1982) argue that people with a higher degree of trust in the government do not feel the need to participate, since they trust that government will make decisions in their best interest. However, generally collaborative governance scholars emphasize that public-private cooperation is necessary to improve government performance and policy activism (Agranoff and McGuire, 2003; Goldsmith and Eggers, 2004; Emerson, Nabatchi, and Balogh, 2011). In other words, government does not act in the interest of people unless they actively participate and make their voices heard. In particular, Ansell and Gash (2008) maintained that building trust by means of dialogue is critical as an initial condition to make actors commit to a collaborative process. On the other hand, some argue that the initial design of collaborative governance between the public and private sectors does not necessarily require government trust, since cross-boundary cooperation between them is possible without mutual trust. Despite these somewhat diverging views, it is certain that as most social-capital theories argue, trust serves to draw all concerned parties to participate and cooperate in solving shared problems. Since Putnam (1993) emphasizes the correlation between social capital (including trust) and good governance with better government performance, many studies find a close relationship between social trust and government trust and also between trust and democratic governance (Boix and Posner, 1998; Braithwait, 1998; Tarits, 2006; Taylor, 1998).

***Previous Participatory Experiences***

As seen in the previous section, many studies on collaborative governance find that citizen participation is likely to induce cooperation between the public and the government. The problem of this thesis is that "participation" is measured broadly by the general attitude of citizens toward engagement with government programs rather than any specific participation experiences that can be repeated in the future. Therefore, it is often difficult to distinguish whether the interaction between citizen participation and cooperation with government is simply a case of correlation or whether there is a causal relationship between the two. The choice of an individual to participate is affected by their specific past experiences. According to the theory of planned behavior put forth by Ajzen (1991), past experiences shape future behavioral choices by means of changing attitudes, subjective norms, and behavioral control. If an individual has a positive experience with political or social participation in the past, this will reinforce their willingness to participate again in the future.

In consideration of this theory, we asked people if they had ever participated in any of a list of nineteen activities either as an individual or as a group representative. Survey participants were asked if they had ever taken part in a residents meeting, a public hearing, a deliberative poll, a signature campaign, a one-man protest, a group rally, an audit request, a press conference, a local referendum, a meeting with a congressional representative, a meeting with a top local government official, a public-private consultative body, an ombudsman system, making a claim on a government website, administrative litigation, a citizen recall of a local government official, or a citizen jury. We assumed that past experiences with these activities would be important factors which would influence people in deciding whether to engage with government when they face social or political conflict.

### *Assessment of Conflict Management System*

Many governments have introduced conflict management tools to respond to rising social conflict. Although their specific forms and actual usage differ, all five East Asian countries dealt with in this chapter have institutionalized such tools. It was our assumption that whether or not citizens engaged with the government to resolve public conflicts would be influenced by their views on these conflict management systems. Accordingly, we asked each survey participant to evaluate five statements on the conflict management tools in terms of their information disclosure, prior consultation with stakeholders, efforts to seek expert scientific opinions, communication with the public, and caring engagement with the socially vulnerable. We posited that positive assessments of these conflict management tools indicate that an individual is more likely to engage with the government to resolve public conflict.

### *Political System*

If conflict management tools are a mechanism to more directly influence the attitudes of citizens regarding government engagement, individual views of political systems are a background factor affecting overall citizen participation. Citizen participation has long been regarded as a key element in making democracy stronger (Verba and Nie, 1972; Barber, 1985). Democratic governments are more responsive to public demands and are willing to actively involve citizens in public governance. Accordingly, people will engage with the government to resolve public conflict when they view their political system as democratic.

Using these three personal factors and two institutional factors as independent variables for participation, the research framework is laid out in Figure 1.

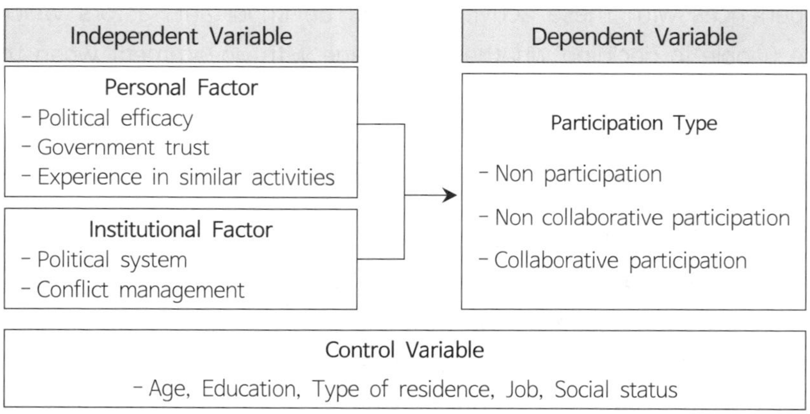


**Figure 1.** Research Framework

## Data

The EACC's cross-national survey is composed of two parts. The first is findings about how citizens of five Asian countries view social conflict categorized by intensity and the realms in which it occurs. The second is findings about the kinds of participatory actions they are taking to resolve such conflicts. All surveys were carried out online with randomly sampled people between the ages of 18 and 64. People age 65 or older, 17 and younger, and those who cannot access the internet were excluded from the sample. This exclusion of older people in online surveys remains a shortcoming of the data. The survey samples in Japan, South Korea, Taiwan, and Thailand were drawn nationally, whereas the Indonesian sample was limited to the two major islands of Java and Sumatra. The surveys of the former four countries were carried out in March 2018, and the Indonesian survey was conducted in January 2019.

**Table 1.** Cross-national Surveys of Five East Asian Countries

| Category | Contents |
|---|---|
| Population | Adults aged 18~64 years in South Korean, Japan, Taiwan, Thailand and Indonesia |
| Sampling | • Access Panel |
| | • A quota sampling method based on region, gender, and age<br>(In Indonesia, only residents of Java and Sumatra are surveyed) |
| Sample size | • South Korea: 1,118 • Taiwan: 1,030 • Indonesia: 1,048<br>• Japan: 1,010 • Thailand: 1,018 |
| Sample error (95% confidence level) | • South Korea : ± 2.9% • Taiwan: ± 3.1% • Indonesia: ± 3.0%<br>• Japan: ± 3.1% • Thailand: ± 3.1% |
| Survey methodology | • Online panel research |
| Weighting method | • Weight by region, gender and age according to the criteria below<br>- South Korea: 2018 Resident registration demographics (http://www.mois.go.kr/)<br>- Japan: 2015 Population and Households (https://www.e-stat.go.jp/)<br>- Taiwan: 2010 Population and Housing Census (https://eng.stat.gov.tw/) |

| | | | | |
|---|---|---|---|---|
| | - Thailand: 2010 Population and Housing Census (http://popcensus.nso.go.th/)<br>- Indonesia: SENSUS PENDUDUK 2010 (https://sp2010.bps.go.id) | | | |
| Response rate | Country | Mail sent | Completed Samples | Response rate (%) |
| | South Korea | 6,824 | 1,118 | 16.4 |
| | Japan | 4,798 | 1,010 | 21.1 |
| | Taiwan | 5,115 | 1,030 | 20.1 |
| | Thailand | 16,896 | 1,018 | 6.0 |
| | Indonesia | 4,622 | 1,048 | 22.7 |
| The period of investigation | • 2018-03-08~2018-03-21/ Indonesia 2019-01-09~2019-01-23 | | | |

## Survey Findings on Social Conflicts

In order to understand how the citizens in each of these five countries perceive public conflict, we asked "In your opinion, how frequently do public

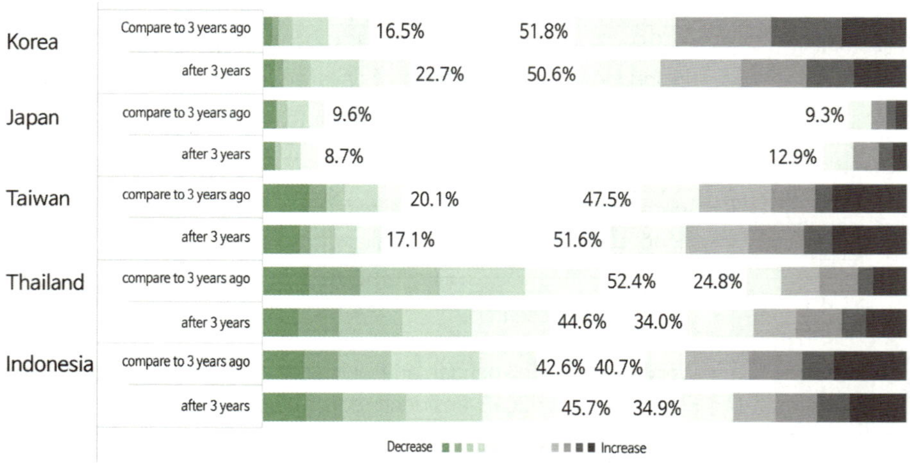


**Figure 2.** Citizens' Perceptions of Social Conflicts

conflicts related to government policies occur now, and how do you expect it to change in the future?" A retrospective view was asked via the question "Compared to three years ago, the current frequency of public conflicts (increased or decreased on a scale of 0~10)." This scale allowed for eleven possible scores ("has decreased" from 0 to 4 and "has increased" from 6 to 10, while a score of 5 indicated that the level of public conflict "has neither increased nor decreased"). To measure the expectations of our survey participants for the future, we asked participants to use the same 11-point scale to indicate "Compared to the present, the frequency of public conflicts three years later will (increase or decrease)."

In South Korea and Taiwan, almost half of the citizens surveyed thought that public conflict has increased over the last three years, and half also believed that public conflict would rise over the next three years. Only about 20 percent of citizens surveyed thought that public conflict had decreased over the previous three years. In addition, just 22.7 percent of Koreans and 17.1 percent of Taiwanese expected future conflicts to decrease. On the other hand, citizens of Thailand and Indonesia were more optimistic than their Korean and Taiwanese counterparts. Only 24.8 percent of Thai citizens thought that public conflict had increased over the last three years, while 52.4 percent thought they had decreased. A margin of 10.6 percent more Thai citizens expected public conflict to decrease compared to the citizens who answered that public conflict will increase over the next three years. Although the margins were small, Indonesian citizens also tended more towards the view that public conflict has decreased and will continue to decrease in the future. Japan appears to be distinctive, since an absolute majority of about 80 percent of the Japanese citizens surveyed thought that the level of public conflict at present was the same as that of three years ago. This *status quo* view also applies to the Japanese view of future public conflict. Only 20 percent of Japanese citizens indicated that public conflicts would either increase or decrease in the future.

Government is an actor and also an expected mediator in diverse inter-group conflicts. In order to compare public conflicts where government is the most powerful actor with other types of social conflicts where the government is not directly involved, we attempted to assess the intensity of different conflicts. In South Korea, Taiwan, and Indonesia, the lowest level of

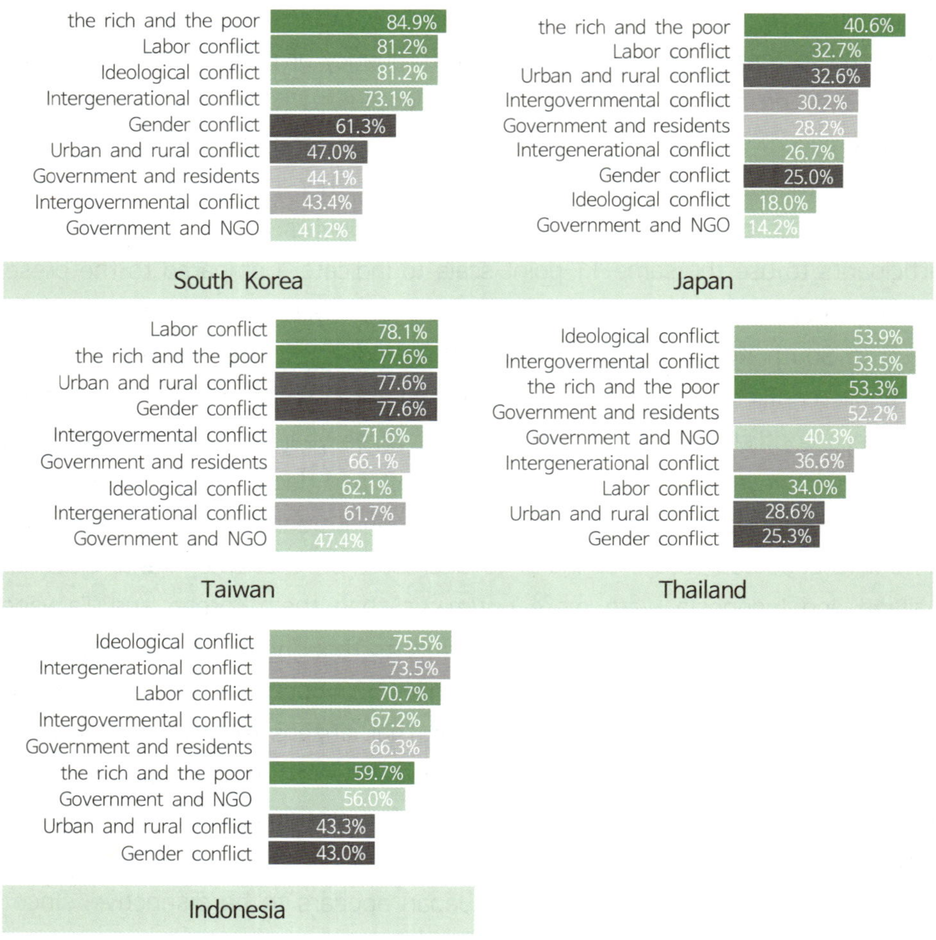


**Figure 3.** Types of Social Conflicts

conflict was still viewed by more than 40 percent of people as serious, whereas the highest level of conflict was viewed as serious by 75 or 85 percent of people. On the other hand, the percentage of people who said a certain conflict was serious ranged from between 40.6 and 14.2 percent in Japan and between 53.9 and 25.3 percent in Thailand. In Japan, there is a tendency for individuals to believe that stating only troublemakers point out the presence of social conflict.

This perception discourages people from stating that a social conflict exists. The choice of the word "conflict" itself is another possible contributor to the perception of a low degree of social conflict where government is a party as opposed to other economic and social conflicts in South Korea, Taiwan, and Japan. For example, respondents in these three countries ranked three types of government- involved conflicts—government-resident conflict, intergovernmental conflict, and government-NGO conflict—as less serious than class (rich-poor) conflict and labor conflict. On the other hand, intergovernmental and government conflicts with either residential groups or NGOs were viewed as relatively more intense in Thailand and Indonesia. Class and labor conflicts were ranked distinctively higher in Korea and Taiwan from among a list of social conflicts between nongovernmental actors. Ideological conflict was viewed as very serious in South Korea, Indonesia, and Thailand. Gender conflict was least important in Indonesia and Thailand, but was viewed as quite serious in Korea and Taiwan.

In terms of conflict saliency, Indonesia, Korea, and Taiwan are similar, with higher levels of conflict. Japan appears to be the least conflict-ridden society. The Japanese culture of emphasizing harmony (*wa*) and the conventional characterization of Japan as a consensus-oriented society seem to suppress open expressions of the existence of conflict. In contrast, civil society in Korea and Taiwan is contentious, and politics are more polarized between competing forces. Indonesia also shows a high level of conflict. Thailand, which has undergone a democratic breakdown, shows a lesser degree of conflict, but the long-time political divide between anti-Takshin and pro-Takshin factions has left Thai citizens with a view of ideological conflict in their society as high. Economic conflict, such as class or labor conflict, is perceived as high among the three Northeast Asian countries, which are also more industrialized and affluent than their Southeast Asian neighbors. Among government-related conflicts, intergovernmental conflict is perceived as high in Thailand, perhaps because of the frequent military interventions into the country's governance.

# Factors Influencing Citizen Participation in Public Conflict

## Dependent Variables

In order to find out how citizens participate when they face public conflict, we asked the question "If you were in a public conflict situation with the government (e.g., a large-scale national project, welfare policy, education policy, city planning, or establishment of undesirable facilities), what kind of approach would you generally take to resolve the conflict?" Among the nine actions listed as possible responses, we chose six actions relevant to influencing public decisions and then divided them into "uncollaborative" participation and "collaborative" participation. Protest, administrative litigation, and press conferences were categorized as uncollaborative activities, which usually entail ignoring, bypassing, or directly confronting the other party. A press conference is an ambiguous action that is difficult to exclusively label "uncollaborative." Nonetheless, a press conference is usually a tactic engaged in by civilian parties when they are critical of the government before or after engaging with it. In this sense, it is closer to being uncollaborative than collaborative. For collaborative actions, we selected visiting a relevant congressperson, negotiating with the government, and participating in a multilateral consultative group. These actions recognize government as a legitimate party to consult and negotiate with. In addition to these six actions, "no participation" was included, since many citizens opt to take no action even when they have a conflict with government. As seen in Table 2, a total of 419 (37.5 percent of total people surveyed) Koreans, 657 (65.0 percent) Japanese, 489 (47.5 percent) Taiwanese, 576 (56.6 percent) Thais, and 784 (74.8 percent) Indonesians either did not participate in any activities or participated in one or more of the six activities we categorized as uncollaborative and collaborative. In the category of "no participation," the Japanese are notably high with 66.2 percent stating they will not engage with their government in the face of a public conflict. In contrast, just 7.1 percent of Indonesians stated they would not engage with the government to attempt conflict resolution, while 32 percent of Koreans and 44.4 percent of Taiwanese respondents stated the same. For collaborative participation, Indonesians are the most willing to engage with the government to resolve conflict with 67.2 percent answering affirmatively, while the number of Japanese who took this position was a mere 11.7 percent. For uncollaborative participation, Thailand (36.5 percent), Taiwan (35.6 percent) and South Korea (33.4 percent) show a similar pattern. Namely, about one-third of the people in these three countries said they would take critical or opposing action against the government. If we limit our view to a comparison of the ratio between uncollaborative and collaborative actions, twice as many Japanese respondents indicated they would engage in uncollaborative actions over collaborative actions. In contrast, four times as many Indonesians said they will engage with government collaboratively to resolve a conflict compared to those who indicated they would engage in uncollaborative actions.

## Independent Variables

As illustrated in the research framework, six independent variables were selected; four as individual factors and two as institutional factors. We took two political efficacy variables as important factors affecting the attitude of individuals towards future participation in public conflict resolution. Responses to the statement "A small number of people control the government and politics regardless of the will of most people in our country" were used to measure external political efficacy. For internal political efficacy, we asked participants to rank their agreement with the commonly used statement of "People like us are not qualified or capable of talking about what the government does." Both internal and external political efficacy variables were used from the mean of the five-point scale. Although the differences were small, external efficacy was stronger in Taiwan and Thailand, with means of 2.6 and 2.57, respectively, whereas Korea scored the lowest at 2.23. On the other hand, internal political efficacy was higher in Taiwan, Korea, and Indonesia, with the respective scores of 3.39, 3.36, and 3.16, whereas Japan scored the lowest at 2.65. Internal political efficacy was higher than external in all five countries, with South Korea showing the biggest gap of 1.13. This suggests that Koreans think they are capable democratic citizens but feel they lack much power to change society. Taiwanese respondents scored higher in both internal and external efficacy, as is desirable for a strong democracy.

Using a scale of 1 (complete distrust) to 10 (complete trust), a government trust score was taken as a mean score of trust in the president or prime minister, trust in the central government, and trust in the local government. Indonesians had a higher level of government trust, while Japanese and Taiwanese participants had relatively less trust in their governments. To assess the influence of previous participation activities on the willingness of citizens to engage in conflict resolution with the government, we calculated the ratio of people who had taken any of the nineteen participatory actions over the last three years. Since these nineteen

**Table 2.** Independent and Dependent Variables for Data Analyses

| Country | Independent Variable (Average) | | | | | | Dependent Variable (Person, %) | | |
|---|---|---|---|---|---|---|---|---|---|
| | External efficacy (1~5) | Internal efficacy (1~5) | Government trust (1~10) | Previous participation experience (0~1) | Evaluation of conflict management system (0~10) | Assessment of democracy (0~10) | Participation for Conflict Resolution: No Participation | Un collaborative participation | Collaborative participation |
| Korea (N=419) | 2.23 | 3.36 | 5.13 | 0.45 | 4.90 | 5.76 | 134 | 140 | 145 |
| | | | | | | | 32.0% | 33.4% | 34.6% |
| Japan (N=657) | 2.38 | 2.65 | 4.31 | 0.79 | 4.07 | 4.94 | 435 | 145 | 77 |
| | | | | | | | 66.2% | 22.1% | 11.7% |
| Taiwan (N=489) | 2.60 | 3.39 | 4.05 | 0.61 | 5.25 | 4.90 | 217 | 174 | 98 |
| | | | | | | | 44.4% | 35.6% | 20.0% |
| Thailand (N=576) | 2.57 | 2.98 | 5.04 | 0.41 | 6.00 | 5.36 | 137 | 210 | 229 |
| | | | | | | | 23.8% | 36.5% | 39.8% |
| Indonesia (N=784) | 2.38 | 3.16 | 6.29 | 0.26 | 6.69 | 5.52 | 56 | 201 | 527 |
| | | | | | | | 7.1% | 25.6% | 67.2% |

participatory actions are different from the future action of participating in public conflict resolution with government, we simply took a previous participation ratio of people who engaged in at least one of the nineteen activities we listed earlier.

For institutional factors, we used the evaluation of the existing conflict management system and of the democratic performance of the political systems of our survey participants. The evaluation of the existing conflict management system used the mean score of five questions about easy and transparent information disclosure; government efforts to consult in advance with stakeholders regarding the participation process, agendas, and other preparatory matters; government efforts to consult with experts on fact finding; government efforts to communicate better; and government efforts to take care of the socially vulnerable. Indonesia (6.7) evaluated its conflict management system most positively, followed by Thailand (6.0), Taiwan (5.25), Korea (4.9), and Japan (4.1). Korea ranked its democratic performance highest on the scale from 0 (completely undemocratic) to 10 (completely democratic), followed by Indonesia, Thailand, Japan, and Taiwan.

## Influential Factors in Citizen Participation in Public Conflict by Country

In this section, we will examine the factors in each country which influence the indicated future willingness of citizens to take participatory action when faced with public conflict. A multiple logistic analysis comparing collaborative and uncollaborative participants with non-participants is used to see which factors make people more likely or willing to engage in collaborative participation.

① South Korea

| | | | Standard error | B | Significance level | Exp (B) |
|---|---|---|---|---|---|---|
| Than non-participation | | | | | | |
| Collaborative participation | Personal Factor | External efficacy | .150 | -.207 | .169 | .813 |
| | | Internal efficacy | .107 | .255 | .017 | 1.290 |
| | | Government Trust | .098 | -.082 | .404 | .921 |
| | | No previous participation experience (than with an experience) | .264 | 1.019 | .000 | 2.769 |
| | Institutional Factor | Evaluation of conflict management system | .083 | .125 | .131 | 1.133 |
| | | Perceived level of democracy | .088 | .233 | .008 | 1.263 |
| | Control Factor | Social status | .087 | -.049 | .576 | .952 |
| | | Age | .117 | .302 | .010 | 1.353 |
| | | Male (than female) | .264 | .303 | .252 | 1.354 |
| | | Less than elementary school (than graduate school) | .000 | -18.405 | .000 | 1.016E-8 |
| | | Less than middle school (than graduate school) | 8206.599 | -18.330 | .998 | 1.095E-8 |
| | | Less than high school (than graduate school) | .549 | -.400 | .466 | .670 |
| | | University educated (than graduate school) | .442 | -.157 | .722 | .854 |
| | | City residence (than village) | .572 | .029 | .960 | 1.029 |
| | | Town residence (than village) | .569 | .004 | .995 | 1.004 |
| Non-collaborative participation | Personal Factor | External efficacy | .147 | -.061 | .677 | .941 |
| | | Internal efficacy | .105 | .198 | .060 | 1.219 |
| | | Government Trust | .099 | -.137 | .167 | .872 |
| | | No previous participation experience (than with an experience) | .261 | .977 | .000 | 2.656 |
| | Institutional Factor | Evaluation of conflict management system | .082 | .064 | .435 | 1.066 |
| | | Level of democracy | .085 | .091 | .285 | 1.095 |

| | | | | | |
|---|---|---|---|---|---|
| Control Factor | Social status | .086 | .076 | .374 | 1.079 |
| | Age | .112 | -.051 | .649 | .950 |
| | Male (than female) | .261 | .420 | .108 | 1.522 |
| | Less than elementary school (than graduate school) | .000 | -18.013 | .000 | 1.503E-8 |
| | Less than middle school (than graduate school) | 8600.815 | -18.657 | .998 | 7.895E-9 |
| | Less than high school (than graduate school) | .512 | .218 | .670 | 1.244 |
| | University education. (than graduate school) | .430 | -.376 | .382 | .687 |
| | City residence (than village) | .559 | -.253 | .651 | .777 |
| | Town residence (than village) | .555 | -.268 | .629 | .765 |
| Chi-squared<br>Nagelkerke R2 | 74.677<br>0.184 | p-value*p<0.05 | | | |

For Korea, the survey finds that internal political efficacy, participation history, assessment of democracy, and age all influence an individual's collaborative attitude in resolving public conflict. The internal political efficacy of people who are willing to engage in collaborative activities was 1.29 times higher than that of the people who had no interest in taking an action. These collaborative engagers viewed their democracy as 1.26 times more democratic compared to non-participants. Older people were more likely to be willing to participate collaboratively than younger people. Interestingly, the survey also found that those without any participatory experience in the last three years were 2.77 times more willing to take collaborative action than those who had a history of participatory action. This negative effect of previous participation upon future willingness to engage in public conflict resolution was also found to hold up for uncollaborative actions such as protests, lawsuits, and press conferences. The question is, why does previous participation experience discourage people from participating in future public conflict resolution efforts? One possible reason may be related to the high costs of participatory activities with lower returns. Citizens who have engaged with the government to resolve public conflict may lose their trust in government, which could discourage them from repeating such engagement. This claim is supported by Kim (2017), who found that individual experiences of public conflict significantly reduced the level of trust in government.

### ② Japan

| | | | Standard error | B | Significance level | Exp (B) |
|---|---|---|---|---|---|---|
| Than non-participation | | | | | | |
| Collaborative participation | Personal Factor | External efficacy | .159 | -.066 | .679 | .936 |
| | | Internal efficacy | .142 | .119 | .403 | 1.126 |
| | | Government trust | .085 | .160 | .060 | 1.173 |
| | | No previous participation experience (than with an experience) | .299 | 1.879 | .000 | 6.547 |
| | Institutional Factor | Evaluation of conflict management system | .089 | -.011 | .899 | .989 |
| | | Perceived level of democracy | .076 | -.038 | .622 | .963 |
| | Control Factor | Social status | .083 | -.166 | .046 | .847 |
| | | Age | .126 | .047 | .710 | 1.048 |
| | | Male (than female) | .274 | -.324 | .237 | .723 |
| | | Less than elementary school (than graduate school) | .000 | -18.175 | .000 | 1.279E-8 |
| | | Less than middle school (than graduate school) | .965 | .142 | .883 | 1.152 |
| | | Less than high school (than graduate school) | .634 | -.440 | .487 | .644 |
| | | University education (than graduate school) | .619 | -.260 | .675 | .771 |
| | | City residence (than village) | .573 | .839 | .144 | 2.313 |
| | | Town residence (than village) | .583 | .751 | .198 | 2.120 |
| Non-collaborative participation | Personal Factor | External efficacy | .134 | -.433 | .001 | .649 |
| | | Internal efficacy | .110 | .156 | .156 | 1.169 |
| | | Government trust | .068 | -.054 | .428 | .947 |
| | | No previous participation experience (than with an experience) | .248 | 1.893 | .000 | 6.639 |

| | | | | | |
|---|---|---|---|---|---|
| Institu-tional Factor | Evaluation of conflict management system | .067 | -.045 | .501 | .956 |
| | Perceived level of democracy | .059 | .043 | .470 | 1.044 |
| Control Factor | Social status | .067 | .036 | .592 | 1.036 |
| | Age | .101 | .046 | .650 | 1.047 |
| | Male (than female) | .218 | .216 | .322 | 1.241 |
| | Less than elementary school (than graduate school) | 8588.708 | -18.266 | .998 | 1.167E-8 |
| | Less than middle school (than graduate school) | 1.208 | -1.570 | .194 | .208 |
| | Less than high school (than graduate school) | .481 | -.567 | .238 | .567 |
| | University education (than graduate school) | .467 | -.263 | .574 | .769 |
| | City residence (than village) | .349 | -.179 | .608 | .836 |
| | Town residence (than village) | .349 | -.168 | .631 | .846 |
| Chi-squared<br>Nagelkerke R2 | | 136.207<br>0.228 | p-value*p<0.05 | | |

In Japan, previous participation experience, social status, and external political efficacy were statistically significant factors affecting collaborative participation. Japanese survey participants were less willing to participate in both collaborative and uncollaborative actions when faced with public conflict. Those who do participate, however, choose to engage in uncollaborative participation twice as often as collaborative participation. In Japan, the number of people with no previous participation experience was 6.55 (6.64) times more likely to be willing to take collaborative (uncollaborative) action in a future conflict compared to those who answered that they would not be willing to engage in participatory action in the future. People who also perceived their family as belonging to a higher status group were less likely to engage in collaborative action than nonparticipants. The external political efficacy of uncollaborative participants was lower than that of non- participants. This finding suggests that when Japanese people think they cannot influence government policies, they are willing to engage in uncollaborative action such as protests and administrative lawsuits.

③ Taiwan

| | | | Standard error | B | Significance level | Exp (B) |
|---|---|---|---|---|---|---|
| Than non-participation | | | | | | |
| Collaborative participation | Personal Factor | External efficacy | .118 | .082 | .487 | 1.085 |
| | | Internal efficacy | .114 | .152 | .182 | 1.164 |
| | | Government trust | .078 | .133 | .091 | 1.142 |
| | | No previous participation experience (than with an experience) | .292 | 1.547 | .000 | 4.698 |
| | Institutional Factor | Evaluation of conflict management system | .066 | .099 | .129 | 1.105 |
| | | Perceived level of democracy | .055 | .084 | .128 | 1.087 |
| | Control Factor | Social status | .082 | -.019 | .816 | .981 |
| | | Age | .124 | -.088 | .480 | .916 |
| | | Male (than female) | .265 | .013 | .960 | 1.013 |
| | | Less than elementary school (than graduate school) | .916 | -1.207 | .188 | .299 |
| | | Less than middle school (than graduate school) | .732 | .136 | .853 | 1.145 |
| | | Less than high school (than graduate school) | .519 | -.198 | .702 | .820 |
| | | University education (than graduate school) | .461 | -.181 | .695 | .835 |
| | | City residence (than village) | .493 | .029 | .952 | 1.030 |
| | | Town residence (than village) | .528 | .394 | .456 | 1.483 |
| Non-collaborative participation | Personal Factor | External efficacy | .106 | -.085 | .424 | .919 |
| | | Internal efficacy | .096 | .094 | .329 | 1.098 |
| | | Government trust | .072 | -.102 | .154 | .903 |
| | | No previous participation experience (than with an experience) | .265 | 2.460 | .000 | 11.701 |
| | Institutional-Factor | Evaluation of conflict management system | .056 | .033 | .560 | 1.033 |
| | | Level of perceived democracy | .049 | .145 | .003 | 1.156 |

| | | | | | | |
|---|---|---|---|---|---|---|
| | Control Factor | Social status | .074 | .033 | .650 | 1.034 |
| | | Age | .112 | .065 | .559 | 1.067 |
| | | Male (than female) | .241 | .107 | .657 | 1.113 |
| | | Less than elementary school (than graduate school) | .736 | -1.080 | .142 | .340 |
| | | Less than middle school (than graduate school) | .710 | -.544 | .444 | .581 |
| | | Less than high school (than graduate school) | .446 | .000 | 1.000 | 1.000 |
| | | University education (than graduate school) | .404 | -.408 | .312 | .665 |
| | | City residence (than village) | .443 | .275 | .535 | 1.317 |
| | | Town residence (than village) | .486 | .542 | .265 | 1.719 |
| Chi-squared<br>Nagelkerke R2 | | 150.775<br>0.302 | p-value*p<0.05 | | | |

Previous participation experience and perceived level of democracy affect the Taiwanese attitude toward collaborative participation for public conflict resolution. The likelihood of having no previous participation experience was 4.7 and 11.7 times higher among collaborative and uncollaborative participants, respectively, than among nonparticipants. Uncollaborative participants were 1.16 times more likely to view their country as being more democratic than non-participants. This is opposite to the Korean case, where the positive perception of democracy encouraged collaborative participation.

### ④ Thailand

| | | | Standard error | B | Significance level | Exp (B) |
|---|---|---|---|---|---|---|
| Than non-participation | | | | | | |
| Collaborative participation | Personal Factor | Externa efficacy | .107 | -.041 | .700 | .959 |
| | | Internal efficacy | .098 | .253 | .010 | 1.288 |
| | | Government trust | .064 | .091 | .153 | 1.095 |
| | | No previous participation experience (than with an experience) | .239 | 1.074 | .000 | 2.927 |

| | | | | | | |
|---|---|---|---|---|---|---|
| | Institutional Factor | Evaluation of conflict management system | .050 | .065 | .190 | 1.067 |
| | | Perceived level of democracy | .058 | -.166 | .004 | .847 |
| | Control Factor | Social status | .085 | -.008 | .922 | .992 |
| | | Age | .122 | -.220 | .072 | .803 |
| | | Male (than female) | .234 | -.018 | .938 | .982 |
| | | Less than elementary school (than graduate school) | .978 | -1.224 | .211 | .294 |
| | | Less than middle school (than graduate school) | .563 | -.352 | .532 | .703 |
| | | Less than high school (than graduate school) | .398 | .437 | .272 | 1.548 |
| | | University education (than graduate school) | .297 | -.184 | .534 | .832 |
| | | City residence (than village) | .318 | .029 | .927 | 1.030 |
| | | Town residence (than village) | .434 | .163 | .708 | 1.177 |
| Non-collaborative participation | Personal Factor | External efficacy | .111 | -.088 | .426 | .916 |
| | | Internal efficacy | .102 | .143 | .160 | 1.153 |
| | | Government trust | .065 | -.010 | .877 | .990 |
| | | No previous participation experience (than with an experience) | .250 | 1.592 | .000 | 4.916 |
| | Institutional Factor | Evaluation of conflict management system | .051 | .033 | .518 | 1.033 |
| | | Perceived level of democracy | .058 | -.125 | .032 | .882 |
| | Control Factor | Social status | .086 | .051 | .557 | 1.052 |
| | | Age | .125 | .047 | .704 | 1.049 |
| | | Male (than female) | .240 | .357 | .136 | 1.429 |
| | | Less than elementary school (than graduate school) | .845 | -.770 | .362 | .463 |
| | | Less than middle school (than graduate school) | .561 | -.233 | .678 | .792 |
| | | Less than high school (than graduate school) | .415 | -.244 | .557 | .783 |

| | | | | | |
|---|---|---|---|---|---|
| | | University education. (than graduate school) | .296 | -.485 | .102 | .616 |
| | | City residence (than village) | .334 | .089 | .791 | 1.093 |
| | | Town residence (than village) | .445 | .512 | .250 | 1.669 |
| Chi-squared Nagelkerke R2 | | 93.983 0.170 | p-value*p<0.05 | | | |

Previous participation experience and the perception of democracy also mattered in Thailand. Thai respondents who said they were willing to participate in collaborative action if faced with public conflict had nearly one-third of the previous participation experience of those who said they wouldn't participate in the future. Building on this, Thai respondents who said they would participate in uncollaborative actions in the future had just one-fifth of the previous participation experience as those who indicated they had no intention of participating again in the future. Interestingly, those who viewed their country as more democratized were less willing to participate in both collaborative and uncollaborative action to resolve public conflict. That is, Thai respondents who view their country as undemocratic are more willing to participate in public conflict resolution efforts, perhaps to defend their interests from the undemocratic government. This is contrary to the Korean case, where the belief in the country's democracy encourages collaborative participation in the future.

### ⑤ Indonesia

| | | | Standard error | B | Significance level | Exp(B) |
|---|---|---|---|---|---|---|
| Than non-participation | | | | | | |
| Collaborative participation | Personal Factor | External efficacy | .125 | -.095 | .445 | .909 |
| | | Internal efficacy | .128 | .156 | .222 | 1.169 |
| | | Government trust | .104 | .142 | .169 | 1.153 |
| | | No participation experience (than with an experience) | .335 | 1.199 | .000 | 3.317 |

| | | | | | | |
|---|---|---|---|---|---|---|
| | Institu-tional Factor | Evaluation of conflict management system | .073 | .146 | .046 | 1.157 |
| | | Perceived level of democracy | .084 | .157 | .063 | 1.170 |
| | Control Factor | Social status | .200 | .248 | .217 | 1.281 |
| | | Age | .186 | .254 | .172 | 1.289 |
| | | Male (than female) | .350 | -.229 | .514 | .796 |
| | | Less than elementary school (than graduate school) | 1.090 | -1.090 | .317 | .336 |
| | | Less than middle school (than graduate school) | .902 | -.528 | .559 | .590 |
| | | Less than high school (than graduate school) | .846 | .200 | .813 | 1.221 |
| | | University education (than graduate school) | .812 | -.084 | .917 | .919 |
| | | City residence (than village) | .469 | .121 | .796 | 1.129 |
| | | Town residence (than village) | .529 | .276 | .601 | 1.318 |
| Non-collabora-tive participa-tion | Personal Factor | External efficacy | .131 | -.054 | .682 | .948 |
| | | Internal efficacy | .134 | .066 | .623 | 1.068 |
| | | Government trust | .108 | -.103 | .342 | .902 |
| | | No previous participation experi-ence (than with an experience) | .356 | 1.456 | .000 | 4.290 |
| | Institu-tional Factor | Evaluation of conflict management system | .076 | .090 | .238 | 1.094 |
| | | Perceived level of democracy | .089 | .134 | .133 | 1.143 |
| | Control Factor | Social status | .209 | .393 | .060 | 1.481 |
| | | Age | .193 | .296 | .125 | 1.345 |
| | | Male (than female) | .366 | -.203 | .580 | .817 |
| | | Less than elementary school (than graduate school) | 1.077 | -1.388 | .197 | .250 |
| | | Less than middle school (than graduate school) | .910 | -1.550 | .089 | .212 |
| | | Less than high school (than graduate school) | .845 | -.849 | .315 | .428 |
| | | University education (than graduate school) | .808 | -1.000 | .216 | .368 |

| | | | | | | |
|---|---|---|---|---|---|---|
| | | City residence (than village) | .496 | -.058 | .907 | .944 |
| | | Town residence (than village) | .553 | .341 | .537 | 1.407 |
| Chi-squared<br>Nagelkerke R2 | | 148.577<br>0.218 | p-value*p<0.05 | | | |

Previous participation experience also negatively influenced the willingness to participate in future public conflict resolution efforts in Indonesia. Indonesians who answered that they would be willing to take part in collaborative or uncollaborative participation in a future public conflict were 3.32 and 4.29 times less likely to have engaged in any participatory action in the past compared to Indonesians who showed no interest in participating in future public conflict resolution efforts. Indonesians with a positive assessment of the existing conflict management system were more likely to be willing to engage in collaborative participation.

**Table 3.** Cross-national Comparison

| Variable | | | Korea | Japan | Taiwan | Thailand | Indonesia |
|---|---|---|---|---|---|---|---|
| Collaborative participation | Personal Factor | External efficacy | | | | | |
| | | Internal efficacy | + | | | + | |
| | | Government trust | | | | | |
| | | Previous participation Experiences | - | - | - | - | - |
| | Institutional Factor | Conflict management | | | | | + |
| | | Democratic political system | + | | | - | |
| | Control Variable | Social status | | - | | | |
| | | Age | + | | | | |
| Non-collaborative participation | Personal Factor | External efficacy | | - | | | |
| | | Internal efficacy | | | | | |
| | | Government trust | | | | | |
| | | Previous participation experiences | - | - | - | - | - |

| Institutional Factor | Conflict management | | | | | |
|---|---|---|---|---|---|---|
| | Democratic political system | | | + | − | |
| Control variable | Social status | | | | | |
| | Age | | | | | |

Table 3. shows the significant factors influencing the participatory attitudes of citizens in the five Asian countries surveyed. First, it was striking to find that previous participation experience discouraged people from future participation in all five countries, regardless of whether such future action was cooperative or oppositional, in public conflict resolution. The literature in collaborative governance has emphasized the role of citizen participation in the collaborative process to reach more binding and effective public decisions. In particular, memories of the participatory process and results of participation provide political efficacy to participants and are linked to ongoing participation. It is paradoxical to observe that participation discourages future participation in public conflict resolution. It looks as if many of the Asians in our survey did not have positive experiences with participatory actions, perhaps because of higher opportunity costs or less rewarding outcomes. This finding needs to be taken seriously by public officials who design participatory mechanisms for collaborative governance.

Second, it is interesting to study the different effects of citizen evaluations of democracy. When Koreans think their political system is more democratic, they are inspired to engage in collaborative participation, whereas Taiwanese are inspired towards uncollaborative forms of participation. In contrast, Thai people tend to participate in resolving public conflicts when they think their government is undemocratic. If the dynamic of a strong democratic performance perception and greater institutional engagement works for Koreans, greater democratic perception of the political system encourages freer and contentious actions among the Taiwanese. People seem to participate in public conflict resolution efforts in Thailand to guard their interests, since they cannot trust an undemocratic government. This diverging effect of people's perception of democracy on their participatory attitude invites further study.

## Conclusion

This study has examined the trends of social and public conflict resolution by means of individual perceptions. It analyzed several factors that influence individual participatory attitudes.

People viewed the level of conflict as serious and likely to worsen in the future in South Korea and Taiwan. On the other hand, people in Thailand and Indonesia viewed the level of conflict somewhat less seriously in comparison. A significant proportion of Thais and Indonesians anticipate a lessening of social conflict in the future. Japan was distinctive in the sense that an absolute majority of people viewed conflict to be lower in their society. In terms of conflict types, Korea, Japan, and Taiwan shared many similarities, whereas Thailand and Indonesia shared a few. The level of socio-economic development and the legacy of developmental history seem to be important in this grouping. The degree of geographical dispersion and differences in religious-cultural attitudes should have also been contributing factors in the willingness of individuals to participate in public conflict resolution. How institutions and, in particular, government are viewed seem to be critical in influencing citizen participation in public conflict. Our study found that government trust was higher in Indonesia and the country's existing conflict-management system was also viewed more positively than comparable systems in other countries.

When several factors for collaborative participation were analyzed using survey data, the "paradox of participation" phenomenon emerged. In all five Asian countries surveyed, previous participation experience was negatively related to future willingness to participate in public conflict resolution. This finding poses a challenge to the popular thesis that more participation experience encourages greater levels of cooperation and collaboration with government. Why people who have actively participated in public affairs to make their voices heard are discouraged from cooperating with government to resolve public conflicts in the future is a critical question. It may be because the experiences individuals had in interacting with the government were not positive for one reason or another. As a result of their experience, people do not regard the government as a collaborative partner. In East Asia, government is still strong vis-à-vis private individuals and groups. For better or worse, government in East Asia is powerful and active in line with its historical legacy and the more recent "developmental state" practices. Governments in East Asia are plan-oriented and tend to impose top-down policies despite ongoing decentralization efforts. In the same context, governments design collaborative policy mechanisms to involve citizens in public governance. This top-down process of creating collaboration with citizens is not likely to reflect the type of true partnership and co-decision making espoused by the collaborative governance studies developed in Western democracies. Unless the state-society relationship of East Asian countries evolves to be sufficiently equal in the governance of public affairs, collaborative governance based on a true public-private partnership is not likely to be realized.

Since the social and political context was not fully considered in this particular glimpse into the paradox, we need to delve more deeply into the politics and public governance of each country. Instead, this study was limited to statistically analyzing data from cross-national surveys of five Asian countries. Despite this shortcoming, our empirical study can contribute to the movement of existing collaborative governance studies towards a comparative approach.

# References

Abcarian, G., & Palmer, M. (1974). Society in Conflict: An Introduction to Social Science. Canfield Press.

Agranoff, Robert and Michael McGuire (2003). *Collaborative Public Management: New Strategies for Local Governments*. Georgetown University Press.

Ajzen, I. (1991). The theory of planned behavior. Organizational behavior and human decision processes, 50(2), 179-211.

Ansell, C., & Gash, A. (2008). Collaborative Governance in Theory and Practice. *Journal of Public Administration Research and Theory*, 18(4), 543-571.

Barber, B. R. (1985). *Strong Democracy: Participatory Politics for a New Age*. University of California Press.

Boix C., & Posner, D. N. (1998). Social Capital: Explaining its Origins and Effects on Government Performance. *British Journal of Political Science*, 28(4), 686-693.

Braithwaite, V. (1998). Communal and Exchange Trust Norms: Their Value Base and Relevance to Institutional Trust. V. Braithwaite and M. Levi, *Trust and Governance*. Russell Sage Foundation, 46-74.

Bryson, J. M., Crosby, B. C., & Stone, M. M. (2006). The Design and Implementation of Cross-Sector Collaborations: Propositions from the Literature. *Public Administration Review*, 66(s1), 44-55.

Campbell, A., Gurin, G., & Miller, W. E. (1954). *The Voter Decides*. Evanston, Ⅲ.; Row, Peterson and Company.

Dahrendorf, R. G. (1959). *Class Conflict in Industrial Society*. Routledge & Kegan Paul.

________. (1968). *Essays in the Theory of Society*. Routledge & Kegan Paul.

Donahue, J., & Zeckhause, R. J. (2011). *Collaborative Governance: Private Roles for Public Goals in Turbulent Times*. Princeton University Press.

Easton, D. (1965). *A Systems Analysis of Political Life*. Wiley.

Emerson, K., Nabatchi, T., & Balogh, S. (2011). An integrative framework for collaborative governance. *Journal of Public Administration Research and Theory*, 22, 1-29.

Finkel, S. E. (1985). Reciprocal effects of participation and political efficacy: A panel analysis. *American Journal of Political Science*, 891-913.

Foa, R. S., & Mounk, Y. (2017). The Signs of Deconsolidation. *Journal of Democracy*, 28(1), 5-16.

Fukuyama, F. et al. (2015). *Democracy in Decline?* The Johns Hopkins University Press.

Galaskiewicz, J. (1979). *Exchange Networks and Community Politics*. Sage Publications.

Gerbaudo, Paolo. (2012). *Tweets and the Streets: Social Media and Contemporary Activism*. London: Pluto Press.

Goldsmith, S., & Eggers, W. D. (2004). *Governing by Network: The New Shape of the Public Sector*. Brookings Institution Press.

Ha, H. Y., & Lee, D. G. (2007). Based on the Case Studies in Korea between 1995 and 2006: The Occurrence and Resolution of Public Conflicts. *The Korea Association for Policy Studies*, 16(4). 329-357.

Hong, S. M., & Kim, K. K. (2008). A Study on the Effectiveness of Inter-governmental Conflict Management Institutions. *Korean Public Management Review*, 22(4), 1-17.

Jeong, J. H. (2012). Institutional Approach on Prevention of Public Conflict: Focused on Introduction of Public Debate Institution. *The Journal of Korean Policy Studies*, 12(2), 311-336.

Kaase, M. (1999). Interpersonal trust, political trust and non-institutionalized political participation in Western Europe. *West European Politics*, 22(3), 1-21.

Ka, S. (2016). An Analysis of Public Opinion on Korean Public Conflicts: Continuity and Change of Age Groups. *Dispute Resolution Studies Review*, 14(3), 129-162.

Kim, J. K. (2010). Problems of installing the social conflict facilities and resolving plan for conflict. *Public Law*, 38(3), 287-310.

Kim, S. I. (2011). A Study on the Policy Conflict and Mediation between Central Government and Local Residents Focused on the Case of Four Dams Construction in Gangwon-Do. *Korean Public Administration and Policy Review*, 9(1). 53-82.

Lah, T. J., & Park, J. H. (2004). *Institutional Approach to Conflict Resolution*. Seoul: Korea Institute of Public Administration.

Levitsky, S., & Ziblatt, D. (2018). *How Democracies Die*, Broadway Books.

Miller, A. H. (1974). Political issues and trust in government: 1964–1970. *American Political Science Review*, 68(3), 951-972.

Moore, S. A. (1996). Defining successful environmental dispute resolution: case studies form public land planning in the United states and Australia. *Environmental Impact Assessment Review*, 16.

Muller, E. N. (1982). An explanatory model for differing types of participation. *European Journal of Political Research*, 10(1), 1-16.

OECD. (2019). *Government at a Glance*. http://www.oecd.org/gov/government-at-a-glance-22214399.html

Papacharissi, Z. A. (2015). *Affective Public: Sentiment, Technology, and Politics*. Oxford University Press.

Pruitt, Dean G., & Jeffrey Z. Rubin, J. Z. (1986). Social Conflict: *Escalation, Stalemate, and Settlement*. Random House.

Putnam, D. (1993). *Making Democracy Work*. Princeton University Press.

Rothstein, B. (2001). Creating trust from above: social capital and institutional legitimacy. In European Consortium for Political Research Joint Sessions of Workshops, Grenoble, France, April.

Tarits, M. (2006). Making Democracy Work More? Exploring the Linkage between Social Capital and Government Performance. *Political Research Quarterly*, 59 (2), 211-225.

Tyler, T. (1998). Trust and Democratic Governance. V. Braithwaite and M. Levi, *Trust and Governance*. Russell Sage Foundation, 259-294.

Verba, S., & Almond, G. (1963). *The Civic Culture: Political Attitudes and Democracy in Five Nations*. Princeton, NJ: Princeton University Press.

Verba, S., & Nie, N. H. (1972). *Participation in America: Political Democracy and Social Equality*. The University of Chicago Press.

Walton, R. E., & Dutton, J. M. (1969). The management of interdepartmental conflict: A model and review. *Administrative Science Quarterly*, 14(1).

Whittaker, W. H. (1965). A study of intergroup conflict in an agency camp setting. Atlanta University Center.

Yang, K. (2005). Public Administrators' Trust in Citizens: A Missing Link in Citizen Involvement Efforts. *Public Administration Review*, 65(3), 273-285.

2

# Towards a Collaborative Governance: Exploring Consequences of Conflict Resolution Initiatives in Asia

Reginald G. Ugaddan, Na Gyeom Yang, and Sung Min Park

## Introduction

Public administration literature has dealt extensively on how public administrators confront multifaceted and complex issues of governance, effective and efficient delivery of services while taking into account the will and demands of the citizens (Lan, 1997; Wilson, 1992). In a democratic state, policy-making has to recognize the interaction of government, citizens, and/or the whole body politic. Governance, as it was differed with government, relates to "the processes of interaction and decision-making among the actors involved in a collective problem that lead to the creation, reinforcement, or reproduction of social norms and institutions" (Marc, 2011; "Governance", n.d.). In the same vein, public policies are designed to manifest citizen's desires, beliefs, and opinions on the country's political course (Farazmand, 2019) that require a collaborative governance framework of communication and consultation between and among stakeholders. In the 20th century, democratic ideals have swept all over the world wherein "public's preferences, and weighting all citizen's equally, has reached a high point of worldwide esteem" (Page & Shapiro, 2010, 2). Meaning, citizen's policy preferences have greatly influenced government's policy choice and actions (Page & Shapiro, 2010; 1993). Many governance policies, if not handled well, may encourage conflict that may affect the whole process of policy implementation. If conflict is handled properly, it can be a powerful vehicle to clarify communications, explain the intention and goals of policies to build stronger working relationships and to reach consensus.

Government and citizens' conflicts may occur when one perceive that its interest is negatively affected by the other (Wall & Callister, 1995); or if one perceives that the other party may frustrate or about to frustrate an important policy initiative; goal incompatibilities are strong between the government and citizens (Poole & Putnam, 1997; Rahim, 2017; Vecchio, 2005). Besides internal conflicts (e.g., institutional, organizational, or jurisdictional conflict), public administrators face conflict with citizens whenever a policy on economic development runs counter with environmental protection, policies for national development against rights for security and life; infrastructural development versus public safety; and among others. The government and leaders do not operate in ultra vires that whatever policies, projects, or developmental efforts they think or plan will be executed without prior approval and acceptance of the citizens. Even in a republican democratic state and with the people's so called "representatives" in the parliament or national assembly has to consult the citizens for support. In various contexts, new laws or government policies are not insulated from people's scrutiny. People will always have the voice before the full implementation or adoption of a new policy. This is a very important component of democracy that allows active interplay between the government and citizens—that citizen's voice is heard and conflicts are resolved within a constitutionally, legally, and morally acceptable mechanism.

In case of policy misunderstanding or conflict, the government engages citizens through various conflict resolution strategies such as public consultation, information drive, and among others. Conflict resolution is an indispensable component of contemporary public administration and that it is time the field started paying serious attention to it. Deutsch, Coleman, and Marcus (2011, 188) mentioned that "conflict resolution refers to both the collaborative process by which differences are handled and the outcomes that are jointly agreed to by the parties." Like in an organizational behavior perspective whereby resolution conflict or dispute management strategy takes negotiation or bargaining (Golembiewski, 2000), the government take similar methods in dealing with possible conflict between government and citizens. The government employs applicable conflict resolution approaches to try to inform and correct the citizen's perception about why a policy is right and needed.

The success of conflict resolution initiatives could enhance citizen's trust in the government (Gottman & DeClaire, 2001) and contingent with external factors, such as political influence. Conflict resolution entails conflict management. Conflict mismanagement may result to mismanagement of trust which would seriously harm trustful relationship. In such instance, instead of resolving conflict, it would rather complicate or widen the gap of any existing differences in views or perspectives of parties. In case of government and citizens conflict, the question that may be asked would be, is it possible to trust the government with their initiatives in resolving possible conflict with the citizen? Or, would these conflict resolution approaches may enhance trust, or rather undermine trust in the central or local government? Deutsch and colleagues (2011, 189) pointed out, "conflict resolution involves a transformation of the relationship and situation such that solution developed by the parties are sustainable and self-correcting in the long term." In transition, the transformation could create a positive exchange between the government and citizens and encourage the emergence of a co-created policy (De Waal et al., 2010; Kelly et al., 2005; Sasser & Koslow, 2008), hence, could possibly enhance trust in the government.

Other factors distinct in power interplay in a political and democratic context that would influence conflict resolution is the political influence that would stem from political or any government entity. For example, political influence includes pressure given to a certain group or individual (Cherunilam, 2010) with the direct relationship between influence and power (Talcott & Mayhew, 1985). The political interplay and influence are political realities in the context of policy identification, development, and implementation. Fairclough and Fairclough (2013, 14) argue that "politics is about arriving cooperatively at decisions about what to do in the context of disagreement, conflict of interests and values, power inequalities, uncertainty, and all these factors can affect the rationality of the decisions that are made."

While there is a growing interest and literature on government's conflict resolution approaches, limited attention has been given to international comparative studies that look at consequences of conflict resolution methods in the Asian governance context. This paper analyzes how conflict resolution methods[1] is related with trust in central and local government, and on the conflict between government and local residents in Korea, Japan, Taiwan, and Thailand. The study argues that the four countries included in the study may have captured some (if not all) major principles of conflict resolution methods available in Asia. For example, Korea, Japan, and Taiwan (Confucian countries) put emphasis on social harmony and conformity based on reciprocity, thus are motivated to avoid conflict (Chua, 1997; Kurtz & Turpin, 1999; Magnan-Park, Marchetti, & Tan, 2018; May & Brown, 2009). While, in most cases, Thailand (non-Confucian country) that has strong central government tradition, conflicts with NGOs or local residents may have been confrontational (Farazmand, 2019). The paper also looks at the moderating effect of political influence of government entities that could be derived from the central government and local government on the relationship between trust in government and government and citizen conflict. The study further explores the intervening role of trust in government on the relationship of conflict resolution methods and the outcome variable. The analysis is based on the 2018 International Survey on the Causes and Effects of Conflicts collected by Sungkyunkwan University in the rural and urban residents of Korea, Japan, Taiwan, and Thailand.

# Literature Review and Hypotheses

## Conflict Resolution Methods

The government has various avenues in dealing with or resolving possible conflict with the citizens caused by new policies. A collaborative and principled conflict management strategy include transparency of information (Ofori & Lujala, 2015), early consultation (Fisher, 1972; 1983; Fields, 1996), objective discussion of issues, undiscriminating, and open communication can contribute to a healthy and inclusive conflict resolution. First, the accessibility and transparency of information is a deeply-rooted good governance principle that advances "frankness, openness and candor in state affairs" (Hood, 2006, 5). Transparency is a key concept in a democratic space and has been at the heart of a numerous governance efforts (Gupta, 2008). Transparency is achieved through the "disclosure of reliable information about administrative processes, decision, activities, outputs, and outcomes" (Mancini, Vaassen, & Dameri, 2013, 78). As a conflict resolution method, transparency and accessibility of relevant information for the public would erase any doubts of corruption, malpractice, and may intelligently inform the public about the intentions and goals of the government (O'Neill, 2006). Citizens should be factually and intelligently informed of all the details of any policy prior its adoption and implementation. Informed citizens may enhance vibrant community, thus reduce conflict with the government.

Second, in most applications, a third party consultative body is composed of interested parties—i.e., leaders of their respective groups, official representative with no direct decision-making power, and informal representatives (Fisher, 1972; 1983). For example in South Korea, consultative body is formed to push for major projects with other countries (e.g., Vietnam, United Arab Emirates) (Yonhap News Agency [Yonhap], 2018) or international institutions (e.g., Inter-American Development Bank [IDB], Asian Infrastructure Investment Bank [AIIB]) (The Korean Herald, 2018; Yonhap, 2018; The Korea Bizwire, 2016). Consultative body functions to enhance and strengthen bilateral cooperation with other countries and institutions. In the context of conflict resolution, third party consultative functions: (1) inducing mutual positive motivation for problem-solving; (2) improving the openness and accuracy of communication; (3) diagnosing the issues and processes of the conflict; and (4) regulating the interaction among the participants (Fisher, 1983, 304).

Third, government conflict management also employ panel of experts in cases when there are complex scientific and technical uncertainties in an issue. The panel of experts may consist of content or lay experts (Zaphiris & Ioannou, 2016), "thought leaders" or "futurists" (Wiklund, Kendler, & Strochlic, 2010), professional and/or citizens knowledgeable pertaining to the issue of focus (Ritchie, Burns, & Palmer, 2005). In a judicial proceeding, experts or expert witnesses act as interface between scientific evidence or trier of fact (O'Malley, 2013); experts were tapped to provide expert advice, program or policy recommendations (Leet, Gillespie, & True, 2010). In conflict resolution, panel of experts (or subject-matter experts) serve as an advisory panel and should be transparent to the parties (Rowe et al., 2013). Experts provide clear and objective information about the possible risks or consequences of a new policy once implemented.

Fourth, government should communicate with citizens about the programs, projects, or policies that may directly affect them. Citizens need to understand and know what are the possible outcomes and consequences of a policy (Mahmud, 2016) specifically on the risk prevention and management. Maintaining an effective communication with the citizens could build broader support and legitimacy of government policies, programs and projects. The World Bank's "The Contribution of Government Communication Capacity to Achieving Good Governance Outcomes" (2009, 1) mentioned that

> Government communication capacity is not just about efficient and effective information dissemination. The ability to "push out" information is necessary, albeit deeply insufficient. The willingness and ability to speak with citizens must be coupled with a willingness and ability to listen to them, incorporate their needs and preferences into the policy process, and engage local patterns of influence and trusted sources of information.

In the context of conflict resolution, good governance recognizes the role of the citizens in the whole governance process. The sustainability of policy and programs of government depends largely on the citizens. Sustainability is ensured when there is legitimacy and acceptability of policies that were crafted in a two-way communication with citizens. Many scholars argue that a meaningful and effective communication may reduce the chances of conflict (Askari et al., 2012; Miller, 2017; Malzia & Jameson, 2018; Rahim, 2017).

Last, conflict could possibly arise whenever a policy, program, or project failed to consider socially disadvantaged group (i.e., elderly, children, physically impaired citizens, and among others) in the risk prevention and management. Adopting Hardina's (2012, 44) connotation, socially disadvantaged group are "some demographic groups by virtue of factors such as age, physical/mental abilities, income, gender, religion, sexual orientation, ethnicity, race, or immigration status may be relatively privileged members of society while others are disadvantaged." In some, if not in most cases, conflict between government and citizens are usually caused by the infringement of human rights (both constitutionally and internationally recognized human rights). The non-recognition and disregard of individual and/or group rights in the adoption and implementation of policy would seriously cause conflict. For example, policies that discriminate and ignore the protection of individual and/or group rights, particularly disadvantaged groups and minorities could invite civil libertarians to call the attention of the government in the issue.

The major argument of this research, taking into account the governance context of South Korea, Japan, Taiwan, and Thailand, is that when handled well, conflict resolution approaches of the government may discourage conflict and enhance trust in government (i.e., central and local government). In essence, the five conflict resolution methods mentioned in this study call for effective, objective, and transparent communication between the government and citizens. The principles of good governance are responsive to the needs of the citizen through policies, programs, and projects that are legitimate and well-communicated to the people. Transparent communication creates value that results to trust (Tapscott & Ticoll, 2003). The contemporary society is in the "show me" era wherein transparency develops trust (organizational effectiveness; Steiber &

Alange, 2015, 240). The silence or non-communication of the details of governmental policy, programs, and projects undermine trust. Wong (2010, 79) mentioned that "trust is shallow when transparency is low." Even in a context of government and citizen conflict, the government has to create a reasonable and acceptable avenue that may allow citizens to understand and appreciate new policies or programs. Transparency allows the public to be heard, have access to all information, including the risk protection and management mechanisms, and easily understand the policy. Through this, transparency can encourage and sustain trust (Raines, 2012). Following these arguments, we propose the following hypotheses:

> **Hypothesis 1**: The level of perceived conflict resolution adoption—i.e., information disclosure ($H1_a$), consultative body ($H1_b$), panel of experts ($H1_c$), communication with the public ($H1_d$), and caring for the socially disadvantaged ($H1_e$) is positively related with trust in central government.
> **Hypothesis 2**: The level of perceived conflict resolution adoption—i.e., information disclosure ($H2_a$), consultative body ($H2_b$), panel of experts ($H2_c$), communication with the public ($H2_d$), and caring for the socially disadvantaged ($H2_e$) is positively related with trust in local government.
> **Hypothesis 3**: The level of perceived conflict resolution adoption—i.e., information disclosure ($H3_a$), consultative body ($H3_b$), panel of experts ($H3_c$), communication with the public ($H3_d$), and caring for the socially disadvantaged ($H3_e$) is negatively related with government and local residents conflict.

## Direct and Intervening Role of Trust in Government

Trust in government would pave the way for participatory governance and engaging citizens (Ugaddan & Calata, 2018). There are various definitions or conceptions for trust in government. Trust per se is defined "as the subjective assessment of one party that another party will perform a particular transaction according to his or her confident expectations, in an environment characterized by uncertainty" (Ba & Pavlou, 2002, 245). To apply it in a context of government and citizen relationship, trust in government refers to the degree of trust and confidence the public has towards its government—executive, legislative, and judicial branches of the government ("Trust in Government", Gallup, n.d.). Trust in government is represented by various policies, programs, and/or actions of the government. According to Organization for Economic Co-operation and Development (OECD, 2017, par. 1), "trust, is both interpersonal trust, and trust in institutions, is a key ingredient of growth, societal well-being and governance." Interpersonal trust includes generalized trust (interpersonal trust not known to a person) and limited trust (interpersonal trust known to a person); while institutional trust refers to all trust directed towards "political, law, and order and non-governmental institutions" (OECD, 2017, 11). Institutional trust can also denote on continues interactions that is based on explicit or implicit rules and norms (Rousseau, Sitkin, Burt, & Camerer, 1998; as cited in Deutsch, Coleman, & Marcus, 2011, 97).

In a governance perspective, institutional trust is a determinant for public value creation (Kelly, Mulgan, & Muers, 2002). Government's performance builds trust in government it manifests legitimacy and acceptability of public policies (Keele, 2007; "Trust in Government", OECD, n.d.). Although widely acknowledged, trust in government strengthens good governance and successful society. It would be impossible for a society to have harmony when citizens perceive that government institutions are not trustful—incompetent, ineffective, and fails to "get things done" for the citizens. As already argued, trust in government has a complex origin (Kim, 2010). Trust is contingent with the past and recent actions of government, in particular performance of government institutions in the executive, legislative, and judicial branch (Keele, 2007). One may argue high trust in government may effectively mediate or intervene on the activities of government, citizens, and the society towards positive outcomes.

Government and citizen relationship is dependent on trust in committing resources, achieving decisions in attaining societal goals, and acquiescence to public policies (Chanley, Rudolph, & Rahn, 2000; OECD, 2017). Grounded on institutional trust, government and citizen conflict could be undermined and mutual agreement can be reached. Along this backdrop, the study proposes the following hypotheses:

**Hypothesis 4**: The level of trust in central government ($H4_a$) and local government ($H4_b$) is negatively related with government and local residents' conflict.

**Hypothesis 5**: The trust in central government ($H5_a$) mediates the relationship of perceived conflict resolution adoption—i.e., information disclosure ($H5_{a1}$), consultative body ($H5_{a2}$), panel of experts ($H5_{a3}$), communication with the public ($H5_{a4}$), and caring for the socially disadvantaged ($H5_{a5}$) and government and local residents conflict.

**Hypothesis 6**: The trust in local government ($H6_a$) mediates the relationship of perceived conflict resolution adoption—i.e., information disclosure ($H6_{a1}$), consultative body ($H6_{a2}$), panel of experts ($H6_{a3}$), communication with the public ($H6_{a4}$), and caring for the socially disadvantaged ($H6_{a5}$) and government and local residents conflict.

## Moderating Role of Political Influence

Political influence is referred to as an exercise of political power by those who do not actually possess political authority or enforce policies or laws. To have political influence is not necessary to have political authority; when a private or public institution was able to persuade an institution or individual with political authority to act on something in their favor, the former public or private institution exercised political power. According to Luhmann (2018), political influence comes in three forms: authority, reputation, and leadership. First, political influence comes in a form of authority when it is grounded from moral or historical authority. For example, individual leaders can possess political influence if they belong biologically or politically affiliated with those political nobles. Second, reputation as a source or form of political influence is best displayed by those who are known for their exceptional skills, intelligence, and/or wit. Last, leadership is a form or source political influence exemplified by the leaders with the capability of influencing others and builds followers.

Using Luhmann's theory on political influence, the relationship of trust in government (i.e., central, local government) and government and local resident's conflict could be explained by the authority, reputation, and leadership of political leaders or nobles of the central and/or local government. However, the so-called post-truth politics that include disdain and distrustful political leadership creates or establishes a negative connotation towards politicians. Thus, whatever interaction they may employ during a conflict weaken the relationship of trust and conflict. Following this argument, we hypothesize:

> **Hypothesis 7**: Political influence of central government ($H7_a$) and local government ($H7_b$) is positively related to conflict between government and local residents.
> **Hypothesis 8**: Political influence of central government ($H8_a$) and local government ($H8_b$) positively moderates the relationship between trust in central government and conflict between government and local residents.
> **Hypothesis 9**: Political influence of central government ($H9_a$) and local government ($H9_b$) positively moderates the relationship between trust in local government and conflict between government and local residents.

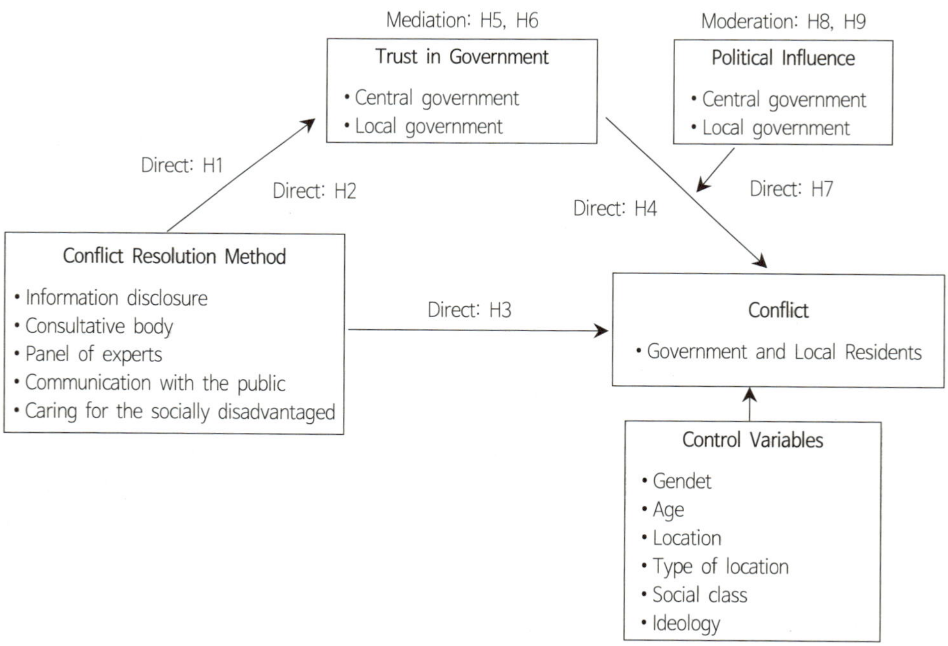


**Figure 1.** Research Model

# Methods

## Data and Instrumentation

The study is a comparative study of four countries including Korea, Japan, Taiwan and Thailand. The data used to verify the hypothesis in the study was an international survey of the causes and effects of the conflict, conducted by Sungkyunkwan University in four countries: Korea, Japan, Taiwan and Thailand. The survey asked respondents about conflicts between government policies, public and group, causes of conflict, approaches and initiatives to resolve conflicts between the government and citizens, trust in the government and their perceptions of government political influence. This was conducted online among four countries between January 2018 and March 2018. The study employed the data collected from Korea ($n$ = 1,118), Japan ($n$ = 1010), Taiwan ($n$ = 1,030) and Thailand ($n$ = 1,018).

## Measures

*Conflict resolution methods (CRM).* There were five items related to respondents' perception of the conflict resolution method. The survey asked the respondent to what extent do they agree on the following statements in a scale of 10 (1 = highly disagree to 10 = highly agree): "For conflict resolution, the government releases the relevant information in an easy and transparent manner", "In forming the consultative body, the government tries to consult with interested parties in advance on the scope, agenda, deadline, location, purpose, and decision-making method", "In the case of conflict situations with complex scientific and technical uncertainties, the government acknowledges the uncertainty and tries to form the fact relation by organizing a public-private expert panel", "The government is communicating its policies to the public on risk prevention and management", and "The Government are considering social disadvantaged groups (e.g., the elderly, children, people with disabilities, etc.) in their risk prevention and management policies."

*Trust in government (TIG).* To measure trust in government, the respondents were asked to what degree do they trust the central government and local government on a scale of 1 (total disbelief) to 10 (total belief).

*Political influence (PI).* To measure political influence of government, the respondents were asked to what extent do they perceive the political influence of the central government and local government. The survey items were asked on a scale of 1 (no impact at all) to 10 (very powerful).

*Government and local resident conflict (GLRC).* The item of for government and citizen conflict, the respondents were asked how serious the conflict between the government and local residents in the society in a scale of 1 (very serious) to 5 (not serious at all).

*Control variables.* The analysis controlled for the effects of gender, age, location, educational attainment, social class, and ideology. The gender was coded 1 for male and 0 for female. Type of age was (1) 18-29, (2) 30-39, (3) 40-49, and (4) 50-64. And location was categorized into 3: City Central, City, Town hall. Educational attainment was no formal education, incomplete elementary school, completed elementary, incomplete secondary school, completed secondary school, incomplete high school, completed high school, incomplete university, completed university or equivalent university degree and diploma, and graduate school or higher. Social class was answered on a scale of 10 (1 = the lowest status to 10 = the highest status). The ideology was denoted either progressive or conservative. Table 1 shows the sample characteristics.

**Table 1.** Sample Characteristics

| Variable | Category | Korea (n = 1,118) | Japan (n = 1,010) | Taiwan (n = 1,013) | Thailand (n = 1,018) |
|---|---|---|---|---|---|
| | | n (%) | n (%) | n (%) | n (%) |
| Gender | Male | 547 (48.93) | 509 (50.4) | 518 (50.3) | 498 (48.9) |
| | Female | 571 (51.07) | 501 (49.6) | 512 (49.7) | 520 (51.1) |
| Age (years) | 18 - 29 | 254 (22.72) | 202 (20.0) | 322 (31.3) | 267 (26.2) |
| | 30 - 39 | 218 (19.50) | 215 (21.3) | 270 (26.2) | 253 (24.9) |
| | 40 - 49 | 276 (24.69) | 256 (25.3) | 247 (24.0) | 250 (24.6) |
| | 50 - 64 | 370 (33.09) | 337 (33.4) | 191 (18.5) | 248 (24.4) |
| Location | City Central | 553 (47.67) | 463 (45.8) | 667 (64.8) | 678 (66.6) |
| | City | 527 (47.14) | 439 (43.4) | 273 (26.5) | 149 (14.6) |
| | Town Hall | 58 (5.19) | 108 (10.7) | 90 (8.8) | 192 (18.8) |
| Education attainment | No formal education | 0 (0.00) | 4 (0.4) | 2 (0.2) | 2 (0.2) |
| | Incomplete elementary school | 2 (0.18) | 1 (0.1) | 12 (1.1) | 4 (0.4) |
| | Completed elementary | 0 (0.00) | 1 (0.1) | 12 (1.2) | 8 (0.8) |
| | Incomplete secondary school | 0 (0.00) | 1 (0.1) | 3 (0.3) | 6 (0.6) |
| | Completed secondary school | 6 (0.54) | 15 (1.5) | 29 (2.8) | 30 (3.0) |
| | Incomplete high school | 5 (0.45) | 32 (3.2) | 37 (3.6) | 28 (2.8) |
| | Completed high school | 148 (13.24) | 417 (41.3) | 189 (18.4) | 124 (12.2) |
| | Some of college university/Incomplete University | 143 (12.79) | 49 (4.9) | 144 (14.0) | 37 (3.7) |
| | Completed university or equivalent university degree and diploma | 701 (62.70) | 448 (44.4) | 482 (46.8) | 527 (51.8) |

| | | | | | |
|---|---|---|---|---|---|
| | Graduate school or higher | 113 (10.11) | 43 (4.3) | 119 (11.6) | 250 (24.6) |
| Job classification | Agriculture, fishery & Forestry | 11 (0.98) | 15 (1.5) | 26 (2.6) | 40 (3.9) |
| | Self-employed business | 90 (8.05) | 58 (5.8) | 68 (6.6) | 194 (19.0) |
| | Sales/service | 58 (5.19) | 69 (6.8) | 96 (9.3) | 57 (5.6) |
| | Function/skilled workers | 29 (2.59) | 27 (2.7) | 116 (11.3) | 35 (3.4) |
| | General work | 18 (1.61) | 26 (2.6) | 32 (3.1) | 8 (0.8) |
| | Office/technical workers | 425 (38.01) | 326 (32.3) | 281 (27.3) | 244 (24.0) |
| | Management/managerial position | 53 (4.74) | 12 (1.2) | 34 (3.3) | 33 (3.3) |
| | 9th-6th grade officials | 18 (1.61) | 3 (0.3) | 18 (1.7) | 142 (14.0) |
| | Officials of grade 5 or higher | 3 (0.27) | 0 (0.00) | 3 (0.3) | 7 (0.7) |
| | Professional/liberal professors | 65 (5.81) | 36 (3.6) | 70 (6.8) | 39 (3.8) |
| | Housewives | 171 (15.30) | 171 (16.9) | 65 (6.3) | 60 (5.9) |
| | Students | 81 (7.25) | 15 (1.4) | 73 (7.1) | 45 (4.4) |
| | Unemployed | 61 (5.46) | 153 (15.1) | 80 (7.8) | 48 (4.7) |
| | Others | 35 (3.13) | 98 (9.7) | 67 (6.5) | 67 (6.6) |

## Analysis

Analysis of variables in this study used SPSS software. Detailed analysis methods are as follows. First, descriptive statistics analysis was performed to determine the demographic distribution of the samples and the level of measured variables. Second, correlation analysis was conducted to confirm the correlation between the study variables. Third, the regression analysis was performed and compared for each country in order to check the significance of dependent variables, independent variables, moderator and mediating variable. Along with an assessment of the intervening variable's effect, this study employed the causal steps approach (Baron & Kenny, 1986). To test for mediation, Baron & Kenny (1986, 1177) suggested, "first regressing the mediator on the independent variable; second, regressing the dependent variable on the independent variable; and third, regressing the dependent variable on both the independent variable and on the mediator." Mediation is indicated when, in the three regression processes, significant effects are observed among the independent and mediator, the independent and dependent, and the mediator and dependent variables (Baron & Kenny, 1986). This approach required two structural models: (1) direct effects between conflict resolution methods and conflict between government and local residents and (2) the structural model with the intervening variable, trust in central and local government, included. However, the causal steps approach is limited in that it assumes the randomness of sampling procedure. To strengthen the robustness of the results, the analysis employed Preacher and Hayes' (2004) bootstrapping mediation technique, which is a non-parametric resampling procedure that adjusts for non-normal distributions (Hayes, 2009).

## Findings and Results

### Descriptive Statistics Analysis

First of all, methods for the government's conflict resolution between government and citizens analyzed information disclosure, consultation, experts' panel, communication with the public and social disadvantage. Trust in government is divided into two: trust in central government and trust in local government. Moreover, there are 2 moderators such as central government political influence and local government political influence. Korea showed that the government social disadvantage is shown to be well-considered for the government to take good care of the socially vulnerable in risk prevention and management policies (mean = 5.06), trust in central government was confirmed by analyzing public confidence in the government (mean = 4.99), and government's political influence was also identified by analyzing its perceptions of central government political influence (mean = 6.96). In Japan, among the government's conflict resolution methods, consultative body had an average of 4.22, and the average of 4.62 was found in trust in local government. And central government political influence had an average of 6.57. Like in Taiwan and Japan, consultative body had the highest average of 5.76 for the government's conflict resolution methods. In addition, the average value of 4.33 was shown in trust in local government and 7.20 in the central government political influence. Finally, Thailand had the highest information disclosure of 7.05 out of five government conflict solutions, trust in central government had an average of 5.23, and central government political influence had an average of 7.07. When looking at conflicts between government and citizens in different countries, the results indicated that citizens were aware that conflicts with the government were serious (Korea's mean = 2.65, Japan = 3.75, Taiwan = 3.95 and Thailand = 3.51). The results showed that citizens' reactions to the government's conflict resolution methods vary slightly from country to country, and that citizens generally trust the government, though not much. It also meant that citizens recognize that the government has great political influence.

**Table 2.** Results of Descriptive Statistics

| Variables | Korea | | | | Japan | | | | Taiwan | | | | Thailand | | | |
|---|---|---|---|---|---|---|---|---|---|---|---|---|---|---|---|---|
| | Min | Max | Mean | SD | Min | Max | Mean | SD | Min | Max | Mean | SD | Min | Max | Mean | SD |
| GCC | 1.00 | 9.00 | 2.65 | 0.98 | 1.00 | 9.00 | 3.75 | 2.09 | 1.00 | 9.00 | 3.95 | 1.12 | 1.00 | 9.00 | 3.51 | 1.26 |
| ID | 0.00 | 10.00 | 4.83 | 2.33 | 0.00 | 10.00 | 3.93 | 2.04 | 0.00 | 10.00 | 5.69 | 2.60 | 0.00 | 10.00 | 7.05 | 3.06 |
| DB | 0.00 | 10.00 | 4.94 | 2.19 | 0.00 | 10.00 | 4.22 | 1.96 | 0.00 | 10.00 | 5.76 | 2.45 | 0.00 | 10.00 | 6.92 | 2.90 |
| PE | 0.00 | 10.00 | 4.92 | 2.16 | 0.00 | 10.00 | 4.19 | 1.93 | 0.00 | 10.00 | 5.69 | 2.50 | 0.00 | 10.00 | 6.67 | 2.86 |
| CWP | 0.00 | 10.00 | 4.96 | 2.26 | 0.00 | 10.00 | 3.78 | 2.01 | 0.00 | 10.00 | 5.22 | 2.80 | 0.00 | 10.00 | 5.23 | 2.87 |
| CSD | 0.00 | 10.00 | 5.06 | 2.16 | 0.00 | 10.00 | 3.80 | 2.07 | 0.00 | 10.00 | 5.50 | 2.73 | 0.00 | 10.00 | 5.70 | 2.91 |
| TCG | 1.00 | 10.00 | 4.99 | 1.91 | 1.00 | 10.00 | 4.19 | 2.12 | 1.00 | 10.00 | 4.06 | 2.06 | 1.00 | 10.00 | 5.23 | 2.51 |
| TLG | 1.00 | 10.00 | 4.61 | 1.73 | 1.00 | 10.00 | 4.62 | 1.86 | 1.00 | 10.00 | 4.33 | 1.98 | 1.00 | 10.00 | 4.70 | 2.30 |
| CGPI | 1.00 | 10.00 | 6.96 | 1.89 | 1.00 | 10.00 | 6.57 | 2.27 | 1.00 | 10.00 | 7.20 | 2.23 | 1.00 | 10.00 | 7.07 | 2.28 |
| LGPI | 1.00 | 10.00 | 6.05 | 1.70 | 1.00 | 10.00 | 5.50 | 1.76 | 1.00 | 10.00 | 6.44 | 2.00 | 1.00 | 10.00 | 5.94 | 2.07 |

Note: ID: information disclosure; CB: consultative body; PE: panel of experts; CWP: communication with the public; CSD: caring for the socially disadvantaged; GCC: government and citizen conflict; TCG: trust in central government; TLG: trust in local government; CGPI: central government political influence; LGPI: local government political influence.

## Correlations Analysis

A correlation analysis of the study variables was performed and the results in Korea are presented in Table 3, in Japan, Taiwan and Thailand are each shown in Table 4, 5 and 6, respectively. In Korea, the dependent variable, Government and Citizen Conflict, was found to have a significant positive correlation with all variables except for the moderator variable, central and local government's political Influence. Japan showed that conflict has a significant negative correlation with all variables except information disclosure, consultative body and Panel of experts. In Taiwan, there is a significant positive correlation with the dependent variable and the mediation variable, trust in the government, and a significant negative correlation with the moderating variable, governance's political influence. In Thailand, the dependent variables have a significant negative correlation with the independent variables, information disclosure and consultation, and a significant positive correlation with communication with the public and social disadvantage; while significantly and positively correlated with trust in the government. These results show that Japan has a direct correlation with the moderator variable, but Korea and Thailand have no any correlation with the intervening variable. It also indicates that there is a correlation with central government's political influence in Taiwan, but not with political influence of local government. The next step was to conduct a regression to verify the causality and effect between variables empirically based on these significant correlation results.

**Table 3.** Correlations Results (Korea)

| Variable | 1 | 2 | 3 | 4 | 5 | 6 | 7 | 8 | 9 | 10 |
|---|---|---|---|---|---|---|---|---|---|---|
| 1. Government and citizen conflict | 1 | | | | | | | | | |
| 2. Information disclosure | -.21** | 1 | | | | | | | | |
| 3. Consultative body | -.23** | .83** | 1 | | | | | | | |
| 4. Panel of experts | -.22** | .77** | .85** | 1 | | | | | | |
| 5. Communication with the public | -.25** | .70** | .77** | .77** | 1 | | | | | |
| 6. Caring for the socially disadvantaged | -.24** | .62** | .69** | .69** | .79** | 1 | | | | |
| 7. Trust in central government | -.27** | .46** | .50** | .49** | .54** | .53** | 1 | | | |
| 8. Trust in local government | -.21** | .34** | .37** | .40** | .40** | .45** | .73** | 1 | | |
| 9. Political influence of central government | .01 | .01 | .03 | .06* | .08** | .12** | .15** | .10** | 1 | |
| 10. Political influence of local government | .03 | .05 | .05* | .10** | .12** | .14** | .18** | .17** | .76** | 1 |

Note: **Correlation is significant at the 0.01 level (1-tailed). *Correlation is significant at the 0.05 level (1-tailed).

**Table 4.** Correlations Results (Japan)

| Variable | 1 | 2 | 3 | 4 | 5 | 6 | 7 | 8 | 9 | 10 |
|---|---|---|---|---|---|---|---|---|---|---|
| 1. Government and citizen conflict | 1 | | | | | | | | | |
| 2. Information disclosure | -0.02 | 1 | | | | | | | | |
| 3. Consultative body | -0.03 | .70** | 1 | | | | | | | |
| 4. Panel of experts | -0.04 | .74** | .72** | 1 | | | | | | |
| 5. Communication with the public | -.05* | .67** | .58** | .69** | 1 | | | | | |
| 6. Caring for the socially disadvantaged | -.06* | .64** | .56** | .63** | .78** | 1 | | | | |
| 7. Trust in central government | -.14** | .36** | .29** | .36** | .41** | .39** | 1 | | | |
| 8. Trust in local government | -.07* | .23** | .20** | .24** | .25** | .24** | .75** | 1 | | |
| 9. Political influence of central government | -.06* | -0.04 | .04 | .01 | -.07* | -.05* | .14** | .18** | 1 | |
| 10. Political influence of local government | -.06* | 0.05 | .07* | .06* | .04 | .02 | .26** | .32** | .67** | 1 |

Note: **Correlation is significant at the 0.01 level (1-tailed). *Correlation is significant at the 0.05 level (1-tailed).

**Table 5.** Correlations Results (Taiwan)

| Variable | 1 | 2 | 3 | 4 | 5 | 6 | 7 | 8 | 9 | 10 |
|---|---|---|---|---|---|---|---|---|---|---|
| 1. Government and citizen conflict | 1 | | | | | | | | | |
| 2. Information disclosure | -.01 | 1 | | | | | | | | |
| 3. Consultative body | -.03 | .81** | 1 | | | | | | | |
| 4. Panel of experts | -.02 | .78** | .83** | 1 | | | | | | |
| 5. Communication with the public | -.09** | .62** | .65** | .68** | 1 | | | | | |
| 6. Caring for the socially disadvantaged | -.09** | .63** | .66** | .70** | .82** | 1 | | | | |
| 7. Trust in central government | -.28** | .20** | .17** | .21** | .28** | .23** | 1 | | | |
| 8. Trust in local government | -.26** | .24** | .23** | .24** | .25** | .23** | .79** | 1 | | |
| 9. Political influence of central government | .08** | .28** | .32** | .30** | .16** | .23** | -.02 | .09** | 1 | |
| 10. Political influence of local government | .03 | .26** | .29** | .26** | .17** | .22** | .05 | .12** | .82** | 1 |

Note: **Correlation is significant at the 0.01 level (1-tailed). *Correlation is significant at the 0.05 level (1-tailed).

**Table 6.** Correlations Results (Thailand)

| Variable | 1 | 2 | 3 | 4 | 5 | 6 | 7 | 8 | 9 | 10 |
|---|---|---|---|---|---|---|---|---|---|---|
| 1. Government and citizen conflict | 1 | | | | | | | | | |
| 2. Information disclosure | .11** | 1 | | | | | | | | |
| 3. Consultative body | .11** | .91** | 1 | | | | | | | |
| 4. Panel of experts | .08** | .85** | .89** | 1 | | | | | | |
| 5. Communication with the public | -.13** | .47** | .44** | .49** | 1 | | | | | |
| 6. Caring for the socially disadvantaged | -.07* | .56** | .58** | .59** | .78** | 1 | | | | |
| 7. Trust in central government | -.29** | .19** | .22** | .26** | .40** | .41** | 1 | | | |
| 8. Trust in local government | -.21** | .13** | .13** | .15** | .31** | .30** | .72** | 1 | | |
| 9. Political influence of central government | .03 | .50** | .54** | .55** | .27** | .34** | .37** | .25** | 1 | |
| 10. Political influence of local government | -.03 | .29** | .32** | .36** | .29** | .29** | .49** | .46** | .64** | 1 |

Note: **Correlation is significant at the 0.01 level (1-tailed). *Correlation is significant at the 0.05 level (1-tailed).

## Regression Analysis on Trust in Government

Four regression analyses were conducted to determine the main effects between independent variables and mediator variables, resulting in the following Tables 7 in the order of Korea, Japan, Taiwan and Thailand. Factors were analyzed for independent variables, conflict resolution methods: information disclosure, consultation, experts' panel, communication with the public and social disadvantage. Then, we added control variables including gender, age, location, type of location, social class, and ideology. Korea showed that trust in central government was significantly predicted by communication with the public ($\beta = .18$, $p < .0.001$) and caring for socially disadvantaged ($\beta = .12$, $p < .001$). Among conflict resolution methods, trust in local government was statistically and significantly predicted by panel of experts ($\beta = .16$, $p < .01$) and caring for socially disadvantaged ($\beta = .30$, $p < .001$). These results supported $H1_d$, $H1_e$, $H2_c$, and $H2_e$.

In Japan, panel of experts ($\beta = -.09$, $p < .05$), communication with the public ($\beta = .19$, $p < .001$), and caring for socially disadvantaged ($\beta = .12$, $p < .01$) had significant effects on trust in central government, especially communication with the public, which had the largest statistically significant effect. On the other hand, only communication with the public ($\beta = .09$, $p < .10$) had a significant impact on trust in local government ($\beta = .27$, $p < .001$). These results supported $H1_c$, $H1_d$, $H1_e$, and $H2_d$. While in Taiwan, only Trust in the government and communication with the public (Central: $\beta = .27$, $p < .001$, Local: $\beta = .10$, $p < .05$) appeared to have a statistically significant effect, thus supporting $H1_d$.

Last, the results for Thailand shows that although trust in central government had statistically significant positive effects with panel of experts ($\beta$ =.15, $p < .01$), communication with the public ($\beta = .18$, $p < .001$), and caring for socially disadvantaged ($\beta = .22$, $p < .001$), but they had negative effects with information disclosure ($\beta = -.22$, $p < .001$). Trust in local government had an 18 percent capacity for explanation ($AdjR^2$=.18), with communication with the public ($\beta = .15$, $p < .001$) and caring for socially disadvantaged ($\beta = .17$, $p < .001$) having a statistically significant positive effect. These results supported $H1_a$, $H1_c$, $H1_d$, $H1_e$, $H2_d$, and $H2_e$.

**Table 7.** Results of Regression Analysis for Trust in Government

| | Korea | | Japan | | Taiwan | | Thailand | |
|---|---|---|---|---|---|---|---|---|
| | CG | LG | CG | LG | CG | LG | CG | LG |
| | *Beta* | *Beta* | *Beta* | *Beta* | *Beta* | *Beta* | *Beta* | *Beta* |
| *Conflict resolution method* | | | | | | | | |
| Information disclosure | .05 | .00 | .05 | .03 | .08 | .10 | -.22*** | -.03 |
| Consultative body | .08 | .01 | -.03 | .00 | -.05 | .00 | .03 | -.06 |
| Panel of experts | .06 | .16** | .09* | .08 | .02 | .07 | .15** | .04 |
| Communication with the public | .18*** | .03 | .19*** | .09° | .27*** | .10* | .18*** | .15*** |
| Caring for socially disadvantaged | .22*** | .30*** | .12** | .06 | -.03 | .03 | .22*** | .17*** |
| *Control variable* | | | | | | | | |
| Gender | -.03 | -.07** | -.13*** | -.05° | .05* | .05 | .03 | .00 |
| Age | .04 | .00 | -.05 | -.03 | -.08** | -.09** | .09*** | -.01 |
| Location | .02 | -.04 | .00 | -.02 | -.01 | -.02 | .02 | .02 |
| Type of location | .02 | .07 | -.07 | -.04 | .04 | .04 | -.02 | .05* |
| Social class | .12*** | .12*** | .10** | .15*** | .18*** | .19*** | .18*** | .18*** |
| Ideology | -.16*** | -.03 | .15*** | .10*** | .03 | .04 | .14*** | .17*** |
| $R^2$ | .37 | .24 | .25 | .12 | .13 | .12 | .28 | .18 |
| *Adjusted* $R^2$ | .36 | .23 | .24 | .11 | .12 | .11 | .27 | .17 |
| *F* | 58.97*** | 31.18*** | 30.52*** | 12.14*** | 13.50*** | 13.04*** | 34.92*** | 20.67*** |

Note: o = p <. 10, * = p < .05, ** p < .01, *** p < .001, two-tailed tests of significance. CG: central government; LG: local government.

## Results of Regression Analysis on Government and Local Residents Conflict

This analysis looked at the relationship between the dependent variable and the independent variable, the dependent variable and the parameters, and trust in government. We looked at the relationship between the dependent variables and the interaction of parameters and the moderator variables. In South Korea, the results of multiple regression analyses show that trust in central government ($\beta = -.14$, $p < .01$) had a negative impact on conflict while local government political influence ($\beta = .13$, $p < .01$) is positively related with conflict. It was shown that there was no effect on the interaction between trust and political influence. These results supported $H4_a$ and $H7_b$. While in Japan, like South Korea, the results reveal that trust in central government ($\beta = -.17$, $p < .001$) had a statistically negative effect on conflict. In addition, local government political influence positively moderates the relationship between trust in central government ($\beta = .16$, $p < .01$). These results supported $H4_a$ and $H8_b$.

In Taiwan, caring for socially disadvantaged ($\beta = -.11$, $p < .05$), trust in central government ($\beta = -.16$, $p < .001$) and trust in local government ($\beta = -.16$, $p < .001$) appeared to have a negative effect on conflict; while central government political influence significantly and positively related with conflict ($\beta = .12$, $p < .01$). The result also shows that central political influence ($\beta = .13$, $p < .05$) positively moderate the negative relationship between trust in local government and conflict. These findings supported $H3_e$, $H4_a$, $H4_b$ and $H7_a$.

Last, the result on Thailand data reveal that communication with the public ($\beta = -.16$, $p < .001$) and trust in central government ($\beta = -.35$, $p < .001$) are negatively and significantly related with conflict; while local government political influence ($\beta = .09$, $p < .05$) is positively related with conflict. These findings supported $H3_d$, $H4_a$, and $H7_a$. See Table 8 for the results.

**Table 8.** Results of Analysis for Government and Citizens Conflict

| | Korea | | Japan | | Taiwan | | Thailand | |
|---|---|---|---|---|---|---|---|---|
| | *Beta* | *t* | *Beta* | *t* | *Beta* | *t* | *Beta* | *t* |
| *Conflict resolution method* | | | | | | | | |
| Information disclosure | -0.01 | -0.17 | 0.06 | 1.11 | 0.10 | 1.78 | 0.08 | 1.17 |
| Consultative body | -0.05 | -0.73 | 0.01 | 0.15 | -0.03 | -0.53 | 0.13 | 1.59 |
| Panel of experts | 0.01 | 0.24 | -0.02 | -0.36 | 0.07 | 1.11 | 0.02 | 0.28 |
| Communication with the public | -0.09 | -1.55 | -0.04 | -0.73 | -0.02 | -0.42 | -0.16 | **-3.43***** |
| Caring for socially disadvantaged | -0.06 | -1.21 | -0.02 | -0.28 | -0.11 | **-1.90*** | 0.03 | 0.52 |
| *Trust and political influence* | | | | | | | | |
| Trust in central government | -0.14 | **-2.80**** | -0.17 | **-3.21***** | -0.16 | **-3.21***** | -0.35 | **-7.21***** |
| Trust in local government | -0.06 | -1.33 | 0.06 | 1.30 | -0.16 | **-3.23***** | -0.03 | -0.63 |
| Central government political influence | -0.01 | -0.17 | -0.05 | -1.18 | 0.12 | **2.09**** | 0.05 | 0.99 |
| Local government political influence | 0.13 | **2.93**** | 0.03 | 0.73 | 0.00 | -0.01 | 0.09 | **2.00*** |
| *Two-way interaction* | | | | | | | | |
| Central trust*central political influence | -0.04 | -0.51 | -0.08 | -1.34 | -0.10 | -1.54 | 0.01 | 0.26 |
| Central trust*local political influence | -0.01 | -0.18 | 0.16 | **2.73**** | 0.01 | 0.13 | -0.02 | -0.41 |
| Local trust*local political influence | 0.11 | 1.57 | -0.03 | -0.46 | 0.02 | 0.26 | 0.04 | 0.71 |
| Local trust*central political influence | 0.08 | 1.17 | 0.03 | 0.59 | 0.13 | **2.05*** | 0.07 | 1.46 |
| *Control variable* | | | | | | | | |
| Gender | 0.04 | 1.45 | 0.11 | 3.52 | 0.07 | **2.27*** | 0.06 | **2.12*** |
| Age | -0.02 | -0.60 | -0.01 | -0.27 | -0.07 | **-2.13*** | -0.11 | **-3.47***** |
| Location | 0.12 | **2.51**** | 0.01 | 0.24 | -0.02 | -0.71 | 0.04 | 1.26 |

| | | | | | | | | |
|---|---|---|---|---|---|---|---|---|
| Type of location | −0.12 | **−2.54**** | 0.07 | 2.11 | 0.00 | −0.10 | −0.05 | −1.55 |
| Social class | −0.08 | **−2.63**** | −0.01 | −0.44 | −0.02 | −0.72 | 0.04 | 1.20 |
| Ideology | 0.02 | 0.69 | 0.02 | 0.70 | 0.02 | 0.70 | 0.04 | 1.13 |
| $R^2$ | .13 | | .06 | | .12 | | .17 | |
| *Adjusted* $R^2$ | .11 | | .04 | | .10 | | .15 | |
| *F* | 8.46*** | | 3.08*** | | 6.97*** | | 10.58*** | |

Note: +$p < 0.10$, *$p < 0.05$, **$p < 0.01$, ***$p < 0.001$.

## Analysis on the Mediation Role of Trust in Government

Employing the Preacher-Hayes bootstrapping mediation analysis, the study determined the intervening role of trust in government (i.e., central and local government). See Tables 9 and 10 for the summary of results. First, testing on the mediating role of trust in central government, the results show that across the four countries, trust in central government mediates the relationship between the CRM and GLRC. In South Korea, there was a significant indirect effect of CRM on GLRC. Indirect effect ranged from 7.9% to 8.7% (*b* values ranged from -.038 to -.048), the maximum value that CRM could have for the GLRC. The results also provide that trust in local government mediates the relationship between CRM and GLRC. There was a significant indirect effect of CRM on GLRC through trust in local government, *b* is from -.020 to -.024 with an indirect effect being from 4.5% to 5.2% of the maximum value. The findings in South Korea show that the indirect effects via trust central and local government is fairly small effect. These results supported H5 and H6.

The findings for Japan provides that only trust in central government mediates the relationship between CRM and GLRC. In the analysis, the *b* values ranged from -.050 to -.066 with the maximum value for indirect effects from 4.5% to 5.7%. These results show a small indirect effect through trust in central government. These findings supported H5.

For Taiwan, there was a significant indirect effect of CRM on GLRC through trust in central and local governments. The findings reveal that the indirect effect ranged from $b=-.025$ to $b=-.030$ (5.5% to 7.4% maximum value of indirect effect of CRM) for trust in central government. While the indirect effect via trust in local government shows that effect ranged from $b=-.023$ to $b=-.028$ with a maximum value from 5.5% to 6.2%. The results show a small indirect effect. Hence, supported H5 and H6.

Last, the results show that trust in central and local government mediate the relationship of CRM and GLRC. For the trust in central government, the indirect effect ranged from $b=-.022$ to $b=-.052$ (5.8% to 11.3% maximum value of indirect effect of CRM) from CRM to GLRC. For the trust in local government, the indirect effect ranged from $b=-.010$ to $b=-.026$ (2.9% to 5.7% maximum

**Table 9.** Bootstrapping Mediation Analysis (Trust in Central Government)

| Country | Independent Variable | Dependent Variable | Mediator Trust in Government | Indirect Effect (*b*) | 95% bias Corrected Bootstrap CI | $k^2$ | 95% bias Corrected Bootstrap CI |
|---|---|---|---|---|---|---|---|
| Korea | Information disclosure | Conflict | Central government | -.048 | -.054, -.022 | .084 | .046, .119 |
| | Consultation | Conflict | Central government | -.041 | -.057, -.023 | .085 | .045, .116 |
| | Experts panel | Conflict | Central government | -.043 | -.060, -.026 | .087 | .048, .119 |
| | Communication with the public | Conflict | Central government | -.038 | -.055, -.017 | .079 | .036, .117 |
| | Social disadvantage | Conflict | Central government | -.043 | -.067, -.024 | .085 | .045, .126 |
| Japan | Information disclosure | Conflict | Central government | -.062 | -.094, -.036 | .056 | .033, .083 |
| | Consultation | Conflict | Central government | -.050 | -.077, -.029 | .045 | .025, .067 |
| | Experts panel | Conflict | Central government | -.059 | -.093, -.031 | .050 | .027, .078 |
| | Communication with the public | Conflict | Central government | -.066 | -.097, -.034 | .057 | .029, .084 |
| | Social disadvantage | Conflict | Central government | -.059 | -.093, -.031 | .054 | .028, .082 |
| Taiwan | Information disclosure | Conflict | Central government | -.026 | -.038, -.018 | .062 | .040, .089 |
| | Consultation | Conflict | Central government | -.025 | -.036, -.016 | .055 | .036, .081 |
| | Experts panel | Conflict | Central government | -.027 | -.038, -.017 | .061 | .037, .084 |
| | Communication with the public | Conflict | Central government | -.030 | -.041, -.021 | .074 | .052, .102 |
| | Social disadvantage | Conflict | Central government | -.025 | -.035, -.017 | .061 | .040, .088 |
| Thailand | Information disclosure | Conflict | Central government | -.022 | -.031, -.014 | .058 | .038, .083 |
| | Consultation | Conflict | Central government | -.029 | -.039, -.020 | .071 | .049, .097 |
| | Experts panel | Conflict | Central government | -.033 | -.044, -.023 | .079 | .057, .106 |
| | Communication with the public | Conflict | Central government | -.051 | -.064, -.039 | .108 | .083, .137 |
| | Social disadvantage | Conflict | Central government | -.052 | -.067, -.037 | .113 | .081, .145 |

**Table 10.** Bootstrapping Mediation Analysis (Trust in Local Government)

| Country | Independent Variable | Dependent Variable | Mediator Trust in Government | Indirect Effect (*b*) | 95% bias Corrected Bootstrap CI | $k^2$ | 95% bias Corrected Bootstrap CI |
|---|---|---|---|---|---|---|---|
| Korea | Information disclosure | Conflict | Local government | -.020 | -.032, -.008 | .048 | .018, .075 |
| | Consultation | Conflict | Local government | -.022 | -.035, -.009 | .048 | .019, .077 |
| | Experts panel | Conflict | Local government | -.024 | -.039, -.012 | .052 | .024, .083 |
| | Communication with the public | Conflict | Local government | -.020 | -.033, -.006 | .045 | .013, .077 |
| | Social disadvantage | Conflict | Local government | -.024 | -.039, -.008 | .050 | .015, .082 |
| Japan | Information disclosure | Conflict | Local government | -.014 | -.033, .001 | .013 | .001, .004 |
| | Consultation | Conflict | Local government | -.012 | -.031, .001 | .011 | .001, .027 |
| | Experts panel | Conflict | Local government | -.013 | -.033, .001 | .012 | .001, .028 |
| | Communication with the public | Conflict | Local government | -.013 | -.031, .004 | .012 | .001, .029 |
| | Social disadvantage | Conflict | Local government | -.012 | -.029, .003 | .011 | .001, .027 |
| Taiwan | Information disclosure | Conflict | Local government | -.027 | -.038, -.016 | .062 | .041, .088 |
| | Consultation | Conflict | Local government | -.027 | -.038, -.018 | .058 | .039, .082 |
| | Experts panel | Conflict | Local government | -.028 | -.038, -.018 | .062 | .040, .085 |
| | Communication with the public | Conflict | Local government | -.025 | -.034, -.017 | .061 | .040, .083 |
| | Social disadvantage | Conflict | Local government | -.023 | -.032, -.015 | .055 | .036, .077 |
| Thailand | Information disclosure | Conflict | Local government | -.010 | -.017, -.005 | .026 | .013, .044 |
| | Consultation | Conflict | Local government | -.012 | -.019, -.007 | .029 | .016, .047 |
| | Experts panel | Conflict | Local government | -.014 | -.021, -.008 | .033 | .019, .051 |
| | Communication with the public | Conflict | Local government | -.025 | -.037, -.016 | .055 | .034, .081 |
| | Social disadvantage | Conflict | Local government | -.026 | -.037, -.017 | .057 | .036, .083 |

value of indirect effect of CRM) from CRM to GLRC. Still, the indirect effect is relatively small. These results supported H5 and H6.

## Discussion and Conclusion

This study found that there are similarities and differences in the effect of conflict resolution methods on trust in government in South Korea, Japan, Taiwan, and Thailand. The results indicate that in the four countries the communication with the public was positively associated with trust in central government and local government (no significant results from South Korea). In South Korea and Thailand, caring for socially disadvantaged group is positively associated with trust in central (findings for Japan is also positive and significant) and local government. Interestingly, the finding on the relationship between information disclosure and trust in central government is negative and significant.

These results on the relationship of conflict resolution methods and trust in government reflect the growing attention on the values and principles of good governance — communication, transparency, and citizen participation. As argued in this paper, the conflict resolution methods mirror the characteristics of transparency and openness with the citizens.

One may argue that information disclosure, forming a consultative body, engaging panel of experts, communication with the public, and caring for socially disadvantaged groups lead towards transparency. Although transparency relate to the degree by which the government reveals important information (Curtin & Meijer, 2006; Welch, Hinnant, & Moon, 2005), one of the objective of conflict resolution method is to address transparency and provide clearer understanding about a policy, program, and project (Cook, Jacobs, & Dukhong, 2010).

In the era of governance, transparency is now taken to address mistrust in government — one of the prevailing issue of democratic governance (Grimmelikhuijsen & Porumbescu, 2013). Previous studies argue that transparency enhances trust in government (De Fine Licht, 2011; Tolbert & Mossberger, 2006). In the findings, however, the conflict resolution approaches that employ communication with the public, caring for the disadvantaged group, and engaging panel of experts accounted positive results for trust in government. These findings suggest that government leaders in their effort to increase trust through conflict resolution mechanisms, they have to prioritize initiatives that engage and inform citizens in a convincing, objective, and without discrimination all policies, programs, and projects that may directly or indirectly affect citizen. The government may activate a communication process that may effectively manage flow of information from the government to the citizens or vice versa: (1) information drive by the government through various medium (i.e., mass media, SNS, and among others); citizen consultation; and citizen dialogue (Rowe & Frewer, 2005). Also, government leaders must endeavor to create a collaborative governance culture that encourages partnership with citizens rather a hierarchical relationship through interactive activities between government leaders and local residents in the community (Bingham, Nabatchi, & O'Leary, 2005; Kim, 2010). Collaborative governance may prosper when the government creates an opportunity for the citizens to actively engage and participate in all governmental activities. It may possibly increase open-communication, thus may enhance affective-based trust relationship between the citizens and government.

The results indicate that among the conflict resolution methods, caring for socially disadvantaged group in Taiwan and communication with the public in Thailand is negatively associated with conflict. In Taiwan, the result mirror's the ongoing government's effort in caring their citizens through comprehensive and uniform health benefits and various programs for the elderly. The structural changes in the country such as the increasing senior population which is projected at 14% in 2018 ("Senior Welfare", 2015) may have influenced the perception of the citizens to address the needs and consider disadvantaged groups. In Thailand, the current military government has been implementing digital transformation 4.0 aims at enhancing citizen's wellbeing (Sagarik, Chansukree, Cho, & Berman, 2018). The effort of the government to enhance the communication between the government and citizens may reduce the chances of conflict (Thanannithichot, 2012).

In terms of trust in government, the study found that trust in central government is negatively associated with conflict in South Korea, Japan, Taiwan, and Thailand; while only in Taiwan shows trust in local government is negatively associated with conflict. Also, the findings show that political influence central government political influence in Taiwan and local government political influence in Korea and Thailand positively affect conflict. Meaning, when political influence from the central or local government they may increase the chances of more conflict. Last, the results indicate that local government political influence positively moderates the effect of trust in central government on conflict in Japan; while central government political influence positively moderate the effect of local trust on conflict in Taiwan. These findings suggest that trust reduce the possibility of conflict between the government and local residents. The study confirmed the mediating role of trust in government in predicting the effect of conflict resolution methods on conflict between government and local residents; except for the no-mediation role of trust in local government in Japan. The findings emphasize the important role of trust in government in the context of conflict management in the public sector.

Last, the findings of the study present important information that may pave the way towards adopting collaborative governance framework in the public sector. Acceptable and resilient public policies—designed in a flexible and divergent opinion—can be achieved through well-entrenched collaborative governance with trust and consensus (Bevir, 2006). Trust has to be promoted and sustained in all levels and areas of collaboration and interaction between and among the government, citizens, and private sector. The network or relationship depends on trust, loyalty, and reciprocity among stakeholders even in the absence of institutional safeguards (Loughlin, Kincaid, & Swenden, 2013). Thus, various mechanisms may be established that may encourage the active participation of citizens and other stakeholders in governance. For example, within local government a "counterpart bureaucracy"—local planning organizations or citizen actions group—can be developed and institutionalized within a local government to actively play the role of aggressively engaging citizens in governance (Yin, 2009).

Although these findings provide straightforward and important implications for conflict management, the results must be interpreted with caution and discussed within the boundaries of the limitations of the study, which reveal a clear need for further research. For example, the analyzed data were cross-sectional, which might provide speculative causal relationships or a sense of reverse causality. Thus, employing objective, longitudinal, and multi-source data might reduce subjective interpretations of the results. The data were prone to common method or social desirability biases, which might lead to inflated observed correlations or relationships. The consequences of self-report data could be reduced with data collected from multiple sources for the dependent and independent variables. To validate the findings and to generalize the lessons from this study, we also plan to continue this study through employing an experimental or quasi-experimental design by which we expect to obtain additional set of theoretical and practical caveats on conflict management, trust in government, and political influence.

## References

Askari, M., B Mohd Noah, S., Aishah Bt Hassan, S., & Bt Baba, M. (2012). Comparison the effects of communication and conflict resolution skills training on marital satisfaction. *International Journal of Psychological Studies*.

Baron, R. M., & Kenny, D. A. (1986) The moderator-mediator variable distinction in social psychological research: Conceptual, strategic, and statistical considerations. *Journal of Personality and Social Psychology*, 51(6), 1173-1182.

Ba, S., & Pavlou, P. A. (2002). Evidence of the effect of trust building technology in electronic markets: Price premiums and buyer behavior. *MIS Quarterly*, 243-268.

Bingham, L. B., Nabatchi, T., & O'Leary, R. (2005). The new governance: Practices and processes for stakeholder and citizen participation in the work of government. *Public Administration Review*, 65(5), 547-558.

Brownson, R. C., Baker, E. A., Leet, T. L., Gillespie, K. N., & True, W. R. (2010). *Evidence-Based Public Health* (2 edition). Oxford University Press. New York.

Chanley, V. A., Rudolph, T. J., & Rahn, W. M. (2000). The origins and consequences of public trust in government: A time series analysis. *Public Opinion Quarterly*, 64(3), 239-256.

Cherunilam, F. (2010). *Elements of Business Environment*. Himalaya Publishing House.

Chua, B. H. (1997). *Communitarian Ideology and Democracy in Singapore* (Vol. 9). Psychology Press.

Cook, F. L., Jacobs, L. R., & Kim, D. (2010). Trusting what you know: Information, knowledge, and confidence in Social Security. *The Journal of Politics*, 72(2), 397-412.

Curtin, D., & Meijer, A. J. (2006). Does transparency strengthen legitimacy? *Information Polity*, 11(2), 109-122.

de Fine Licht, J. (2011). Do we really want to know? The potentially negative effect of transparency in decision making on perceived legitimacy. *Scandinavian Political Studies*, 34(3), 183-201.

Del Vecchio, F. (2005). *Statistica per la ricerca sociale*. Cacucci.

Deutsch, M., Coleman, P. T., & Marcus, E. C. (Eds.). (2011). *The Handbook of Conflict Resolution: Theory and practice*. John Wiley & Sons.

De Waal, F. (2010). *The Age of Empathy: Nature's Lessons for a Kinder Society*. Broadway Books.

Farazmand, A. (Ed.). (2019). *Handbook of Comparative and Development Public Administration*. CRC press.

Fields, B. S. (1996). The molecular ecology of legionellae. *Trends in microbiology*, 4(7), 286-290.

Fisher, R. J. (1983). Third party consultation as a method of intergroup conflict resolution: A review of studies. *Journal of Conflict Resolution*, 27(2), 301-334.

Golembiewski, R. T. (2000). Handbook of organizational behavior, revised and expanded. CRC Press.

Gottman, J. M., & DeClaire, J. (2001). *The Relationship Cure: A 5 Step Guide for Building Better Connections with Family, Friends, and Lovers*. NY: Crown Publisheers.

Grimmelikhuijsen, S., Porumbescu, G., Hong, B., & Im, T. (2013). The effect of transparency on trust in government: A cross-national comparative experiment. *Public Administration Review*, 73(4), 575-586.

Gupta, A. (2008). Transparency under scrutiny: Information disclosure in global environmental governance. *Global Environmental Politics*, 8(2), 1-7.

Hardina, D. (2012). *Interpersonal Social Work Skills for Community Practice*. Springer Publishing Company.

Hayes, M. H. (2009). *Statistical Digital Signal Processing and Modeling*. New York: John Wiley and Sons.

Hood, C. (2006). *Transparency in Historical Perspective*, 135, 3-23. Oxford University Press.

Hufty, M. (2011). *Investigating Policy Processes: the Governance Analytical Framework (GAF)*.

Ietcu-Fairclough, I., & Fairclough, N. (2013). *Political Discourse Analysis: A Method for Advanced Students*. Routledge.

Keele, L. (2007). Social capital and the dynamics of trust in government. *American Journal of Political Science*, 51(2), 241-254.

Kelly, G., Mulgan, G., & Muers, S. (2002). *Creating Public Value: An Analytical Framework for Public Service Reform*. London: Strategy Unit, Cabinet Office.

Kelly, N. J. (2005). Political choice, public policy, and distributional outcomes. *American Journal of Political Science*, 49(4), 865-880.

Kim, S. (2010). Public trust in government in Japan and South Korea: Does the rise of critical citizens matter? *Public Administration Review*, 70(5), 801-810.

Kurtz, L. R., & Turpin, J. (Eds.). (1999). *Encyclopedia of Violence, Peace, and Conflict* (Vol. 1). Academic Press.

Magnan-Park, A. H. J., Marchetti, G., & Tan, S. K. (Eds.). (2018). *The Palgrave Hand-*

*book of Asian Cinema*. Palgrave Macmillan.

Mahmud, Adnan. (December 7, 2016). "How should government communicate with citizens? https://www.govloop.com/community/blog/government-communicate-citizens/

Mahmud, H. (2016). Impact of the destination state on migrants' remittances: A study of remitting among Bangladeshi migrants in the USA, the UAE and Japan. *Migration and Development*, 5(1), 79-98.

Malizia, D. A., & Jameson, J. K. (2018). Hidden in plain view: The impact of mediation on the mediator and implications for conflict resolution education. *Conflict Resolution Quarterly*, 35(3), 301-318.

Mancini, D., Vaassen, E. H., & Dameri, R. P. (2013). Trends in accounting information systems. In *Accounting Information Systems for Decision Making*, 1-11. Springer, Berlin, Heidelberg.

May, L., & Brown, J. (Eds.). (2009). *Philosophy of Law: Classic and Contemporary Readings*. John Wiley & Sons.

Miller, P., & Rose, N. (2017). Political power beyond the state: Problematics of government. *In Foucault and Law*, 191-224. Routledge.

OECD. (2017). *Guidelines on Measuring Trust*.

Ofori, J. J. Y., & Lujala, P. (2015). Illusionary transparency? Oil revenues, information disclosure, and transparency. *Society & Natural Resources*, 28(11), 1187-1202.

O'Malley, L. S. S. (2013). *Indian Caste Customs*. Cambridge University Press.

O'neill, B. E. (2006). *Insurgency and Terrorism: From Revolution to Apocalypse*. Manas Publications.

Page, B. I., & Shapiro, R. Y. (1993). The rational public and democracy. *Reconsidering the Democratic Public*, 35-64.

_________. (2010). *The Rational Public: Fifty Years of Trends in Americans' Policy Preferences*. University of Chicago Press.

Poole, M. S., Putnam, L. L., & Seibold, D. R. (1997). Organizational communication in the 21st century. *Management Communication Quarterly: McQ*, 11(1), 127.

Preacher K. J. & Hayes A. F. (2004) SPSS and SAS procedures for estimating indirect effects in simple mediation models. *Behavior Research Methods*, 36(4), 717–731.

_________. (2008). Asymptotic and resampling strategies for assessing and comparing indirect effects in multiple mediator models. *Behavior Research Methods*, 40(3), 879–891.

Rahim, M. A. (2017). *Managing Conflict in Organizations*. Routledge.

Raines, J. (2012). The Digital Accountability and Transparency Act of 2011 (DATA): *Using Open Data Principles to Revamp Spending Transparency Legislation*. NYL Sch. L. Rev., 57, 313.

Ritchie, B. W., Burns, P. M., & Palmer, C. A. (Eds.). (2005). *Tourism Research Methods: Integrating Theory with Practice*. Cabi.

Rousseau, D. M., Sitkin, S. B., Burt, R. S., & Camerer, C. (1998). Not so different after all: A cross-discipline view of trust. *Academy of Management Review*, 23(3), 393-404.

Rowe, G., & Frewer, L. J. (2005). A typology of public engagement mechanisms. *Science, Technology, & Human Values*, 30(2), 251-290.

Rowe, S., Alexander, N., Weaver, C. M., Dwyer, J. T., Drew, C., Appelbaum, R. S., ... & Westring, M. E. (2013). How experts are chosen to inform public policy: Can the process be improved? *Health Policy*, 112(3), 172-178.

Sagarik, D., Chansukree, P., Cho, W., & Berman, E. E-government 4.0 in Thailand: The role of central agencies. *Information Polity* (Preprint), 1-11.

Sasser, S. L., & Koslow, S. (2008). The Creative Advertising Development Process: Is Organizational Politics a Recipe for Disaster or a Dysfunctional Antidote? *New Trends in Advertising Research*, 103-119.

Steiber, A., & Alänge, S. (2015). Organizational innovation: verifying a comprehensive model for catalyzing organizational development and change. *Triple Helix*, 2(1), 14.

Tapscott, D., & Ticoll, D. (2003). *The Naked Corporation: How the Age of Transparency Will Revolutionize Business*. Simon and Schuster.

Thananithichot, S. (2012). Political engagement and participation of Thai citizens: the rural-urban disparity. *Contemporary Politics*, 18(1), 87-108.

Tolbert, C. J., & Mossberger, K. (2006). The effects of e-government on trust and confidence in government. *Public Administration Review*, 66(3), 354-369.

Ugaddan, R., & Calata, E. (2016). Interpretive and Disposition Effect of Democratic Policies and Political Propensity on Political Engagement: A Test of Policy Feedback in the Philippines. 2016, 1-22.

Wall, Jr, J. A., & Callister, R. R. (1995). Conflict and its management. *Journal of Management*, 21(3), 515-558.

Welch, E. W., Hinnant, C. C., & Moon, M. J. (2004). Linking citizen satisfaction with e-government and trust in government. *Journal of Public Administration Research and Theory*, 15(3), 371-391.

Wong, C. A., Spence Laschinger, H. K., & Cummings, G. G. (2010). Authentic leadership and nurses' voice behaviour and perceptions of care quality. *Journal of Nursing Management*, 18(8), 889-900.

Zaphiris, P., & Ioannou, A. (2018). Learning and Collaboration Technologies. Design, Development and Technological Innovation. Springer.
5th International Conference, LCT 2018, Held as Part of HCI International 2018, Las Vegas, NV, USA July 15-20, 2018, Proceedings.

## Notes

1. (a) Transparent information disclosure, (b) public consultation, (c) setting up a fact-finding body of experts, (d) public communication on risk prevention and management policies, and (e) consideration of socially disadvantaged groups on risk prevention and management policies.

## Appendix

### Construction of Indices

<u>Conflict Resolution Methods</u> (5 items)

To what extent do you agree with the following?

a. For conflict resolution, the government releases the relevant information in an easy and transparent manner.
b. In forming the consultative body, the government tries to consult with interested parties in advance on the scope, agenda, deadline, location, purpose, and decision making method.
c. In the case of conflict situations with complex scientific and technical uncertainties, the government acknowledges the uncertainty and tries to form the fact relation by organizing a public-private expert panel.

d. The government is communicating its policies to the public on risk prevention and management.
e. The government are considering social disadvantaged groups (e.g. the elderly, children, people with disabilities, etc.) in their risk prevention and management policies.

<u>Government and Citizen Conflict</u> (1 item)
How serious do you think the conflicts between people or groups shown below are in our society today?
a. Government and local residents

<u>Trust in Central and Local Government</u> (2 items)
How strongly do you trust the following organizations or groups? Please check the level of trust each organization or organization has.
a. Central government
b. Local government

<u>Political Influence of Central and Local Government</u> (2 items)
How much do you think the following organization or organizations have political influence?
a. Central government
b. Local government

3

# Comparative Analysis of the Nuclear Energy Policy Process in South Korea and Japan:

## Focusing on Citizen Participation Systems Enhancing Coexistence

Jeong Ho Yoo and Rosa Minhyo Cho

## Introduction

Social and political conflict structures that often occur in modern society are generally caused by a lack of communication or by blocked communication (Landwehr, 2010). Conflicts can be amplified when social actors fail to convey each other's will, whether intentionally or spontaneously, or when information about each other is insufficient or inaccurate. As a result, citizen participation and communication with greater openness is being highlighted to create alternatives to address difficult public issues more effectively (Kim, 2006). Promoting the voluntary participation of citizens in the policy-making process and encouraging a collective policy-making process through public deliberation are efforts to change the typical top-down communication style of East Asian governments. Such changes in communication is expected to (1) minimize social conflicts and costs that may arise from government-led policy-making and resolution of policy issues, (2) strengthen citizen participation in an open society, and (3) create synergies of collaborative governance in which a more dynamic and effective policy process can be developed (Fischer, 1998; Yoon, 2012).

Citizen participation has developed in various forms, especially in the United Kingdom and the United States since the early 1900s, when local government systems provided opportunities for citizens to participate in the local community's policy processes. Specifically, in the 1960s and 1970s, as efficiency in allocation of resources deteriorated due to frequent government failures and nationalization of private companies, concerns about a crisis in representative democracy emerged and thus the United States enacted a law obligating citizen participation (Burns et al., 1994; Park, 2002; Thomas, 1995). For example, the United States began institutionalizing citizen participation in the National Environmental Policy Act (NEPA) in 1967 and expanded it to various areas including transportation, urban planning, and river refurbishment (Lee & Lee, 2018).

Yet, the development of citizen participation in the political processes of East Asian democratic countries such as Korea and Japan are different from that of the West. Specifically, in both Korea and Japan, elite public officials in the central government were in charge of making decisions to promote efficient economic development during the modernization process of post-World War Ⅱ. For example, after the opening of ports for the West in 1854 and the Meiji Restoration, Japan adopted the bureaucratic model of Prussia with the goal of becoming a rich prosperous country. In the case of Korea, after achieving independence from Japan, the Park Chung-hee government (1961~1979) implemented an economic development model in 1961 based on the Japanese development model characterized as efficient economic development based on a strong centralized system. The centralized and authoritative policy-making process was an efficient method toward economic development in the early stages of development, but this led to a lack of citizen participation in the policymaking process as well as a sense of superiority of government officials over the people (Lee, 1999, 112; Park, 2002).

Since the 1990s, however, both Korea and Japan began to notice the limitations of solving complex social problems with simply their central government and National Assembly alone, and thus started to expand and institutionalize opportunities for citizens to participate in the policy process. In the beginning, public hearings and opinion polls were the preferred policy tool, but this effort gradually developed into policy tools with higher levels of participatory engagement such as advisory committees and referenda etc. In both countries, efforts to engage citizen participation began at the local government level, and such a tendency was quite pronounced during the 1990s in the case of Korea as its democratic political system matured (Lee & Lee, 2018, 272). In either Korea or Japan, the citizen participation system at the national (central government) level has not been fully activated.

In March 2011, a radioactive leak occurred at a nuclear power plant in Fukushima Prefecture, Japan. This shocked the whole world and triggered a radical shift in nuclear energy policy among countries around the world. Prime Minister Naoto Kan, Democratic Party of Japan, declared to abandon nuclear power and conducted the 'Deliberative Poll on Energy and Environmental Policy Options in Japan' from March 2012 to October 2012 based on the principles of deliberative democracy. Shortly after, the Cabinet decided to officially 'exit nuclear energy policy' in November 2012. However, Prime Minister Shinzo Abe of the Liberal Democratic Party, who took office in December 2012, overturned the original decision to exit nuclear energy policy and regressed back to a nuclear energy-dependent state in 2014 (Lim, 2018).

On the other hand, in Korea, despite the Fukushima nuclear accident the Lee Myung-bak administration was strongly promoting the development of nuclear power plants as a viable source of energy and exported nuclear power plants to the United Arab Emirates. Yet, in the 2012 presidential election, the opposing party candidate, Moon Jae-in, made a vigorous pledge to exit nuclear energy policy for the first time in the political sphere but was defeated. However, Moon Jae-in was elected in the following presidential election in 2017 and officially pledged to abandon nuclear energy policy. One of the first efforts related to abandoning nuclear energy policy was to form a public deliberation committee based on a deliberate polling model and use its results to decide whether the construction of Shin-Gori Nuclear Reactors No. 5 & 6 should be put to a stop. The public deliberation committee conducted the 'Participatory Surveys for Public Deliberation on Shin-Gori Nuclear Reactors No. 5 & 6' and concluded that although efforts to exit nuclear energy policy should be maintained at a macro level, the construction of Shin-Gori Nuclear Reactors No. 5 & 6, which was suspended, should resume. This decision was a result of compiling opinions of expert committee members and citizen participants at the public deliberation meetings.

Interestingly, both the Korean and Japanese governments used a citizen participation system called deliberative polling to determine the direction of their nuclear energy policy following the Fukushima nuclear accident. In Japan, deliberative polling was first used at the national level for pension reform in 2011, and the deliberative polling to exit nuclear energy policy in 2012 was its second effort. In Korea, the use of deliberative polling to revisit its national nuclear energy policy in 2017 was the first deliberative polling effort initiated by the central government that used a nationally representative sample with procedural legitimacy.[1)] Despite similarities in the decision making processes related to nuclear energy policy, these two countries have diverged in their policy trajectories since then. For example, the Abe government of conservative Liberal Democratic Party in Japan declared to abandon the results from the deliberative poll and resume production of nuclear energy, whereas in Korea although nuclear reactors are be built following the decision of the national deliberative poll some of the NGOs continue to criticize this decision.

In both cases, it appears that policies determined by the people through deliberation continue to be challenged and (in the case of Japan) short-lived. It should be noted that generally there are large social and economic costs associated with implementing citizen participatory systems. For example, it is reported that the Korean government spent 4.6 billion won (about 4 million US Dollars) on both the deliberation process (with 471 people participating) and the Participatory Surveys for Public Deliberation on Shin-Gori Nuclear Reactors No. 5 & 6 (with 20,000 people participating). In addition, the process of stopping and resuming construction of the Shin-Gori Nuclear Reactors No. 5 & 6 for four

1) Deliberative polling was first implemented in Korea by the Ministry of Finance and Economy to map out real estate policies in 2005, but was later severely criticized for methodological problems associated with lack of representativeness of the sample and procedural issues etc. Since then, there have been smaller scale use of deliberative polling (e.g., SBS Broadcasting company on the Korea-U.S. FTA in 2006; Busan port authority on the redevelopment project of the northern port of Busan in 2007) at the local government or individual institution levels.

months incurred a loss of 270 billion won (about 230 million US Dollars) (Jang, 2018). The huge social and economic costs associated with using these participatory channels warrants an examination into whether the citizen participation system is an effective policy option in the East Asian socio-political context.

Therefore, in this study, we examined the function and limitation of deliberative polling as a citizen participation system in the policy-making process and compared how the mechanism of increased citizen participation worked in each country. We also focused on how the policy context evolved overtime to further examine whether policy making through deliberative polling lasted in the context of East Asia.

## Citizen Participation System in the Policy-making Process

### Citizen Participation System in Korea and Japan

Japan achieved national development through strong centralization and policy making by elites in the 1900s. That is, Japan achieved economic development through the exclusive policy decisions of the central government's elite bureaucracy, members of the National Assembly, and the Japan Business Federation (Japan Business Federation). Yet, by the 1990s, with the recognition that the central government alone cannot solve all social problems effectively, citizen participation at the local government level was first institutionalized. Specifically, the policy advisory committee, citizen opinion surveys, online policy forums, and referendum systems were created in the policy-making process of local governments (Masao Kikuchi, 2010). This meant that local governments were able to experience grassroots democracy and enhance their political efficacy. In addition, increased cooperation between local governments and nonprofit organizations has led to more than 30,000 NPOs nationwide. Yet, still at the central government level, the indirect democracy system through parliament was the only way for ordinary citizens to participate in the policymaking process. In other words, although civic participation was encouraged at the local government level, it has not been active at the central government level.

In Korea's case, following the Korean War and during the military regime, Korea decided to focus on economic development based on administration through elite bureaucrats. So, there was no system for ordinary citizens to participate in the national policy process. In 1993, the Kim Young-sam government implemented the local government system, and the Roh Moo-hyun government (2003~2007) declared 'Participatory Government' as the presidential policy paradigm which embraced citizen participation in the policy process. Yet, efforts to institutionalize citizen participation was not strong during the Roh administration and as a result non-institutionalized forms of citizen participation increased since (Ju, 2010). That is, there have been no cases in which results of citizen participation directly influenced the policy of the central government.

Thus, the use of deliberative polling in determining the direction of a nation's energy policy can be seen as an important event in the citizen participation system in both Korea and Japan. Although there are many ways for citizens to participate in the policy making process, such as public hearings, opinion polls, national referendums, and public opinion surveys, the main focus of this study is on deliberative polling used by both Korea and Japan in the process of making nuclear energy policy.

## Deliberative Polling

For a long time, administrative or policy studies have emphasized citizen participation in the policy making process (Irvin & Stansbury, 2004). How citizens' opinions are reflected in policy making can be divided into two ways — one that reflects their opinions as they are and the other that reflect the refined opinions of participants during deliberations (Fishikin, 2009, 14). There has been much research on the method of using public hearings and public opinion polls in the policy-making process, but deliberative polling based on deliberative democracy has not been sufficiently studied as a policy making method (Halpin & Cintula, 2014, 69).

Public opinion is interpreted differently from general opinion. Contrary to general opinion, which seeks opinions from various people passively, public opinion emphasizes active communication (Kim, 2004, 119). To actively reflect citizens' opinions in policy, it is necessary to go through a public discussion process that allows various people to gather together on an issue to form refined and agreed opinion by having them go through a process of learning and discussion (Kim, 2004, 123). Deliberative polling is a model designed in 1988 by Professor James S. Fishikin of Stanford University. Fishikin (2009) argued that this method, which reflects refined public opinion in its policy decisions, represents the opinions of citizens and complements the limitations of the way in which citizens' opinions are usually summed up through majority vote (Fishikin, 2009). Specifically, public opinion, which is the refined public opinion of citizens formed through deliberation, learning and discussion, can be considered as one important policy making method that can both increase the representativeness in policy making and promote collective rationality (Kim, 2018).

Public opinion has significant implications for policy practitioners who determine and enforce actual policies (Halfin & Cintula, 2014, 70). In addition, as the process of public debate is a process of conveying citizens' refined public opinion to the government, it can be an important way to justify governmental policy. If citizen participation in policy making through deliberative polling is comprehensive, voluntary, rational and equal, it can be said that deliberative polling has gained legitimacy in the process of reflecting citizens' opinions in policy (Barrett et al., 2012, 186).

In Table 1, the characteristics of various methods of collecting opinions are presented. As is shown, deliberative polling may look similar to general opinion surveys and to the parliamentary system. However, the key difference between deliberative polling and the parliamentary system is that members of Congress are elected through elections. Parliament therefore has political justification. On the other hand, deliberative polling has statistical representation through the randomization process, unlike public statements and public hearings. That is, statistical representation is based on the way in which participation occurs. There is a difference between voluntary participation and randomization. Voluntary participation can be attended by stakeholders as well as ordinary citizens, so opinion can be distorted by the opinions of strongly asserted stakeholders at public hearings and public announcements. This is the case where the paradox of citizen participation could arise (Sone, 2016). In deliberative polling, some randomly selected participants may also have a skewed voice. However, deliberative polling can be adjusted by identifying differences between relatively small groups and populations through weighing the gap between the participants in the deliberative polling and the population. Another feature of deliberative polling is that participants go through a deliberative process after verifying that the information they have on the related issue is objective. Therefore, deliberative polling has an advantage over other methods of gathering opinions in that it provides statistical representation, provides sufficient information on the relevant policy issues, and has participants acquire knowledge of the issues and change their opinions during the discussion process.

By constructing a representative sample like this, it is possible to secure a justification of the final results through deliberative polling. In addition, providing participants in the deliberative polling with discussion opportunities related to specific issues (while providing balanced information) can ensure justification of the decision and increase the acceptability of the results of the deliberation process. Deliberative polling can have a legitimacy that is similar to that in the parliamentary system in that it meets the conditions of representativeness, sufficient information, and deliberation through discussion, unlike other methods of collecting opinions. Deliberative polling was proposed to overcome the limitations of traditional methods of collecting opinions and to satisfy both representativeness and deliberation (Cho, Cho, & Yoon, 2006). Therefore, it is important to ensure that the sample appropriately presents the population and that fairness is obtained in the deliberation process. It is also crucial for deliberation to actually have occurred in order for this process to be successful.

Many countries, including the United States, the United Kingdom, Australia, China, Japan, and Mongolia, use deliberative polling to determine the directions of policies on a variety of issues, including tax increases, abolition of capital punishment, maintenance of monarchy, government spending priorities, nuclear energy and constitutional amendments (Center for Deliberative Democracy, 2019). Forty-seven cases of deliberative polling in various countries were examined

**Table 1.** Characteristics of Methods for Collecting Opinions

| | Representativeness | Sufficient Information | Accessibility | Discussion |
|---|---|---|---|---|
| Public Comments | × | ▲ | ○ | × |
| Public Hearings | × | ▲ | ○ | ▲ |
| Opinion Survey | ○ | × | × | × |
| Deliberative Polling | ○ | ○ | × | ○ |
| Parliamentary System | ○ | ○ | × | ○ |
| Referendum | ○ | ▲ | ○ | × |

Note: ○: Excellent, ▲: Relatively Poor, ×: Poor
Source: Yasunori Sone, 2016 (reconstructed).

based on the nation, political system and ruling regime involved (Kim, 2018). Specifically, 18 cases (38.3%) of deliberative polling were conducted in parliamentary cabinet systems; 16 cases (34%) were conducted in countries with a presidential system; and 6 cases (12.7%) were conducted in nations with a semi-presidential system, which is a compromise between the presidential system and the parliamentary system. In general, the parliamentary cabinet system, which is politically sensitive to public affairs and thus actively reflects public opinion, is more likely to use deliberative polling than the presidential system. In addition, results were analyzed based on the ideology of the national policy making system, i.e., whether the ruling administration was progressive or conservative at the time of the deliberative polling. The frequency of progressive regimes (24 cases, 51.1%) is much higher than the conservative regimes (9 cases, 19.1%). In other words, it is highly likely that deliberative polling will be implemented in the policy making system of progressive regimes that recognize a culture of discussion (Park, 2000).

These findings are in line with the results of this study, given that it was the first use of deliberative polling at a time when progressive parties such as 'The Democratic Party of Korea' and 'Democratic Party of Japan' took power. The Democratic Party of Japan first came to power after the end of World War Ⅱ, breaking away from the unilateral rule of the Liberal Democratic Party until 2009. In 2011, deliberative polling was conducted for the first time at the central government level on the direction of pension reform due to the effects of an aging society. Based on the results, the Japanese House of Representatives held a discussion and voted on the policy (Maeil Business News, Nov. 1, 2017). In addition, the government expanded citizen participation in policy making on nuclear energy through deliberative polling in 2012. Korea's participatory surveys for public deliberation on Shin-Gori Nuclear Reactors No. 5 & 6 were highly political issues and were related to the pledge made by the Moon Jae-in government, the progressive-led government that took office after the impeachment of the conservative President Park Geun-hye. In other words, the newly launched regime tried to obtain political legitimacy through citizen participation. In the early process of public deliberation, the Moon Jae-in government announced that the central government would directly incorporate the results of participatory surveys of public deliberation committee in the policy thereby delegating all decision making authority as well as responsibility. However, the public deliberation committee argued that the committee can only consult, while the government had the authority and responsibility to make the final decision (Chae, 2017). Despite such events, the process still allowed the Moon Jae-in regime to obtain political legitimacy to continue to pursue abandoning the nuclear energy policy. Overall, scholars and critics have criticized some theoretical flaws or methodological weaknesses of the participatory surveys, but no one has argued that there are definitive flaws in the methodology of participatory surveys for public deliberation on Shin-Gori Nuclear Reactors No. 5 & 6 (Rhee, 2017).

Professor Fishikin's basic model of deliberative polling is described above, but each country adapted modified models depending on the case and the political and social environment of each country. Next, we will examine specifics related to the nuclear policy-making process through deliberative polling on energy and environmental policy options in Japan and participatory surveys for public deliberation on Shin-Gori Nuclear Reactors No. 5 & 6 in Korea.

### *The Deliberative Poll on Energy and Environmental Policy Options in Japan*

'The deliberative poll on energy and environmental policy options' in Japan was based on Professor Fishikin's deliberative polling model, but the specific details were modified to make them suitable for the Japanese context. The Japanese government conducted the deliberative polling using three main methods (Yasunori Sone, 2016): holding public hearings, a deliberative poll, and public comments (via Internet homepage, email and FAX). In other words, the deliberative polls on energy and environmental policy options used the basic model of the deliberative polling, but also supplemented the process with public hearings and public comments to make sure that they could collect and verify public opinion on energy and environmental policy options. Such additional measures were taken to overcome any limitations that may result from the limited number of participants involved in the polling process itself.

In Japan, prior to the Fukushima nuclear accident there was little, if any, conflict between the political sphere and citizens regarding nuclear energy policy with the majority view supporting nuclear energy. However, following the March 11, 2011 Great East Japan Earthquake and the Fukushima nuclear accident, the public's perceptions of nuclear power plants changed dramatically. To overcome the crisis, the Naoto Kan government of the Democratic Party of Japan established 'the Energy and Environment Council' on June 7, 2011. The Energy and Environment Council sought to reexamine Japan's existing energy policies and to establish new energy plans and policies. On July 29, 2011, the Energy and Environment Council published 'The Innovative Energy and Environment Strategy' with three principles to reduce reliance on nuclear power plants, transform energy into a distributed system, and expand public discussion of energy policies (Energy and Environment Council, 2012a). Specifically, they decided that nuclear power plants must be secured, and by 2030, nuclear power plants are to be completely decommissioned, at the same time fossil fuel energy will be supplied to provide stable energy while realizing the green energy revolution.

On December 21, 2011, the Energy and Environment Council announced the basic policies of energy reform, including the 'Revolution of Power Systems', which changed the energy supply and demand structure (Minister of Economy,

Trade and Industry, 2012). Accordingly, on June 29, 2012, the Energy and Environment Council named three scenarios in which nuclear energy rates were quantitatively defined as 'energy and environment options' and presented these to the public (Energy and Environment Council, 2012a). The first option was the 'zero scenario', in which the ratio of nuclear power generation will be zero by 2030, 35 percent for renewable energy and 65 percent for thermal energy. The second option was the '15 Scenario', in which the ratio of nuclear power will be 15 percent by 2030, new and renewable energy will be 30 percent, and thermal energy will be 55 percent. The third option was the '20~25 scenario', in which the ratio of nuclear power is 20~25 percent, renewable energy is 25~30 percent, and thermal energy is 50 percent.

The first stage of the deliberative poll, 'Public hearings on energy and environmental options', began in Saitama City on July 14, 2012 and was conducted in a total of 11 locations through August 4, 2012. The public hearing was selected through a lottery of between 100~200 participants per session. At the start of the public hearings, a government official explained three scenarios for energy in 2030, with participants expressing their opinions. As the second stage, the government established 'The Executive Committee of the Deliberative Poll on Energy and Environmental Policy Options' to conduct the national deliberative poll on July 7, 2012. Several committees including the executive committee in charge of planning and operation, the supervisory committee, the expert committee for providing opinions and advice, and the third-party verification committee were formed to conduct this deliberative poll led by the Japanese government (Center for Deliberative Democracy, Stanford, 2019). From July 7 to July 22, 2012, telephone opinion surveys were conducted on men and women over the age of 20 nationwide through random sampling, and 285 respondents willing to participate in the two-day general debates from August 4 to 5 were selected. The third stage of this process involved collecting public comments on energy and environment options from July 2, 2012 to August 12, 2012 using the internet homepage, email, and FAX.

The results showed the highest approval rate for the 'zero scenario' across all methods including public hearings, deliberative polling, and public comments. In the public hearings, 70% of the 1,400 people who expressed their opinion supported the zero scenario (The Nihon Keizai Shinbun, Aug. 10, 2012). Furthermore, in the deliberative polling process, about 32.6 percent of telephone poll respondents supported the zero scenario, while among the 285 participants of the two-day general debates 41.1 percent and 46.6 percent were found to support the zero scenario before and after the general debates, respectively (Executive Committee of the Deliberative Poll on Energy and Environmental Policy Options, 2012). In addition, 87% of the 89,124 public comments also supported the zero scenario (Energy and Environment Council, 2012b). On the basis of these public deliberations, the Democratic Party government finally decided on September

**Table 2.** Timeline of the Deliberative Polling on Energy and Environmental Policy Options

| Date | Contents |
|---|---|
| March 11, 2011 | Great East Japan Earthquake and the Fukushima nuclear accident |
| June 7, 2011 | The Naoto Kan government of the Democratic Party established the Energy and Environment Council |
| July 29, 2011 | The Energy and Environment Council published the 'Innovative Energy and Environment Strategy' with three principles for reducing reliance on nuclear power plants |
| December 21, 2011 | The Energy and Environment Council announced the basic policies of energy reform, including 'Revolution of Power Systems' |
| June 29, 2012 | The Energy and Environment Council named three scenarios in which nuclear energy rates are quantitatively defined as 'energy and environment options' and presented these to the public |
| July-August, 2012 | 'Public hearings on energy and environmental options' were conducted at 11 locations |
| July 7-22, 2012 | The government established 'The Executive Committee of the Deliberative Poll on Energy and Environmental Policy Options' to conduct the national deliberative poll. |
| July-August, 2012 | A survey using the Internet homepage, email, and FAX was conducted |
| September 14, 2012 | Democratic Party government finally decided on the innovative energy and environmental strategy with zero nuclear power plant ratio by 2030 |
| December 26, 2012 | Regime changed to Prime Minister Shinzo Abe, the Liberal Democratic Party |

Source: Japan Atomic Industrial Forum, September 5, 2019. reconstructed.

14, 2012 to pursue an innovative energy and environmental strategy with zero nuclear power plant production by 2030.

### *Participatory Surveys for Public Deliberation in Korea*

The Moon Jae-in administration which came into power on May 7, 2017 tried to implement his presidential election pledge to stop the construction of the Shin-Gori Nuclear Reactors No. 5 & 6 thereby exiting nuclear energy policy. However, it was important to gain legitimacy and base the policy decision on public opinion. On June 27, 2017, a public deliberation committee was formed at the Cabinet meeting chaired by the president to promote public deliberation on the Shin-Gori Nuclear Reactors No. 5 and 6 issue. On July 17, 2017 The Office for Government Policy Coordination (under the office of the prime minister) laid out 'Regulations on the Formation and Operation of the Public Deliberation Committee on Shin-Gori Nuclear Reactors No. 5 & 6' and as a result the Public Deliberation Committee on Shin-Gori Nuclear Reactors No. 5 & 6 was officially launched on July 24, 2017.

In the beginning, there was disagreement between the government and the public deliberation committee on the nature and authority of the committee. The government sought a Citizen's Jury system that would delegate substantive policy-making authority to the committee and defer responsibility for the decision, but the committee argued that the final policy-making authority was the government's responsibility and that they were merely an advisory organization (Presian, Dec. 6, 2017). Eventually, the committee was agreed upon to serve as mainly an advisory organization, implying that the government would receive results of the participatory surveys for public deliberation and try to make a final decision based on such results but would take ultimate responsibility for these actions.

Difference between an administrative committee and an advisory committee is important here. An administrative committee, similar in character to that originally proposed by the government, can be established on the basis of Article 5 of 'the Government Organization Act' and has the authority to decide and externally announce the will of the State. On the other hand, an advisory committee is established by a Presidential Decree or the Prime Minister's Decree and is meant to assist in the decision-making of administrative agencies such as deliberation, coordination, and consultation in the context of providing professional opinions or consulting (Government Organization Management Information System, 2019). In other words, decisions made by administrative committees are legally binding whereas those made by advisory committees are not.

The participatory surveys for public deliberation on Shin-Gori Nuclear Reactors No. 5 & 6 was conducted based on Fishikin's model of deliberative polling, but the surveys were customized to make them more suitable for the Korean context. The participatory surveys for public deliberation aimed to educate participants to have complete information so that they could select the best option through discussion and deliberation. Therefore, the selection of participants representing the public and the implementation of a mature process of forming knowledgeable opinions through learning were key attributes emphasized in the Korean deliberative polling process (Rhee, 2017).

To form the citizen participation groups, a two-stage stratified sampling method was applied. In the first stage, a stratified random sample based on 160 stratifications of region, gender, and age were applied. In the second stage, 30 stratifications were formed based on gender, age, and the first survey opinion of whether to continue with construction, suspend construction, or reserve any judgment. Through this process 500 people were sampled and of these 471 people participated in the deliberation process. In other words, the Korean participatory surveys for public deliberation constructed a sample through stratified two-stage sampling to ensure representativeness which is commonly pointed out as a weakness of most citizen participation systems such as the referendum. However, this method was still not completely free from controversies associated with representativeness due to its relatively small sample size.

On September 21, 2017 citizen participants were provided lectures on pros and cons of nuclear power plants and other related issues through the e-learning system. Citizen participants' opinions on nuclear energy policy were collected four times throughout the entire process of which they gradually acquired more information and had more time to deliberate. Also, any change in opinions were analyzed. The final opinion of the citizen participants were obtained at the general debate where participants were required to stay for two nights and three days to deliberate beginning on October 13, 2017. On October 20, 2017, the public deliberation committee announced that the construction of Shin-Gori

**Table 3.** Timeline of the Public Deliberation on Shin-Gori Nuclear Reactors No. 5 & 6

| Date | Contents |
| --- | --- |
| June 27, 2017 | In a cabinet meeting (session 28) chaired by the president, it was decided that a Public Deliberation Committee be established to build consensus by carrying out a public deliberation process based on deliberative polling concerning the issue of construction of Shin-Gori Nuclear Reactors No. 5 & 6 as part of a process of consensus-building and that construction on the reactors would be temporarily suspended. |
| July 7, 2017 | The Office for Government Policy Coordination began the process of organizing the Public Deliberation Committee (temporary designation) on Shin-Gori Nuclear Reactors No. 5 & 6. |
| July 17, 2017 | The Office for Government Policy Coordination (under a directive by the prime minister) laid out "Regulations on the Formation and Operation of the Public Deliberation Committee on Shin-Gori Nuclear Reactors No. 5 & 6." |
| July 24, 2017 | The Public Deliberation Committee on Shin-Gori Nuclear Reactors No. 5 & 6 was officially launched. |
| August 25, 2017 | The 1st survey was conducted.<br>A televised debate was broadcast on Ulsan MBC. |
| September 7, 2017 | A regional open debate was conducted in Gwangju. |
| September 13, 2017 | An expanded participatory deliberation group of 500 was selected. |
| September 21, 2017 | The 1st lecture of the e-learning system that focused on understanding the public deliberation process was opened. |
| October 13-15, 2017 | General debate (two nights, three days long) |
| October 13, 2017 | The 3rd survey was conducted. |
| October 15, 2017 | The 4th survey was conducted. |
| October 20, 2017 | The regular meeting was held, and recommendations were submitted by the committee. |

Source: The Public Deliberation Committee on Shin-Gori Nuclear Reactors No. 5 & 6., October 20, 2017. reconstructed.

Nuclear Reactor No. 5 & 6 should resume yet the government should also continue to pursue the policy of abandoning nuclear energy (The Report of the Public Deliberation Committee for Verification, 2017).

Moon Jae-in's government incorporated the polling results of the citizen participation groups and decided to resume the construction of the Shin-Gori Nuclear Reactor No. 5 & 6, but to completely dispose of nuclear power plants by 2070. Since the 2000s, Korean society has experienced many social conflicts over the construction of nuclear power plants and radioactive waste disposal facilities. These conflicts involved not only local residents, but also various actors such as environmental NGOs, the central government, local governments, and the Korean Hydro & Nuclear Power Company. The fact that various participants were able to provide objective information equally within the system and citizen participation groups were able to present and accept their opinions through mutual deliberation is quite meaningful. Given that the results of this deliberation was reflected in policy without much opposition or conflict also suggests that social costs of conflict may have been decreased.

## Continuity of Policy — Local Government's Right to Consent to the Construction of Nuclear Power Plants

### The Local Government Systems in Korea and Japan

Korea and Japan have developed in different historical and cultural contexts in terms of local governmental systems. Korea had a political system characterized by a strong centralized system for 600 years from the Joseon Dynasty to the modern era. After the founding of the Republic of Korea, due to the legacy of governance led by a strong central government in South Korea, its local government system has been weak. Since the first local government election was held in 1995, there has been a stronger demand for the power devolution to local governments. The Confucian philosophy that influences Koreans from the Joseon Dynasty to the present day emphasizes loyalty and filial piety, especially in the historical and cultural context of centralized power, which equates filial piety with parents at home and loyalty to the king. On the contrary, Japan has maintained a feudal system for a long time before modernization and the Meiji Restoration. As a result, Japan to this day has a relatively strong local government system compared to Korea, and the Japanese local governments tend to have independent authorities separate from the central government.

Interestingly, when we look at the structure and authority of the local government system across the two countries, Korea and Japan both appear to have a two-tiered system comprised of a regional local government and a basic local government. Local governments in Korea are composed of metropolitan city governments such as Seoul and Busan etc., provincial governments that include regional local governments, and basic local governments called si (city), goon (county), and gu (district) located within provinces. In Japan, the prefectures are regional local governments, consisting of Tokyo, Hokkaido, Osaka, Kyoto, and other prefectures. Under prefectures, there are basic local governments, called the municipality, which include shi (city), machi (town), and mura (village).

The functions (tasks) of local governments are divided into three types, "local autonomy functions", "statutory entrusted functions", and "delegated functions" (Lee J., 2009). Local autonomy functions refer to functions that the local government can autonomously execute without any interference or monitoring from the central government usually related to issues on local resident welfare. Among the functions entrusted to local governments through laws or ordinances, statutory entrusted functions are functions that were originally the responsibility of the central government. Once entrusted these functions operate with supervision of the local council but the central government still retains responsibility for ensuring their proper implementation. Lastly, delegated functions are those that the chief executive of the local government implements and manages legally under the jurisdiction of central government ministries and agencies. Such functions are under the strict oversight of central government with local council's role being limited to expense management. In Korea and Japan, the central government has given local governments large amounts of delegated functions and thus effectively controlled them (Masao Kikuchi, 2010). Increasingly, however, the relationship between the state and local governments has shifted from a vertical model to a more horizontal and complementary model (Muramatsu, 2006).

Japan's local government system re-established the relationship between the central government and local governments through the decentralization reform under the "Omnibus Local Autonomy Law" in 1999, and the authority of local governments is being continuously reformed. Japan recognized local governments as equal subjects who share the role with the central government as agents responsible for regional comprehensive administration. Japan revised or abolished a number of institutions formed on the basis of vertical relations. In addition, the delegated functions were abolished through ongoing negotiations between the central and local governments. In other words, the central government's intervention and control methods have begun to change to meet the expectations of new roles for local governments (Ha, Joo, & Choi, 2011). After the Omnibus Local Autonomy Law amendment, local governments held authority over almost all administrative areas except those that require a unified national implementation such as diplomacy, security, trials, and prosecutors. This meant that the central government takes charge of affairs in foreign affairs, defense, highways, national roads, higher education, social insurance, and economic policies, while regional local governments are in charge of affairs in policing, port management, high school education, child welfare, public health centers, regional development policies, and job security. The basic local governments are in charge of firefighting, resident registration, local roads, ports, sewage control, primary and secondary education, water supply, waste disposal, and regional development policies which greatly expanded their functions and responsibilities (Ministry of Internal Affairs and Communications, Local public finance in Japan, 2007).

Meanwhile, in creating its local government system Korea benchmarked the Japanese system in 1995 and has since practically maintained its core features with a lot of delegated functions (as of 2018) being used as a tool to control local governments (Ha, Joo, & Choi, 2011). Although the Roh Moo-hyun government (2003~2007) attempted decentralization of the central authority by increasing the local grant tax and giving authority to autonomously manage administrative organizations and personnel quotas, the existence of delegated functions limited the actual degree of autonomy. President Moon Jae-in, who served as senior secretary to president Roh Moo-hyun, passed the 'Omnibus Local Transition Act' at the Cabinet Council in October 2018, benchmarking Japan's Omnibus Local Autonomy Law (Ministry of the Interior and Safety, October 23, 2018). The act has currently passed the plenary session of the National Assembly in January 2020, and is scheduled to go into effect in 2021. The act contains a broad expansion of local autonomy and the decentralization of finance. However, the passage of this act does not automatically imply that local governments will have greater discretion related to the operation of nuclear power plants.

## Authority and Role of Japanese Local Governments in the Policy Process of Restarting Nuclear Power Plants

As mentioned earlier, after the administration of Prime Minister Shinzo Abe of Liberal Democratic Party took over on December 26, 2012, the circumstances around nuclear energy policy began to change. The conservative Liberal Democratic Party has lot of interests in electric power companies who are the operators of nuclear power plants (Kim & Chung, 2018). In addition, the cost of importing energy sources increased to US$40 trillion between 2011 and 2013, resulting in a trade deficit of US$227.9 billion from April, 2011 to April, 2014, shortly after the Fukushima nuclear accident (Global Risk Insight, 2019.07.05). This lead the Abe government to revise the 'zero scenario' nuclear energy policy by removing contents of the 'energy and environmental options' in the 'Energy White Paper 2013' (Choi, 2013).

Specifically, the Abe government created a Nuclear Regulatory Authority (NRA) and promoted the restart of nuclear power plant construction. This meant that the administration scrapped the 'zero scenario' policy of nuclear power generation determined by the 'deliberative polls on energy and environmental policy options'. Japan became divided in its view on nuclear energy with the government and industries being in favor of nuclear power plants for economic and energy security purposes, while the people generally opposing it (Suzuki,

2019). As of June, 2019, nine reactors at five plants have met the new standards set by the Abe government and resumed operations. The five plants are Ōi and Takahama (Kansai Electric Power Company), Genkai and Sendai (Kyūshū Electric Power Company), and Ikata (Shikoku Electric Power Company) (Nippon.com, 2019).

It is interesting to point out that the nine reactors at the five nuclear power plants that have resumed are located in localities where the governor of the prefecture comes from the conservative party and thus local residents vote predominantly conservative. The remaining six reactors are blocked from reactivation by the local governments. This phenomenon can be better understood in relation to the local government system in Japan since the local governments have an "informal" authority to veto nuclear power plants from restarting. In order to restart nuclear reactors in Japan, the electric power company must first submit a request to restart the nuclear power plant and then the NRA makes a determination on its readiness and safety to confirm that the reactor meets the new safety standards. This is a formal regulatory approval process. The final stage to this process requires the approvals of the governor of the prefecture and the mayor of the municipality in which the nuclear power plant is located. This is an informal, but recognized, step to approve or reject the reopening (Brain Efird et al., 2018). The approval process of the local government is unique in that it is a normalized but informal process that is not based on the law. In addition, the electric power companies are unable to restart their nuclear reactors with central government permission only since the governor of the prefecture may impose indirect restrictions on the operation of the plant based on the permission to reclaim the sea, and the mayors of municipalities may impose indirect restrictions based on laws related to firefighting and roads (Kim et al., 2014). In fact, obtaining approval from the local government is a necessary step in even the construction phase of nuclear power plants. Again, the construction agreement of the governor of the prefecture is not based on legal requirement but rather on 'implicit rules' (Kim M., 2017).

Another possible mechanism to block the restart of a nuclear power plant is through its legal system. In a few cases, advocacy organizations have filed an injunction to block the reactors from restarting and this gives the judiciary an opportunity to intervene. In fact, recently in January, 2020, the Japanese court has been reported to have ruled against the operation of Ikata nuclear reactor No. 3 in Ehime Prefecture (Kyodo News, January 17, 2020).

In sum, although nuclear energy policy is a national affair that requires unified promotion nationwide, local governments in Japan have been able to influence this process. Specifically, they have been able to intervene indirectly through their local autonomy functions such as management of local roads, firefighting, and waterworks. Also, the governor and mayor of local governments who are accountable to local residents have an informal (but recognized) ability to veto nuclear power plants from restarting. This means that the central government must obtain the consent of prefectures and municipalities in the nuclear power plant-based region when executing their national energy policy. In other words, the mature and well established Japanese local government system may function as a safeguard to drastic changes in central government policies and better align nation policies with the people's will.

## Authority and Role of Korean Local Governments in the Policy Process of Restarting Nuclear Power Plants

In South Korea, the policy of nuclear energy policy has been considered entirely as a state affair. This is because the nuclear energy policy was viewed as a highly specialized and technical area and a task that should be carried out uniformly at the national level (Kim M., 2017). Article 11 of the current Local Government Act lists affairs that are difficult to handle with the technical and financial capabilities of local governments, such as development and regulation of nuclear facilities which requires highly sophisticated technology. However, since the construction of nuclear facilities is not only related to national energy supply concerns but also to the development of the region with direct implications on environment, safety, and welfare of the local people, the relevance to local governments should not be ignored.

The decision process for the plans associated with nuclear power plant development in Korea is as follows (Ministry of Industry and Energy, 2018). The Korea Hydro & Nuclear Power Company (KHNP) prepares an approval plan and applies for approval to the Ministry of Trade, Industry and Energy (MOTIE, formerly the Ministry of Knowledge Economy). The Ministry of Trade, Industry and Energy approves and reviews the implementation plan. Subsequently, the 11 central government agencies are consulted, and the MOTIE finally approves the implementation plan (see Figure 1). It should be pointed out that the current system does not have an effective channel for local residents to voice their opinions. That is, recognizing the opinions of local governments is more of a formality and, in contrast to the Japanese case, there is no procedure involving the consent of local governments and local residents.

Of course, there have been instances where local governments held referendums regarding the decision to build nuclear power plants and/or radioactive waste management facilities. However, in Article 7 paragraph 2 of the Resident Referendum Act, there is a provision that "It cannot be put to a referendum on matters belonging to the authorities or functions of the central governments or other local governments." Thus, the outcome of the referendum cannot be legally binding on the nuclear energy policy, which belongs to state affairs. In other words, Korean local governments do not have the right to consent to (or veto) the central government's decision to construct or resume nuclear power plants either by law or custom.

From this perspective, the continuity of the decision to abandon nuclear energy is questionable in the Korean context. For example, if the succeeding administration decides to revoke the exit nuclear energy policy and restart nuclear power plants, there is little means to stop such effort. That is, the policy determined by the participatory surveys for public deliberation on the Shin-Gori Nuclear Reactors No. 5 & 6 may not last for long since the local government cannot function as a safeguard to such decisions as in the Japanese case. In fact, Korea is currently implementing the exit nuclear energy policy with the voluntary support of the Korean Hydro & Nuclear Power Company in terms of abandoning its business. Of course, such policy is not based on any legislation but rather pursued as simply an administrative plan. This implies that the policy can fluctuate rapidly with changes in internal and external environments such as regime change and/or massive blackouts.

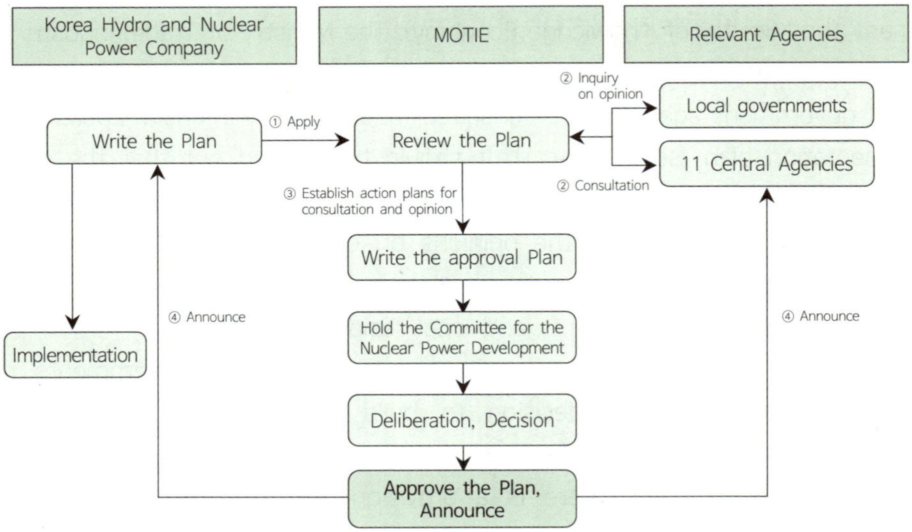


**Inquiry on opinion:** Relevant local governments.
**Consultation:** 11 Central Agencies
Ministry of Economy and Finance, Nuclear Safety and Security Commission, Ministry of National Defense, Ministry of the Interior and Safety, Ministry of Agriculture, Food and Rural Affairs, Ministry of Environments, Ministry of Trade, Industry and Energy, Ministry of Land, Infrastructure, and Transport, Korea Communications Commission, National Fire Agency, National Forest Service.

**Figure 1.** The Decision Process for Nuclear Power Plant Development Plans

Source: Ministry of Trade, Industry and Energy, The Decision Process for the Plan of Nuclear Power Plant Development, 2018.

## Conclusion and Implications

Public opinion in Korea and Japan regarding the exit nuclear energy policy was influenced by the 2011 Fukushima nuclear accident. The Democratic Party of Japan declared it would follow an exit nuclear energy policy and conducted the 'Deliberative Poll on Energy and Environmental Policy Options' as a citizen participation system from March 2012 to October 2012. Based on the results of the deliberate polling, the Japanese parliament voted and adopted the exit nuclear energy policy in October 2012. However, in December 2012, the conservative

Liberal Democratic Party's Abe government was launched and the exit nuclear energy policy was abolished. This meant that the country returned to a policy of nuclear energy dependence.

In 2017, with the launch of the Moon Jae-in government, Korea conducted the 'Participatory Surveys for Public Deliberation on Shin-Gori Nuclear Reactors No. 5 & 6' in which citizens participated in the process of evaluating the exit nuclear energy policy. The decision was reflected in the policies to resume construction of Shin-Gori Nuclear Reactors No. 5 & 6 but maintain the national agenda of exit nuclear energy policy and reduce nuclear energy dependence.

In terms of continuity of the decisions resulting from deliberate polling, both Korea and Japan have limitations in that they lack legal grounds to support the results. This is because the results of the deliberate polling in both countries were not made legally binding through parliamentary legislation. Therefore, it is highly likely that policies will change drastically at the national level due to changes in internal and external circumstances. This actually already happened in Japan where restarting nuclear power plants is being supported by the current Abe government. However, in our analysis, we found that continuity of the deliberate polling results regarding exit nuclear energy policy is closely related to one's local government system. In the case of Japan, obtaining indirect consent of local governments on the basis of customary agreements as well as exercising local authority based on positive laws such as firefighting law and reclamation authority of the sea seem to function as a measure to check the central government. Such measures are not quite available to the Korean local governments which limit their influence drastically.

Deliberative polling is a mechanism for coexistence and conflict resolution. It is important in terms of collecting public opinion and making sure that such results of deliberations are reflected in public policy. However, we must keep in mind that poorly executed deliberative polling and citizen participation systems with insufficient deliberation time and/or low representativeness etc. may actually increase or simply postpone conflicts. The deliberative polling periods in both Korea and Japan were relatively short, three months and six months, respectively. Moreover, during general debates there were conversations that appealed to emotions and some proactive participants would try to dominate the debate leading to issues of procedural legitimacy (The Public Deliberation Committee for Verification, 2017). Lastly, it should be important to consider mechanisms that may improve the continuity of decisions reached through deliberative polling.

## References

Barrett, G., Wyman, M., & Schattan, V. (2012). Assessing the policy impacts of deliberative civic engagement. In T. Nabatchi, J. Gastil, M. Weisner and M. Leighninger (eds). *Democracy in Motion. Evaluating the Practice and Impact of Deliberative Civic Engagement.* Oxford University.

Brain Efird et al. (2018). The Policymaking process to restart Japanese Nuclear Power Plants. The King Abdullah Petroleum Studies and Research Center (KAPSARC).

Burns, D., Hambleton, R., & Hoggett, P. (1994). *The Politics of Decentralisation.* Houndmills, Macmillan.

Chae, Jong Hun. (2017). The Success or Failure of the New Government's Nuclear Power Plant Policy and Public Deliberate. *Kore Institute of Public Administration,* Issue Paper. 52.

Cho, Sung Kyum., Cho, Eun Hee., and Yoon, Jeong-Ro. (2006). The Validity of the Deliberate Procedure in Deliberate Polling. *Korean Journal of Journalism & Communication Studies.* Spring Conference.

Choi, Seung-Eun. (December 20, 2013). Japan's Energy Basic Plan Amendment. Korea Energy Economics Institute. *World Energy Market Insight.*

Fishkin, James S. (2009). *When the People Speak: Deliberative Democracy and Public Consultation.* Oxford University Press.

Government Information Agency in Korea. (2008). *The White Paper on the Management of State Affairs* under the Roh Moo-hyun Government, Vol. 7 of the Government Innovation. The Government Information Agency in Korea.

Ha, Dong-Hyun, Joo, Jae-Bok, & Choi, Heung-Suk. (2011). An Analysis of Organizational Managements of Japan's Local Governments and Its Implications. *The Korea Local Administration Review,* 5(1), 277-314.

Halpin, Darren R., and Cintula, Juraj. (2014). Interests, Public Policy and Deliberation. In S. Elstub and P. McLaverty (Ed.). *Deliberative Democracy: Issues and Cases,* 69–81. Edinburgh University.

Irvin, Renee, and Stansbury, Jonh. (2004). Citizen Participation in Decision Making: Is It Worth the Effort? *Public Administration Review,* 64(1), 55–65.

Jang, Soo Chan. (2018). The Evaluation on Participatory Surveys for Public Deliberation on Shin-Gori Nuclear Reactors No. 5 & 6: *The Philosophy and Background of Participatory Public Policy Decision.* The ChungNam Institute.

Japan Atomic Industrial Forum. (September 5, 2019). Current Status of Nuclear Power

Plants in Japan. https://www.jaif.or.jp>jp-npps-operation20190905_en

Ju, Chang Bum. (2010). Civic Engagement, Cognitive Legitimacy, and Long Tail Politics. *The Korean Journal of Local Government Studies*, 22(4), 363-379.

Kim, Chang-Soo, Lee Kang-Ung, & Heu, Chul-Hang. (2014). The Dilemma of Local Governments in Building Nuclear Safety Systems: Focusing on the Case of Busan Metropolitan City. *The Korean Journal of Local Government Studies*, 18(2), 427-450.

Kim, Dae-Young. (2014). Two Strategies for Public Judgement in Political Critique. *Korean Political Science Review*, 38(2), 117-141.

Kim, Jungin. (2018). The Applicability of Deliberative Democracy in Policy Decision Making: Focusing on National Characteristics, Representatives, and Collective Rationality of Deliberative Poll. *Journal of Governmental Studies*, 24(1), 343-375.

Kim, Minhoon. (2017). *Nuclear Power and Local Autonomy*. Korean Nuclear Society.

Landwehr, Claudia. (2010). Discourse and Coordination: Modes of Interaction and their Roles in Political Decision-making. *The Journal of Political Philosophy*, 18(1), 1-42.

Lee, Jong-Soo. (2009). *Dictionary of Public Administration*. Seoul: Daeyoung Company.

Lee, Kongju. (2013). A Revitalization Measure of Referendum System for Realization of Popular Sovereignty. *Law Review, Korean Law Association*, 49, 253-275.

Lee, Min-young & Lee, Yong-sook. (2018). Participatory Governance and Public Involvement: An Assessment of Seoul Station 7017 Project. *Journal of Governmental Studies*, 24(2), 267-302.

Lee, Seung Jong. (1999). Participation in Local Autonomy and Citizen Education. *Korea Journal of Public Administration*, 37(2), 99-118.

Lim, Eunjung. (2018). Changes in Japans Energy Policy during the Era of Abe: Focusing on Liberalization of Energy Market and Nuclear U-turn. *Journal of Asiatic Studies*, 61(1), 177-216.

Masao Kikuchi. (2010). Public Policy Processes and Citizen Participation in Japan. In Berman, Evan., Moon, Jae E., and Choi, Heungsuk. (Ed), *Public Administration in East Asia: Mainland China, Japan, South Korea, Taiwan*. CRC Press.

Minister of Economy, Trade and Industry in Japan (2012). *White papers on Energy*.

Muramatsu, Michio. (2006). *Textbook Local Government (テキストブック地方自治)*. Toyo Keizai Shinbun.

Nippon.com. (July 8, 2019). Japan's Nuclear Power Plants. https://www.nippon.com/en/features/h00238/japan%E2%80%99s-nuclear-power-plants.html

Park, Chun Oh. (2002). An Empirical Study on the Acceptability of the Bureaucracy for Citizen Participation in Korea: Surveying Perceptions of Civil Servants. *Korea Journal of Public Administration*, 40(2), 1-28.

Park, Seung-Gwan. (2000). The Significance of Civility in Deliberative Democracy. *Korean Journal of Journalism & Communication Studies*, 45(1), 162-194.

Prime Minister of Japan and His Cabinet. (2012.06.08). Speeches and Statements by the Prime Minister. https://japan.kantei.go.jp/noda/statement/201206/08kaiken_e.html

Rhee, June Woong. (2017). Participatory Surveys for Public Deliberation that Shows the Power of Citizens to Adjust and Compromise Social Conflicts. In *The Whitepaper of the Public Deliberation Committee*, 188-190.

Sone, Yanase, Uekihara & Shimada. (2013). *Deliberative Polling: Lean, Think, Talk*. Sotokoto Shinsho.

Sone, Yasunori. (2016). Nuclear Energy Policy and the National Deliberative Poll. *Public Policy and Public Consultation: Deliberative Democracy in Asia*.

Suzuki, Tatsujiro. (2019). Nuclear Energy Policy after the Fukushima Nuclear Accident: An Analysis of "Polarized Debate" in Japan. IntechOpen. DOI: http://dx.doi.org/10.5772/intechopen.83435

The Energy and Environment Council. (June 29, 2012). Options for Energy and the Environment.

The Global Risk Insight. (July 5, 2019). Nuclear energy challenges in Japan. https://globalriskinsights.com/2019/07/japan-nuclear-energy

The Korea Economic Daily. (January 12, 2015). Japan's Abe government lost in the election for governor of Saga Prefecture. https://www.hankyung.com/international/article/201501127226g

The Ministry of Internal Affairs and Communications in Japan. (2007). Local public finance in Japan, 2007. http://www.soumu.go.jp/

The Ministry of the Interior and Safety in Korea. (October 26, 2017). The Roadmap for Local Transition (Proposal).

_________. (October 23, 2018). The Omnibus Local Transition Act, passed by the Cabinet Council, Press release.

The Public Deliberation Committee for Verification. (December 22, 2017). The Report of the Public Deliberation Committee for Verification on Shin-Gori Nuclear Reactors No. 5 & 6.

The Public Deliberation Committee on Shin-Gori Nuclear Reactors No. 5 & 6. (October 20, 2017). Results of Participatory Surveys for Public Deliberation on Shin-Gori

Nuclear Reactors No. 5 & 6.

Thomas, John Clayton. (1995). *Public Participation in Public Decision*. San Francisco: Jossey-Bass.

Yanase, Noboru. (2013). The Implementation of the Deliberative Forum for Public Policy Making: Report on the National Deliberative Polling on Energy and Environmental Policy Options. *Journal of the Faculty of Law*, Komazawa University, No. 71 March 2013.

Part 2

# Government-Citizen Collaboration in a Public Program

4

# Good Practices in Collaborative Governance: Local Governments and Galing Pook in the Philippines

Alex B. Brillantes Jr. and Karl Emmanuel V. Ruiz

## Overview

The praxis[1] of collaborative governance is alive and well in the Philippines. This is especially true at the sub-national level where we have seen good and best practices among local governments engaged in the area of active collaboration and cooperation towards the common objective of providing improved basic services to the people, in various sectors be they in the area of law and peace and order, environmental and ecological protection, delivery of basic social services and more. The role of strong institutions, leadership and active citizen engagement, among others has been central in advancing collaborative governance in the Philippines.

It will be recalled that in 1991, a Local Government Code was enacted in the Philippines. It transferred massive functions, powers and authorities to the sub-national (local) governments through a process of decentralization and devolution. It has been over 25 years now since the Code was enacted. While the operationalization of the Code has had some major issues and concerns, ranging from capacities, to finance to reluctance of national government agencies to

1) Praxis in this context refers to the "theory and practice."

pursue devolution[2] the process has also seen the emergence of many good and best practices among local governments as they rose to confront the many challenges brought about by process of devolution. It was within this context that a program was launched by the Local Government Academy of the Department of Interior and Local Government (DILG) in 1993 called the Galing Pook[3] Awards Program that documented and recognized many good and best practices in local governance throughout the country. This program continues up to the present and is one of the most successful and sustainable awards program for local governments in the Philippines. It is one of the most prestigious awards for local governments that has recognized various innovations and initiatives at the local level. By itself, Galing Pook is a model of collaborative governance considering that its conceptualization, and implementation has been one of cooperative partnership between the Local Government Academy[4] of the Department of Interior and Local Government, together with leaders from the academic and private and business sectors including the media.

This paper examines the many good and best practices and innovations that emerged out of Galing Pook. It paper suggests that the elements of the collaborative governance, and related frameworks such as network governance, can be among the major factors that enabled such innovations. The lenses of collaborative governance are used to examine the specific cases of the winners of the Galing Pook innovations program in the Philippines. Collaborative governance as defined within the context of *Galing Pook*, is a collaborative arrangement, whether in a formal, regular way or ad-hoc basis, where local governments, the private commercial sector, the media, civil society organizations, religious groups, the academic community, international organizations, and the local people

2) See for instance, Brillantes, *Innovations and Excellence. Understanding Local Governments in the Philippines*. Center for Local and Regional Governance, National College of Public Administration of the Philippines, 2003.

3) *Galing Pook* literally means "clever" or "excellent place." By extension it means excellent local government.

4) Alex Brillantes, one of this paper's authors, was in fact the Executive Director of LGA. Galing Pook was launched in partnership with the international organization, the Ford Foundation, a private academic institution, the Asian Institute of Management, and other partners including government agencies, the academic community and the media.

themselves, work together to craft sustainable governance solutions for different localities.

Collaborative governance has been defined as a multi-sector procedure which comprise various participants such as government agencies, private firms, civil society organizations and even labor unions (Finkelstein, 1995; Rosenau, 1992). According to Ansell and Gash (2007), it is a type of public management in which government and private firms act together in unique ways, in certain sequences, to institute shared rules and guidelines in delivering public goods. It is about facilitating operations in multi-organizational environments to resolve very complex challenges. Collaborative means to unite to accomplish mutually beneficial goals, constantly working across different disciplines that require an intricate web of human relations where reciprocity is prized (Amsler and O'Leary, 2017).

Collaborative governance has always been present, in a different name, context, extent, and form of practice. In the 1970s, the New Public Management (NPM) gained traction call learn from the lessons that corporations had faced (Thatcher, 1995). The movement underscored a government's size and high operational costs as signs of inefficiency and pushed for downsizing (Moon and Hwang, 2013). It also called on leaders to genuinely engage stakeholders in all steps of the process and not be accused of being out of touch with reality. Entrepreneurial management in public institutions was put forward (Osborne, 2010, 3). Monitoring and assessing the quality of inputs and outputs were emphasized. It was all about business-like changes in public agencies institutions. Including encouraging private sector competition and the belief that market forces will improve public services, the introduction of an open culture intended to strengthen accountability and so on (Klenk and Reiter, 2019).

In the 1990s, there were calls to shift the thinking from government to governance (Rhodes, 1997) has been presented as a solution for the excessiveness of government interventions (Bardach and Kagan, 1982). Different people around the world think that that governments should not be the only primary authority in almost all human affairs (Van der Heijden, 2014). Collaboration, not supervision, has been gaining momentum in scholarly discourses in public administration. There are many definitions that attempt to comprehensively describe collaborative governance and the usual elements are the participants, process, structure, and the desired result Among all the descriptions given, the one posited by Ansell and Gash (2007, 544) is among the most popular:

> A governance setting, where many government institutions directly engage different societal stakeholders in a collective decision-making process which is official, widely agreed upon, and contemplative, that aspires to construct and execute public policies and oversee governmental programs and resources.

Collaborative governance is very much affected by necessity and various incentives. Ritz, Brewer, and Neumann (2016) found out that the belief that people are willing to do some self-sacrifice to help achive common goals and aid the society in general, finds strong basis in many scholarly writings that tackle factors about public service motivation. Many individuals who work in public service agencies are compelled not just by their own desires but also a strong sense of altruisim and liking to help realize public good (Choi and Robertson, 2018). There are findings that public service or pro-society thinking is correlated to higher incidences of honorable conduct and selflessness in different institutions (Esteve, Van Witteloostuijn, and Boyne, 2015).

Amsler and O'Leary (2017, 630) suggest that collaborative governance is an "umbrella term" that conveys a plethora of governance practices puts significant value on consultation and cooperation among government agencies, private corporations, civil society organizatons, and/or the citizens themselves to accomplish public projects. The appearance of collaborative governance, by emphasizing the people's voice and role to partake in public affairs in both procedure and application, is a proof that various societies are adapting to powerful pressures on public and private sectors to help resolve today's complicated problems.

Collaborative governance engagements became essential due to a host of governance shortcomings which the era of globalization has made (Rasche, 2010). According to Van der Heijden (2014), the main feature of a real collaborative public management occurs when public authorities, companies and non-governmental organizations and the people act together in public affairs. This is a significantly distinct form of leading the society that the conventional one where the government exercises general supervision over non-state entities considered to be ordinary subjects. This arrangement is generally better because practitioners of a particular field have in-depth, tacit knowledge of their daily situation and of their peers than governments can ever acquire. It gives *cooperative benefits* because these are created to solve policy and coordination challenges that an organization, or a government ministry can never on its own (Doberstein, 2015).

*A notable value of collaborative governance is the augmented acceptability of authority.* It arose partially as an answer to unilaterally crafted definite codes of conduct which are often perceived as illegitimate, mainly because of the lack of consultation from other potential participants (Albareda, 2008). By contrast, cooperative solutions to governance benefit from bolstered input and legitimacy, because a plethora of actors are included in the process of norms creation and acceptance (Roloff, 2008). Amsler (2016) concurs by stating that cooperation signifies a broader approval of a policy choice and implementation. And so, collaboration in governance is a valuable way to attain a goal. It is significant because it can help foster goodwill among partners instead of having antagonism which may spur many challenges for current and future ventures (Amsler, 2017). Boerzel and Risse (2005) stress that another advantage of collaborative governance activities is their heightened potential to find effective answers for administrative problems. By combining finances and assets and by promoting knowledge processes among contributors, cooperative forms of governance are able to address community and ecological challenges, especially since many solutions necessitate specialized knowledge and skills (Rasche, 2010).

## Enabling Collaborative Governance

There are very many productive partnerships in the world today with concerns at the national or global level (Zadek, 2008) that can be seen within the framework of collaborative governance. It necessitates data sharing, action and movement synchronization, supply sharing, and capacity-building activities among participants. In time, actors move from interaction through coordination, teamwork and collaboration, to enable ample time to get to know each other, earn trust, become acquainted with each other's sphere of influence and so on (Sale, 2011; 2012).

Klijn and Koppenjan (2012) emphasize inter-sectoral collaboration in the provision of public goods. It presumes that institutions and societies require access to finances, knowledge, skills, and assets from other groups. The emphasis is on coordination tools and the construction of tangible products results, and services (Hjern and Porter, 1981).

The following section discussions some examples of institutions and forms that enable collaborative governance: (1) open systems and a democratic environment; (2) public-private partnerships; (3) transnational advocacy networks; and (4) knowledge production.

## Open Systems and a Democratic Environment

This is one of the most basic cooperative forms of governance. It is where experts, private firms, government actors, NGOs, and CSOs and other players can network with each other. When institutionalized, it facilitates knowledge sharing to bridge the gaps between distinct and often conflicting interests and viewpoints (Yang, 2016). This can also be a platform where confidence-building activities can be implemented, whether formal or informal. Klijn and Koppenjan (2012) point out that trust alleviates ambiguities in the long term, eases suspicions of different actors on each other because players consider all parties' concerns and objectives.

Collaborative governance is acknowledged as a form of leading organizations through open discussion, and collective decision-making instead of the traditional "command and control" (Amsler and O'Leary, 2017, 629). Open, democratic governance is a fertile ground that enables a free-flowing, unhampered, flow of information through multiple channels which enable vigorous consultations between the government and the public. A two-way communication showcase democracy's power: unlimited feedback loops. With strong public participation and flexible arrangements, there can be realistic issue identification, formation of the right plans, and constant evaluations during implementation of governmental programs to assure suitability in different local contexts (Tanchai, 2012). In essence, this can be considered not just an early form of collaborative governance, but its foundation.

## Public-Private Partnership

Public-private partnership (PPP) pertains to formal arrangements between the public sector and the private firms where some services and jobs that are done by the former will be taken on by latter based on an enforceable contract of shared goals to provide public goods and/or infrastructure (Carbonara, Costantino, and Pellegrino, 2014). The aim is to realize alignment of interests rather than to attain some decision-making accord. It may just signify a contract between government and private actors to bring certain public goods or accomplish definite tasks (Ansell and Gash, 2007). Sale (2015, 23) stated an example which is the "build-operate-finance-transfer (BOFT)" where the risks for private firms when it comes to help public projects materialize are higher. This signifies the change from government to governance where public agencies and private business engage in partnerships arrangements and networking. The conventional government and hierarchy only is being set aside.

Both the public and private sectors have long histories, and government authorities have been collaborating with private enterprises for most of human history. In spite of our renewed interest, public-private partnerships, scholars are right when they said that it is not new at all (Hodge, Greve, and Biygautane, 2018). It is very much underpinned by democratic governance because of the popular mandate of the government to fulfil public service provision even if they no longer provide it themselves (Reynaers, 2012). Democratic governance is a political system that is underpinned by democratization. Marsh (2015) describes it as a process where non-democratic governments are replaced by democratic ones. Democratic politics is kept in good order by strong institutions (March and Olsen, 2006). To put it simply, democratic governance can be defined as a capable administration based on the values, ethics and procedures of a modern democratic polity. It facilitates the interdependence of running and monitoring of an entire organization to effectively and efficiently materialize policy choices and convey the process to everyone, especially non-state stakeholders (Reynaers, 2012).

After the consolidation of democratic governance, the openness of information channels had fostered vibrant discourses and had built considerable social trust in different societies. Networks and network theories are not novel because we humans have always created and modified social networks shape together large polities, markets, wealth, material production, incubation of ideas, people's social status, places in a varying configurations that constantly modifies itself. According to Keast (2016), network governance represents a social, well-knit organization where human relational elements like goodwill, reciprocity and the quest for common progress all interact dynamically to form a widely accepted rules to produce favourable societal outcomes. It emphasizes horizontal over vertical manner in policymaking where open communication and knowledge sharing are alive and well. And so, network governance is a natural development of democratic governance, which also enriches the theory and practice of collaborative governance.

Different countries' private commercial sector and administrative structures have transformed over the past few decades where ethics and efficiency has been emphasized. This revolution compelled led businesses to be more open and cooperative. A reason for this change has to do with the adoption of "Corporate Social Responsibility" (CSR) which requires corporations to do their part towards the advancements of societal welfare by means of contributing to public programs in different ways. It soon became mainstream and incetivized companies because it is a way to cultivate and maintain a positive image among its customers and clients (Pirnejad, 2017, 41). With this in mind, the public and private sector have become collaborators.

## Transnational Advocacy Networks

These are cooperative, loose linkages that have common ideals, and in the possession of specialized expertise that facilitate better communication and exchange of best practices (Keck and Sikkink, 2004) that build and consolidate lasting connections in pursuit of public good (King, 2015). Civil society organizations tend to get involved in these arrangements and occasionally enter into coalitions with the government (Tsujinaka, Ahmed, and Kobashi, 2013).

Different groups usually pursue this option because of alignment of interests and the potential incentives (real or perceived) that may be gained after a period of time. Once they are involved in a partnership, participants, usually agents of groups with similar or conflicting interests, have to tend to common concerns that facilitate attainment of mutual dividends and cultivate good connections. Certain objectives that actors advocate and how they relate with others in order to arrive at a negotiated settlement, will be contingent on the nature of their own and their group's "social motivation" (Choi and Robertson, 2018, 3). Social motivation pertains to the desire to secure favorable results between oneself and other group members and can be for one's own welfare (worried about outcomes' effects on self) or for the common good (wants beneficial results for many in the spirit of fairness) (De Dreu, Nijstad, and Van Knippenberg, 2007, 23). Hence, social motivation has a significant influence on the process and outcome of a collaborative governance arrangement.

Confidence-building activities tend to be involved along the way which build and consolidate goodwill among different actors that wish to partake in a collaborative arrangement. Over time, due to successes and challenges that members of transnational advocacy networks have faced and overcame, King (2015) points out that their bond grows strong so there are more opportunities to synchronize their activities, harmonize objectives and exchange data. When the network becomes large and tough enough, it has the potential to become a major actor that can help shape the results of politics and policy choices. Collaborative governance arrangements require participative decision-making where active group intelligence sharing and handling to be effective (Choi, 2014) and partnerships with a strong trust can easily do this.

## Knowledge Production

Iris Marion Young (2000) explains that the practice of collaborative governance becomes not about just articulating inclinations, but about transforming them through learning new best practices and acknowledging unfamiliarity which is vital identifying points for policy improvements. Nevertheless, not just knowledge, but applying it in real situations. Leaders should inspire creativity by fusing the knowledge of various members so the group can create novel designs (Ansell and Gash, 2007).

Collaborative governance which needs high levels of trust needs proactive exchange of information. In fact, Klijn and Koppenjan (2012), cooperative ventures of private companies, government authorities and the academic community to build up a high level of productivity, like the creation of industrial parks, significantly improved the innovative capacity of different regions which gave them the boost for their economic development. This welcome development had received considerable attention from the society. Open spaces are needed to make people comfortable to communicate openly and create knowledge. Doberstein (2015) pointed out civil society organizations who are intimately familiar to the facts on ground than government employees may possess valuable diversity of experience, and the knowledge they have can difficult, if not impossible to codify. This valuable information, when incorporated in policy discussions and implementation, will be very much worthwhile.

Knowledge-creation theory attempts to synthesize existing interdisciplinary theories and concepts of the past and present from different national traditions to truly comprehend different human societies. It combines various disciplines such as philosophy, character education, history, traditions, and culture. It posits the process of *phronesis* in different leaders. It is where people in administrative capacities develop explicit and tacit knowledge, apply and share them with different people. It does not come easily as it is only built up in many years of experience, study and interaction with people. Most important, it can only be facilitated where there is *ba* (space) that is conducive for knowledge creation and exchange (Nonaka et al., 2018). In addition, people should study different fields in order to learn different bits of information and then apply it in a problem. It is learning transfer where an individual learns from a field and then apply it to another discipline. Many people who became successful are voracious learners and extensive generalists, not specialists (Simmons, 2018).

Without knowledge circulation, social inequalities are quickly created and widened which political and economic control becomes concentrated in the few elites and puts the people at a great disadvantage. Vibrant democracies can only development when data is open and accessible to everybody (Koltay, Špiranec, and Karvalics, 2016). Thus, when there is knowledge-intensive management in the government and the society, it can enlighten everyone concerned on how to build up people's capacity, cultivate worthwhile pursuits, and attain equitable prosperity for a country.

In the quest for knowledge, collaborative governance is always present. Pirnejad (2017) stated that when there is accessible data, citizens can see all the world's knowledge and information to build new services, craft new ideas, and identify critical errors in the public infrastructure and services. It has even led to creative, unsolicited solutions to multifaceted social challenges, in which polities may not be able to tackle on their own due to limited budget, resources, or lack of technical capacity. Presently, public participation only needs a laptop and a good internet connection. Now, with civic innovation at its core, people can work together from across the world, and scale rapidly.

The above are some examples of how collaborative governance have been enabled by various mechanisms and institutions. The next section discusses the experience of the Philippines at the local level and suggests how these may have been operationalized and enabled by sub-national local governments as documented by the Galing Pook Awards Program.

## Good and Best Practices in the Philippines

This section discusses mostly cases at the local level — among local governments — which are frontline institutions where the "rubber hits the ground" and where collaborative governance practices are imperative. The following are some cases — good and best practices — drawn from various sectors that somehow illustrate and operationalize the importance of collaborative governance.

## Good Citizenship: Gawad kalinga

In the past few years, the Gawad Kalinga (GK), (meaning "to take care of others") has become a promising style of a public welfare program in the Philippines (Brillantes and Fernandez, 2008). According to its founder, Antonio Meloto "it is an initiative to alleviate extreme poverty that has generated enormous altruism and volunteer work" (Meloto, 2009). It is a native development case which can be spread globally that promotes the "new politics of looking after each other. It follows the traditional Filipino viewpoint called "bayanihan" which means "cooperativism or communal work." The GK way is one of a drastic citizenship and nationalistic development. It takes a whole-of-society approach that takes into account prevalent cultural norms, moral values, and social arrangements. It loves the poor and also recognizes the contributions of well-off groups and individuals who care for them. Men and women who volunteer their time, talents, and resources literally build homes for the needy and even those who serve in the armed forces. Gawad Kalinga has fostered a network called "Answering the Cry of the Poor" (ANCOP), consisting of a rising number of international societies covering countries like the US and in West Europe. (Brillantes and Fernandez, 2008). It goes to show that most people, rich or poor, can do their jobs, give back to communities, and pay it forward.

The spirit of collaborative governance is very much alive in the this case of the Gawad Kalinga due to several reasons. The leadership exhibited by its founder is more of being compassionate, wise, and in serving others. The program also seeks to create the spirit of unity among different communities by looking out for each other. In addition, they build support from as many potential partners as possible, like local governments, student volunteers, privat firms and others to help willingly and without compensation, a reflection of restoring trust in goodness of humanity. In addition, it also sought to become inclusive because they treat the poor, and even former prisoners, as human beings with dignity. In essence, this practice of building a whole-of-society approach towards poverty alleviation, by enlisting as many possible stakeholders as possible, is a clear testament of a successful collaborative governance.

## Education

Sarangani is among the 20 least developed in the Philippines. Confident that a good education can uplift one from being poor, the provincial government commenced the *Quality Education for Sarangani Today (QUEST)* program last 2007 as an attempt to advance children's access to primary and secondary schooling. QUEST put in place ways to stimulate the active participation of societies and the private businness sector in visualizing, organizing, implementing and examining educational designs. This differed with the old method where there was only meager involvement from the province in the Education Ministry's undertakings (DepEd) (Galing Pook, 2012).

In order to assure the education reforms' viability, QUEST was established as a special unit of the Provincial LGU through a local legislative act in 2009 (Provincial Executive Order 2). School authorities, teachers and societal leaders taught parents and collaborated with volunteers to create a system to inculcate desirable learning habits for children whether in the classroom or at their houses. Moreover, the business sector was commited to provide school materials annually and to even help build desirable facilities such as the school cum dormitories (SchoolDorm) for indigenous peoples' (IPs) kids. The initiative succeeded in providing school books for all Grades I and II students and guidebooks for all their instructors (Galing Pook, 2012).

The collaborative governance here was started by a very important catalyst—strong political leadership and a genuine desire for public good. The provincial government here invested in a long-term benefit for the future generations because of significant support for education to the children of both poor families and those from the indigenous tribal communities. It also utilized the spirit of communal work (bayanihan) by solicitng support from many possible benefactors and communicating it to them. Many volunteered and even private businesses contributed in the form of material assistance like constructing buildings and school supplies. In addition, they strived to know the facts on the ground by enlisting the help of good educators and some students in helping to revise learning materials, a sign of being aware of the local educational needs of young students. In sum, the collaborative governance exhibited in this case was about being consultative, inclusive, and compatible towards local needs.

## Environment

The Clean Water Act has been in force since 2004. Developed cities were ordered that septage management systems to be built if sewerage systems are not feasible. At the same time, USAID picked Dumaguete City as one of first laboratories for the program "Local Initiatives for Affordable Wastewater Treatment." This drove an inter-sectoral assembly to organize a research on the city in terms of both current and potential sources of sewage, water supply that can be polluted, its own clealiness practices and ecological managemen legislation (Galing Pook, 2012).

A salient challenge that was rasied was the hazard to the city's ground water resource from the approximately 20,000 unsuitably built and maintained septic tanks in the area. Aterwards, in 2006, local government implemented Septage Management Ordinance which required the right plan, construction and maintenance of septic tanks, periodic declogging, payment collection to generate revenues, promotion, information campaign and the creation of a septage administraton. The city government started assembling the waste treatment facility using its own development finances. Few months later, it entered into an agreement with the Dumaguete City Water District to operate the septage management system. The pact specifies fair allocation between the two operational expenditures and any forthcoming profits (Galing Pook, 2012).

This is another exercise of collaborative governance where strong political will was shown. Another good move they did was to become transparent with the local people by coducting a massive awareness campaign for the need to have a good sanitation system in the city. As a result, the residents, who are also stakeholders, became empowered by receiving such important health information. It also highlighted that because of strong political commitiment, a local government (Dumaguete City government) and a government-owned corporation (Dumaguete City Water District) have learned to cooperate. The city had proven their mettle to an international organization, the USAID (United States Agency for

International Development), that they are worth assisting in the quest for public welfare. They have also been shown to engage in information exchange, a feature of collaborative governance, by sharing to different local governments, schools, and NGOs, about their successful project.

## Good Governance

Thirst for outstanding governance and a business friendly environment led Valenzuela City's LGU to formulate its Simple and Speedy Public Service Program or 3S in Public Service. The program aims to root out corrupt practices, restructure the city government's leadership, streamline transactions, and encourage its constituents to provide opinions on how to further improve government services. With 3S in place, it now takes only 20 minutes to acquire a business license. A robust post-audit system has been in force to allow commercial activities to be set up easily. A Task Force keeps them in check and offenders are prohibited from conducting business. A sleek organizational structure was adopted by the city to lessen bureaucratic layers in order to be more effective. The work environment was redesigned to foster greater acountability (Galing Pook, 2012).

Team meetings have been regularly held to foster collaboration and communication among officials and employees. Consultations workshops with citizens are complemented with texting, email, and social media so that people can report problems and suggestions directly to the local chief executive. The Mayor responds personally to every mail received and leads appropriate agencies for immediate action. An officer to handle feedback raised through the social media sites and to endorse complaints to concerned departments for suitable response. To ensure the long term viability of the initiative, the City passed relevant legislation for the program to acquire legal basis in order to obtain regular allocation from the local treasury (Galing Pook, 2012).

Collaborative governance here is once again advanced by the local government through strong political leadership. By having a solid desire for clean public service and to become a real provider for its people, it capacitated itself by availing the latest technologies to simplify the public goods provision like business licensing and document processing. active feedback on its services. It also conveyed a clear direction in its actions by making a simple acronym as its slogan. It also exercised a good communication to become more in touch with its constituents by encouraging active feedback to fine-tune the changes. To ensure that they are genuinely collaborating, they held regular team consultations with other local government employees and officials. To ensure the legitimacy and sustainability of their reforms, they also passed the needed legislation for those services.

## Health

Poor families seldom benefit from the services of formal health facilities because they do not have the means. The Quezon Provincial government responded with the Lingap Kalusugan sa Barangay or the Barangay Health Assistance program to improve the needy families' access to health services. Basically, the project involves the delivery of coupons to identified families, with the assistance of informal leaders assigned by the village governments. The recipients use these as full or partial payment for medical services at the hospitals. The Provincial Government reimburses the hospitals based on medical expenses covered by the health coupons (Galing Pook, 2012).

The distribution of coupons instead of actual cash to beneficiaries ensures that these are not alloted for aims other than addressing medical and health needs. There is also no transfer of cash between the Provincial Government and the community hospitals — the LGU simply replenishes the medicines and helps develop the hospitals' facilities. As a result, it can also curb the corruption at the city and even village level (Galing Pook, 2012).

Collaborative governance was shown by the Quezon provincial government by deciding to work with good service provders — the hospitals. Then, they also exhbited strong political leadership by becoming commmited to provide better access to healthcare for their poor residents. They also exhibited wisdom by not giving a lot of money to beneficiaries to ensure that they will only use it to receive needed medical attention. This is also a clever way they came up with to reduce corruption By giving the people service coupons, they can get health services for free while the provincial authorities pay the hospitals. In addition, local authorities showed inclusivity by being considerate to allow these people to pay for medical services by offering their farm produce to the hospitals. In turn, the people likely felt empowered and free of debt to the government because even if they have little to offer, what they are giving has been honored.

## Peace and Order

Kauswagan, Lanao del Norte has been caught in the crossfire of violent groups and the military for several decades due to armed clashes between warring forces—between the Blackshirts (Maranao fanatics) and the Ilagas (Christian fanatics). In 2008, Moro Islamic Liberation Front (MILF) and the state forces had a skirmish. Collectively, these confrontations resulted in large scale death and destruction and displacement of many people (Galing Pook, 2014).

The new local aministration started to organize a participatory approach in the governance to incentivize rebels to return to the mainstream society. The LGU commenced the initiative "From Arms to Farms." Peace activities and confidence-building measures such as Peacepath workshops were pursued in coordination with the populace and with the aid of local NGOs (nongovernmental organizations) and POs (peoples' organizations) and even the religious groups. Even the armed forces helped in arranging the surrenderees into socio-economic organizations. Program design, financing, and control was implemented through a bottom-up way, with the societies and rebel returnees choosing activities that are suited to their wishes (Galing Pook, 2014).

The Agriculture Ministry (DA) and the Agricultural Training Institute (ATI) funded some of the programs and activities identified by the communities, and helped educate the farmers in organic farming methods. More MILF rebels began to participate in the socio-economic activities. Four MILF commanders and 100 of their men returned to the fold and now do organic agriculture. They nurtured various plants, raised livestock and looked after fish farms. Sooner than later, these former fighters have been earning decently. Capacity-building played a vital role in enhancing the skills of the farmers. It improved the confidence of the younger generation to venture in the farming business (Galing Pook, 2014).

The Kauswagan local government, even in the face of imminent danger, chose to become decisive and exercise strong political leadership, a vital impetus of collaborative governance. With this, they started honestly communicate with the local ceasefire personnel to help stop sporadic warfare in their area. Afterwards, they proceeded to engage everyone concerned including the rebels in a participative manner. In this way, they conducted many confidence-building measures and led the local people into the same narrative. They also engaged the Department of Agriculture to help capacitate the surrenderees to a new way of livelihood — farming. They also communicated with the government forces and convinced them of the promising option of settling the insurgency peacefully. Once they have secured the pledge and trust of everyone, the initiative of securing peace and bringing better living became a reality.

## Tourism

The municipality of Loboc, Bohol have exhibited features of good collaborative governance in improving lives through tourism. It was a 2012 Galing Pook awardee. In 2004 to 2005, the local government organized several dialogues with village officials, citizens' associations, NGOs and the commercial sector to understand what they have to do the needed enhacements. The meetings resulted in the restructuring of income-producing activities and the capacity-building, centralization, and streamlining of public and tourism facilities and services. Formulation and enforcement of new guidelines and binding rules over-seeing tourism and the promotion of ways of sustainable ecological management (Galing Pook, 2012).

The LGU also perfomed rounds of awareness campaigns about desirable environmental and tourism practices and held consistent communication with the relevant participants, i.e. the residents, societal leaders, boat drivers, and other tourism employees. Local officials, department managers, and tourism staff operators were also introduced to other tourism practices to stimulate better appreciation of environmental factors crucial to tourism development and the impact of tourism (Galing Pook, 2012).

LIT HOPE (Livelihood, Infrastructure, Tourism, Health and Sanitation, Organization Strengthening, Peace and Order, and Education) became the local government's advocacy and also encapsulated their economic development plan for the municipality. With the significant backing from the Ministries of Trade and Finance, the local government was able to connect with and avail financing from several international organizations from Canada, Australian, and the World Bank. With sufficient funding at its disposal, constructing a modern docking port and tourism are became the local goverment's main project. This facility was intended to conform with safety standards as well as provide comfortable lodging to visitors. It also expedited the supervision of tourist arrivals and the collection of payments (Galing Pook, 2012).

Collaborative governance, in this case, was also lead by strong political commitment from the Loboc local government. They immediately formed a common goal of improving the livelihoods of their locality and the only way to do that effectively is to engage all the possible stakeholders and potential benefactors. NGOs, tourism personnel local government employees, and officlals resolved to work together for this loftly aim. The practice is very much participative and aimed to build rapport amongst different actors. Moreover, they took capacity-building seriously by placing all personnel including public managers and tourism workers in learning programs about tourism and the environment. They also conducted information campaigns to show transparency to the local people and societal leaders about the program. When the news of the initiative spread around, they received generous help not only from the Philippine Finance and Trade Departments, but also from Western international aid agencies to build a modern port in their locality. All of this happened because all of them are on the same page which made this collaborative partnership work well.

## Women Empowerment

In Cebu City, the local government commenced the program Bantay Banay (Family Watch) program in the 1990s. It taps in the spirit of volunteerism where there are many who offer their time and talents who help and shelter battered wives, women, and their children. The volunteers were also trained in gender sensitivity issues, violence against women adn children, family dialogue and legal processes on women's problems. There are thousands of cases reported to the task force but most were settled out of court through mediation, reconciliation, and counseling at the village level. Very few turned to legal action. They provided support to victims by attending court hearings and seeking media coverage in the possible shotcomings of the legal system in adjudicating the cases. Cebu City was also the first to pass a local Gender and Development Code which serves as guideline for gender development in the city. In order to ensure its effectivity, the mayor signed an agrrement with barangay officials to allot five percent (5%) of the local budget for gender-oriented welfare activities (Galing Pook, 2003).

Again, the primary characteristic in the success of this program is robust leadership inherent in the collaborative governance partnership for women's welfare. Second, capacity-building was given to all relevant personnel which also made them commited to the same goal. There is also honest communication by enacting information campaigns and dialogue with reporters. They also courted support from employees and judges of courts who handle cases that involve violence against women. When the women's rights groups were able to marshal popular support in the city, the local government passed relevant law in order to institutionalize women protection. It goes to show that leadership not only comes from local authorities but also from NGOs and activists. Everyone working vigorously for a common noble cause is an exercise of collaborative governance.

## Justice

Legal action is so expensive that ordinary mumble that justice is only for the privileged. When Barangay (Village) Justice System in Cebu City sprang into action, people of humble origins now have way to settle disputes for free. In July 27, 2003, the Lupong Tagapamayapa (Peace Council) were the first personnel. Known as the Liga Ng Mga Lupong Tagapamayapa of Cebu City (or League of Peace Councils of Cebu City), they spearheaded the creation of a not-for-profit organization for this purpose. Their program "Strengthening Justice System in the Grassroots" have been put into operation. It has been intended to help realize peaceful and progressive communities by aiding residents to resolve fights cordially in a skilled manner. The reconciliation committees conducted dialogue, site visits, realistic exercises, and comparative study of relevant programs from other places. This allowed them to evaluate and cultivate the proficiency of the officers, instill suitable principles, instruct relevant personnel in various conflict settlement methods, and obtain resources to maintain and bolster the program (Galing Pook, 2007).

This is a classic yet local way of exercising collaborative governance — an inexpensive but inclusive administration of justice in a local community. Collaborative governance, once again, was jumpstarted by a strong leadership, not just from the local government but from concerned practitioners of local justice. In addition, they sought to keep the dispute resolution inclusive by mediating grieving parties in a local setting. They also availed capacity-building programs supported by their city to enhance their skills. And so, commitment for the common good was instilled in the peace officers.

## Local Intergovernmental Cooperation in Infrastructure

Usually, constructing a sturdy concrete highway would cost a million — the fee charged by private contractors which is too costly for a town. In Cotabato, several of them along with the provincial authorities, combined their means and persevered to create roads at about P30,000 per kilometer. It became known as the Kabalikat PALMA Infrastructure Project. It began in February 2002, the project has renovated old roads and built new ones of almost 300 kilometers, costing about P8 million. A remarkable point about the initiative is that the people have mindful of their responsibility for the project so they are immersed in designing, executing, supervising and suporting it. The locality offered lodging for the drivers and heavy equipment workers, protecting the machineries, cooking food for the manpower, and the maintenance of roads in their locality. While the local governments set up equipment to the host town or village guarantee that these are functioning for building roads in their respective jurisdictions. To assure that the program will persist in the future, facilitating procedures have been established that include a well-delineated administrative configuration, citizen cooperation, information sharing, relevant laws and sufficient financing (Galing Pook, 2007).

Collaborative governance, in this area, was realized not just because of a strong political commitment from a single local government but a united leadership from multiple local authorities. From the start, they had the sharp, single-minded focus that the only way to build good infrastructure is to collaborate together. Due to being adjacent societies, they had good trust amongst each other. Having a common interest and a good legal basis, the Local Government Code of 1991, which sanctioned their collective actions, they immediately built their road networks. What they practiced is the common resource pooling that was started by intergovernmental cooperation. Hence, they practiced the spirit of real collaborative partnership.

## Povery Reduction

Siayan, Zamboanga del Norte was designated as the most deprived municipality back in 2003. It is now in the past as the local government unveiled its Community Enterprise Development Program through Pangkabuhayan (Livelihood) Centers (CEDP-PCenter). This provided workable livelihood potential that led to significant growth in the incomes of its poor residents. The CEDP-PCenter program involves the creation of small community-owned and community-managed merchandise stores across several villages of the municipality. The program encourages the most needy residents to combine their resources together with financing from the LGU in starting and running these businesses or Pangkabuhayan Centers (PCenters). These stores would sell commodities at a much lower cost and purchase agricultural crops at a higher expense than proprietary business owners. The incomes are reinvested and part are plowed back as payments to the members. It is intended to become a cooperative so that these PCenters are strucutured in this way. The local government also constructed infrastructure to reduce transportation fees and accelerate the mobility of farm produce. It also even delivered a series of capacity-building on sound business management practices like accountability and transparency to inspire the people and change their preconveived notions and confidence in a good way (Galing Pook, 2015).

Once again, the collaborative governance was jumpstarted by strong political leadership by the local government. Then, they started resource pooling in a form of a cooperative. The locality, driven by a desire for a better livelihood, and support from the local government, started a cooperative so they can all borrow money and start small businesses. In this act, the local residents showcased resourcefulness and a commitment for their common good by growing their cooperative. In this way, they all have the same goal of escaping poverty together, a sign that they have a strong social capital. This must have been underpinned by good friendships and honest communications in their area. This success story in a locality with limited resources and knowledge, is a de facto exercise of collaborative governance.

## Factors for Collaborative Governance

Taking off from the above, this section discusses the emerging factors that contribute to the success of these programs from the framework of collaborative governance. These are the following.

### A Common, Shared Understanding

Clear direction is needed that all parties need before they give their commitment in an undertaking. It is defined in different writings as a "joint task" (Alexander, Comfort, and Weiner, 1998). It is always desirable to have an amicable start in any cooperative undertaking. Nonetheless, under some conditions, even the most bitter of adversaries can be influenced or forced to join forces. Definitely, if there is a common and strong discontentment with the status cuo among all participants, rivals may decide to set aside fundamental differences and unite. Under settings of disappointment and urgency—because of an imminent crisis or catastrophe, a policy deadlock or dreary policy options—a coalition to attain the mutually advantageous aims of the collective (Booher, 2004). Deciding a collaborative arrangement's direction happens when stakeholders identify a common objective, jointly design an approach, process the information and institute common rules, then assign task forces to study more challenging issues in a deeper manner. Individuals leave eventually, so interested institutions and public agencies always be cognizant of the external and internal factors that influence affect the collaborative governance arrangement like different interests, incentives, goals, values, and viewpoints which are necessary in ensuring that everyone is on the same page (Cheng et al., 2015).

Shared understanding of poverty among the stakeholders of Gawad Kalinga (GK) certainly played a key to the success of GK. It was both a bottom-up and top down approach with all stakeholders sharing a common value of vision of "walang iwanan" (no one gets left behind).

Legal authority of local government and public agencies to enter and/or leave cooperative arrangements. Before embarking on governance partnerships, government officials and employees must contemplate the legal basis that may guide their acts. There are different potential implications as the construction and interpretation of law and their exceptions are very diverse amongst nations (Amsler, 2016). But in general, cooperation and dialogue are conducted due to legal necessity and as custom, because it is seen to be useful (Batory and Svensson, 2019b). In addition, in a study by Albrecht (2016) about flood risk mitigation, found out that, government authorities in the European Union have recognized the need of citizen input for public initiatives because of the potential of different polities combining their resources to bring major benefits for all.

In the context of Filipino local governments, collaborative governance has been thriving because it can be facilitated easily by the law. In the Philippine Local Government Act (1991), in Section 33 of the law, it allows partnerships with different local government units. For Section 35, the local government can team up with people's associations and non-governmental organizations in terms of economic development. Under the Sections 498, 501 and 504, in their "g" paragraphs, local administrations (i.e., municipalities, cities, and provinces) are encouraged to communicate and cooperate with the central government and the private commercial actors to attain and improve prosperity in their jurisdictions. The advent of the Galing Pook Awards through the Galing Pook Foundation ensured that cases of collaborative governance among different localities are analyzed, synthesized, shared and preserved for posterity.

### Short-term Tangible Results

Aside from trust, small steps leading to modest achievements will go a long way for it builds the momentum for different potential participants to be willing to venture into bigger projects (Rogers et al., 1993).

Short term, tangible results were among the factors that were seen in the Galing Pook winners that were awarded for their accomplishments in the education, environment and health sectors. Indeed, tangible results — sometimes referred to as "proof of concept" — were key not only to the process of "buy in" by the citizens, but more importantly is further supporting the programs that were key to their sustainability. It will be recalled that a key criterion of awarding a GP winner is sustainability, and transferability.

### Confidence-building Measures

Constant communication is important. It is where it can be assessed whether a person or a group is worth of one's time and effort. The open nature of policymaking procedure, with steady exchanges between different players resulted in much less adversarial viewpoints and more confidence in each other.

They comprehended their interdependence, acknowledged other parties' ambitions and concerns and constantly aspired to arrive at win-win resolutions paving the way to a more amicable partnership in the future (Van Buuren, Edelenbos, and Klijn, 2007). A leader in a collaborative governance setting has to be bold: to communicate his/her expectations, show sincerity, to use a reward and punishment system to promote collaboration and to raise the stakes of the initiative (Linden, 2010).

The primary aim of conducting these activities is necessary to secure commitment and goodwill — trust. Warsen, Nederhand, Klijn, Grotenbreg and Koppenjan (2018) pointed out that good faith in partnerships is supremely important to work well. When it is strong enough, different participants' concerns and suspicions will be considerably alleviated because they can be assured that their interests will be seriously considered by other parties. But once it is lost, it is unlikely that actors can willingly face potential hazards because there are opportunists who can easily take advantage of them. So, it becomes more problematic to arrive at acceptable results. Hence, we can say that confidence-building measures have always been key to the success of peace and order programs that were cited as Galing Pook winners. The case of Lanao del Norte and the "farms to arms" program would not have been as successful if the surrenderees and the armed forces did not have confidence in the peace process. Confidence-building led to lowering of guards and enabled mutual trust among the stakeholders.

## Incentives to Encourage Participation

Cooperation in collaborative governance is largely by a group's own free will which is why a financial reward is very useful. Incentives grow as sponsors see a direct correlation between their participation and concrete, tangible, favorable results (Brown, 2002). But they decrease if stakeholders perceive their own effort to be just optional and/or symbolic in nature (Futrell, 2003).

Participants may not have a motivation to partake, specially, if they see alternate means to attain their goals (Ansell and Gash, 2007). Watching out for the right moment will be significant: organizations that believe that their influence and resources are increasing will be unlikely to want to bind themselves to collaboration (Gray, 1989). This may be something that they may see as something that can limit their freedom of action, a sign of growing confidence and prestige that comes with it.

There are many incentives, like potential access to resources and increased social prestige for a group and the likely disadvantages like bigger conflicts and social exclusion, which can motivate various actors to enter into collaborative governance arrangement. According to McDougall and Banjade (2015), when there is genuine involvement in decision-making for all members, shared rapport between groups, and improvements in guidelines and rules can always minimize animosities and prevent them from being a full-blown armed clash. Even if there are hidden wounds amongst actors that when suddenly exposed, provoke increased conflicts, the potential incentives, participative decision-making, and use of various conflict management techniques, can keep simmering tensions between participants at bay. In fact, when their grievances are successfully addressed, the collaborative partnership will enjoy greater confidence not only from the benefits it can offer, but also the strengthened social cohesion of its members will make it stronger in responding to inside and outside dangers.

People participation — or citizen engagement, as we will discuss later — is a key factor that cut across most of our good and best practices, from Gawad Kalinga to peace building to the delivery of basic services. To a certain extent, the good and best practices in local governance — have had people participation, ownership of the process, citizen engagement — as a bedrock. Pushing participation even further is the imperative of continuously consulting the people. In the Philippines, an Indigenous People's Rights Act (IPRA) law was passed. At the heart of the IPRA law is a principle called the "free and prior informed consent" principle. It says that no outside programs and projects and activities may be designed and implemented in the area if the indigenous peoples are not only consulted, but more importantly, asked for their consent in the implementation of such activities.

## Institutional Structures

Nobel Prize awardee Alfred North (1991, 97) explains institutions as the following.

> Institutions are the man-made systems that organize political, monetary, social, and diplomatic relations. They comprise of both informal checks (penalties, forbidden topics, habits, traditions, and moral codes), and official regulations (national charters, laws, civil liberties). Over the centuries, institutions have been invented by people to peace and order and minimize unpredictability in exchange.

Indeed, the recognition of the role of institutions — formal and informal — in the design of *appropriate* interventions underscore the need to recognize the unique context of the situation that may warrant any intervention in the name of "development." In other words, context should be recognized and it should matter. This is key to the success of Gawad Kalinga and key to the many peace and order interventions in the Muslim populated areas in southern Philippines where local laws, traditions and customs are not only recognized but more importantly, respected.

Institutional designs are the simple conventions for cooperation, which is indispensable for the technical acceptability of the collaboration progress (Ansell and Gash, 2007). Every nation has organizations and political traditions that enjoy confidence of its constituents (North et al., 2009). The right to partake in the decision-making process that collaborative governance offers is the main question. Openness and transparency influence participation as only the parties that can sense that they have had a legitimate opportunity to join and shape the policy outcome are the most probable to cultivate an interest and then "pledge to the entire endeavor" (Ansell and Gash, 2007).

## Importance of Roles

Recognizing the problem and crafting solutions is a good start. But in order to apply it on the ground, the different functions that each person and group must undertake to ensure that most, if not all of them, are 'on the same page.' There will be some challenges, according to Johnston et al. (2010), there is a need for shared responsibility, and a preparedness to face perils along the way. Peter Pirnejad (2017) stated, "The vital positions consist of an advocate, organizer, benefactor, and a chief. Each job has a unique set of tasks and attributes, in a particular form by a capable individual or a group over time."

Pirnejad (2017) added, "It is someone who is the most dedicated to the routine of the partnership, guaranteeing the aims of the collaboration are being achieved; a custodian. The second one is responsible for the key assets and logistics essential to sustain the alliance such financing, manpower, provisions, and all the rest. The third one, are the ones who enable consultations, build agreements at critical junctures in the process. They assure that all stakeholders remain updated and included in all the developments, as choices and concessions are made. They are frequently cognizant of all participants' requirements, and the suitable means of acquisition during the period of cooperation.

This is what is present in all collaborative governance organizations and the Galing Pook programs are no different. All players, explicitly or implicitly, understood what each of them should do. Sometimes, these functions tend to overlap. The ones who championed a program is usually the Local Government Unit, a group of concerned citizens, or an NGO. The directive role is normally taken by a local chief executive. A facilitator is someone who is an informal but an influential individual. The ones who provide the means are the national government and even international institutions. Once all of them have become accustomed and started working together, it is only a matter of time before they can get good results.

## Capability for Institutional Adjustment

The capacity to acclimate is exhibited by people or a group on how they plan, improvise, and react by means of study, experience and suppleness to uphold or increase a preferred situation and outcome (Folke et al., 2005). When it comes to multi-sectoral administrative arrangements, the aptitude to get accustomed to different challenges may be viewed as a desirable feature of a collaborative governance system to modify in-house procedures and configure structural essentials to offset potential problems (i.e., change of internal and external factors, different metrics for success of implementing a program) and even take advantage of experienced or expected contigencies in a given setting (Pahl-Wostl, 2009).

Current and former members, especially influential individuals must have the means to keep and sustain their social connections to the group so they can share their explicit and tacit know-how, specifically, those with expertise on technical matters and resource management to help a collaborative partnership keep its overall flexibility and efficiency. Furthermore, they can also function as trusted facilitators or even as informal leaders are vital because once they completely leave, the alliance's adaptability may greatly diminish and led to disappointments and reluctance for any future joint venture (Cheng et al., 2015).

The participants of different collaborative governance programs in the Galing Pook cases are knowledgeable and experienced individuals and organizations such as business people, outside experts, learned advocates, and seasoned government officials. As a result, they have learned on how to live with adversity and uncertainty. They have the awareness, grit, knowledge, and resources, to push though these projects because they know that if they have unity, they can overcome any challenge that may seem insurmountable.

Building upon the above discussion and cases, we suggest the following collaborative governance model shown as Figure One. We highlight the imperative of cooperation and collaboration among the following institutions if collaborative governance is to be successful and would lead to innovations at the local level: the national government, the local governments, civil society, NGOs people's organizations, the private sector, academic institutions and the international community.

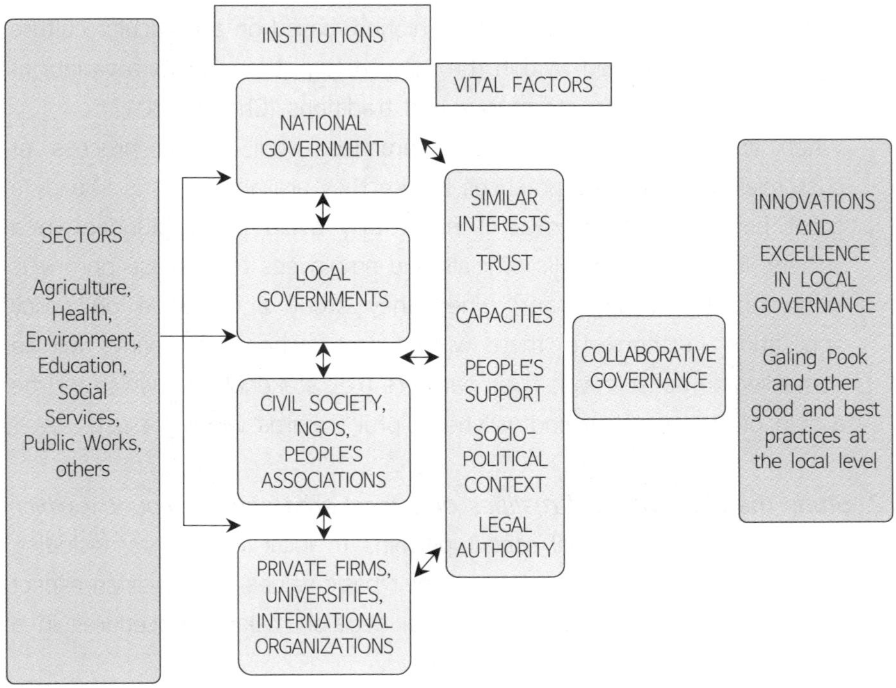


**Figure 1.** Collaborative Governance Model

The Galing Pook cases compile best practices from local governments in the Philippines. There is always the possibility of learning from other countries' experiences and then studying whether it can be adapted in a particular polity, and when it is judged to be so, how is a governance practice *contextualized* in order to become viable for a locality in a different nation-state.

Some factors that ought to be examined with regards to adaptability of the Galing Pook's best practices are:

1. ***Contextualize governance lessons***. Wang and Liu (2018) described trans-border learning transmission pertains to the diffusion of tried and tested policy choices, administrative structures and exemplary practices are imitated by various countries. The governance model largely influenced by Western traditions and experiences are not always compatible with other

nations. As such, some Asian countries have started to view them with doubt. Governance is contextually fashioned, based on a particular culture and is socially ingrained. Within the Asian region, there exists a variety of administrative cultures, structures, and traditions (Cheung, 2013).

When collaborative governance is practiced well in the process of customizing governance practices before they are applied, it is already a great help to help minimize if not totally avoid policy blunders in a society. It also helps public officials and employees to exercise phronetic leadership (wise judgement) when they study and decide on policy application. Furthermore, there will be times when participants will be compelled to consult with their partners (i.e., stakeholders) which will be a sign of transparency and will be helpful towards winning trust.

2. *Study the socio-political realities of a local area and the country which it is a part of.* The social aspect pertains to local inhabitants, including their social networks, resources and their basic values. The decision aspect relates to its politics and the practical decision-making procedures in a government (Park and Weible, 2017).

   This is equally important before attempting to implement a local governance experiment. When participants of a collaborative governance arrangement are aware of this, they can much more easily adjust their programs and pay attention to a locality's unspoken rules which will make their programs much more acceptable to the local inhabitants and public authorities there.

3. *Use resources with care and foresight.* The innovative local governance practices in the Philippines have always exercised not just intense cognizance of the distinct conditions in a locality but also inventiveness and resourcefulness. In a study of the OECD (2011), to develop rural livelihoods, public policies are intended to empower small businesses based in a practical use of native natural resources. Steering resources wisely is constant one that becomes more fruitful when the foundations for learning and adaptive capacity was adopted from the beginning. Mid-course policy changes in resource management affect livelihoods, social networks, because governments and other stakeholders commu-

nicate and decide on how to allocate limited resources, create products, produce income under constantly changing surroundings (Funder, Mweemba, and Nyambe, 2017).

Competition for resources can become very fierce if conflicts are not handled early and skilfully. Striving to use resources as careful as possible can minimize waste in a governance initiative while granting other interested parties to have their share. By engaging in a respectful give and take transactions, all parties will feel empowered and respected and will feel positive about continuing a fruitful collaborative partnership.

4. *Make sure that any local collaborative governance program that will be implemented can be adjusted along the way in the light of changing interests and times.* When there is institutional diversity and disintegration in a country, the government agencies' ability to govern people and natural resources is not fixed. It needs endless adjustments because it can always be disputed and demanded by various entities. Hence, the people's support for the current governance structures is important to secure and maintain legitimacy (Funder, Mweemba, and Nyambe, 2017).
   There are always challenges that will appear in the face of collaborative governance arrangements so its legitimacy and practicality will be on the line. As a partnership goes on, its rules and objectives will guide it on how flexible it will be when the situation demands it. And so, the collaborative governance qualities of having honest communications, transparency, trust, and adequate capacities will enable it to decide what are its non-negotiable goals and help it respond effectively to inside and outside pressures.

5. *Conduct pilot projects in small areas.* Local governments must participate actively in a preliminary implementation of a local governance program to study and ensure its sustainability. A way to help realize their involvement is the creation of task forces regarding all relevant public officers down to the village-level, if needed (Wirakartakusumah, Purnomo, and Dewanti-Hariyadi, 2014). Public authorities have also recognized the importance of seriously considering the responses in their locality by involving relevant non-state interested parties (i.e., people, civil society organizations, private

sector) with a particular significance in policy application (Ahlers, Heberer, and Schubert, 2016).

The purpose of implementing pilot projects is to see if a policy helps in cost-saving, the viability of a program when applied on a national scale, on how to enact good policies, how to overcome challenges when they appear, and develop the policy process in a polity (Ettelt, May, and Allen, 2013). This is totally compatible with collaborative governance because small-scale policy applications not only give government authorities the practice to accumulate leadership experiences, but also help them get familiar with a locality's conditions. It also helps non-state stakeholders to feel empathy for public employees and officials. All of this contributes positively for them to save necessary energy, resources, and time, build up their capacities, and strengthen their personal and professional bonds (trust) by facing an overcoming challenges together in the development arena.

## A Word of Caution:
## Some challenges in collaborative governance

We have discussed the factors of how collaborative governance initiatives (the Galing Pook cases) have succeeded in the Philippines. Nevertheless, the common faults that are ever-present must also be taken into account so partnerships in the future will know on what these pitfalls are in order to avoid or minimize the impact.

According to Simonin (2017), there are no fully self-sufficient creatures on Earth. The drive to team up with others and take part in collective actions is the most primal natural force. In our present organizations, this characteristic may be very active but are no less omnipresent. There will always be changes, from rivalry to an alliance, back and forth, as the only permanent in this world is interest.

### *Recognize When is the Proper Time to Enter into a Partnership*

The trend now shows that, at least on the surface-level, collaborations have become so predominant it is now considered as a custom. More and more, there is a popular notion that those who do not take part in this cooperative arrangements an organization will be left behind. Getting on the collaborative fashion can be perilous in the absence of a well-crafted strategy; it can be confusing and exacerbate an already delicate position, and divert precious assets away from critical undertakings (Simonin, 2017). In essence, inadequate preparation and further study can be fatal.

### *A Good Plan on How to Amicably Leave a Cooperative Arrangement*

First of all, cancelling a partnership is not exactly an impending fiasco, but can also be a sign of accomplishment. Parties have attained their goals and have to carry on, until another chance arrives. Intensely aware that alliances can lead to failures signalled by a quick dissolution, institutions must prudently contemplate about the conclusion and formulate a clear departure blueprint (Simonin, 2017). These may be informally called as "acid-reflux moments" as it is often present during contract termination.

### *Misjudgement of Cultural Differences (Both National and Organizational-level)*

When collaborating with people of different nationalities, even in the public sector, both clashes and mistakes are embedded in cultural variations. These changes manifest themselves in a variety of ways: linguistic, priorities, and seemingly distant disposition of the parties involved. These can be hindering in terms of working effectiveness and causes tension between associates (Simonin, 2017). People behave differently according to their country's culture. Their manner of dressing, speaking, conduct of business, pace, and work ethics are very different. Especially, among Asians and Europeans, this cannot be overstated. Collaborating with multinational professionals who have experience abroad can be both a privilege and a challenge. Instituting common rules promptly with all participants will go a long way (Tomalin and Nicks, 2007).

### *Inability to Trust Adversaries and Rivals*

This is always a severe risk that a collaborative partnership may become undermined and incapable to perform functionally due to so much infighting resulting in little confidence. Due to the general volatility of collaborative networks, participants must learn to prevail over mutual suspicions and to effectively settle ongoing skirmishes of objectives that unavoidably occur with the parties regardless of the reality they need each other. But with skilful hands-on facilitation of functional cooperation and setting aside of differences, they will learn on how to look at the bigger picture (Sorensen, 2007).

### *Keep in Mind That There is No Panacea*

Especially, in our times that is also known as the rise of wicked challenges, there is no one-size-fits-all. Ostrom (2007) stated, "The answers are not easy to obtain because we have just started to develop the ideas and the means that can solve, or at least remedy the broad origins of our difficulties." Today's challenges tend to be structural-oriented, where human responses are intricate and erratic and where reasons, occasionally straightforward, are often manifold. They appear in all directions randomly, transcends boundaries, and may develop exponentially. The line of thinking that there is one solution to everything is not right way. It is tantamount to thinking of old-fashioned solutions to new, complicated problems. Reyes (2017) in his study explained, simplistic answers can disrupt initiatives created with noble purposes for it may restrict the recognition of a multifaceted problem where dormant and unanticipated consequences of a set of responses may be overlooked due to so much attention to expected results. That is why collaborative governance participants have to learn on how to plan the core values and desired outcomes for the initial phases, but also learn on how to customize the implementation as they progress.

Drawing from our earlier work, the following are some of the major factors that brought about innovations at the local level that may be seen from the framework of collaborative governance as shown in Figure 2:

These include the following:

1. Leadership
2. People Participation and Support

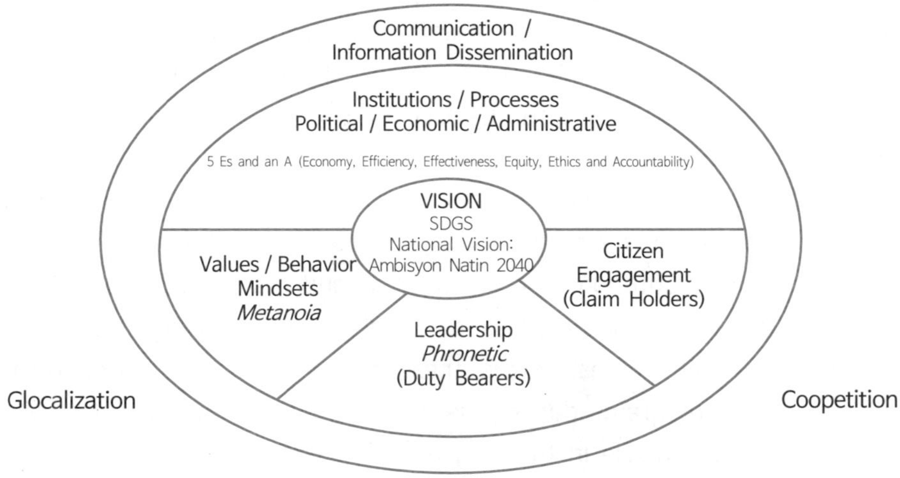


**Figure 2.** Reform Governance Framework

3. Multi-sectoral Cooperation
4. Media and Information Dissemination
5. Support from International Institutions

Indeed, success in innovations — and collaborative governance — among the Galing Pook winning programs discussed earlier have to mainly rely on leadership, people's participation and support, and multi-sectoral cooperation. It could be argued that these three components are highly vital in determining the success and longevity of the programs as it shows the need for leadership (in a community or in the local government), the commitment and the participation concerning the program, and the involvement and cooperation of various groups and civil society organizations. The combination of these three components show the interconnection of the government, people, and the civil society in supporting a common goal — pursuing peace in a community.

On the other hand, there are also winning programs that had to heavily mobilize people's participation and support, and multi-sectoral cooperation only. While it did not have leadership by the government itself, the commitment of the people and other sectors showed that the program objectives could be achieved, especially if their lives are at stake. It exemplifies how ordinary citizens, who have the will to make changes in their community, could partner with civil society to push for their agenda, even with the lack of support from their government officials.

On the other side of the spectrum, support from external international institutions greatly help the start and implementation of the winning program. These international institutions provide funding and resources for the LCEs to realize their programs and implement it. While not all programs could be sponsored by international institutions, these institutions still play a huge role in the fruition of the programs due to the massive support they could provide—which could still be tangible in the long run of the program.

Analysis of the above can be further deepened by using the Governance Innovations Framework developed by Brillantes and Calina (2013). These include innovations that emerged as a result of reforms in the following areas:

1. Reforms in Institutions, Processes and Procedures
2. Reforms in Mindsets, Paradigms and Behavior
3. Reforms enabled by Leadership and Political Will
4. Reform enabled by Active Citizen Engagement
5. Reforms are consciously communicated to stakeholders to enable ownership and sustainability

The context within which these reforms are to be undertaken should be recognized. This includes the global—yet local—context in accordance to the universally accepted principle to "think global, yet act local," hence "glocalization." Equally important is the imperative to recognize the need to cooperate and—certainly collaborate—with other stakeholders to attain a common purpose, yet be *driven* by a sense of competition, hence "coopetition."

We end with some principles that enable the emergence of innovative practices and collaborative governance as applied across various sectors.

Leadership is key. This leadership is characterized by curiosity, boldness, non-conformity and one that is daring to question authority and the status quo.

It is willing to venture into the unknown with limited but accurate information, daring to "muddle through" (Lindblom, 1959) and "grope along" (Behn, 1988). It is not reckless but is confidently willing to take calculated risks. Equally important, this leadership is characterized by phronesis (Aristotle) marked by practical wisdom.

Citizen engagement is imperative. The participation of the people—citizen's engagement—is sine-quo non for innovations to be sustained, at least in the peace and order sector. This is also true for the social sector.

The innovation should be within the context of a legitimate enabling framework such as a law or a policy or the Constitution. While innovators may be risk takers—they consistently push the envelope as they try to introduce "new ways of doing things"—they innovation should always be within the bounds of the law.

Strong institutions matter. This is where the continuous capacity building become very important for collaborative governance. Capacity building can be at the level of individuals, or at the level of refining and structures and procedures in the organizations and aligning them to the specific unique needs of the people.

Finally, collaborative governance is a dynamic and continuous process. Like all innovations, the fundamental principle of continuous improvement is built in the process. And this is fuelled by a built in monitoring and assessment systems, with a recognition that there is always a better way, considering the rapidly changing environment, one that is vulnerable, uncertain, complex and ambiguous (VUCA). It is within this context that, as our good and best practices at the subnational level have shown, collaborative governance is critical and indeed, as noted at the outset of this paper, alive and well.

## References

Albareda, L. (2008). Corporate responsibility, governance, and accountability: from self-regulation to co-regulation. *Corporate Governance*, 8(4), 430-439. DOI: 10.1108/14720700810899176

Albrecht, J. (2016). Legal framework and criteria for effectively coordinating public participation under the Floods Directive and Water Framework Directive: European requirements and German transposition. *Environmental Science & Policy*, 55, 368-375. DOI: 10.1016/j.envsci.2015.07.019

Ahlers, A. L., Heberer, T., and Schubert, G. (2016). Whither local governance in contemporary China? Reconfiguration for more effective policy implementation. *Journal of Chinese Governance*, 1(1), 55-77. DOI: 10.1080/23812346.2016.1138700

Alexander, J. A., Comfort, M. E., and Weiner, B. J. (1998). Governance in public-private community health partnerships: a survey of the Community Care Network: SM demonstration sites. *Nonprofit Management & Leadership*, 8, 231-332. DOI: 10.1002/nml.8402

Amsler, L. B. (2016). Collaborative Governance: Integrating Management, Politics, and Law. *Public Administration Review*, 76(5), 700-711. DOI: 10.1111/puar.12605

Amsler, L. B., and O'Leary, R. (2017). Collaborative public management and systems thinking. *International Journal of Public Sector Management*, 30(6/7), 626-639. DOI: 10.1108/ijpsm-07-2017-0187

Ansell, C., and Gash, A. (2007). Collaborative Governance in Theory and Practice. *Journal of Public Administration Research and Theory*, 18(4), 543-571. DOI: 10. 1093/jopart/mum032

Bardach, E., and R. A. Kagan (1982). *Going By the Book: The Problem of Regulatory Unreasonableness*. Philadelphia, Pennsylvania: Temple University Press.

Behn, R. D. (1988). Management by Groping along. *Journal of Policy Analysis and Management*, 7(4), 643-663. DOI: 10.2307/3323485

Boerzel, T. A., and Risse, T. (2005). Public-private partnerships: effective and legitimate tools of transnational governance. In Grande, E., and Pauly, L. W. (Eds.). *Complex Sovereignty: Reconstituting Political Authority in the Twenty-first Century*. Toronto, Canada: University of Toronto Press, 195-216.

Bradford, N. (1998). Prospects for associative governance: Lessons from Ontario, Canada. *Politics & Society*, 26, 539-573. DOI: 10.1177/0032329298026004005

Brillantes, A. B., Jr. (2003). *Innovations and Excellence. Understanding Local Govern-*

*ments in the Philippines*. Quezon City, Philippines: Center for Local and Regional Governance, National College of Public Administration of the Philippines.

Brillantes, A. B., Jr., and Fernandez, M. T. (2008). Is There a Philippines Public Administration?: Or Better Still, For Whom is Philippine Public Administration? *Philippine Journal of Public Administration*, 52(2-4) (April-October).

________. (2011). Good Governance, Social Quality, and Active Citizenship: Gawad Kalinga in the Philippines. *International Journal of Social Quality*, 1(2), 19-30. DOI: 10.3167/ijsq.2011.010203

Brown, A. J. (2002). Collaborative governance versus constitutional politics: Decision rules for sustainability from Australia's South East Queensland forest agreement. *Environmental Science and Policy*, 5, 19-32. DOI: 10.1016/S1462-9011(02)00022-9

Carbonara, N., Costantino, N., and Pellegrino, R. (2014). Concession period for PPPs: A win-win model for a fair risk sharing. *International Journal of Project Management*, 32(7), 1223-1232. DOI: 10.1016/j.ijproman.2014.01.007

Cheung, A. B. L. (2013). Can there be an Asian model of public administration? *Public Administration and Development*, 33(4), 249-261. DOI: 10.1002/pad.1660

Cheng, A. S., Gerlak, A. K., Dale, L. and Mattor, K. (2015). Examining the adaptability of collaborative governance associated with publicly managed ecosystems over time insights from the Front Range Roundtable, Colorado, USA. *Ecology and Society*, 20(1), 1-35. Retrieved from https://www.jstor.org/stable/26269758

Choi, T. (2014). Rational and Compassionate Information Processing: A Conceptual Framework for Authentic Dialogue. *Public Administration Review*, 74(6), 726-735. DOI:10.1111/puar.12277

Choi, T., and Robertson, P. J. (2018). Contributors and Free-Riders in Collaborative Governance: A Computational Exploration of Social Motivation and Its Effects. *Journal of Public Administration Research and Theory*, 1-20. DOI: 10.1093/jopart/muy068

De Dreu, C. K. W., Nijstad, B. A., and Van Knippenberg, D. (2007). Motivated Information Processing in Group Judgment and Decision Making. *Personality and Social Psychology Review*, 12(1), 22-49. DOI: 10.1177/1088868307304092

Doberstein, C. (2015). Designing Collaborative Governance Decision-Making in Search of a "Collaborative Advantage." *Public Management Review*, 18(6), 819-841. DOI: 10.1080/14719037.2015.1045019

Esteve, M., van Witteloostuijn, A., and Boyne, G. (2015). The Effects of Public Service Motivation on Collaborative Behavior: Evidence from Three Experimental Games.

*International Public Management Journal*, 18(2), 171-189. DOI: 10.1080/10967494.2015.1012573

Ettelt, S., May, N., and Allen, P. (2013). *The Multiple Purposes of Policy Pilots and Why They Matter: An Analysis of Three Examples from Health and Social Care in England.* Paper presented at the European Health Policy Group Meeting, London, on September 19-20, 2013. Retrieved April 22, 2020 from https://www.kingsfund.org.uk/sites/default/files/Paper2_The_multiple_purposes_of_policy_pilots_why_they_matterSept13.pdf

Finkelstein, L. S. (1995). What is global governance? *Global Governance*, 1(3), 367-372. Retrieved from http://www.good-governance-debates.de/wp-content/uploads/2015/03/What-is-global-governance-by-Lawrence-S.-Finkelstein_1995.pdf

Folke, C., Hahn, T., Olsson, P., and Norberg, J. (2005) Adaptive governance of social-ecological systems. *Annual Review of Environment and Resources*, 15(30), 441-473. DOI: 10.1146/annurev.energy.30.050504.144511

Funder, M., Mweemba, C., and Nyambe, I. (2017). The Politics of Climate Change Adaptation in Development: Authority, Resource Control and State Intervention in Rural Zambia. *The Journal of Development Studies*, 54(1), 30-46. DOI: 10.1080/00220388.2016.1277021

Futrell, R. (2003). Technical adversarialism and participatory collaboration in the U.S. chemical weapons disposal program. *Science, Technology, & Human Values*, 28, 451-482. DOI: 10.1177/0162243903252762

Galing Pook Foundation. (2003). *Gawad Galing Pook 2003: A Tribute to Innovation and Excellence in Local Governance*. Retrieved from http://www.galingpook.org/Websites/GalingPook/images/GP_Magazine/Gawad_Galing_Pook_2003.pdf

__________. (2007). *Galing Pook: The Ten Outstanding Local Governance Programs for 2007.* Retrieved from http://unpan1.un.org/intradoc/groups/ public/documents/eropa/unpan031880.pdf

__________. (2012). *Outstanding Local Governance Programs for 2012.* Retrieved from http://www.galingpook.org/Websites/GalingPook/images/GP_Magazine/Galing_Pook_Awards_2012_Magazine.pdf

__________. (2014). *Ten Outstanding Local Governance Programs.* Retrieved from http://www.galingpook.org/Websites/GalingPook/images/GP_Magazine/Galing_Pook_Awards_2014_Magazine.pdf

__________. (2015). *Mamamayan, Mamamayani: Exercising Citizenship to Make Government Work: 10 Outstanding Local Governance Programs and 3 Citizenship Award Winners.* Retrieved from http://www.galingpook.org/Websites/GalingPook/images/

GP_Magazine/Galing%20Pook%20Awards%202015%20Magazine.pdf

________. (2017). *Galing Pook 2017: The Ten Outstanding Local Governance Programs for 2017*. Retrieved from http://www.galingpook.org/Websites/GalingPook/images/GP_Magazine/Galing%20Pook%20Awards%202017%20Magazine.pdf

Gash, A. (2016). Collaborative governance. In Ansell, C. and Torfing, J. (Eds.). *Handbook on Theories of Governance*. Cheltenham, UK: Edward Elgar Pub. DOI: 10.4337/9781782548508

Gray, B. (1989). *Collaborating: Finding Common Ground for Multi-party Problems*. San Francisco, California: Jossey-Bass.

Hjern, B., and Porter, D. O. (1981). Implementation structures: a new unit for administrative analysis. *Organizational Studies*, 3, 211-237. DOI: 10.1177/017084068100200301

Hodge, G., Greve, C., and Biygautane, M. (2018). Do PPP's work? What and how have we been learning so far? *Public Management Review*, 20(8), 1105-1121. DOI: 10.1080/14719037.2018.1428410

Howlett, M., Kekez, A., and Poocharoen, O. O. (2017). Understanding Co-Production as a Policy Tool: Integrating New Public Governance and Comparative Policy Theory. *Journal of Comparative Policy Analysis: Research and Practice*, 19(5), 487-501. DOI: 10.1080/13876988.2017.1287445

Huxham, C., and Vangen, S. (2000). Leadership in the shaping and implementation of collaboration agendas: How things happen in a (not quite) joined-up world. *Academy of Management Journal*, 43, 1159-1175. DOI: 10.5465/1556343

Johnston, E. W., Hicksy, D., Nanz, N., and Auer, J. C. (2010). Managing the Inclusion Process in Collaborative Governance. *Journal of Public Administration Research and Theory*, 21, 699-721. DOI: 10.1093/jopart/muq045

Keast, R. (2016). Network governance. In Ansell, C., and Torfing, J. (Eds.). (2016). *Handbook on Theories of Governance*, 442-453. Cheltenham, UK: Edward Elgar. DOI: 10.4337/9781782548508

Keck, M. E., and Sikkink (2004). Transnational Advocacy Networks in International Politics. In Mingst, K. A., and Snyder, J. L. (Eds.). *Essential Readings in World Politics*. 2nd ed. New York: Norton.

King, B. (2015). Transnational Actors in World Politics. In Kavalski, E. (Ed.). *Encounters with World Affairs: An Introduction to International Relations*. Surrey England: Ashgate.

Klenk, T., and Reiter, R. (2019). Post-New Public Management: reform ideas and their application in the field of social services. *International Review of Administrative*

*Sciences*, 1-8. DOI: 10.1177/0020852318810883

Klijn, E. H., and Koppenjan, J. (2012). Governance network theory: past, present and future. *Policy & Politics*, 40(4), 587-606. DOI: 10.1332/030557312x655431

Koltay, T., Špiranec, S., and Karvalics, L. Z. (2016). *Research 2.0 and the Future of Information Literacy*. Amsterdam, The Netherlands: Elsevier.

Lane, C., and Bachman, R. (Eds.). (1998). *Trust within and Between Organizations: Conceptual Issues and Empirical Applications*. Oxford: Oxford University Press.

Lindblom, C. E. (1959). The Science of "Muddling Through." *Public Administration Review*, 19(2), 79-88. DOI: 10.2307/973677

Linden, R. M. (2010). *Leading Across Boundaries: Creating Collaborative Agencies in a Networked World*. 1st ed. San Francisco, California: Jossey-Bass.

Maragah, H. D., and Corredoira, R. A. (2002). Al Gore's Initiative of Reinventing the Government: The Real Story of Total Quality Management in the Federal Government. *Quality Engineering*, 14(2), 279-291, DOI: 10.1081/QEN-100108685

March, J. G., and Olsen, J. P. (2006). The Logic of Appropriateness. In Moran, M., Rein, M., and Goodin, R. E. (Eds.). (2006). *The Oxford Handbook of Public Policy*, 689-708. Oxford, UK: Oxford University Press.

Marsh, K. (2015). The History of Global Politics. In Kavalski, E. (Ed.). *Encounters with World Affairs: An Introduction to International Relations*, 13-35. Surrey England: Ashgate.

McDougall, C., and Banjade, M. R. (2015). Social capital, conflict, and adaptive collaborative governance: exploring the dialectic. *Ecology and Society*, 20(1), 1-44. DOI: 10.5751/es-07071-200144

Meloto, A. (2009). *Builder of Dreams*. Mandaluyong City: Gawad Kalinga Community Development Foundation.

Moon, M. J., and Hwang, C. H. (2013). The State of Civil Service Systems in the Asia-Pacific Region: A Comparative Perspective. *Review of Public Personnel Administration*, 33(2), 121-139. DOI: 10.1177/0734371X13484831

Murdock, B., Wiessner, C., and Sexton, K. (2005). Stakeholder participation in voluntary environmental agreements: Analysis of 10 Project XL case studies. *Science, Technology & Human Values*, 30, 223-250. DOI: 10.1177/0162243904266104

Nonaka, I., Nishihara, A. H., and Kawada, H. (2018). Knowledge-Based Management Theory. In Nishihara, A. H., Matsunaga, M., Nonaka, I., and Yokomichi, K. (2018). (Eds.). *Knowledge Creation in Public Administrations: Innovative Government in Southeast Asia and Japan*, 1-21. Cham, Switzerland: Palgrave Macmillan. DOI: 10.1007/978-3-319-57478-3

North, D. C. (1991). Institutions. *The Journal of Economic Perspectives*, 5(1), 97-112. Retrived September 20, 2019 from http://www.jstor.org/stable/1942704

North, D. C., Wallis, J. J., and Weingast, B. R. (2009). *Violence and Social Orders: A Conceptual Framework for Interpreting Recorded Human History*. Cambridge: Cambridge University Press.

OECD. (2011). *The Economic Significance of Natural Resources: Key Points for Reformers in Eastern Europe, Caucasus and Central Asia* (Report). Paris, France: Author. Retrieved April 20, 2020 from http://www.oecd.org/env/outreach/ 2011_AB_Economic%20significance%20of%20NR%20in%20EECCA_ENG.pdf

Osborne, S. P. (2010). Introduction: The (New) Public Governance: a suitable case for treatment? In Osborne, S. P. (Ed.). (2010). *The New Public Governance: Emerging Perspectives in the Theory and Practice of Public Governance*, 1-17. London: Routledge.

Ostrom, E. (2007). A diagnostic approach for going beyond panaceas. *Proceedings of the National Academy of Sciences*, 104(39), 15181-15187. DOI: 10.1073/pnas.0702288104

Pahl-Wostl, C. (2009). A conceptual framework for analysing adaptive capacity and multi-level learning processes in resource governance regimes. *Global Environmental Change*, 19(3), 354-365. DOI: 10.1016/j.gloenvcha.2009.06.001

Park, K., & Weible, C. M. (2017). Developing policy theories in South Korea: lessons from the advocacy coalition framework. *Journal of Asian Public Policy*, 11(2), 136-150. DOI: 10.1080/17516234.2017.1412904

Philippines (1991). *Republic Act No. 7160: An Act Providing for a Local Government Code of 1991*. Retrived from https://www.officialgazette.gov.ph/1991/10/10/republic-act-no-7160/

Pirnejad, P. (2017). *Elements of a Successful Multi-sectoral Collaborative from a Local Government Perspective: A Framework for Collaborative Governance -dimensions Shared by Award Winning Multi-sectoral Partnerships* (Doctoral dissertation). Retrieved from https://search.proquest.com/docview/1914676917?accountid=47253

Porio, E. (2017). Citizen Participation and Decentralization in the Philippines. In Berenschot, W., Schulte-Nordholt, H., and Bakker, L. (Eds.). *Citizenship and Democratization in Southeast Asia*. Leiden, The Netherlands: Brill.

Rasche, A. (2010). Collaborative Governance 2.0. *Corporate Governance: The International Journal of Business in Society*, 10(4), 500-511. DOI: 10.1108/14720701011069713

Reyes, D. D. L. R. (2017). The Sustainable Development Goals and the Dangers of

Policy Reductionism. *International Journal of Policy Studies*, 8(1), 21. Retrieved from http://www.kaps.or.kr/en/src/board/view.php?page=1&code=IJPS&mode=&no=4543&s_kind=&s_type=1&s_text

Reynaers, A. M. (2012). *Public-Private Partnerships and Democratic Governance: Results from a Case Study* (Conference paper). Presented at the Symposium "Neither Public nor Private: Mixed Forms of Service Delivery around the Globe", on May 17-18, 2012 at the School of Economics, University of Barcelona, Spain. Retrieved from http://www.ub.edu/graap/Final%20Papers%20PDF/Anne-Marie%20Reynaers.pdf

Rhodes, R. A. W. (1997). *Understanding Governance: Policy Networks, Governance, Reflexivity, and Accountability*. Philadelphia, Pennsylvania: Open University Press.

Ritz, A., Brewer, G. A., and Neumann, O. (2016). Public Service Motivation: A Systematic Literature Review and Outlook. *Public Administration Review*, 76(3), 414-426. DOI: 10.1111/puar.12505

Roehrich, J. K., Lewis, M. A., and George, G. (2014). Are public-private partnerships a healthy option? A systematic literature review. *Social Science & Medicine*, 113, 1-28. DOI: 10.1016/j.socscimed.2014.03.037

Rogers, T., Howard-Pitney, B., Feighery, E. C., Altman, D. G., Endres, J. M., and Roeseler, A. G. (1993). Characteristics and participant perceptions of tobacco control coalitions in California. *Health Education Research, Theory & Practice*, 8, 345-357. DOI: 10.1093/her/8.3.345

Roloff, J. (2008). Learning from multi-stakeholder networks: issue-focused stakeholder management. *Journal of Business Ethics*, 82, 233-250. DOI: 10.1007/s10551-007-9573-3

Rosenau, J. N. (1992). Governance, order, and change in world politics. In Rosenau, J. N., and Czempiel, E. O. (Eds.). *Governance without Government: Order and Change in World Politics*, 1-29. Cambridge: Cambridge University Press.

Sale, J. P. (2011). *The Governance of Decision Making and Labor Dispute Settlement in the Philippines: Shifting Methods from Command to Collaboration or Vice-Versa?* (Doctoral dissertation). Quezon City: UP National College of Public Administration and Governance, 08 March 2011.

__________. (2012). Labor Market Governance and Regional Development in the Philippines: Uneven Trends and Outcomes. *World Technopolis Review*, 1(3), 192-205. DOI: 10.7165/wtr2012.1.3.192

__________. (2015). Collaborative Governance in Philippine Science and Technology Parks: A closer look at the UP-Ayala Land Technohub. *World Technopolis*

*Review*, 4, 23-32. DOI: 10.7165/wtr2015.4.1.23.

Scherer, A. G., and Palazzo, G. (2008). Corporate social responsibility in global context', in Crane, A., McWilliams, A., Matten, D., Moon, J., and Siegel, D. (Eds.). *The Oxford Handbook of Corporate Social Responsibility*, 413-431. Oxford: Oxford University Press.

Scherer, A. G., Palazzo, G., and Baumann, D. (2006). Global rules and private actors: toward a new role of the transnational corporation in global governance. *Business Ethics Quarterly*, 16, 505-532. DOI: 10.2307/3857794

Sidel, J. T. (2004). Bossism and Democracy in the Philippines, Thailand, and Indonesia: Towards an Alternative Framework for the Study of 'Local Strongmen.' In J. Harriss, K. Stokke, and O. Tornquist (Eds.). *Politicizing Democracy: The New Local Politics of Democratization*. New York: Palgrave Macmillan.

Simmons, M. (2018 Dec 8). How Elon Musk Learns Faster and Better Than Everyone Else. *Medium* (News site). Retrieved from https://medium.com/accelerated-intelligence/learn-like-elon-musk-fe8f8da6137c

Simonin, B. L. (2017). The darker side of collaborations: 12 common mistakes. *The Fletcher Forum of World Affairs*, 41(1), 7-26. Retrieved from https://search.proquest.com/docview/1914089346?accountid=47253

Sorensen, E. (2007). Local Politicians and Administrators as Metagovernors. In Marcussen, M., and Torfing, J. (2007). *Democratic Network Governance in Europe*. Hampshire, London: Palgrave Macmillan. DOI: 10.1057/978023059628

Sorensen, E., and Torfing, J. (2005). The Democratic Anchorage of Governance Networks. *Scandinavian Political Studies*, 28(3), 195-218. DOI: 10.1111/j.1467-9477.2005.00129.x

Stokke, K., and O. Tornquist (Eds.). (2005). *Politicizing Democracy: The New Local Politics of Democratization*. New York: Palgrave Macmillan.

Tanchai, W. (2012). Thailand: People-centric leadership and management. In *The Second Policy Forum on Leadership and Management Development in Asian Countries Transcript* (2012) (Conference proceedings). Presented at the Policy Forum on Leadership and Management Development in Asian Countries on March 26-27, 2015. Tokyo, Japan: National Graduate Institute for Policy Studies (GRIPS).

Thatcher, M. (1995). *The Downing Street Year*. London: Harper Collins.

Tomalin, B., and Nicks, M. (2007). *The World's Business Cultures and How to Unlock Them*. London: Thorogood Publishing.

Tsujinaka, Y., Ahmed, S., and Kobashi, Y. (2013). Constructing Co-governance between

Government and Civil Society: An Institutional Approach to Collaboration. *Public Organization Review*, 13(4), 411-426. DOI: 10.1007/s11115-013-0260-9

Van Buuren, A., Edelenbos, F., and Klijn, E. H. (2007). Interactive Governance in the Netherlands: The Case of the Scheidt Estuary. In Marcussen, M., and Torfing, J. *Democratic Network Governance in Europe*. New York: Palgrave Macmillan.

Van der Heijden, J. (2014). *Governance for Urban Sustainability and Resilience Responding to Climate Change and the Relevance of the Built Environment*. Cheltenham, UK: Edward Elgar.

Vangen, S., and Huxham, C. (2003). Enacting leadership for collaborative advantage: Dilemmas of ideology and pragmatism in the activities of partnership managers. *British Journal of Management*, 14, 61-76. DOI: 10.1111/j.1467-8551.2003.00393.x

Voorberg, W. H., Bekkers, V. J. J. M., and Tummers, L. G. (2014). A Systematic Review of Co-Creation and Co-Production: Embarking on the social innovation journey. *Public Management Review*, 17(9), 1333-1357. DOI: 10.1080/14719037.2014.930505

Wang, T. Y., and Liu, H. (2018). An emerging Asian model of governance and transnational knowledge transfer: an introduction. *Journal of Asian Public Policy*, 11(2), 121-135. DOI: 10.1080/17516234.2018.1477030

Warsen, R., Nederhand, J., Klijn, E. H., Grotenbreg, S., and Koppenjan, J. (2018). What makes public-private partnerships work? Survey research into the outcomes and the quality of cooperation in PPPs. *Public Management Review*, 20(8), 1165-1185. DOI: 10.1080/14719037.2018.1428415

Xu, R. Y., Sun, Q. G., and Si, W. (2015). The Third Wave of Public Administration: The New Public Governance. *Canadian Social Science*, 11(7), 11-21. DOI: 10.3968/7354

Yang, L. (2016). Types and Institutional Design Principles of Collaborative Governance in a Strong-Government Society: The Case Study of Desertification Control in Northern China. *International Public Management Journal*, 20(4), 586-623. DOI: 10.1080/10967494.2016.1141812

Young, I. M. (2000). *Inclusion and Democracy*. Oxford: Oxford University Press.

Zadek, S. (2008). Global collaborative governance: there is no alternative. *Corporate Governance: The International Journal of Business in Society*, 8(4), 374-388. DOI: 10.1108/14720700810899121S

5

# Collaborative Local Governance in Japan: Configuration and Practical Development

Masao Kikuchi

## Introduction

Collaborative governance is not a new way of governing but the need for it has increased over the past several decades. Following a series of policy failures and socioeconomic changes including the emergence of more active civil society organizations, many governments are facing increased pressure to provide better services with less resources. Accordingly, most current democratic governments are making efforts to develop effective and efficient collaborative governance in both decision-making and service delivery. Collaborative governance involves communication and collaboration between the government, the community, and private sector actors in order to achieve common goals that any single sector actor cannot achieve on its own. Ansell and Gash (2007, 544) defines the concept of collaborative governance as "A governing arrangement where one or more public agencies directly engage non-state stakeholders in a collective decision-making process that is formal, consensus-oriented, and deliberative and that aims to make or implement public policy or manage public programs or assets." It involves the government (governing issues), process orientation on consensus, and management and delivery issues. The emergence of collaborative governance literature reflects the fact that neither managerialism represented by the New Public Management approach nor traditional meritocratic bureaucracy theory is useful in guiding government to meet increasingly complex public demands.

Collaborative governance is distinct from the "small government" approach that attempts to scale down government programs. In collaborative governance, the expected roles and activities of government in policy-making or service delivery may undergo transformation. Unlike privatization, however, collaborative governance requires new government capacity to coordinate and harness stakeholders to achieve shared goals and deliver targeted outcomes (Emerson, Nabatchi, and Balgoh, 2012). In other words, the government is expected to facilitate, coordinate, and deliver its aims through a collaborative process. This is a new capacity challenge for government. The government's primary practices can be traced back to the pre-modern traditional style of public management (O'Leary and Bingham, 2009), where institutionalized and capacitated "government" was not yet formed and shared resources were governed by "citizens" through participatory processes. Stakeholders made decisions and independently managed and implemented them. In Japan, during the *Edo* era (1603~1868), village farmlands were co-owned and managed so that shared interests were kept intact. Such land, the "commons", was managed by a special-purpose local government (*Zaisanku*, or property ward) through collaboration between the government and landowners, who were, in many cases, residents of former municipalities that were merged during the *Meiji* and *Showa* municipal merger campaign period. *Zaisanku* is a legal entity acting as a local government but also served as a mechanism for management of common-pool resources by property owners, with the government establishing the legal framework for managing properties through owner participation (McKean and Cox, 1982; Ostrom, 1990; Tanaka and Inoue, 2015). This Japanese case demonstrates that an earlier form of today's collaborative governance was practiced in the past.

Against this background, this chapter examines the current state and characteristics of collaborative governance in Japan in terms of its levels, areas, processes, and related issues. The following section provides a broad overview of the current state of collaborative governance in Japan and discusses its major drivers. The final section presents several case studies that highlight the characteristics of Japanese collaborative governance and offers some policy-relevant concluding remarks.

## Areas and Levels of Collaborative Governance in Japan: Configuration and practice

### Background to the Rise of Collaborative Governance in Japan

Collaborative governance in Japan is largely practiced at the local government level. Only certain cases of collaborative governance are found at the central government level, such as deliberative polling on nuclear energy policy choices and participatory project planning for national infrastructure projects. More recently, central government ministries have been actively attempting to collaborate with the technology sector for the rapid advancement of the Internet of Things, artificial intelligence, and other areas. However, local governments hold a larger share of public expenditure and have more extensive roles in providing basic public services to citizens than the central government. Accordingly, numerous and various cases of collaborative governance can be found at the local government level rather than the central government level.

The rise of collaborative governance at the local government level has been influenced by several factors. The first is power devolution from the central government to local governments. Many social and welfare services have become the responsibility of local governments (Ministry of Internal Affairs and Communications, 2019). Since decentralization reforms began in 2000, local governments have had substantial discretionary power in determining standards and covering various public services (Muto, 2010). For example, the national government's share of all government expenditures on school education in the fiscal year 2017, was a mere 13% — the remaining 87% was spent by local governments. Local governments are no longer arm's-length bodies that simply implement centrally decided services. Under this decentralization, local governments are required to manage and provide services through collaboration with stakeholders to identify and meet local needs (Pekkanen, Tsujinaka, and Yamamoto, 2014).

The second factor in the larger role of local governments in collaborative governance is demographic changes, which have resulted in fiscal consequences. Japanese society is rapidly aging and experiencing depopulation. The total Japanese population has been steadily decreasing because the birth rate has been too low to sustain the population since 2008. Furthermore, the population is getting older, with senior citizens (aged 65 years or more) accounting for nearly 28% of Japan's total population in 2018. There is also a huge disparity in the distribution of senior citizens throughout the country. Senior citizens comprised 21% of the total population of Okinawa in 2017 but more than 35% of the total population of Akita Prefecture, which is located in the north of Japan's main island (National Institute of Population and Social Security Research, 2018). This ongoing demographic change places local governments under growing fiscal pressure to sustain public services including welfare demands, while resources based on tax revenue are inevitability on the decline. In 2006, Yubari City in Hokkaido declared "bankruptcy" and decided to enter a fiscal rehabilitation process. The city once enjoyed economic prosperity as one of Japan's coal-mining centers. After the last coal mine closed in 1990, the population began to decline, dwindling to less than 10,000 from its peak of 120,000 in 1960. As the case of Yubari demonstrates, local governments especially in rural areas must transform their governance and service styles by collaborating more with stakeholders to enhance the effectiveness of public services and sustain them (Kikuchi, 2009). In addition to financial constraints, local governments in Japan are facing a shortage of human resources. Although demand for government services have been increasing and becoming more diverse due to the problems of a super-aging society, there has been a sharp decline in the number of local civil servants over the last 15 years. In 1998, more than 3.2 million local civil servants were employed throughout Japan. This number dropped to less than 2.73 million in 2018.

The third factor in the rise of collaborative governance at the local government level is the growth of the voluntary and nonprofit sector, which cooperates with the government in the delivery of public services. Even though human resources in local government have been shrinking, the country's voluntary and nonprofit sector has been rapidly growing since the 1990s, especially after the Law to Promote Specified Nonprofit Activities, known as the "NPO Law", was enacted in 1998. This law was put in place after nonprofit organizations and voluntary citizen groups responded efficiently to the disaster caused by the Great Hanshin-Awaji Earthquake in 1995. The law has allowed many civil service organizations and voluntary groups to apply for recognition as a legal entity as a specified nonprofit organization (corporation). The number of NPOs has been increasing ever since, reaching more than 50,000 in 2018 (Cabinet Office, 2018), as shown in Figure 1. In addition to these specific NPOs that gained new legal status under this law, there has been an increase in conventional types of organizations that have a different corporate and legal status. Public interest corporations (public interest foundations and public interest associations), which

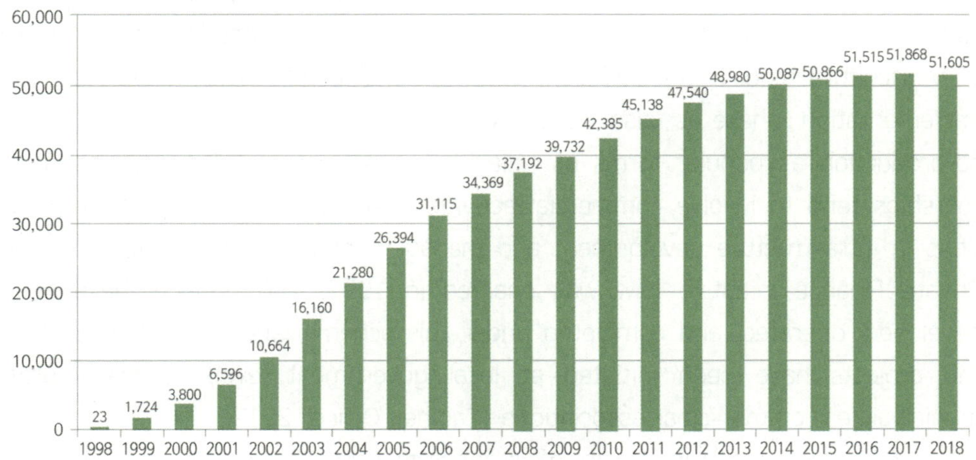


**Figure 1.** Number of Registered NPOs (Specified Nonprofit Corporations) between 1998 and 2018

Source: Cabinet Office (2018). *Ninsyou NPO no suii [Trend of certified NPOs].*

usually have a long history and large regional scope, are given legal status and regulated under the Civil Code of Japan. Social welfare corporations, private school corporations, medical corporations, and religious corporations follow a parallel special law. These corporate categories enjoy tax exemptions and receive tax-deductible contributions in the same way as the widely known 501(c)(3) and 501(c)(4) nonprofit corporations in the United States. The introduction of a new category of nonprofit organizations through the NPO Law reflects the fact that Japanese government increasingly began to look to partnerships with private actors and pursued collaborative governance in policy-making and service delivery.

## Forms of Collaborative Governance in Japan

Various forms and institutions of collaborative governance exist at the local government level in Japan. Local governments commonly carry out a decision-making phase, including participatory budgeting (e.g., Ichikawa City), deliberative polling (e.g., the national government, Fujisawa City, and Mitaka City), consensus development conferences or technology assessment (e.g., the Ministry of Agriculture and Kawasaki City), and citizens panels and workshops. An implementation phase is also conducted, with public-private partnership and co-production as popular forms of collaborative governance. Public-private partnerships tend to involve commercial activities, so partners are mostly corporations in infrastructure development and management (Nemoto, 2015). After the Private Finance Initiative Law was enacted in 1997, 740 projects have been developed, operated, and completed under this scheme, and more than 82% of the projects have been initiated at local government level, by prefectures, municipalities, or municipal associations (Cabinet Office, 2019).

The most common form of collaborative governance in the Japanese context is thought to be "co-production" (*Kyodo* in Japanese). It seeks greater collaboration mainly in the service delivery phase through partnerships with various organizations such as citizen groups, voluntary groups, and NPOs (Brandsen and Pestoff, 2006; Ostrom, 1996). In co-production, actors with different roles in the same sector are expected to work together toward the same objective. Local governments exert much effort into fostering co-production cases in disaster management; environmental protection including recycling and waste management; management of roads, parks, and other public facilities; and social welfare programs for the elderly, people with disabilities, the poor, foreign citizens, gender minorities, and other marginalized citizens (Tsukamoto and Nishimura, 2006). All these programs need to take into account various voices and interests of stakeholder citizens in deciding their scope, standards, and coverage. They also rely on cooperation with stakeholders for efficient and effective service delivery. In other words, stakeholder citizens are not mere recipients or "consumers" of public programs. They are rather the "producers" of public programs and thus partners with whom local governments collaborate.

Co-production is an increasingly common form of collaboration between local governments and NPOs. The Cabinet Office found via a survey that 66% of municipalities and 100% of prefectures had co-production experiences with NPOs as early as 2004 (Cabinet Office, 2004). The most common form of co-production was project outsourcing to NPOs (100% of prefectures, 80% of municipalities), followed by nominal support provided to NPO projects (87% of prefectures, 41% of municipalities), and project and event co-hosting with NPOs (82% of prefectures, 46% of municipalities). The main areas of co-production were welfare (40% of prefectures, 52% of municipalities), environmental protection (52% of prefectures, 28% of municipalities), and community development (30% of prefectures, 38% of municipalities). These main policy areas of co-production hold a greater share of local government expenditures. Accordingly, service delivery through these co-production programs requires collaboration driven by efficiency and effectiveness for the sake of budget rationality.

# Collaborative Governance Practiced by Japanese Local Governments

This section illustrates the features of collaborative governance through notable case studies. The first case is environmental protection practiced by Shibushi City in Kagoshima Prefecture, which achieved the highest recycling rate in Japan for more than the past 10 years. Recyclable materials comprise almost 80% of all waste in Shibushi and the city aims to increase that percentage even further. Since 1998, the city's landfill sites were projected to reach capacity within the next 10 years. A large-scale incinerator was proposed but entailed a high investment cost. Furthermore, the city's local government faced ongoing running costs at the time when it was already experiencing severe financial difficulties. Awareness of climate change issues was growing, and after a series of citizens workshops, the local government decided to increase recycling rates rather than attempt to go down the route of reducing the amount of waste destined for landfill. This required the active participation of citizens in separating and sorting their waste and the local government put a great deal of effort into ensuring every citizen was ready to recycle and actually recycled. The mayor and city government staff participated in many community meetings with neighborhood citizens groups to discuss the importance of this project for environmental protection.

After years of consultation, the city initiated a new waste management system in 2005. Since then, household waste in the city has been separated into 28 categories. Every household receives a booklet explaining the system and when and how to dispose of waste (Figure 2). Furthermore, recycling support groups were set up in each neighborhood to provide assistance to senior citizens and others who had difficulties in independently complying with the system in their household. As a result, the city earned the title of highest recycling city from 2007 and has retained its top position in subsequent years. Furthermore, not only has landfill waste disposal decreased by 80%, which means that designated landfill sites are now estimated to last another 30 years, but the city's waste disposal cost per person has also fallen below the nationwide average.

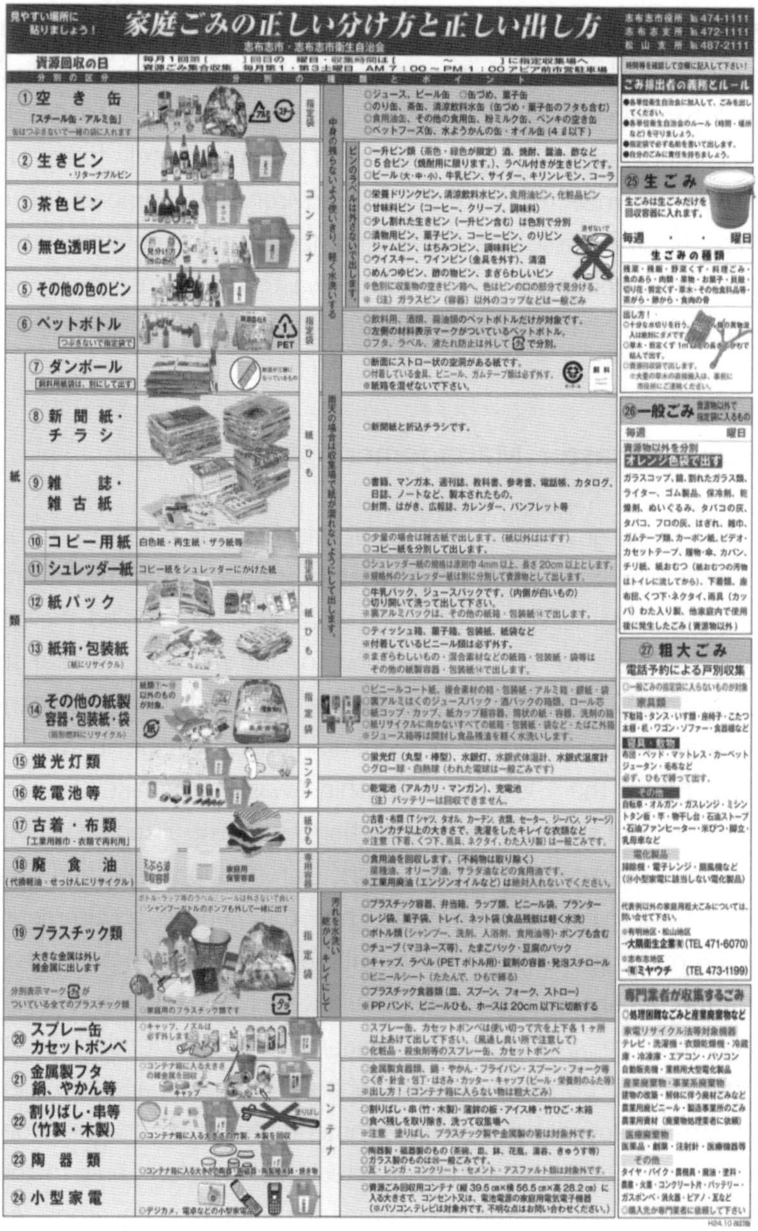


**Figure 2.** Shibushi City Booklet on Sorting of Household Waste

Source: Shibushi City.

The local government and citizens have announced a goal of reaching a 90% to 95% recycling rate in near future. Efforts to achieve this bold goal include calling for further collaboration, especially with the industrial sector. In 2019, the city signed a partnership agreement with Unicharm Company to develop a pilot diaper recycling operation. This pilot operation could ultimately form a nationwide program in an attempt to decrease the environmental impact of disposable diapers. Shibushi City is also sharing its knowledge and experience internationally by participating in projects dealing with waste problems in Fiji and other developing countries.

## Collaborative Disaster Management

The Japanese government has dealt with various disasters throughout its history. Japan is one of the countries most prone to natural disasters, including earthquakes, so critical lessons from each disaster have enabled the government to determine how best to mitigate, respond to, and manage crises. For instance, the basic national institutional framework for disaster management was established after major typhoons brought immense damage in the 1960s. The lessons learned from the 1995 Great Hanshin-Awaji Earthquake strengthened the Japanese government's information collection and centralized risk management, which led to the establishment of the Cabinet Information Collection Center in the Cabinet Secretariat. Local governments, not the central government, are the primary government agencies that deal with disasters and protect the lives and property of the Japanese public. For example, as of 2019, only 172 staff are employed by the Fire and Disaster Management Agency under the Ministry of Internal Affairs and Communications, whereas more than 160,000 full-time firefighters are employed by local governments to work on the frontline. The Japan Self-Defense Force dispatches disaster relief missions only in the event of large-scale disasters and at the request of a prefectural governor. Accordingly, local governments have a far larger crisis management capacity than the central government (OECD, 2009).

An important factor in sustaining Japan's crisis management capacity is the trichotomy of the country's crisis management into self-help, co-help, and public assistance, and collaboration among these. Under self-help, securing safety and protecting one's life are considered to be the responsibility of individuals. This is the fundamental philosophy of crisis management. In the case of large-scale natural disasters, the government cannot be expected to provide an immediate rescue response. Instead, the foundation of crisis management is self-help preparedness and actions, including preparing survival and stockpiled goods, checking evacuation areas, and participating in emergency drills. Co-help refers to community or association-based mutual aid activities such as those run by voluntary disaster management organizations and the distribution of community maps to identify disaster-prone areas and vulnerable people such as the elderly, people with disabilities, and those living alone (Table 1). Strengthening community resilience through self-help and co-help is key to transferring crisis management capacities away from the government sectors. Networking and collaboration with the private sector and NPOs also contribute to making up for the weakening capacities of local governments.

**Table 1.** Collaborative Disaster Management and the Trichotomy of Self-help, Co-help, and Public Assistance

| | |
|---|---|
| Self-help | Prepare survival and stockpiled goods, check evacuation area, participate in emergency drills, and others |
| Co-help | Form a self-help organization in the community, identify vulnerable people such as elderly persons living alone, identify vulnerable areas in the community, prepare business continuity plans, and others |
| Public Assistance | Fire brigade, police force, Self Defense Force, and others |

The crisis management approach suggests that during the initial 72 hours (3 days) after a natural disaster has occurred, it is critical to have victims themselves practicing self-help and co-help. Citizens and the community as a whole must prepare to mitigate and respond to possible disasters in the initial 72 hours. In large-scale disasters, the government may take up to 72 hours to identify the extent of damage and deploy rescue teams — most survivors in need of help under stressful circumstances and without food or water can survive only within this time period. In the case of the Great Hanshin-Awaji Earthquake in

1995, 85% of survivors in need of help were rescued by fellow citizens and 5% by fire brigades.

The central government of Japan focuses more on coordination tasks, whereas local governments play a vital role in crisis management. The national framework for crisis management allocates local governments, especially municipalities, as the fundamental public bodies for establishing evacuation orders and hazard areas and carrying out natural disaster-prevention measures. In the case of large-scale disasters that are beyond the capacities of small local governments, neighboring local governments work together by sharing resources. In addition, the local public finance situation has deteriorated, which has recently seen governments try to share responsibilities with private actors. This trend is considered irreversible due to fundamental socioeconomic change in Japan's population structure. Thus, an important lesson from the Japanese collaborative governance experiences is the necessity of developing a new approach of establishing sustainable public-private partnerships in order to complement weakening government capacities.

## Evidence-based Policy Making and Randomized Control Trials in Collaborative Governance Practice

The final case study of Japanese collaborative governance is evidence-based policy making (EBPM) and randomized control trials (RCTs). EBPM involves examining the effectiveness of policies implemented in the past and possible future policy options. It is based on empirical findings and thus increases the effectiveness of policy plans. It ensures that best available evidence from research is central to policy development and implementation to guide people in decision-making on policies, programs, and projects. One of the keys of effective collaborative governance lies in information sharing and common understanding. Information sharing on policies or projects through EBPM helps develop common understandings and ensure everyone aims for the same goals. Following the successful example of the United Kingdom, momentum is building for Japan to introduce an EBPM approach. RCT is an experimental form of impact evaluation in which the population receiving the program or policy intervention is chosen at random from the eligible population, and a control group is also chosen at random from the same eligible population. It tests the extent to which specific, planned impacts are being achieved. One of its strengths is that it provides a very powerful response to the question of causality, helping program implementers and evaluators to know that what is being achieved is resulted from not anything else than the policy intervention(White, Sabarwal, and Hoop, 2014).

A successful application of an RCT is illustrated in the recyclable waste collection station project of Hayama Town in Kanagawa Prefecture. The town has a population of approximately 30,000 and started a community-based recyclable waste collection station system in 2014. The new system led to a decrease in the amount of waste generated in the town and also an increased in its recycling rate. However, eventually a town-wide issue became evident, namely, improper use of the recyclable waste collection stations, such as improper separation or dumping after collection hours. After consultations with citizens, a collaborative project for the eradication of improper use of stations was initiated in 2015.

First, to accurately grasp the situation at the time, town and community groups regularly monitored the state of use of the collection stations. Of all 475 stations, they selected 158 stations and monitored citizens' recycling behaviors for 22 days. More than 1,200 monitoring episodes in total were recorded. The results of this basic monitoring survey were analyzed, with both town staff and community groups working together at workshops to investigate the causes of improper use. They identified two different causes: improper separation and dumping after collection hours. Then, the RCT approach was implemented to identify the impact of two proposed ways for deterring the improper use of the collection stations. A total of 160 stations were selected to represent the entire population of collection stations. These stations were randomly separated into three groups. Group Ⅰ consisted of 54 stations for which flyers were distributed to citizens explaining how to sort waste and use nearby collection stations. Group Ⅱ consisted of 53 stations at which a "Today's Collection is Over" signboard was placed after collection hours. Group Ⅲ was treated as the control group, meaning no intervention (Figure 3). All three groups of stations were again monitored for the next 1 month; more than 1,600 monitoring episodes in total were recorded.

After the 1-month trial period, analysis of the results revealed that Group Ⅰ initially had a notable impact, decreasing improper separation by 80%, but the effect did not last long. Group Ⅱ had a more sustainable impact, decreasing improper use of the collection stations by 15%, with the effects lasting beyond the trial period. Accordingly, the town decided in 2017 to apply the policy of Group Ⅱ to all 475 stations.

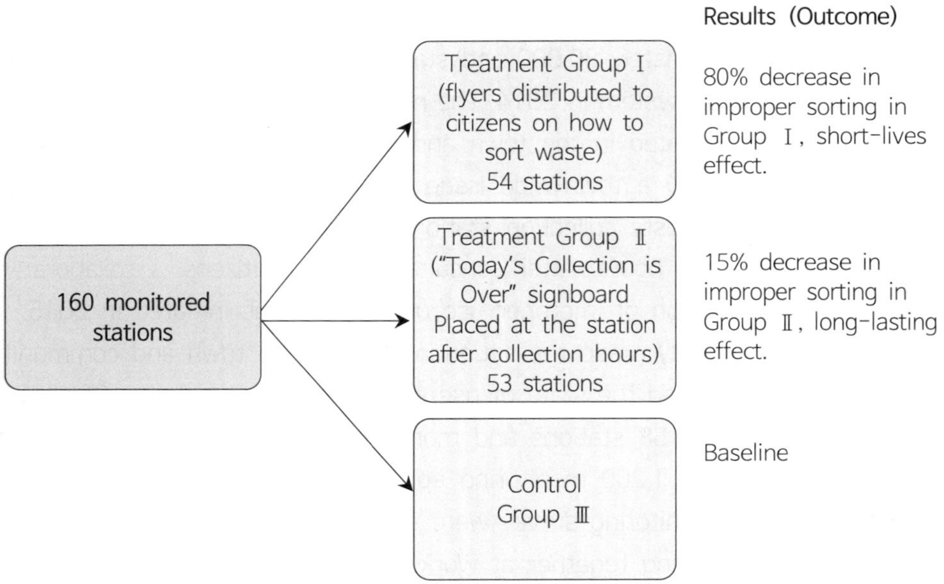


**Figure 3.** Hayama Town Randomized Control Trial on the Use of Recycling Stations

Source: Hayama Town (2019).

The town government later asked citizen participants to respond to an opinion survey on their experience with the collaborative RCT project: 87% of the participants expressed willingness to take a more active role in the project. The city's citizens came to better understand the problems surrounding the use of the collection stations and cooperated in using the stations properly. The impact of the RCT interventions (i.e., response alternatives to the improper use of the collection stations) was useful in steadily improving the town's recycling rate.

## Lesson Learned and Concluding Remarks

The case studies in the areas of environmental and disaster management discussed in the previous section illustrated the overall characteristics of collaborative governance in Japan and the factors involved. First, as in other countries, collaborative governance practices can be observed across different levels of government. Japanese collaborative governance is developed and practiced primarily at the local or community levels, which may reflect the institutional and functional distribution of the government apparatus. Even before the decentralization reform took place in 2000, many basic government services were provided by local governments, not the central government. This wider role of local governments to maintain the daily life of ordinary citizens may explain the uneven practices of collaborative governance.

Japan's public administration literature uses the term collaborative governance interchangeably with community governance, local governance, and co-production. It has been discussed in the context of local and community governance transformation after the decentralization reform (Pekkanen, Tsujinaka, and Yamamoto, 2014). Also, collaborative governance is primarily considered in implementation processes rather than policy decision-making, which is often done at the central level. Most of the functions of central agencies involve establishing public service guidelines and standards in order to ensure the citizens have equal access and a minimum level of public service provisions nationwide; their collaborative governance practices are lagging far behind those of local governments. Therefore, there is room to explore the collaborative governance approach for the Japanese central government in its policy developments both in theory and practice.

Various theoretical models have been constructed based on practices in efforts to identify critical variables for "successful" collaboration (Ansell and Gash, 2007; Doberstein, 2016; Donhaue and Zeckhauster, 2011; Klijn and Koppenjan, 2000). Many academics and practitioners point out the following "successful" factors for effective and efficient collaborative governance: participatory processes, stakeholder engagement, a multisector approach, and administrative leadership. Nevertheless, few empirical studies have tested these factors, especially outside of the United States and United Kingdom where most studies of collaborative governance have been carried out. Accordingly, Japanese innovative practices of EBPM and RCT collaborative governance deserve to be explored and tested in other countries.

Most studies suggest that the collaborative process is not merely about negotiation but also about building mutual trust. Trust building is often the most prominent aspect of the early collaborative process but the most difficult to cultivate (Ansell and Gash, 2007). Trust in government is a fundamental element of the democratic "contract" and its decline may have considerable negative impacts on government activities. It may also be regarded as the foundation of good governance. The importance of trust building in forming the collaborative process is also related to the starting conditions of collaborative governance among stakeholders. If there is no initial level of trust and participants have "uneven" power, resources, and asymmetrical burdens both in real and perceived terms, then negotiation would not begin with collaboration in reaching a new equilibrium and improved outcomes. This implies that the initial level of trust among stakeholders and trust building measures are key factors for effective collaborative governance in action (Kim, 2010; OECD, 2017).

## References

Ansell, C., & Gash, A. (2007). Collaborative governance in theory and practice. *Journal of Public Administration Research and Theory*, 18, 543-571.

Brandsen, T., & Pestoff, V. (2006). Co-production, the third sector and the delivery of public services. *Public Management Review*, 8(4), 493-501.

Brassard, C., Giles, D. W., & Howitt, A. M. (Eds.). (2014). *Natural Disaster Management in the Asia-pacific: Policy and Governance*. Springer.

Cabinet Office. (2004). *Community saikou ni muketa kyodo no arikata ni kansuru tyousa [Research report on the role of co-production for community redevelopment]*.

__________. (2018). *Ninsyou NPO no suii [Trend of certified NPOs]*.

__________. (2019). *PFI jigyo no jishijyoukyou [PFI projects status in Japan]*.

Doberstein, C. (2016). Designing collaborative governance decision making in search of a 'Collaborative Advantage'. *Public Management Review*, 18(6), 819-841.

Donhaue, J. & Zeckhauser, R. (2011). *Collaborative Governance: Private Roles for Public Goals in Turbulent Times*. Princeton University Press.

Emerson, K., Nabatchi, T., & Balogh, S. (2012). An integrative framework for collaborative governance. *Journal of Public Administration Research and Theory*, 22(1), 1-29.

Hayama Town. (2019). *Hayama cho kireina sigen staton kuoudou project [Hayama Town recycle station collaboration project]*.

Kikuchi, M. (2009). Fiscal retrenchment and local public finance reforms in Japan: in search of sustainable local public finance in EROPA Local Government Center (Eds.). *Local Governance Under Stress: Fiscal Retrenchment and Expanding Public Demands on Government*. EROPA Local Government Center. 213-228.

Kim, Soonhee. (2010). Public trust in government in Japan and South Korea: does the rise of critical citizens matter? *Public Administration Review*, 70(5), 801-810.

Klijn, E., & Koppenjan, J. (2000). Public management and policy networks: foundations of a network approach to governance. *Public Management*, 2(2), 135-158.

McKean, M., & Cox, T. (1982). The Japanese experience with scarcity: management of traditional common lands. *Environmental Review*, 6(2), 63-92.

Ministry of Internal Affairs and Communications. (2019). *White Paper on Local Public Finance, FY 2017 Settlement Illustrated*.

Muto, K. (2010) Intergovernmental relations in Japan. in Berman, E., Moon, J., & Choi,

H. (Eds.), *Public Administration in East Asia*. CRC Press. 233-250.

National Institute of Population and Social Security Research. (2018). *Population Projections by Prefecture*.

Nemoto, Y. (2015). Public private partnership in Japan. In Akintoye, A., Beck, M., & Kumaraswamy, M. (Eds.). *Public Private Partnerships: A Global Review*. Routledge. 219-227.

O'Leary, R., & Bingham, L. (2009). *The Collaborative Public Manager: New Ideas for the Twenty-first Century*. Georgetown University Press.

Organisation for Economic Cooperation and Development. (2009). *OECD Reviews of Risk Management Policies Japan: Large-Scale Floods and Earthquakes*. OECD.

_________. (2017). *Trust and Public Policy: How Better Governance Can Help Rebuild Trust*. OECD.

Ostrom, E. (1990). *Governing the Commons: The Evolution of Institutions for Collective Action*. Cambridge University Press.

_________. (1996). Crossing the great divide: governing the commons: the evolution of institutions for collective action. *World Development*, 24(6), 1073-1087.

Pekkanen, R., Tsujinaka, Y., & Yamamoto, H. (Eds.). (2014). *Neighborhood Associations and Local Governance in Japan*. Routledge.

Tanaka, M., & Inoue, M. (Eds.). (2015). *Collaborative Governance of Forests: Towards Sustainable Forest Resource Utilization*. University of Tokyo Press.

Tsukamoto, I., & Nishimura, M. (2006). The emergence of local nonprofit-government partnerships and the role of intermediary organizations in Japan: contractual relationships and the limits to co-governance. *Public Management Review*, 8(4), 567-581.

White, H., Sabarwal, S., & Hoop, T. de. (2014). Randomized controlled trials (RCTs) *Methodological Briefs: Impact Evaluation*, 7, UNICEF Office of Research, Florence.

6

# Conflict and Collaboration in Korean Energy Policy in the Era of Climate Change: Actor, Process, and Governance*

Youhyun Lee, Minhyuk Cho, and Hyung Jun Park

## Introduction

Energy policy is a complex issue in every society. Recent energy policies are primarily the topic of climate change (Mackerron, 2009). The starting point was the 1997 Kyoto Protocol and the 2015 Paris Agreement, aimed at combating global warming. Combustion is the actual source of $CO_2$ emissions in most countries. To achieve reductions in $CO_2$ emissions, the focus must be on the energy sector (GGGI, 2016). Abandoning efforts to combat climate change will further damage ecosystems and biodiversity. Therefore, it is essential that energy policy is managed sustainably, to ensure environmental protection.

While energy policy is important for climate change, it is also significant,

* This article is a partially unpublished doctoral dissertation by Youhyun Lee (Les politiques de l'énergie renouvelable et nouvelle en Corée du Sud et en France, Université de Paris 1, Panthéon-Sorbonne) and is inspired by Hyung Jun Park's original research entitled "Study of participant's perception in Energy Policy Governance," conducted from December, 2018 to August, 2019.

from a macro perspective, for a country's economy, industries, and energy diplomacy. Therefore, energy policy should include climate policy (Lee & Seo, 2018). However, this classification is only applicable for industrialized countries, where the connection between energy and environmental policies is more obvious. Traditionally, these energy and environmental policies are considered separate entities; sometimes controversially, because fossil fuels are the largest pollutants. In recent years, however, energy and environmental policies have become heavily associated with the growing problems of climate change. The "energy triangle" of supply security, competition, and the environment represent the common points between these policies (Cotton & Devine-Wright, 2012).

This level of complexity challenges South Korea to form decisive energy policies. This chapter describes the key players in Korean energy policy, the process of policymaking, and the governance system. Through these presentations, we will approach the core problems of energy policy in South Korea, to derive the common and distinctive features of energy policy governance, in order to overcome conflicts and, ultimately, achieve collaboration.

## Key Energy Policy Actors in Korea

To understand the Korean policymaking system for the energy sector, one must first understand the number of diverse stakeholders in energy policy. Under the paradigm of development, the Ministry of Energy was the only decision maker for Korean energy policy. However, with the growing issue of global climate change and the paradigm shift toward multivalued systems, it has become essential to involve every area of society. Korea now faces this trend. This section identifies key decision makers for energy policy in South Korea. More specifically, we examine the role of the Ministry of Trade, Industry and Energy (MOTIE) and the Ministry of the Environment (MEV), the role of local governments, public enterprises, NGOs, and the direct involvement of citizens through public participation.

## Central Government

### *Ministry of Trade, Industry and Energy (MOTIE)*

The Ministry of Trade and Industry (MTI) was created at the birth of the Republic of Korea, in 1948 and was responsible for regulating economic policy. In 1993, the MTI merged with the Department of Energy and Resources, an organization established in 1977 to ensure a stable supply of energy. This spawned the MOTIE.

In 2008, the Lee Myung-bak government (2008~2012) established the Ministry of Knowledge Economy (MKE), which combines the key elements of the former MOTIE, the Ministry of Information and Communication, and the Ministry of Science and Technology. After taking office in 2013, President Park Geun-hye (in office from 2013 to 2017) reinstated trade policy as the role of the MKE and designated it as the MOTIE. The MOTIE has partners, including 12 public enterprises, 15 quasi-public agencies, and 13 other bodies of mainly research institutes and centers (MOTIE, 2019).

In principle, the MOTIE manages all energy policies, including new and renewable energy sources. The MOTIE leads most of Korea's energy policies with its partner, the Korea Energy Agency (KEA); including new and renewable energy that is being processed at the New and Renewable Energy Center (NREC), owned by KEA (KEA, 2019).

### *Ministry of Environment*

In the Korean system, the MOTIE leads energy policies, including renewable energy. However, there are exceptions. Over the past decade, the MEV has shown a rivalry between renewable energies, as well as between climate change programs.

The history of the MEV originates from the Ministry of Pollution and Health, established in 1967. The ministry was expanded in 1973, to the pollution division, in charge of environmental administration. After several reforms and the expansion of environmental authority, the Environment Bureau was integrated into the Ministry of Health and Welfare, in 1980. In January 1990, as per the

Office of the Prime Minister, the Environment Bureau was attached to the MEV to effectively integrate and coordinate environmental issues. In December 1994, the MEV was given greater authority to establish and implement its own policies (Kim et al., 2014).

The mission of the MEV is to protect the territory from the threats of environmental pollution and improve quality of life, for people to enjoy their natural environment. Additionally, it aims to facilitate global efforts to protect Earth. In February 2008, the Korean Meteorological Administration became a departmental ministry to promote action on climate change. In some countries, the environmental ministry is responsible for the energy policy (e.g., France, U.K.). However, with the strong historical development paradigm of the 1970s and 1980s, the Korean MEV cannot make important decisions in the area of energy policy, despite its competence to intervene.

### *Korea Energy Agency (KEA)*

The KEA is a government agency responsible for implementing energy conservation policies and energy efficiency measures, as well as climate change mitigation activities. Founded in 1980 by the MOTIE, as part of the law on the rationalized use of energy, KEA's main function is the management of national energy by providing various services, such as technical and financial support for administrative services in pursuit of ultimately building a respectful socio-economic structure. The KEA conducts important activities and projects related to energy, climate change, and green growth.

Typically, the KEA is responsible for the energy management of industry and buildings, establishing energy efficiency standards, industrial equipment, home and office appliance-labelling programs, energy demand management, financial support for energy management, climate change mitigation, and other activities, such as public relations, stakeholder engagement and international cooperation. The NREC was established as a subsidiary of the KEA to support and promote new and renewable energy.

## Local Government

The local government in Korea was activated as a result of the democratization movement in the 1980s and early 1990s, continued after the 1991 local council election, and survived the first local general election in 1995 (Choi, 2009). Nevertheless, the situation in the energy sector is worsening due to the slow process of decentralization. According to Kwon (2013), regional energy policies have been criticized as "local autonomy, without autonomy", because of the excessive extent to which local authorities depend on the central government.

In South Korea, regional authorities play a limited role in the energy sector (So, 2011). According to Cheon (2011), the role of regional authorities is seen as secondary, because civil servants are not experts. In principle, local authorities propose small renewable energy projects in the region, the MOTIE assesses their relevance, and the government allocates grants to the local government for each renewable energy project. Therefore, most renewable energy policies are led by the central government, particularly the MOTIE. Local governments are only the recipients of subsidies.

As a result, conflicts between the central and regional administrations are rapidly increasing on issues such as installing a nuclear waste treatment facility or the construction of a nuclear power station. The search for a site for managing radioactive waste is still controversial in Korean society. There have been several attempts to find a treatment site for radioactive waste at a low to medium level since the mid-1980s, but suitable options have been consistently objected to, by local residents and the local government. This is still an unresolved social problem in Korean society.

## Public Enterprises

### *Korea Electric Power Corporation (KEPCO)*

KEPCO is the primary stakeholder in South Korean energy policy. All electricity processes, including power generation, transmission, and distribution, have long been dominated by KEPCO, and, to date, it is the only company authorized to transport and distribute power in Korea. Concerning production, six subsidiaries of KEPCO are responsible for the majority of electricity generation in South Korea. KEPCO owns 100% of these six subsidiaries, which brings KEPCO's installed capacity to 65,383 MW, as of 2016. The Korean government owns a 51% stake in KEPCO. The six KEPCO subsidiaries are the result of the first stage (production) of the KEPCO reform. For network management, the KEPCO Knowledge Data and Network (KDN) provides a full range of electrical services, including power generation, trade, transportation, and sales (KEPCO, 2018).

KEPCO also plays an important role in setting the electricity prices in Korea. According to the Electricity Act, the MOTIE regulates the economy of the power sector, and KEPCO must submit rate recommendations to the MOTIE. After consultation with the Minister of Finance and the Economy (and, if necessary, the Council of Ministers and the President), these recommendations determine the tariffs that will be granted. The law stipulates that tariffs must cover costs and provide fair remuneration for investments (OECD, 2000). In fact, electricity pricing in Korea is determined by negotiations between KEPCO and the central government. This shows the robust power of KEPCO in Korean energy policy.

### *Korea Hydro & Nuclear Power (KHNP)*

KHNP is a subsidiary of KEPCO that generates 30% of Korea's electricity. This company runs six nuclear power plants (Gori, Shin-Gori, Hanbit, Hanul, Wolsong, and Shin-Wolsong), as well as pumped storage, hydro, solar, and wind power plants. Although their main energy resource is nuclear, the Korean Renewable Portfolio System (RPS) system forces power companies to meet renewable generation rates, several of which, KHNP now owns.

## Civil Society

### *Non-Governmental Organizations (NGOs)*

Regarding energy policy, there are three NGOs in South Korea that are most prominent. As an environmental NGO, the Korean Federation for Environmental Movement (KFEM) is one of the largest. Founded in 1993, it is committed to the ecology and biodiversity of the territory, as well as to promoting renewable energy (KFEM, 2015). "Green Korea United" is also a major environmental NGO, established in 1994. It focuses mainly on environmental cooperation with North Korea (Green Korea, 2015).

Korea NGOs' Energy Network is a network of NGOs that focuses on energy issues. It consists of 245 NGOs addressing social issues, including those of consumer, gender, and the environment. This solidarity network founded in 2000 conducts training courses and runs promotional campaigns on the energy economy, climate change, and the consumption of environment-friendly products. Additionally, there is Green Peace Korea, WWF Korea, international environmental NGOs, and religious environmental organizations, such as Protestant NGOs, Eco-Buddha, and Won-Buddhism.

### *People, Citizens, the Rise of Public Deliberation*

The power of the people, that is, the citizens involved in energy policy development, is increasing rapidly. The Moon Jae-in government recently declared Korea "a safe nation" and, since his presidential candidacy, Moon has included "the suspension of construction on the fifth and sixth reactors at the Shin-Gori Nuclear Power Plant" as part of his political agenda. However, due to the many complex issues involved, the implementation of his original agenda proved complicated and the government commenced the process of public deliberation to address the many implications of constructing nuclear power plants, including energy security, residents' quality of life, and construction contracts (PDC, 2017).

Public deliberation is the process of making policy decisions by gathering public opinion. The core intent behind public deliberation is a fair and objective system for solving problems. The Korean government has established a public deliberation committee; an independent organization of nine experts in human and social sciences, science and technology, research and statistics, and conflict management. The public deliberation process lasted three months, and, after thorough study and discussion in terms of the policy, deliberative polling was conducted (PDC, 2017).

The deliberation process was divided into two stages. Stage one: 20,000 people participated in a poll to capture their region, age and gender. Stage two: 500 participants from the first poll were selected to form a public participation group, and they took part in the final poll after careful discussion and public hearings (PDC, 2017).

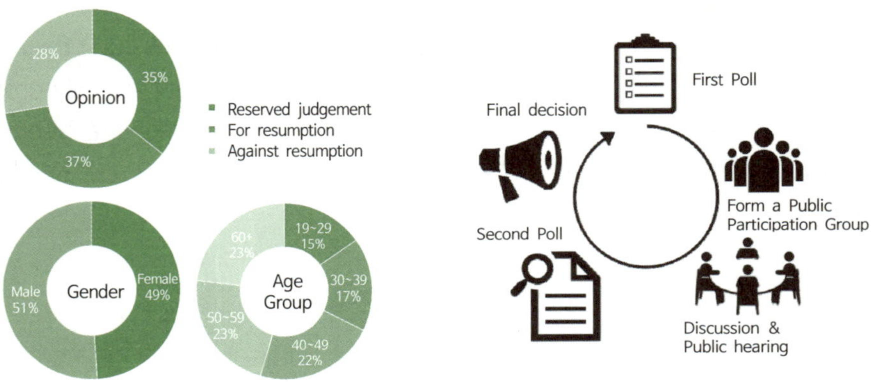


**Figure 1.** Public Deliberation in Korea

Source: PDC Homepage.

## Energy Policymaking Process

Scholars in public policy often use a successive model to analyze the implementation of specific policies. However, this is not a suitable model for the energy sector, because each public policy has been established based on varying cultural, legal, and political conditions, It is possible, and more understandable, to analyze and summarize the characteristics of renewable energy policy with successive political steps, because policymaking includes the combination of various conditional factors at a particular time. Characterizing policies step by step helps to better understand the general characteristics of Korean energy policy.

## The Process of Policymaking

Various problems that exist in society evolve as social issues, and these social issues can be chosen as a target for public policy. The political process corresponds to certain procedural steps, and public policies, including energy policy, are established through certain political processes. According to Anderson (1993), these process can be generally divided into four or five stages, in what is considered as the classic model of political process. These stages are Agenda Setting, Policy Formation, Policy Implementation, Policy Evaluation, and Feedback. Dror (1968) and Lasswell (1951), respectively, proposed three and seven stages in public policymaking. Sabatier (1986) argued that successive models cannot explain cause and effect, and that the "status quo" of administration requires a multi-aspect approach.

First, the implementation stage (Agenda Setting): Problems are raised by society and the government considers whether they can be resolved politically. If so, the first step in policymaking is implemented. The implementation stage can follow official and unofficial paths, which include the media, institutions, and schools. In the case of environmental policy, one of the most important channels of communication is environmental NGOs.

Second, the formation stage (Policy Formation): The decision-making mechanism of public policy enables the creation of laws or regulatory resolutions addressing the issues raised in the first stage.

Third, the application stage (Policy Implementation): The administration implements the policy, established in the previous two stages, by integrating the required administrative and financial processes to support the policy. The application of this stage thus realizes public policy.

Fourth, the evaluation stage (Policy Evaluation): This stage involves the evaluation of the policy's effects, or anticipated effects, on the projects established to achieve the political objective. In other words, this stage measures the current effects or policy outcomes. The evaluation criteria include efficiency, performance, correspondence, equity, and cleanliness (Ko, 2001).

Fifth, the Feedback stage: The information gathered from this stage distinguishes the most effective policies. Concerning renewable energy policy, technologies evolve rapidly and the energy status can change unpredictably, making this stage crucial for sustaining policies.

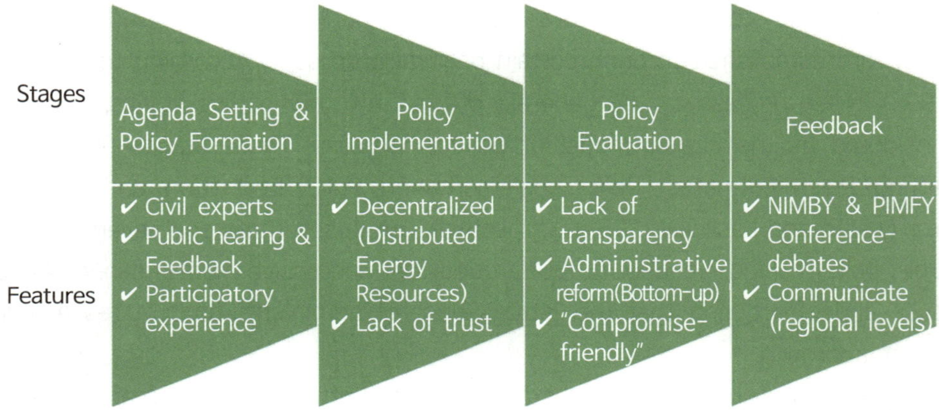


**Figure 2.** Stages and Features of Energy Policymaking Process

### *Agenda Setting and Policy Formation*

Historically, South Korea, which has no natural resources, places considerable emphasis on energy, especially coal and oil imports. In the 1980s, the only concern of the Ministry of Resources and Energies was energy policy. The expertise of civil servants in the ministry, at that time, was much higher than it is today. With the administrative reform, the Ministry of Resources and Energies was absorbed by the MTI, which reduced the size of the energy department. A lack of expertise within the department should be an open invitation for civilian expertise. However, the Korean government retains the prerogative over energy policy decisions (Kim et al., 2014).

According to Article 41 of the Framework Act on Low Carbon, Green

Growth, in the third National Energy Master Plan (20 years, renewed every five years), the MOTIE must recognize "the importance of the process." Thus, unlike the 2008 and 2014 energy plans, a public-private working group of civil experts, teachers, and MOTIE officials participated in making the first draft of the energy plan. Additionally, public hearings were held to gather feedback on the adoption of the final plan. Despite some criticism from NGOs, this participatory experience has been positively evaluated to improve the relevance of Korea's policies in practice. Moreover, it increases the residents' acceptance of renewable energy. The Korean government now invites civilian experts to participate in energy policymaking but retains the final decision-making authority.

***Policy Implementation***

There are two problems in the policy implementation process: The dependence of local governments on the central government, and a lack of trust between these two governments. In Korea, apart from larger cities like Seoul, Gyunggi, and Ulsan, most local governments rely on the central government for more than 70% of their budget for energy policy. To meet all the needs of the country, there is a minimum requirement for energy production, particularly for Korea's industrial sector, where energy consumption is high. Therefore, replacing the share of nuclear and thermal coal with renewable energy is not feasible in the short term; this remains the ideology of ecologists.

The merit of renewable energy policy lies in its "decentralized" nature. Unlike nuclear or carbon power plants, it facilitates small dispersed plants (Distributed Energy Resource: DER) with the production of small power. Environmental problems are caused by large power plants that significantly destroy the landscape, ecosystem, and quality of life of the inhabitants (e.g., noise pollution by the facilities).

Local governments in South Korea hold little authority in the enforcement process, with the exception of cities like Seoul and Gyunggi. However, the role of local governments will increase as the use of renewable energy continues to develop.

Trust in government is the foundation for the legitimacy and sustainability of a political system (Putnam, 2000). It also facilitates the effective deployment of public policy (Seo & Park, 2012). Therefore, trust is considered a crucial component of social capital (OECD, 2013). Confidence in a government might decline, but citizens generally continue to accept the government's guidelines. However, if the mistrust continues, mutual trust among citizens will also deteriorate, which fragments the country (Hong, 2015). Contextually, trust in the government's public policies has become increasingly pivotal for political success.

### *Policy Evaluation*

The lack of transparency in policymaking does not necessarily mean that democracy is lacking in Korean society. Although the planning of energy policy is initiated by MOTIE officials, the additional corrections and feedback are actively matched between interested officials and unofficial political stakeholders. Fortunately, the Korean government has continued to establish a non-authoritarian culture in administration, and administrative reform has been approached from the bottom-up.

According to Article 6 of the Presidential Decree of the Energy Law (Presidential Decree No. 26359, June 30, 2015; date of application July 1, 2015), important political actions are subject to public hearings that are organized by the MOTIE, to gather public opinion and reduce conflict. This might include the announcement of a new plan, or the change of policy instrument (e.g., Purchase Price to RPS). Through these types of remedies, the MOTIE has, at least, shown a "compromise-friendly" attitude. Nevertheless, the final decision rests with the central government.

### *Feedback*

The Feedback stage focuses on communication with citizens. Not In My Backyard (NIMBY) and Please In My Front Yard (PIMFY) are issues that are among the most difficult to solve in terms of new and renewable energy. For example, the inhabitants of the Ga Ro Rim Gulf strongly oppose the construction of a tidal power plant that will preserve the sea and landscape (Kim & Lee, 2019). On the other hand, in Incheon, which is one of the largest autonomous cities to include an international airport, the inhabitants themselves insist on the construction of a tidal power plant, to save the city money and solve local financial problems. Of course, all countries have problems with NIMBY or PIMFY; these phenomena are recurrent. However, in the Korean context, these phenomena are overextended, and, in some cases, there are unresolved conflicts between the government and people. Therefore, conference debates are required to communicate at regional levels, for the duration of the policy implementation.

Another important issue is regarding conflicting elements to be addressed before a policy's implementation. The Korean government tends to solve the problems raised by citizens individually. Further efficiency could be achieved by reducing conflicting elements upstream, through stakeholder communication, including local communities, unions, NGOs, and local residents. Once a policy has been implemented, its reversal is complicated (Lee & Seo, 2018), and to re-plan an alternative policy is prohibitively expensive. By studying the case of energy policy, we can avoid repeating issues in future policymaking.

## Governance in Korean Energy Policy

The issue of energy is a so-called "wicked problem", that is, difficult or impossible to solve (Rittel and Webber, 1973; Sabatier, 2007). This section examines the several forms of governance inherent in Korean energy policy, starting with the inherited traditional theory and environmental governance and the transition to an open and participatory structure of governance. Second, we examine collaborative energy governance, inspired by the model of Ansell & Gash (2008). Finally, we consider the governance model of Confucian reflexivity (Lee & Bae, 2019) to address the possibility of merging Confucianism and governance theory and better understand the unique culture of Korean public administration.

## Energy Policy Governance

The concept of energy governance derives from environmental governance and governance theory. In the 1970s, "governance" was considered synonymous with "government." The interest at the time was in the management capacity of the country. In the 1980s, global interest in governance increased, along with the evolution of public-private partnership (PPP). In the 1990s, the role and participation of civil societies and non-governmental organizations came into focus, emphasizing democracy. Since the 2000s, governance has adapted to specific problems, serving as an alternative mechanism for resolving new social issues.

As this mechanism evolves, so too does the reliance on "Good Environmental Governance" (Lee, 2003). Since the 1992 Earth Summit, environmental governance has been systematically seen as a principle of environmental policy, integral to sustainable development. The concept of environmental governance has improved the cooperative relationship between governmental and non-governmental organizations, offering the opportunity to establish specific interdependencies and restore the decision-making balance.

Although less known than environmental governance, the concept of energy governance is used by scholars and many in civil society. South Korea's energy policies show conservatism with a strong closed nature, especially in the first stage of policymaking. Energy policy requires environmental knowledge, as well as scientific knowledge and technical expertise. Due to the history of its development paradigm, the South Korean government ruled the core decision-making of energy policy, from the 1950s to the 1990s.

Against this background, Korea's energy policy governance can be summarized in three points: First, from a theoretical perspective, energy governance originates from environmental governance. Second, energy governance inherited a culture of central expert-oriented approaches to energy policy. Third, even considering the several points mentioned above, Korea's energy policy decision-making system will shift toward a participatory decision making system, that is, the so-called civilian governance.

In particular, the current energy committee consists of various stake-

**Table 1.** Energy Committee as Part of Energy Policy Governance

| Committee | The fifth energy committee | Electricity policy committee | The Working group of the 3rd energy basic plan |
|---|---|---|---|
| Number of members | 19 | 25 | 15 |
| Member's affiliation | Professor<br>Accountant<br>Lawyer<br>The secretariat of NGO<br>Research institute | Professor<br>CEO<br>NGO<br>Lawyer<br>Public officer<br>The head of association<br>Research institute<br>Korea electric power change<br>KEPCO | Conflict management expert<br>Professor<br>CEO<br>Industry<br>NGO |

holders from a variety of backgrounds. As shown in Table 1, the fifth energy committee consists of government officers, as well as professors, accountants, lawyers, NGOs, and researchers. The electricity policy committee consisted of civil servants, professors, enterprises, NGOs, lawyers, associations, researchers, and public institutions. Finally, the third basic energy plan working group consists of conflict managers, professors, researchers, enterprises, and NGOs.

## Collaborative Energy Governance

Collaborative governance is counter to conflictual governance. Whereas conflictual governance instigates hostility among a network, collaborative governance creates symbiotic networks, based on common interest and conciliated opinion (Kim, 2017). Collaborative governance focuses on interpersonal relationships and organizational arrangements (Milward & Provan, 2000). The core of collaborative governance is its network of stakeholders, based on cooperative relationships. Stakeholders in collaborative governance seek solutions for specific issues through other stakeholders and networks (deLeon & Varda, 2009). Goldsmith &

Eggers (2004) pointed out that there is merit in the use of collaborative networks in (1) various fields of expertise; (2) liberal innovation, regardless of the old system; (3) flexibility and promptness; and (4) accessibility for citizens.

There are six important criteria for collaborative governance: "(1) forums are initiated by public agencies or institutions, (2) forum participants include non-state actors, (3) participants engage directly in decision-making and are not merely consulted by public agencies, (4) forums are formally organized and each meets collectively, (5) forums aim to make decisions by consensus, and (6) the focus of collaboration is public policy or public management" (Ansell & Gash, 2008).

However, the growing importance of collaborative governance does not necessarily diminish the role of the central government (Lee, 2007). In some cases, the role of the central government can extend to facilitating the maintenance of close relations between various participants in the governance system. Its role, particularly in the energy sector, is not a zero-sum relationship

**Figure 3.** Government's Role on Collaborative Energy Governance

with the role of stakeholders, such as local governments, civil society, and organizations. Rather, central government needs to act as a facilitator, or mediator, between policy stakeholders. A good example is the establishment of the public deliberation committee for the construction of the Shin-Gori 5 & 6 nuclear reactors. In delivering ordinary citizens' opinion and value, the central government plays an important role by designing the public deliberation mechanism and by offering the space for debate and discussion.

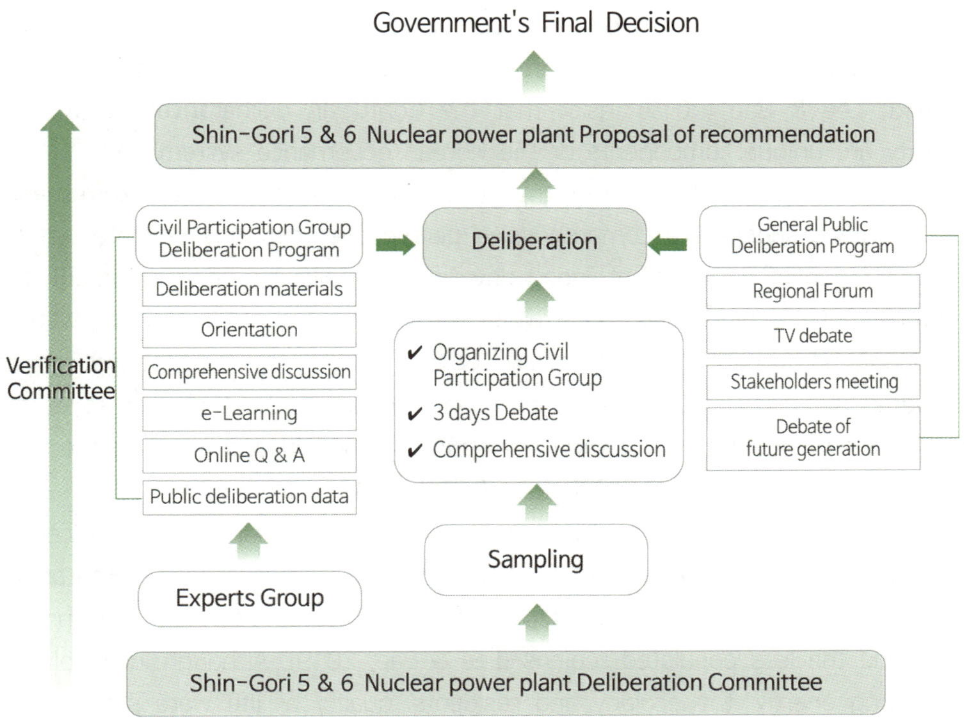


**Figure 4.** Public Deliberation as Collaborative Energy Governance

Source: Committee of Shin-Gori 5 & 6 Reactor Deliverative Poll (2017).

## Confucian Reflexive Governance Model[1)]

Confucianism has long been the dominant governing philosophy in East Asian countries, such as China, Singapore, and South Korea. Former Singaporean chancellor, Lee Kwan Yew, argued that "Western democracy is not applicable for East Asian politics in its direct form, and it needs to be modified in the Asian model" (Verweij et al., 2013). In Korean public administration, Confucianism still has strong explanatory power in analyzing the public administration system (Loader, 2000; Landeta-Manzano et al., 2018). Additionally, many empirical studies have proven the correlation between Confucian value and the culture of public administration in Asia (Park and Kim, 2015; Tian, 2017; Kim, 2018). From this context, Lee & Bae (2019) insist that the Confucian deliberativeness and reflexivity are unique components of the Korean governance system.

Lee & Bae (2019) verify the fusion of Confucianism and governance theory, which suggests a comprehensive perspective that may ultimately affect the realization of a system of "good governance." Following their argument, the Confucian perspective raises three radical questions: what was important, what is important, and what will be important in the future? These questions can be answered by following the correct path and examining the time frames of the past, present, and future (溫故而知新; rethinking the old and knowing the new, The Analects of Confucius, 2: 11) (Lee & Bae, 2019).

Throughout Korean history, energy policy has oriented around central government, which was necessary for energy security. However, during the period of the "Miracle of Han River", discrimination aggravated between metropolitan cities and the less populated regions (Lee & Bae, 2019). Although inevitable for generating energy, the ecology and residents' quality of life were sacrificed in specific regions. Unconsciously and without question, individuals obeyed the central government energy dogma (Lee & Bae, 2019).

Lee & Bae (2019) state that "the present problem of the present is different from that of the past because individuals can ask what is problematic,

1) This section includes Youhyun Lee's original work entitled "Collaboration and Confucian Reflexivity in Local Energy Governance: The Case of Seoul's One Less Nuclear Power Plant Initiatives."

and why it matters." Therefore, in their work, "if all things are considered to be related to each other and to have a symbiotic relationship, pursuing energy justice is not only for the benefit of humans but for the earth and its resources" (Lee & Bae, 2019). Future energy governance will produce optimal and balanced energy with minimal harm to nature, ultimately enabling sustainable energy production for all living things (Lee & Bae, 2019). Table 2 provides an overview of the Confucian Reflexive governance model and presents a new perspective that integrates existent collaborative governance, with new components derived from Confucianism (Lee & Bae, 2019).

**Table 2.** Confucian Reflexivity and Deliberativeness in Energy Governance

| *Time Frame* | *溫故而知新 (Rethinking the old and cultivating the new)* | | |
|---|---|---|---|
| | *Past* | *Present* | *Future* |
| *Reflexive Individual* | Unconscious and ignorant | Conscious & observing<br>Regarding the conditions of others | Will of settlement<br>Regarding symbiotic relationship |
| *Governance Structure* | Closed-governance structure driven by the central government<br>Aggravation of regional inequality and injustice with dogma | Public-private partnership<br>Connected Governance<br>Intervention of Locals | Extended governance<br>Pursuing energy justice with regional balance<br>Inclusiveness of diverse and hetero networks |
| *Relationship with Collaboration* | Absence of collaboration | Creation of intermediate governance model<br>Promoting participation<br>Feedback | Co-evolution and Integration of collaboration and reflexivity<br>Continuous feedback based on learning and practice |
| *Energy Path and Character-istics* | Hard energy system (central government driven, mass production, nuclear and coal thermal energy focused) | Transition process (combination of hard and soft energy systems) | Soft energy system (community based, decentralized, democratic and renewable-energy focused) |

Source: Lee & Bae (2019).

## Concluding Remarks

The Korean governance of energy policy is facing certain change. The need for this change stems from two causes. First is global warming. We are living in the era of climate change. Energy policy, usually the concern of economic policy, now directly relates to environmental policy. Second is the growing demand for stakeholder participation. The energy policy paradigm is shifting from a hierarchical system to participatory policy governance, and various stakeholders are facing conflicting problems in policy design and at the stage of implementation. From this perspective, energy policy governance must appropriately consider, from an environmental and social context, the core issues in energy-related problems.

This study addresses South Korea's energy policy from the perspective of the stakeholders, the process, and governance. Several issues of conflict and collaboration were derived from each of these perspectives as table 3 below. We presented the important stakeholders with influence in energy policymaking. However, there are still conflicting issues. For example, formerly, the MOTIE was in charge of energy policy, but in the era of climate change, the Ministry of Environment is constantly involved in energy policymaking. Another problem is the issue of central and local governance. The central government MOTIE was the decision maker throughout the development paradigm. However, with the promotion of renewable energy, local governments are also considered key stakeholders in policy decision making, which sometimes leads to conflicts. In the case of public debate, the government designed and offered a system to gather public opinion and provided the opportunity for ordinary citizens to participate in the energy policymaking process. However, collaboration problems can be found between this process and the public debate committee.

For process, lack of trust and transparency is a major challenge. As well as overcoming NIMBY and PIMFY, there are general communication issues. However, the increasingly compromise-friendly attitude embodied by the policy-making process, and the expansion of renewable energy itself, facilitates opportunity for collaboration.

**Table 3.** Issues of Conflict and Cooperation in Korean Energy Policy

| Unit of Analysis | Contents | Issue of Conflict | Issue of Collaboration |
|---|---|---|---|
| *Main Stake-holders* | Central Government<br>Local Government<br>Public Enterprises<br>Civil Society | Energy vs. Environment<br>Central vs. Local | Public Debate and Committee |
| *Process* | Agenda Setting & Formation<br>Policy Implementation<br>Policy Evaluation<br>Feedback | Lack of trust and transparency<br>NIMBY and PIMFY<br>Communication problems | Compromise-friendly attitude<br>Expansion of the renewable energy sector |
| *Govern-ance* | Energy Policy Governance<br>Collaborative Energy Governance<br>Confucian Governance Model | Actual decision-making power of the government | Collaborative Energy Governance<br>Adding Confucian value to governance |

Finally, three types of governance for Korean energy policy were presented: traditional policy governance, collaborative energy governance, and the Confucian Reflexive governance model. Although there are no specific issues of conflict, there is, nevertheless, doubt as to whether the various policy stakeholders share decision-making authority with the government equally. In the context of Korea, more time is needed to transition from government-oriented governance to a horizontal governance structure. Nevertheless, the Korean governance system provides useful insight for other East Asian countries, as they prepare the new energy paradigm for the era of climate change.

## References

Agranoff, R., & McGuire. M. (2004). *Collaborative Public Management: New Strategies for Local Governments*. Georgetown University Press.

Anderson, C. W. (1993). Recommending a Scheme of a Reason: Political Theory, Political Science, and Democracy. *Policy Science (Us)*, 26(3), 215-227.

Ansell, C. (2012). *Collaborative Governance*. The Oxford handbook of governance.

Ansell, C., & Gash, A. (2008). Collaborative governance in theory and practice. *Journal of Public Administration Research and Theory*, 18(4), 543-571.

Cheon, D. Y. (2011). The Task of Local Government for Green Growth. *Local Policy Review*, 25(2), 37-56.

Choi, J. W. (2009). *Local Government and Public Administration in Korea*. Ministry of Public Administration and Security.

Committee of Shin-Gori 5 & 6 reactor deliverative poll. (2017). Shin-Gori 5 & 6 reactor deliverative poll report.

Cotton, M., & Devine-Wright, P. (2012). Making electricity networks "visible": Industry actor representations of "publics" and public engagement in infrastructure planning. *Public Understanding of Science*, 21(1), 17-35.

Deleon, P., & Varda, D. M. (2009). Toward a Theory of Collaborative Policy Networks: Identifying Structural Tendencies. *Policy Studies Journal*, 37(1), 59-74.

Dror, Y. (1968). *Public Policy Making Reexamined*. San Francisco, C.A. Chandler.

GGGI. (2016). Korea's Green Growth Experience: Lessons Learned and Outcomes. GGGI Report.

Goldsmith, S., & Eggers, W. (2004). *Governing by Network: The New Shape of The Public Sector*. Washington, D.C.: Brookings Institution Press.

Green Korea United, Introduction. webpage http://www.greenkorea.org [accessed July 2019]

Hong, J. H. (2015) *What Decide the Trust in Politics and Government*. Seoul, Policy Network Nae-Ⅱ, 3-5.

Kim, B., & Lee, Y. (2019). Barriers to Renewable? Case of Garorim Tidal Plant Project in Korea.

Kim, C., Kim, H., Moon, T., Park, M., Park, Y., Oh, S., Yoon, S., Ha, H., & Hong, J. (2014). *Environmental Administration*. Seoul, Daeyoung Company.

Kim, G. (2017). A Case Study on the Failure of the Building in Collaborative Governance, *Korean Autonomous Administration Review*, 31(1), 1-23.

Kim, S. (2018). Public service motivation, organizational social capital, and knowledge sharing in the Korean public sector. *Public Performance & Management Review*, 41(1), 130-151.

Ko, J. K. (2001). *Governement Failure in Environmental Policy*. Seoul National University Press.

Korea Electric Power Corporation. (KEPCO). webpage http://www.kepco.co.kr [accessed July 2019]

Korea Energy Agency. (KEA). webpage http://www.energy.or.kr [accessed July 2019]

Korea Environment Institute. (2013). *New Government: The Pathway of Environmental Policy*. KEI Annual Report.

Korean Federation For Environmental Movement. webpage http://kfem.or.kr [accessed July 2019]

Kwon, O. S. (2013). *Local Energy Policies And The Meaning*. Resume of Effect of Enactment of Local Ordinance, 1-5.

Landeta-Manzano, B., G. Arana-Landín, Calvo, P. M., and Heras-Saizarbitoria, I. (2018). Wind energy and local communities: A manufacturer's efforts to gain acceptance. *Energy Policy*, 121, 314-324.

Lasswell, H. D. (1951). *The Policy Orientation*. San Francisco, C.A. Stanford Univ Press.

Lee, M. (2003). Comparative Analysis on Environmental Governance, *Korea Public Administration Assoiciation*, 201.

Lee, M. S. (2007). Governing by Network: The New Shape of the Public Sector. *Journal of Governance Study*. 2(1), 241-249.

Lee, Y., & Bae, S. (2019). Collaboration and Confucian Reflexivity in Local Energy Governance: Case of One Less Nuclear Initiatives in South Korea. *Journal of Contemporary East Asia*, 18(1), 153-174.

Lee, Y., & Seo, I. S. (2018). Achieving Procedural Energy Justice Through Citizen Participation. *Journal of Dispute Resolution*, 16(3), 37-79.

Loader, I. (2000). Plural policing and democratic governance. *Social & Legal Studies*, 9(3), 323-345.

Mackerron, G. (2009) *Energy for the Future a New Agenda*. London, Palgrave, 3-4.

Milward, H. B., & Provan, K. G. (2000). Governing The Hollow State. *Journal of Public Administration Research and Theory*, 10(2), 359-380.

Ministry of Trade Industry and Energy. (MOTIE). webpage http://www.motie.go.kr [accessed July 2019]

OECD. (2000). Regulatory Reform in Korea: Regulatory Reform in the Electricity Sector. OECE (Paris), 1.

________. (2013). *Trust in Government*. Government at a Glance. Paris. OECD Report.

Park, S. M., and Kim, M. Y. (2015). Accountability and public service motivation in Korean government agencies. *Public Money & Management*, 35(5), 357-364.

Putnam, R. D. (2000). *Bowling Alone: The Collapse and Revival of American Democracy*. New York. Simon and Schauster.

Sabatier, P. A. (1986). Top-Down and Bottom-Up Approches to Implementation Research: A Critical Analysis and Suggested Synthesis. *Journal of Public Policy*, 6(1), 21-48.

Sabatier, P. A., & Jenkins-Smith, H. C. (1993). The Advocacy Coalition Framework: Assessment, Revisions, and Implications for Scholars and Practitioners. *Policy Change and Learning: An Advocacy Coalition Approach*, 211-236.

Seo, I. S., & Park, H. J. (2012). A Study on Relationships of Public Sector Corruptions and Trust in Government via Transaction Cost Theory. *Korea Policy Review*, 21(3), 291-324.

So, J. Y. (2011). Study of Promoting New and Renewable Energy in Region. *Korea Energy Economic Institute Annual Report*.

Tian, X. (2017). Accountability without democracy: evidence from Confucian accountability. *Australian Journal of Political Science*, 52(1), 126-142.

Verweij, S., Klijn, E. H., Edelenbos, J., & Van Buuren, A. (2013). What makes governance networks work? A fuzzy set qualitative comparative analysis of 14 Dutch spatial planning projects. *Public Administration*, 91(4), 1035-1055.

7

# Democratic Subjectivities in Collaborative Governance:

## A Q Methodology Study on Participants of a Local Placemaking Program in Taiwan

Milan Tung-Wen Sun, Jessica Yu-Wen Lin, and Windy Thi-Ngoc-Minh Phan

## Introduction

Over the last two decades, a new strategy of governing called "collaborative governance" has been initiated for dealing with cross-boundaries issues. This mode of governance brings multiple stakeholders together in common forums with public agencies to engage in consensus-oriented decision making (Ansell and Cash, 2008), and participants must actively work together to address what they recognize as an emerging problem or issue of mutual concern which they individually cannot address (Booher, 2004). Weale (2011, 58) defines the mechanisms of collaborative governance as "ways of governing that are non-hierarchical and involve networks of actors, both public and private, determining policy thought negotiation, bargaining and participation."

In contrary to hierarchy, collaborative settings are not based on a central authority and cannot be guided by a single organizational goal. The primary activities of the managers in such settings are to select the appropriate actors and resources, to shape the operating context of the network, and to develop ways to cope with strategic and operational complexities. Through collaboration, each player brings and keeps his or her authority, while managing together with others (Agranoff and McGuire, 2003, 34). The notions of networks, participation and democratic procedure of decision-making are essential for collaborative governance. One can argue that the exercise of collaborative governance may simultaneously enhance the idea of democracy among participants (Barnes et al., 2003; Skelcher et al., 2005).

Since collaborative governance is initiated by public agencies or institutions (Ansell and Cash, 2008), the approach to managing the network is quite essential. Jeffares and Skelcher (2011) noted that there are gaps in knowledge about how public managers themselves construct their roles as actors in a democratic arena, which would impact their roles in shaping and designing the arrangements for collaborative network governance. On the other hand, participants also varied in their awareness of the democratic implications of collaborative governance, and they did not appear to be concerned with how the forms of governance that they were designing had lost some of the basic aspects of transparency and accountability that form the bedrock of representative democratic government (Skelcher et al., 2005).

As argued by Newman, Barnes and Knops (2004), one reason for the considerable interest in collaborative governance is that representative democracy is viewed as too hierarchical, bureaucratic and party-bound to be able to deal effectively with "wicked questions"—a term coined by Rittel and Webber (1973) to describe challenges that are dynamic, complex and hard to address, along with their potentially complicated solutions (Emerson & Nabatchi, 2015; Gray & Purdy, 2018; Termeer, Dewulf, Breeman, & Stiller, 2015).

However, little is known about how individual participants in collaborative governance think about democracy. Jeffares and Skelcher (2011) empirically identified several democratic discourses among English and Dutch public managers regarding the relations between democracy and networks. By replicating Jeffares and Skelcher's research, this paper attempts to reveal the democratic subjectivities of collaborative governance among local participants in Taiwan. The two basic research questions are: (1) How do participants who have been collaborating with each other for several years in local community development projects think about democracy based on their subjective experiences? (2) How do these Taiwan-based inter-subjectivity discourses compare to those of the English and Dutch public managers?

To address these two questions, the "Local Placemaking Program" by a collaborative network in Puli, Taiwan, is used as an example. Puli Township suffered a severe earthquake in 1999; local governments, National Chi Nan University (NCNU), private businesses and NGO have been partners working on many local recovery efforts and community revitalization projects ever since. NCNU established the Center of Humanity Innovation and Social Practice in 2016 for designing courses to involve faculty members and students in local community development projects, to promote community development issues (for example, air and water pollution), and to initiate projects and coordinate efforts from different sectors by serving as a starting engine. Throughout these years, a network of participants collaborating with each other for solving community-level problems has been firmly established. Recently, they've teamed up for a local placemaking program designed to deal with the problem of brain drain as young adults migrate from rural areas to metropolitan cities.

This research is structured in five parts. This introduction is followed by reviews on literature about collaborative governance and its relations with democracy. Next up is the research design and data collection section describing Jeffares and Skelcher's study and introducing the procedure for Q method research. The next section interprets the results of Q analysis, while the last section explains the research results through which the research questions are addressed from a comparative perspective.

## Collaborative Governance and Democratic Quality

### Definitions of Collaborative Governance

The term "collaborative governance" was first published in 1978 (Emerson

& Nabatchi, 2015), in which the "collaborating" approach (Gray, 1989) was perceived as revolutionary then by policy-makers and public administration scholars, providing an alternative answer for figuring out and solving problems besides traditional methods (Gash, 2016). In short, governments should loosen control over the provisions of public goods and services and enhance cross-boundary collaboration. Collaborative governance, in the opinion of many public administration scholars, comes across as a new governing paradigm applicable to democratic systems (Emerson et al., 2011; Jun, 2002).

Public sectors should collaborate with citizens, communities, private sectors and non-profit organizations as a procedure to alleviate the pressure related to limited resources, resolve problems and secure improvements (Gray & Purdy, 2018; Sørensen & Torfing, 2011; Walker & Senecah, 2011), rather than monopolize the distribution of public goods and public services. Consequently, more forms of governance have been proposed throughout this wave of calling for collaboration, such as:

- Co-governance or new governance (Bingham, Nabatchi, & O'Leary, 2005)
- Multiple-stakeholders partnership (Gray & Purdy, 2018)
- Interactive governance or cross-sector collaboration (Bryson, Crosby, & Stone, 2006)
- Multi-sectoral governance (Emerson, 2018)
- Collaborative public management (Agranoff & McGuire, 2003; O'Leary & Bingham, 2007)
- Networked governance (O'Toole Jr. & Meier, 2011; Provan & Kenis, 2008)
- Collaborative governance (Ansell & Gash, 2008; Donahue & Zeckhauser, 2011; Emerson & Nabatchi, 2015; Jing, 2015; Marwell & Calabrese, 2014; Morse, 2011; Mosley & Jarpe, 2019; Purdy, 2012; Scott & Thomas, 2017; Shrestha, 2012; Tang & Tang, 2014)
- Collaborative governance is used as an umbrella term incorporating some to all of the important elements of the aforementioned concepts.

Every public administration scholar has his or her own way of defining "collaborative governance." Ansell and Gash (2008) defined it by emphasizing the formal forms of engagement between state and non-state stakeholders that are initiated by governments. Emerson et al. (2015) expanded the concept by covering a broader set of agents, processes and structures that could send collaborative ideas traveling across jurisdictions, sectors and organizations. As mentioned before, this study adopts Weale's (2011) definition that takes into consideration the networks, participation and democratic procedure of decision-making.

## Collaborative Governance and Democracy

Presumably, collaborative governance meant that the institutions of representative democracy have been supplemented by systems of governance that are established with an emphasis on lateral relationships among networks of public, private, and civil society actors (Mathur and Skelcher, 2007). Dahl (1998), for example, argues that, as the size and complexity of the institutions of democracy increase, opportunities for direct citizen participation shrink accordingly. Along the same line of reasoning, it is argued by Wachhaus (2017) that promoting public participation, which is one of the core elements of collaborative governance, can facilitate robust democracy; community-based models in particular, may be able to rejuvenate democracy (Stivers, 2008).

However, the relations between collaborative governance and democracy can be approached from many different perspectives. Papadopoulos (2012, 514) argued that policy networks in collaborative governance are "more or less uncoupled from the institutions of representative democracy"; Booher (2004, 41) cautiously reminded the advocates of collaborative governance that it is not legitimate because "it is outside of the traditional institutions of authority and accountability." In addition, Papadopoulos (2012) suggested the processes of collaborative governance are encountering several key deficits — a possible lack of inclusiveness of governance networks; a potential of normalizing and dominating state logic while weakening social movements; as well as a lack of transparency, codification and visibility of collaborative mechanisms.

Although collaborative governance is likely to reduce the democratic quality of policy-making, it can be compensated by enhancing the problem-solving capacity of governments and by improving the quality of political decisions

(Papadopoulos, 2011). Furthermore, the practice of collaborative governance can yield new understanding and information to serve as the basis for more democratic decision-making (Booher, 2004, 43). In other words, the practice of collaborative governance may enhance each participant's understanding of the essence of democracy.

Klijn and Skelcher (2007) suggested that there are four conjectures on the relations between democracy and network governance. Taking policy network as an important element of collaborative governance, these conjectures can serve as a comprehensive summary of the potential ties between democracy and collaborative governance:

1. The "complementarity" conjecture suggests that there are more stakeholders involved in the networks than through representative democracy. Therefore, it will enhance the democratic quality of the system and the quality of information for decision-making.
2. The "incompatibility" conjecture stresses the potential conflicts between democracy and collaborative governance because they are running on different sets of institutional rules.
3. The "transitional" conjecture proposes that the governing system is in a process of evolution from the representational democracy, which emphasizes vertical distribution of authority and accountability, to collaborative governance, which stresses the horizontal distribution of power and accountability.
4. The "instrumental" conjecture accentuates the contribution of collaborative governance as a medium through which the problem-solving capacity of its participants, especially government officials, can be enhanced.

Despite the fact that there are abundant literature and research on this topic, relatively little empirical projects have been conducted to examine the relations between collaborative governance and democracy. The practice of collaborative governance should proceed carefully but welcome new research that can generate useful lessons for democracy (Booher, 2004).

# Research Design and Data Collection

## Democratic Subjectivities in Network Governance

As most literature notes, actors from public, private and nonprofit organizations interact directly in a network, posing theoretical and practical problems via linkage to preexisting democratic institutions and processes (Mathur and Skelcher, 2007). Jeffares and Skelcher (2011) argue that it is important to find out how public institutions or public managers view their roles in a democratic arena when initiating a network. Using the four *a priori* conjectures mentioned above as the theoretically grounded frame, they applied the Q methodology to detect the democratic subjectivities in network governance, and identified five democratic subjectivities: Realists and Adaptors (complementary), Progressive Optimists and Radical Optimists (transitional), and Pragmatists (which is beyond the scope of the four conjectures).

Pragmatists have little concern for democracy. Realists regard networks as one of a number of arenas in which the politics are played out. Adaptors identify the potential for greater inclusiveness. Progressive Optimists think that network governance will fill the gap between the theory and practice of representative democracy, while Radical Optimists focus on its potential for enabling direct dialogue.

This study replicates Jeffares and Skelcher's research (2011) to examine the relations between collaborative governance for the following six reasons. First, they utilized the Q methodology in their study, which was introduced by William Stephenson in 1935. Q methodology provides a foundation for the systematic study of subjectivity—a person's viewpoints, opinion, beliefs, attitudes, and the like (Brown, 1996; Watts and Stenner, 2012). This study attempts to examine the relations between collaborative governance and democracy from the participant's point of view. The underlying implications are that not only the democratic subjectivities of participants will influence how they behave in the process of collaboration, but also their subjective collaborative experiences tend to affect how they perceive democracy.

Second, network is an essential part of collaborative governance. Booher (2004) talked about *collaborative network structures* which go beyond network, defined here as formalized linkages and coordination among actors, in which participants must interact with each other as a team to achieve shared objectives. The functioning of collaborative governance relies on an active network of participants. Therefore, the concourse of statements about the public manager's individual views regarding network governance and democracy is valid for applying to this study.

Third, Jeffares and Skelcher (2011, 1258-1259) incorporated a rigorous statement sampling grid for selecting a Q sample. The sampling grid consists of two dimensions: form and discursive quality. Statements in the first dimension are about the definitions, claims of fact/opinion, or normative prescriptions of collaborative governance; those in the second dimension concern the natural relationships between entities, degrees of agency, or clues on an agent's underlying motivation for collaboration. The utility of such a sampling grid had been demonstrated by Dryzek and Berejikian (1993) and Ockwell (2008). Statements in the concourse was sorted according to the 3×3 matrix, and 4 statements were selected from each of the 9 cells; it ended up with 36 statements as the Q sample.

Fourth, the P sample in Jeffares and Skelchers' study (2011) is primary made up of public managers, for they were interested in how these managers think about democracy and how these subjectivities affect their exercises in shaping networks. However, the success of collaborative governance depends on a team of committed and interdependent participants who are interacting with each other on an equal and transparent basis. The subjectivities of all the participants should be investigated so that the relations between collaborative governance and democracy can be better understood. Furthermore, there is no indication that these public managers are interacting with each other on a regular basis. To replicate the study by focusing on participants whom have collaborated with each other regularly, our research findings should have further practical applications.

Lastly, the original study asked 49 public managers from England and Netherlands to perform the Q sorting. Although the purpose of this study is to analyze the democratic subjectivities of participants of collaborative governance within the contexts of Taiwan, by combining the five Western factors into local Q sorts as original data, a comparative study is possible. The results may reveal the similarities and differences of the democratic discourses in Western Europe and Taiwan.

In this study, a Q sample of 36 statements (see Appendix) developed by Jeffares and Skelcher (2011) was adopted.[1] The P sample consists of 16 people from public (civil servants, university researchers) and private (local business owners) sectors, or representatives of local NGOs in Puli Township, Taiwan. These participants have not only worked together for promoting various community-development projects in Puli for many years, they are currently network members of a local placemaking program launched by the central government in 2019.

On November 28, 2019, 16 people were invited to a meeting in which the purpose of this research and the procedure for sorting the statements were explained. They finished the Q sorting on site, and a brief interview was conducted each afterwards to ask why some statements were categorized as "most agreed" or "most disagreed." In addition, the factor Q sort values of the five factors from the original study are also included as data for second-order analysis. So the total number of Q sorts for analysis is 21 (Table 1).

These 21 Q sorts were analyzed first by using the principle components factor analysis; a five-factor solution was decided for a Varimax rotation to maximize the variance among the five factors. Q sorts with a loading of .43 and above were flagged as significant ones that define the meaning of the factors. The factor matrix with defining sorts is presented in Table 1, and factor arrays of each statement associated with the five factors are presented in the Appendix.

---

1) These statements were modified by replacing the term "network governance" by "collaborative governance" for addressing the research question without changing the meaning of the statement. The text is translated from English into Mandarin by two of the co-authors working independently, and the final Mandarin Q sample is decided by mutual agreement between the two translators.

## Results and Analysis

These five factors can explain about 70% of the data variance; 15 respondents have significant loading on one factor, 5 on 2 factors, and 1 on 3 factors (Table 1). There are at least two immediate observations that can be made: (1) Factors associated with the transitional conjecture (FQ03 and FQ04) and the Pragmatists (FQ05) are significantly loaded on Factor A; and the complementary factors (FQ01 and FQ02) and Pragmatists (FQ05) are significant in Factor B. Although the Q methodology is not designed to test *a priori* hypotheses (Jeffares and Skelcher, 2011, 1269), the significant loading of all five previous factors on two factors respectively in this study nevertheless validates our interpretation to follow the same approach. (2) Factor E has only one respondent with significant loading, although it somewhat violates the standard condition for defining a factor (i.e., there are at least two or more people with significantly loading), it is presented here because it, to certain extent, reflects the "incompatibility" conjecture. The five factors describing the democratic discourses among participants of collaborative governance in Puli are named as Transitional Optimists, Complementary Realists, Grassroots Instrumentalists, Incompatible Utilitarians, and Incompatible Functionalists (Table 1).

**Table 1.** Factor Loadings with Defining Sorts

| | Transitional Optimists (A) | Complementary Realists (B) | Grassroots Instrumentalists (C) | Incompatible | | Sector backgrounds |
|---|---|---|---|---|---|---|
| | | | | Utilitarians (D) | Functionalists (E) | |
| FQ03 | **0.77** | 0.26 | 0.16 | 0.06 | 0.22 | **Progressive Optimists** |
| FQ04 | **0.76** | 0.24 | 0.24 | 0.16 | -0.10 | **Radical Optimists** |
| FQ05 | **0.54** | **0.54** | 0.17 | 0.07 | 0.26 | **Pragmatists** |
| DQ01 | **0.63** | 0.12 | **0.55** | 0.03 | 0.09 | Elected P.O. |
| DQ06 | **0.58** | 0.06 | 0.24 | **0.53** | -0.30 | NPO |
| DQ15 | **0.55** | 0.41 | 0.27 | 0.35 | -0.13 | University |
| DQ05 | **0.53** | 0.17 | **0.47** | **0.51** | -0.12 | Private |
| FQ01 | 0.25 | **0.78** | -0.17 | -0.01 | -0.07 | **Realists** |

| | | | | | | |
|---|---|---|---|---|---|---|
| FQ02 | 0.26 | **0.74** | 0.41 | -0.01 | 0.18 | Adaptors |
| DQ14 | 0.11 | **0.52** | **0.73** | 0.19 | -0.10 | University |
| DQ12 | 0.36 | -0.03 | **0.80** | 0.18 | -0.08 | University |
| DQ03 | 0.24 | -0.05 | **0.74** | 0.34 | 0.07 | Private |
| DQ11 | 0.27 | 0.32 | **0.58** | 0.32 | -0.14 | University |
| DQ10 | 0.26 | -0.05 | **0.54** | **0.53** | 0.19 | NPO |
| DQ16 | 0.13 | 0.34 | **0.51** | 0.39 | 0.28 | Private |
| DQ09 | -0.04 | 0.18 | 0.16 | **0.82** | 0.17 | Private |
| DQ02 | 0.11 | -0.15 | 0.03 | **0.74** | 0.23 | Civil S. |
| DQ07 | 0.24 | -0.10 | 0.28 | **0.62** | 0.05 | NPO |
| DQ08 | 0.09 | 0.27 | 0.41 | **0.61** | -0.38 | Civil S. |
| DQ17 | 0.13 | 0.38 | 0.28 | **0.57** | 0.04 | Private |
| DQ13 | 0.26 | 0.38 | 0.38 | **0.50** | 0.28 | University |
| DQ04 | 0.02 | 0.09 | -0.01 | 0.30 | **0.80** | NPO |
| % Expl. Var. | 16 | 12 | 18 | 18 | 6 | |

## Factor A: Transitional optimists

On the basis of trust (s30, +5), Factor A respondents are very optimistic about new forms of democracy that will emerge out of collaborative practice (s12, +4).[2] Collaborative governance can open up the policy process by encouraging more participation and involvement (s36, +4; s26, +3; s7, +2; s3, +2); citizens and managers can have direct communications and input (s25, +2), thus participants can have more influence on the decision-making process (s2, +3; s34, +2).

For transitional optimists, collaborative governance might not have a very clear view of what is expected to achieve (s21, -3), but it is a flexible approach to problem solving (s19, +3). Although collaborative governance may involve managerial and political issues (s14, -3), it is not a fundamental threat to local government (s11, -5), since the transparency of collaborative governance can be

2) Numbers in the parentheses are statement numbers and their factor loading.

ensured (s15, -4). Moreover, the accountability of collaborative governance to government (s33, -4; s6, -2) or to the elected politicians (s31, -3; s1, -2), should not be the major concerns, since this new form of governance emphasizes direct (s27, -2) and equal (s16, -2) participation.

## Factor B: Complementary realists

The complementary realists perceive that collaborative governance as an inherent component of the political process; they do not have a clear view of what it is expected to achieve (s21, -5), because representative democracy can still give directions as the main decision-making system (s10, +2). For this group, accountability in collaborative governance involves reporting to outsiders (s8, +3), particularly elected politicians who are perceived as committed to wider public interest (s29, +2).

Realists believe that flexibility and inclusiveness are the major concerns of collaborative governance rather than advancements in democracy. Although exclusion of participation (s35, +2; s24, -2; s9, -2) and conflict (s18, +4) are inevitable in collaborative governance, it is a flexible problem-solving approach (s19, +3) that can include major stakeholders (s7, +4), in which participants can influence the elected politicians (s34, +2) rather than handing control over to them (s31, -3). Building on the relationship of trust (s30, +5), collaborative governance may develop new forms of democracy (s12, +3).

Because collaborative governance is complementary to the current representative democracy, it poses no fundamental threat to local governments (s11, -4). Collaborative governance is not without constrains on policy-making (s28, -2) because it deals with both managerial and political issues (s14, -4), so elected politicians have to be held accountable (s1, -3; s22, -2), and the normal administrative procedures have to be observed (s6, -3).

### Factor C: Grassroots instrumentalists

Factor C is closely associated with the instrumental conjecture. This factor takes collaborative governance as a medium for problem-solving at the grassroots level. From this perspective, decision-making process in collaborative governance is essentially democratic (s16, -3; s1, -2; s15, -2), but if special care can be taken to open up the decision-making process in collaborative government and make it more transparent to all participants—such as involving stakeholders (s7, +3), disadvantaged groups (s36, +4; s26, +2), and elected politicians (s22, -4)—conflicts can be avoided (s18, -2).

However, this form of collaborative governance is primarily functioning at the grassroots level. Founded upon building trust (s30, +5) and harmony (s20, +1) through face-to-face communications (s25, +2), this flexible approach to solving problems (s19, +3; s6, +3) can really get things done (s4, +1). Therefore, democracy in collaborative governance has to be created on a day-to-day basis (s17, +4). In the long run, new forms of democracy can be further developed through the practice of collaborative governance (s12, +2).

Collaborative governance is emphasized for its instrumental values; it is not a threat to local governments (s11, -5), so governments need not try to control collaborative governance (s33, -2), and its democratic qualities should not be a major concern (s31, -4; s10, -2). On the other hand, elected politicians are committed to the wider public interest (s29, +2), even though this new form of governance may be dealing with complicated issues (s14, -3), they will only turn to collaborative governance when traditional forms of government are ineffective (s5, +1).

### Factor D: Incompatible utilitarian

Factor D and Factor E are two variants of the incompatibility conjecture. According to Jeffares and Skelcher (2011, 1255), the incompatibility conjecture asserts that representative democracy and collaborative governance will come into conflict "because each is predicated on a different set of institutional rules."

The Incompatible Utilitarian is primarily concerned about the potential benefits (and likely results) of practicing collaborative governance, rather than improving its democratic functions (s32, -3). According to the utilitarian factor, the utility of collaborative governance is very clear (s21, +2) — it is expected to maximize its democratic gains, to build trust among participants (s30, +4), to promote involvement and direct communications among stakeholders (s25, +4; s22, -2), to provide easier access for people to participate in the networks (s3, +3), to facilitate new forms of democracy (s12, +2) and to help people to influence the delivery of services (s2, +2).

These democratic gains can only be realized by practicing collaborative governance on a daily basis (s17, +5). On the other hand, the practical benefits of collaborative governance include its flexibility in problem-solving (s19, +3) so that managers can get things done (s4, +3).

Although from a consequentialism perspective, these activists accentuate the importance of maintaining some internal rules for making and delivering policies (s28, -2). These rules include: decisions should be made in open networks (s1, -4), internal procedures should be followed (s6, -3), participants should be held accountable (s8, -2); and power should be distributed and balanced among participants (s16, -2). But to maximize its utility, collaborative governance should not be a threat to government (s11, -4) while avoiding being controlled by the government (s33, -3) or by elected politicians (s31, -5).

## Factor E: Incompatible functionalist

The Incompatible Functionalist is different from the utilitarian perspective by focusing on the functions of collaborative governance rather than its likely benefits, for collaborative governance only deals with managerial issues (s14, +4). It is very clear of what it is expected to achieve (s21, +2); politicians turns to collaborative governance when traditional forms of government are ineffective (s5, +2); the public are concerned with what can collaborative governance achieve (s13, +4); and it should be flexible for problem solving (s19, +3).

Obviously, conflict is inevitable (s18, +2), because everyone in a collaborative governance should be able to have their say (s24, +3). Only by building trust (s30, +3) on a day-to-day basis (s17, +2) can the functioning of collaborative governance be realized. In this regard, the democratic elements are not essential for collaborative governance: legitimacy (s31, -5), the articulative role of politicians (s27, -4), the transparency of policy making (s36, -4; s1, -2), the accountability (s33, -2), and the inclusiveness of the policy process (s26, -3; s2, -3; s7, -3; s16, -2) are irrelevant to collaborative governance. The most important objective is trying to improve the functioning of collaborative governance, rather than arguing about its democratic quality (s32, +5), for collaborative governance is not a threat to local governments (s11, -2).

### Consensus Statements

In this study, there are four statistically significant consensus statements (s5, s19, s23, s28). However, if it is broadly defined by using Jeffares and Skelcher's criteria, there can be 12 consensus statements.3) The reasons for the consensus across factors vary between factors, but broadly speaking, all factors agree that collaborative governance is about problem-solving (s5, s19, s23); collaborative governance should emphasize equal participation among all potential stakeholders (s31, s22, s16, s15) and transparency (s1); it is not a threat to local governments (s31) and accountability does not necessarily have to be enforced vertically (s33). These issues can be the foundations for future discussion about collaborative governance and democracy, at least within the Taiwan context.

## Discussions and Conclusion

This study analyzes the democratic subjectivities among participants of a

3) Statement 28 is excluded because the sign of its factor values are negative on factor B, C and D, but is positive on factor E and is neutral on Factor A.

local placemaking program in Taiwan in relation to collaborative governance. The replication of Jeffares and Skelcher's Q methodology research (2011) of the democratic subjectivities of public managers in relation to network governance reveals that there are five types of attitudes regarding the research question. The Transitional Optimists are optimistic that, through the practice of collaborative governance, new forms of democracy may emerge. The Complementary Realists view collaborative governance as a complementary part of the representative democracy. The Grassroots Instrumentalists believe that the process of collaborative governance is essentially democratic; they take collaborative governance as the means for solving community-level problems.

The Incompatible Utilitarian and Incompatible Functionalist are two related factors of the Incompatibility conjecture. They take the position that collaborative governance and democracy are operating according to different sets of rules. The former is primarily concerned about the potential benefits (and likely results) of practicing collaborative governance, whereas the latter emphasizes the functional aspects of collaborative governance for policy-making. Essentially, the first two factors focus on the democratic gain of practicing collaborative governance, followed by three that consider collaborative governance as a functional requisite in problem-solving.

All four conjectures about the relations between collaborative governance and democracy have been identified in this study. Jeffares and Skelcher (2011) have recognized that the Q methodology is not designed to test *a priori* hypotheses. However, since this study replicates their research and takes their research results (i.e., the factor array of every statement in each of the factors) as raw data, and the results of our data analysis indicate that Progressive and Radical Optimists are associated with the Transitional Optimists factor in this study, and the Realists and Adaptors are defining parts of the Complementary Realists factor, our interpretations inevitably lean toward the positivistic logic of hypothesis testing.

However, to certain extent, the complex and uncertain relations between collaborative governance and democracy have not been clarified too much by this study. It can be argued that, in addition to verifying that the four conjectures about the collaborative governance and democracy do exist as proposed, the only theoretical advancement is that there are two related but different types of opinions of the incompatibility conjecture. Of course, the verification of the existence of four conjectures empirically does shed some light on this subject, but it is the comparison of the two studies and the proposed explanations for their differences that may contribute to future studies.

Jeffares and Skelcher (2011) argued the absence of the incompatibility conjecture in their study may be due to the underlying pro-democracy position of public managers. For the same token, the absence of the instrumental conjecture is because the pervasion of the instrumental nature of their work, that is to manage the new forms of governance. The opposite may explain why incompatibility and instrumental conjectures are revealed in this study. Most of the respondents in this study are not public managers; they are university researchers, local business owners and NPO representatives who have been working together to solve community development problems at the grassroots level for a long period of time. It can be seen from the consensus statements that, according their shared experiences, they work together because the traditional form of government is no longer effective (s5), collaborative governance is not about deliberation (s23), and because it is a flexible approach to problem solving (s19). Their grassroots experiences have directed their attentions to the functional and instrumental characteristics of collaborative governance.

These five factors should be perceived as contextually located discourses; the common experiences of these respondents have a profound influence on their attitudes about collaborative governance and democracy. At the macro level, Taiwan government lifted martial law in 1987 and a government reinvention program was launched in 1998; the notion of New Public Management has prevailed since, and decentralization or localization has been one permanent approach for reinventing governance in Taiwan.

At the micro level, an Integrated Community Development Program was initiated by the central government in 1994. The program encourages local communities to take all aspects of development issues into their own hands, as the central government will only provide policy guidelines and financial support. Within these social and political contexts, our respondents have participated in many community development projects after the earthquake of 1999. Their experiences indicate that government is unresponsive, inefficient and ineffective in disaster relief projects. They prefer to design and implement community development projects by themselves.

At the same time, NCNU began participating in these local projects, facilitating the establishment of a collaborative network that include university researchers and staffs, local businesspeople and NPO representatives for solving community problems. Under these circumstances, how to improve democracy as a governance form is not our respondents' primary concern. Given their actual life experiences, they would like to enhance the democratic quality of collaborative governance, but it is the ability of collaborative governance to resolve community issues that encourages their devotion and participation in the network.

Another potential reason contributing to the difference between Western-European discourses of the relations between governance and democracy and those of Taiwan is the perceived role played by the government in the process of governance. The ultimate concern of Jeffares and Skelcher (2011, 1253) is "how public managers themselves construct their role as actors in a democratic area and what implications this has for their role in shaping and designing the managements for network governance." Implicitly, it is about the role of the government in network governance. In this study, all five discourses explicitly or implicitly de-emphasize or ignore the role and functions of the government in local collaborative settings. As previously described, the political development in Taiwan and the evolution of the nation's community empowerment policy may have contributed to this phenomenon. Collaborative governance in Taiwan has been recognized by our respondents as a grassroots civic forum through which community problems can be solved. This kind of understanding tends to reinforce the functional requisite of collaborative governance.

In this regard, problem-solving ability will be a significant consideration for collaborative governance, and this is the area where higher education can offer the most contributions. Recently, the local collaborative network in Puli is involved in a local placemaking program, in which NCNU's Center of Humanity Innovation and Social Practice is working with regional communities to promote local initiatives, to take stock of local resources, to generate community consensus and to initiate and implement local revitalization projects.

The recent promotion of "University Social Responsibility (USR)" by Taiwan's Ministry of Education may contribute to these efforts; the notion of "engaged scholar" (Boyer, 1996) or "public scholarship" (Kezar et al., 2018) may also encourage university researchers to reach out and collaborate with diverse stakeholders with the intent of making a difference in society. Through collaborative governance, the objective of public scholarship is to "support an equitable, diverse democracy and to promote social justice" (Kezar et al., 2018, 3).

Collaborative governance has been increasingly practiced in many communities all across Taiwan. With or without the assistance from the government, more and more local communities are coming to the understanding that they can deal with their own development problems according to their own preferences. Given the problem-solving potential of collaborative governance and its essentially democratic characteristics in practice, it is argued that the successful practices of collaborative governance at the community level tend to encourage participatory democracy or deliberative democracy — i.e. new forms of governance that can be viewed as a bottom-up approach towards strengthening democracy — in the long run.

## References

Agranoff, R., & McGuire, M. (2003). *Collaborative Public Management: New Strategies for Local Governments*. Washington, D.C.: Georgetown University Press.

Ansell, C., & Gash, A. (2008). Collaborative Governance in Theory and Practice. *Journal of Public Administration Research and Theory*, 18(4), 543-571.

Barnes, M., Newman, J., Knops, A., & Sullivan H. (2003). Constituting the public for public participation, *Public Administration*, 81(2), 379-399.

Bingham, L. B., Nabatchi, T., & O'Leary, R. (2005). The New Governance: Practices and Processes for Stakeholder and Citizen Participation in the Work of Government. *Public Administration Review*, 65(5), 547-558. DOI: 10.1111/j.1540-6210.2005.00482.x

Booher, D. E. (2004). Collaborative governance practices and democracy. *National Civic Review*, 93(4), 32-46.

Brown, S. R. (1996). Q Methodology and Qualitative Research. *Qualitative Health Research*, 6(4), 561-567.

Bryson, J. M., Crosby, B. C., & Stone, M. M. (2006). The Design and Implementation of Cross-Sector Collaborations: Propositions from the Literature. *Public Administration Review*, 66(s1), 44-55. DOI: 10.1111/j.1540-6210.2006.00665.x

Dahl, R. A. (1998). *On Democracy*. New Haven, CY: Yale University Press.

Donahue, J. D., & Zeckhauser, R. J. (2011). *Collaborative Governance: Private Roles for Public Goals in Turbulent Times*. Princeton and Oxford: Princeton University Press.

Dryzek, J. S., & Berejikian, J. (1993). Reconstitutive Democratic Theory. *American Policial Science Review*, 87(1), 48-60.

Emerson, K. (2018). Collaborative governance of public health in low-and middle-income countries: lessons from research in public administration. *BMJ Global Health*, 3 (Suppl 4), e000381-e000381. DOI: 10.1136/bmjgh-2017-000381

Emerson, K., & Nabatchi, T. (2015). *Collaborative Governance Regimes*. Washington, D.C.: Georgetown University Press.

Emerson, K., Nabatchi, T., & Balogh, S. (2011). An Integrative Framework for Collaborative Governance. *Journal of Public Administration Research and Theory*, 22 (1), 1-29. DOI: 10.1093/jopart/mur011%J *Journal of Public Administration Research and Theory*.

Gash, A. (2016). Cohering Collaborative Governance. *Journal of Public Administration*

*Research and Theory*, 27(1), 213-216. DOI: 10.1093/jopart/muw047%J *Journal of Public Administration Research and Theory*

Gray, B. (1989). *Collaborating: Finding Common Ground for Multiparty Problems*. San Francisco: Jossey-Bass.

Gray, B., & Purdy, J. (2018). *Collaborating for Our Future: Multistakeholder Partnerships for Solving Complex Problems*. Oxford: Oxford University Press.

Jeffares, S., & Skelcher, C. (2011). Democratic subjectivities in network governance: A Q methodology study of English and Dutch public managers. *Public Administration*, 89(4), 1253-1273.

Jing, Y. (2015). *The Road to Collaborative Governance in China*. New York: Palgrave Macmillan US.

Jun, J. S. (2002). *Rethinking Administrative Theory: The Challenge of the New Century*. Westport, CT: Praeger.

Kezar, A., Drivalas, Y., & Kitchen, J. A. (2018). *Envisioning Public Scholarship for Our Time: Models for Higher Education Researchers*. Sterling, VA: Stylus Publishing, LLC.

Klijn, E. H., & Skelcher, C. K. (2007). Democracy and Network Govrnance: Compatible or Not? *Public Administration*, 85(3), 587-608.

Marwell, N. P., & Calabrese, T. (2014). A Deficit Model of Collaborative Governance: Government–Nonprofit Fiscal Relations in the Provision of Child Welfare Services. *Journal of Public Administration Research and Theory*, 25(4), 1031-1058. DOI: 10.1093/jopart/muu047%J *Journal of Public Administration Research and Theory*

Mathur, N., & Skelcher, C. (2007). Evaluating Democratic Performance: Methodologies for Assessing the Relationship between Network Governance and Citizens. *Public Administration Review*, 67(2) (March-April), 228-237.

Morse, R. S. (2011). The Practice of Collaborative Governance. *Public Administration Review*, 71(6), 953-957. DOI: 10.1111/j.1540-6210.2011.02448.x

Mosley, J. E., & Jarpe, M. (2019). How Structural Variations in Collaborative Governance Networks Influence Advocacy Involvement and Outcomes. *Public Administration Review*, 79(5), 629-640. DOI: 10.1111/puar.13037

Newman, J., Barnes, M., Sullivan, H., & Knops, A. (2004), Public Participation and Collaborative Governance. *Journal of Social Policy*, 33(2) (April), 203-223.

Ockwell, D. (2008). "Opening Up" Policy to Reflexive Appraisal: A Role for Q Methodology? A Case Study of Fire Management in Cape York, Australia. *Policy Sciences*, 41(4), 263-292.

O'Leary, R., & Bingham, L. B. (2007). *A Manager's Guide to Resolving Conflicts in Collaborative Networks*. Washington, D.C.: IBM Center for the Business of Government.

O'Toole Jr., L. J., & Meier, K. J. (2011). *Public Management: Organizations, Governance, and Performance*. New York: Cambridge University Press.

Papadopoulos, Y. (2012). The Democratic Quality of Collaborative Governance, in David Levi-Faur, ed. *The Oxford Handbook of Governance*. DOI: 10.1093/oxfordhb/9780199560530.013.0036

Purdy, J. M. (2012). A Framework for Assessing Power in Collaborative Governance Processes. *Public Administration Review*, 72(3), 409-417. DOI: 10.1111/j.1540-6210.2011.02525.x

Rittel, H. W. J., & Webber, M. M. (1973). Dilemmas in a general theory of planning. *Policy Sciences*, 4(2), 155-169. DOI: 10.1007/bf01405730

Scott, T. A., & Thomas, C. W. (2017). Winners and Losers in the Ecology of Games: Network Position, Connectivity, and the Benefits of Collaborative Governance Regimes. *Journal of Public Administration Research and Theory*, 27(4), 647-660. DOI: 10.1093/jopart/mux009%J *Journal of Public Administration Research and Theory*

Shrestha, M. K. (2012). Internal versus External Social Capital and the Success of Community Initiatives: A Case of Self-Organizing Collaborative Governance in Nepal. *Public Administration Review*, 73(1), 154-164. DOI: 10.1111/j.1540-6210.2012.02622.x

Skelcher, C., Mathur, N., & Smith, M. (2005). The public governance of collaborative spaces: Discourse, design and democracy. *Public Administration*, 83(3): 573-596.

Sørensen, E., & Torfing, J. (2011). *Enhancing Collaborative Innovation in the Public Sector*, 43(8), 842-868. DOI: 10.1177/0095399711418768

Stivers, C. (2008). *Governance in Dark Times*. Washington, D.C.: Georgetown University Press. DOI: 10.2307/j.ctt2tt756

Tang, C. -P., & Tang, S. -Y. (2014). Managing Incentive Dynamics for Collaborative Governance in Land and Ecological Conservation. *Public Administration Review*, 74(2), 220-231. DOI: 10.1111/puar.12190

Termeer, C. J. A. M., Dewulf, A., Breeman, G., & Stiller, S. J. (2015). Governance Capabilities for Dealing Wisely With Wicked Problems. *Administration & Society*, 47(6), 680-710. DOI: 10.1177/0095399712469195

Wachhaus, A. (2017). Platform Governance: Developong Collaborative Democracy. *Ad-*

*ministrative Theory & Praxis,* 39, 206-221.

Walker, G. B., & Senecah, S. L. (2011). Collaborative governance: Integrating institutions, communities, and people. In E. F. Dukes;, K. E. Firehock;, & J. E. Birkhoff (Eds.). *Community-based Collaboration: Bridging Socio Ecological Research and Practice*, 111-145. Charlottesville and London: University of Virginia Press.

Watts, S., & Stenner, P. (2012). *Doing Q Methodological Research: Theory, Method and Interpretation*. Thousand Oaks, CA: Sage.

Weale, A. (2011). New Modes of Governance, Political Accountability and Public Reason, *Government and Opposition*, 46, 58-80.

## Appendix: Factor Arrays for Each Statement

| | Factor | | | | |
|---|---|---|---|---|---|
| | A | B | C | D | E |
| 1. In Collaborative governance, decision making takes place in closed networks that are not accountable to elected politicians. | -2 | -3 | -3 | -4 | -2 |
| 2. In collaborative governance, networks help people to become involved in influencing how services are delivered. | 3 | 1 | 1 | 2 | -3 |
| 3. People should be able to find out about networks in collaborative governance and make a contribution to decisions. | 2 | 1 | 1 | 3 | -1 |
| 4. In collaborative governance, networks allow managers to get things done. | -1 | 0 | 1 | 3 | 1 |
| 5. Politicians turn to collaborative governance when traditional forms of government are ineffective. | 0 | 0 | 1 | 1 | 2 |
| 6. The value of collaborative governance is that they cut through the usual red tape. | -2 | -3 | 3 | -3 | -1 |
| 7. Networks in collaborative governance should include people who deliver public programmes as well as those who benefit from them. | 2 | 4 | 3 | 1 | -3 |
| 8. In collaborative governance, accountability involves reporting to people who are not my managers. | -1 | 3 | -1 | -2 | 0 |
| 9. In collaborative governance, networks are creating direct democratic involvement by people outside political parties and government. | 1 | -2 | -1 | 0 | 1 |
| 10. Representative democracy should be the main way of making public policy decisions. | -1 | 2 | -2 | -1 | 1 |
| 11. Collaborative governance poses a fundamental threat to local government. | -5 | -4 | -5 | -4 | -2 |
| 12. Collaborative governance can help new forms of democracy to develop. | 4 | 3 | 2 | 2 | 0 |
| 13. The public are concerned with what collaborative governance achieve, not how it make decisions. | -1 | 0 | -1 | 0 | 4 |
| 14. Collaborative governance deals with managerial, not political, issues. | -3 | -4 | -3 | 1 | 4 |
| 15. Most of the decisions made in collaborative governance will involve only a few people and take place behind closed doors. | -4 | 0 | -2 | -1 | -1 |

| | | | | | |
|---|---|---|---|---|---|
| 16. Collaborative governance gives community leaders more power and make it difficult for ordinary people to get involved. | -2 | -1 | -3 | -2 | -2 |
| 17. Democracy in collaborative governance has to be created on a day to day basis. | 1 | -1 | 4 | 5 | 2 |
| 18. Conflict is inevitable in collaborative governance. | 1 | 4 | -2 | 0 | 2 |
| 19. Collaborative governance should have a flexible approach to problem solving. | 3 | 3 | 3 | 3 | 3 |
| 20. Collaborative governance needs to contain strong members who can challenge things which with they don't agree. | 0 | 1 | 1 | -1 | -1 |
| 21. Collaborative governance has a very clear view of what it is expected to achieve. | -3 | -5 | 0 | 2 | 2 |
| 22. Collaborative governance can be democratic without involving elected politicians. | 0 | -2 | -4 | -2 | -1 |
| 23. If collaborative governance can't improve the level of debate between their members, they will lose legitimacy with citizens. | 0 | 1 | 0 | 0 | 1 |
| 24. Everyone in a collaborative governance should be able to have their say in whatever way they think is best. | 1 | -2 | 0 | 1 | 3 |
| 25. The value of collaborative governance is that citizens and managers get to talk face to face. | 2 | -1 | 2 | 4 | 0 |
| 26. Special steps need to be taken to include disadvantaged groups in collaborative governance. | 3 | 0 | 2 | 0 | -3 |
| 27. The politicians' role is to bring the ideas of people into networks of collaborative governance. | -2 | -1 | 0 | 0 | -4 |
| 28. Collaborative governance should be free to implement overall political goals in the way they think is best. | 0 | -2 | -1 | -2 | 1 |
| 29. Politicians are committed to the wider public interest. | -1 | 2 | 2 | 2 | 0 |
| 30. Building trust is the key to a successful collaborative governance. | 5 | 5 | 5 | 4 | 3 |
| 31. Collaborative governance has legitimacy when it is controlled by elected politicians. | -3 | -3 | -4 | -5 | -5 |
| 32. Instead of treating collaborative governance as undemocratic, we should try to improve its functioning. | 1 | 1 | -1 | -3 | 5 |
| 33. Government controls collaborative governance to make sure that what it does fit with their policy. | -4 | -1 | -2 | -3 | -2 |
| 34. In collaborative governance networks, people can influence elected politicians and make a difference to their community. | 2 | 2 | 0 | -1 | 0 |

| | | | | | |
|---|---|---|---|---|---|
| 35. It is inevitable that collaborative governance will exclude some people. | 0 | 2 | 0 | -1 | 0 |
| 36. Collaborative governance helps to open up policy-making to groups who would otherwise not have a voice. | 4 | 0 | 4 | 1 | -4 |

Part 3

# Inter-Governmental Collaborative Governance

8

# How Does the Regional Collaborative Governance Mechanism of Air Pollution in China Operate Well?:

## Evidence from the Yangtze River Delta

Jiannan Wu, Qianqian Liu, Zitao Chen, and Zhao Qin

## Introduction

The spatial diffusion of air pollution requires that the prevention and control of air pollution needs to break the administrative division restrictions and establish an integrated control mode at the regional level (Yang and Sun, 2009; Wang Jinnan et al., 2012). Since 2013, the central government has issued a series of policies such as Action Plan for Air Pollution Prevention and Control and Three-Year Action Plan for Winning the Defense of the Blue Sky , to promote the nation's air pollution governance (Yang and Chang, 2016; Wang Jinnan et al., 2018). After the Action Plan for Air Pollution Prevention and Control was promulgated, key regions have gradually established collaborative governance mechanisms. In particular, the 2018 Three-Year Action Plan for Winning the Defense of the Blue Sky calls for strengthening joint prevention and control of regional air pollution, clearly defined that "continue to play the role of the Air Pollution Prevention Collaboration Group in the Yangtze River Delta", while other key regions need to further establish or improve the collaboration mechanism of air pollution prevention and control, to some extent, which reflects the central government's recognition of the collaborative governance mechanism of air pollution prevention and control in the Yangtze River Delta.

The collaborative governance mechanisms is the systematic regulation of collaborative governance, which is very important for the practice of collaborative governance (Wu and Sun, 2019), and the related research has been paid attention to at least three aspects. First, the mechanism selection and cause analysis of air pollution collaborative governance. Cai (2019) discussed the collaborative governance mechanism for air pollution prevention and control in Guangdong-Hong Kong-Macao Greater Bay Area and the reasons for choosing different collaborative governance mechanisms, pointed out that the low transaction cost and cooperation risk are the possible reasons for choosing network embeddedness mechanism and binding contracts mechanism in Guangdong-Hong Kong-Macao Greater Bay Area. Suo (2018) based on the theory of institutional collective action, through quantitative coding of Sichuan provincial intergovernmental agreements, presents the formation and evolution of the intergovernmental cooperation mechanism. Yi et al. (2018) empirically investigated the influence of urban characteristics and provincial government participation on the choice of collaborative governance mechanism among local governments.

Second, the effectiveness of collaborative governance mechanism for air pollution. Wei et al. (2018) based on the analysis framework of "structure—process—effect", investigated the mechanism and effect of air pollution collaborative governance in the Beijing-Tianjin-Hebei Region, presenting the overall picture of the mechanism. He et al. (2019) reviews the historical process on air pollution joint prevention and control mechanism in the Beijing-Tianjin-Hebei region. The effect on air pollution joint prevention and control mechanism is systematically discussed, including the perspectives of target effect, institutional framework and control measures in the Beijing-Tianjin-Hebei region.

The third is the optimization analysis of collaborative governance mechanism for air pollution. Guo et al. (2016) based on the theory of inter-governmental relations, pointed out that the collaborative governance mechanism of air pollution in Beijing-Tianjin-Hebei region should be built through the construction of partnership, the coordination of inter-governmental interests, the guarantee of laws and regulations and the sharing of governance information. Han et al. (2017) from the perspective of holistic governance theory, proposed to improve the cooperation mechanism by establishing special leadership, daily organization, coordination and participation and other operational mechanisms. Zhao et al. (2019) proposed that based on the theoretical framework of collaborative governance, the mechanisms of air pollution needs to be transformed from a campaign-style to a normalized collaborative governance in the Beijing-Tianjin-Hebei region.

The above research provides a reference for the governance subjects to choose to build or improve the collaborative governance mechanism in the real situation, but there is no research on how the constructed collaborative governance mechanism plays its role. From the perspective of research objects, previous researches mainly focused on Beijing-Tianjin-Hebei, Pearl River Delta/ Guangdong-Hong Kong-Macao Greater Bay Area and other regions. For the research on the collaborative governance of air pollution in the Yangtze River Delta region, for example, Mao (2016) and Yu (2017) et al. conducted a descriptive analysis on the difficulties and solutions in the practice of collaborative governance. However, there has not yet been a review of the overall picture of collaborative mechanism and function logic for air pollution prevention and control in the Yangtze River Delta.

As one of the regions with a long history of cooperation, the integrated development of the Yangtze River Delta has risen to a national strategy in 2019, and the collaborative governance in the Yangtze River Delta has attracted widespread attention. Therefore, this study asks the following two questions. (1) What is the current state of the collaborative governance mechanism for managing air pollution in the Yangtze River Delta? (2) Why the collaborative governance mechanism for air pollution in the Yangtze River Delta operate efficiently? The second section proposes an analytical framework based on the theories of collaborative governance and institutional collective action. The third section reviews the structural and procedural mechanisms, presenting an overall picture of the collaborative governance mechanism for air pollution in the Yangtze River Delta. The fourth section uses institutional collective action theory to show how well the collaborative governance mechanism for air pollution in the Yangtze

River Delta operates, and finally summarizes the research findings and policy implications.

## Theoretical Basis and Analytical Framework

### Collaborative Governance Theory

For some time, research results on collaborative governance have continuously emerged, among which the collaborative governance model proposed by Ansell and Gash (2008) and Emerson et al. (2012) has been widely recognized and applied. Ansell and Gash (2008) pointed out that collaborative governance is a collective decision-making process involving multiple stakeholders, which is consensus-oriented, including starting conditions, institutional design, facilitative leadership, collaborative processes, and outcomes. Among them, the collaborative processes are the core, and the starting conditions, institutional design, facilitative leadership are the supporting factors for the collaborative processes to play effectively. Emerson et al. (2012) emphasized that collaborative governance, as a form of governance, is a process and structure of public policy decision making and management across different subject boundaries, including the general system context, the collaborative governance regime, and its collaborative dynamics and actions. Collaborative governance regime consists of three interactive components: principled engagement, shared motivation and capacity for joint action. These studies provide an important basis for the analysis of the collaborative governance mechanism.

### Institutional Collective Action Theory

Feiock (2009, 2013) proposed the Institutional Collective Action Framework (ICA Framework) based on the institutional framework and collective action analysis. On the one hand, the theoretical framework points out that in the situation of information asymmetry and lack of coordination, the behavior of multiple actors pursuing their own interests will lead to the inefficiency of collective results, especially according to the degree of regional autonomy, the complexity of problems and the number of participants, puts forward a variety of possible cooperation mechanisms (Feiock, 2013). On the other hand, the theoretical framework gives an explanation of the rational choice of regional cooperation, that is, when the net income exceeds the transaction cost, and according to the transaction cost and cooperation risk faced by different mechanisms (see Table 1), then the cooperation mechanism can be selected dynamically (Feiock, 2007, 2009). The ICA framework also clearly points out that cooperation mechanisms will also influence each other, and existing cooperation mechanisms may promote or hinder the functioning of new cooperation mechanisms (Feiock, 2013). it can be seen that, based on the hypothesis of "bounded rational person" of local governments, the ICA framework reveals important variables in cooperation, such as transaction costs, cooperation risks and their mutual relations (Jiang and Yang 2018), which provides an important basis for us to understand and promote practical intergovernmental cooperation mechanisms.

**Table 1.** The Type and Description of Transaction Costs and Cooperation Risks

| Content | Type | Description |
|---|---|---|
| Transaction costs | Information/ coordination cost | The cost of understanding information on the preferences of all participants over possible outcomes, and their resources must be common knowledge |
| | Negotiation/ division cost | The costs of reaching an agreement on the rules or procedures, and the parties must be able to agree to a division of their mutual gains |
| | Enforcement/ monitoring cost | The cost of implementing collective agreements and actions, and there can be at most low costs associated with monitoring and enforcing the agreement |
| | Agency cost | The cost of preventing an agent from deviating from the preferences of the principal, bargaining agents must well represent the interests of their constituents |

| | | |
|---|---|---|
| Cooperation risks | Coordination risks | Cooperative participants are faced with the risk that it is difficult to establish contact with key actors that possess critical information or form "weak-tie" relationships, which will affect the coordination decision |
| | Division risk | Cooperative participants face the risk of disagreement on the distribution of joint benefits or perception of unequal or disproportionate benefits, pose barriers to collaboration |
| | Defection risk | Cooperative participants are at risk of possible defaults and opportunistic behavior in policy decisions or cooperative commitments |

Source: Feiock (2007, 51-52) and Feiock (2013, 406-407).

## Analytical Framework

The "structure-process" model proposed by the Organization for Economic Cooperation and Development (OECD) has been widely used to analyze collaborative governance mechanisms (Meng et al., 2018). It divides collaborative governance mechanisms into two categories: structural mechanisms and procedural mechanisms (OECD, 2000). Structural mechanisms are the organizational components of collaborative governance; that is, the structural arrangements designed for realizing cross-sector collaboration, such as central policy groups, inter-ministerial joint meetings, and special task groups. Procedural mechanisms focus on procedural arrangements and technical methods for achieving collaboration, such as agenda determination and decision-making procedures in the face of "transboundary issues", and the selection of financial and control tools to promote collaboration (OECD, 2000). The structure-process model is very suitable for explaining the basic operation of collaborative governance and can accommodate different collaborative governance theories. In the collaborative governance model proposed by Ansell et al. (2008), institutional design and facilitative leadership mainly correspond to structural mechanisms, and collaborative processes correspond to procedural mechanisms. In the collaborative governance model proposed by Emerson et al. (2012), principled engagement and shared motivation mainly correspond to procedural mechanisms, and capacity for joint action correspond to structural mechanism. In terms of explaining the "why", the institutional collective action theory emphasizes that transaction cost and cooperation risk are impediments to regional cooperation. Suo et al. (2018) reviewed the research on domestic regional governance and found that the institutional collective action framework can explain the complex selection and overall performance of collaborative governance mechanisms. Therefore, the theory of collaborative governance and the theory of institutional collective action complement each other, and can together provide a theoretical basis for understanding collaborative governance mechanisms.

In the follow-up content, this study is based on the realistic situation of collaborative governance for air pollution prevention and control in the Yangtze River Delta, presents the structural and procedural mechanisms from "structure-process" model. At the same time, it further analyzes how the structural mechanism and procedural mechanism change the different types of transaction costs and cooperation risks to explain how the collaborative governance mechanism for air pollution operate well in the Yangtze River Delta.

## Characteristics of the Collaborative Governance Mechanisms

This study has collected the work briefs of the Air Pollution Prevention Collaboration Group Office in Yangtze River Delta published on the website of the Shanghai Municipal Bureau of Ecology and Environment (referred to as "work briefs"), covering 49 issues from February 28, 2014 to September 2, 2019, as an analytical material for the collaborative governance mechanism of air pollution in the Yangtze River Delta. These work briefs reflect the dynamic of regional cooperation and the progress of local provinces and cities, and are the official materials regularly produced and actively disclosed by the Air Pollution Prevention Collaboration Group Office in Yangtze River Delta. Considering that the work briefs did not fully reveal the operation status of the collaborative governance mechanism, further in-depth interviews were conducted with the Ministry of Ecology and Environment and the Eco-Environment Department of the Yangtze River Delta. The interviewees covered "national level, regional level, provincial and municipal level", including the workers at the central ministries level for the air pollution collaborative governance, the staff of Air Pollution Prevention Collaboration Group Office in Yangtze River Delta, and the local provincial and municipal first-line environmental law enforcement personnel. The interview was mainly conducted in a small forum with the interviewees, each of which lasted at least one and a half hours. The interview lasted from 2018 to 2019, and more than 90,000 words of interview materials were formed, which provided first-hand information for opening the structural and procedural "black box" of the collaborative governance mechanism for air pollution prevention and control in the Yangtze River Delta.

## Structural Mechanisms

The groups that make up the structural mechanism of the collaborative governance for air pollution in Yangtze River Delta include a decision-making agency, namely the Air Pollution Prevention and Control Collaboration Group in Yangtze River Delta (APPCCGYRD), an executive agency, namely the Air Pollution Prevention Collaboration Group Office in Yangtze River Delta (APPCCGOYRD), and guarantee agencies, namely the Air Quality Forecasting Center in Yangtze River Delta, Air Pollution Prevention Collaboration Expert Group in Yangtze River Delta (APPCEGYRD), and Key Laboratory of Causes and Prevention of Combined Air Pollution (KLCPCAP) (Figure 1). The APPCCGYRD is responsible for overall consultation and decision-making, the APPCCGOYRD is responsible for the implementation of specific decisions, and the AQFCYRD and KLCPCAP are mainly responsible for providing data, systems, and technical support.

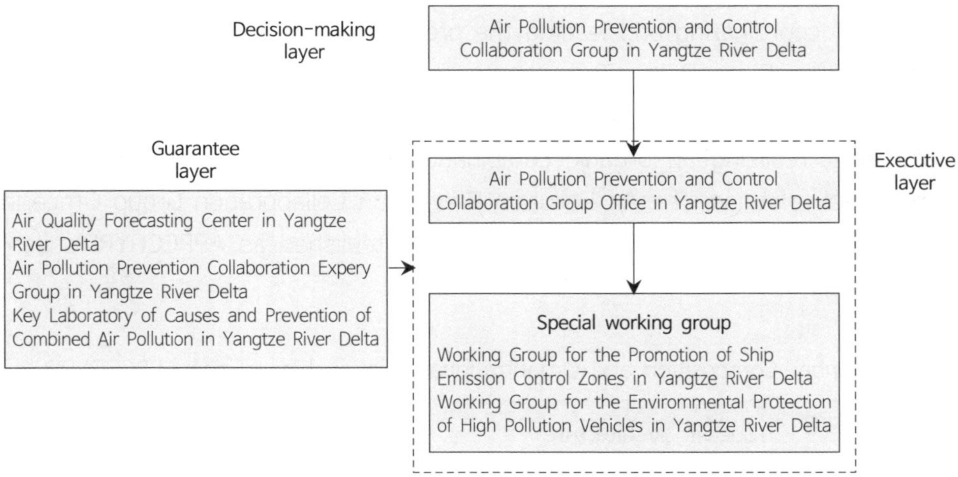


**Figure 1.** Collaborative Structure of Air Pollution Prevention and Control in the Yangtze River Delta

## Decision-making Agency: Coordinating the prevention and control work

Under the policy requirements of the "12th Five-Year Plan for Air Pollution Prevention and Control in Key Regions" and the "Action Plan of Air Pollution Prevention and Control", the Ministry of Ecology and Environment reported to the state council in December 2013 that "the request for the establishment of APPCCGYRD was approved." In January 2014, the APPCCGYRD was formally established. The Ministry of Science and Technology was subsequently added as a member. Currently, the APPCCGYRD is composed of "nine ministries, one city and three provinces" (Table 2), and the working regulations of the APPCCGYRD is its organizational specification. The collaborative governance of air pollution prevention and control in the Yangtze River Delta involves not only collaborations between local governments at the same administrative level, but also collaborations between local governments at different administrative levels. The

Secretary of the Shanghai Municipal Party Committee serves as the leader of the APPCCGYRD, coordinating and leading the prevention and control of air pollution in the Yangtze River Delta. The deputy team leaders and members include relevant leaders of national ministries and relevant leaders of city and provincial governments, realizing an organic combination of vertical and horizontal inter-governmental relations. The Air Pollution Prevention Collaboration Group Office in Yangtze River Delta (APPCCGOYRD) has been established as APPCCGYRD's permanent office.

**Table 2.** Member Composition and Organizational Relationships of the APPCCGYRD

<table>
<tr><th>Decision-making Agency</th><th colspan="2">Specific Architecture</th><th>Content</th></tr>
<tr><td rowspan="4">Air Pollution Prevention Collaboration Group in Yangtze River Delta (APPCCGYRD)</td><td rowspan="3">Organization members</td><td>Team leader</td><td>Secretary of the Shanghai Municipal Committee (member of the Political Bureau of the Central Committee)</td></tr>
<tr><td>Deputy head</td><td>Minister of Ecology and Environment, Mayor of Shanghai, Governor of Zhejiang, Governor of Jiangsu, Governor of Anhui</td></tr>
<tr><td>Specific members</td><td>Deputy Secretary-General of the State Council, Deputy Director of the National Development and Reform Commission, Deputy Minister of Industry and Information Technology, Deputy Minister of Finance, Deputy Minister of Ecology and Environment, Deputy Minister of Housing, Urban-Rural Development, Deputy Minister of Transport, Deputy Minister of Science and Technology, Director of China Meteorological Administration Director of National Energy Administration, Deputy Mayor of Shanghai, Deputy Governor of Zhejiang, Deputy Governor of Jiangsu, Deputy Governor of Anhui</td></tr>
<tr><td>Organizational relationship</td><td>Sub-group</td><td>Air Pollution Prevention Collaboration Group Office in Yangtze River Delta (APPCCGOYRD)</td></tr>
</table>

## Executing Agency: Implementing the policy requirements

The APPCCGOYRD is the permanent office of the APRCEGYRD, responsible for making decisions, implementing policies, guaranteeing services, and coordinating the daily work of air pollution prevention and control in the Yangtze River Delta. The second issue of the work briefing introduced the eight operating mechanisms of the APPCCGOYR, including conference consultation, coordination and promotion, work liaison, information transmission, situation report and notification, research exchange, research evaluation, document and archive management. The APPCCGOYRD membership is composed of the people responsible for the regional ecological environment system (Table 3). As front-line managers, these people are directly responsible for the implementation of policies. In terms of organizational relations, the APPCCGOYRD operates within the General Planning Department of the Shanghai Municipal Bureau of Ecology and Environment, which has the main responsibility for the daily work. The APP-CCGOYRD promotes various tasks by setting up special working groups, such as the Working Group for the Promotion of Ship Emission Control Areas in the Yangtze River Delta and the Working Group for the Environmental Protection of High Pollution Vehicles in the Yangtze River Delta, or other organizations. Thus, the Yangtze River Delta region has ensured the normality, standardization, and specialization of policy implementation by constructing structural mechanisms with office institutions and special working groups dedicated to the execution of the policies.

**Table 3.** Members and Organizational Relationships of the APPCCGOYRD

| Executing Agency | Specific Architecture | | Content |
|---|---|---|---|
| Air Pollution Prevention Collaboration Group Office in Yangtze River Delta (APPCCGOYRD) | Organization members | Director | Deputy Mayor of Shanghai, Deputy Minister of Ecology and Environment |
| | | Executive deputy director | Deputy Secretary-General of Shanghai Municipal Government, Director of Shanghai Municipal Bureau of Ecology and Environment, Director of the Air Department of the Minister of Ecology and Environment |

| | | | |
|---|---|---|---|
| | | Deputy director | Director of the Department of Ecology and Environment of Zhejiang Province, Director of the Department of Ecology and Environment of Jiangsu Province, Director of the Department of Ecology and Environment of Anhui Province |
| | | Concrete members | Deputy Director of the relevant ministries and departments of the Central Committee |
| | | Staff | Staff of General Planning Department of Shanghai Municipal Bureau of Ecology and Environment |
| | Organizational relationship | Entrusted agency | General Planning Department of Shanghai Municipal Bureau of Ecology and Environment |
| | | Sub-group | Working Group for the Promotion of Ship Emission Control Areas in the Yangtze River Delta<br>Working Group for the Environmental Protection of High Pollution Vehicles in the Yangtze River Delta |

## Guarantee Agency: Executing the service decisions

The Yangtze River Delta region has not only decision-making and execution agencies, but also a series of agencies to guarantee air quality, such as the Air Quality Forecasting and Forecasting Center in Yangtze River Delta (AQFFCYRD), Air Pollution Prevention Collaboration Expert Group in Yangtze River Delta (APPCEGYRD), and Key Laboratory of Causes and Prevention of Combined Air Pollution (KLCPCAP). The sixth issue of the work briefing introduces that relying on the "one regional center and four sub-centers" structure, the AQFCYRD has established a regional air quality data sharing platform, a regional pollutant emission inventory, a visual business consultation system, and a forecast and early warning business platform. This guarantee agency includes data centers, research and assessment centers, consultation centers, and forecast centers, and provides integrated services for the collaborative governance of air pollution in the Yangtze River Delta. The APPCEGYRD and KLCPCAP are mainly responsible for researching and judging air environmental problems, improving the scientific diagnosis and prevention of air pollution, improving the quality of scientific decisions and providing technical guidance.

**Table 4.** The Guarantee Agencies and Functions of Air Pollution Prevention and Control in the Yangtze River Delta

| Guarantee Agencies | Functions | Institutions |
|---|---|---|
| Air Quality Forecasting and Forecasting Center in Yangtze River Delta (AQFFCYRD) | Data, consultation and forecast service | Shanghai Environmental Monitoring Center |
| Air Pollution Prevention Collaboration Expert Group in Yangtze River Delta (APPCEGYRD) | Problem research and judgment, scientific decision | Air Pollution Prevention Collaboration Group Office in Yangtze River Delta (APPCCGOYRD) |
| Key Laboratory of Causes and Prevention of Combined Air Pollution (KLCPCAP) | Scientific diagnosis and technical guidance | Shanghai Academy of Environmental Sciences |

## Procedural Mechanism

In the collaborative governance mechanism of air pollution in the Yangtze River Delta, the procedural mechanism has four parts: determinate agendas, formulate programs, policy implementation, and policy evaluation (Figure 2). There is a close relationship among determinate agendas, formulate programs, policy implementation and policy evaluation. The determination of agenda defines the governance tasks for the formulation of programs, and the formulation of programs lays the governance means for the policy implementation. The policy implementation is the premise of the policy evaluation, and the policy evaluation provides guarantee for the policy implementation. This study takes ship emission control in the Yangtze River Delta as an example to illustrate the procedural mechanisms for governing air pollution in the Yangtze River Delta.

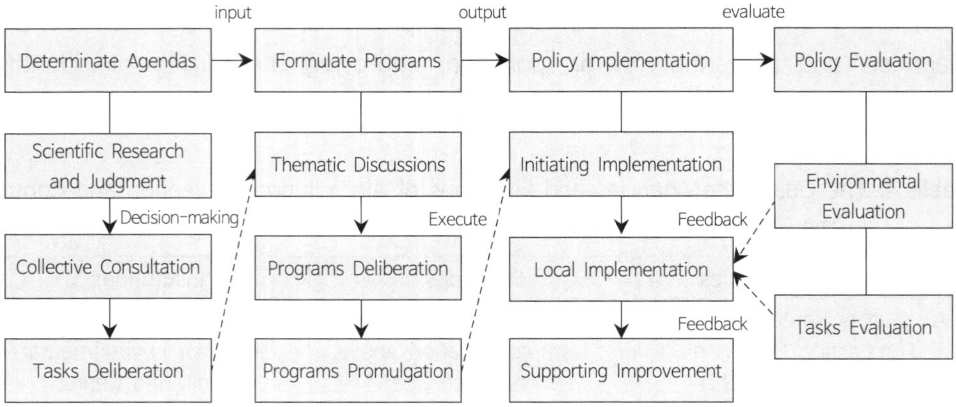


**Figure 2.** Collaborative Process of Air Pollution Prevention and Control in the Yangtze River Delta

## Determinate Agendas: Negotiating the overall working arrangement

The determination of agenda is developed based on scientific research and judgement, collective consultation, and tasks deliberation. Scientific research includes the APPCEGYRD's in-depth analyses of the key sources of energy, industry, volatile organic compounds, motor vehicles, non-road mobile machinery, and ships in the Yangtze River Delta. During the collective consultation, all members of the APPCCGYRD negotiate the choice of key regional issues, targets, and tasks for joint action on air pollution prevention and control. The tasks deliberation refers to the release of the results of the collective negotiation by the APPCEGYRD to all members of the APPCCGOYRD, which is then responsible for determining the overall work arrangements.

Taking the determination of agenda for the ship emission control area in the Yangtze River Delta as an example, in 2014, after examining the scientific data, the APPCEGYRD developed prevention and control ideas that focused on the enhanced control of mobile sources and increased regulation of volatile organic compounds. In the interview, several interviewees mentioned that "the contribution of PM2.5 pollution sources in the Yangtze River Delta mainly comes from ship emissions, and the major economic cities, including Shanghai, Nanjing, Suzhou, have shipping functions." At the second APPCCGYRD meeting, all of the members reached a consensus on strengthening research on key issues and continuing to advance the prevention and control of ship pollution, approving the 2015 Key Work Proposals for the Collaboration of Air Pollution Prevention and Control in the Yangtze River Delta.

## Formulate Programs: Reaching regional agreements using minister-province linkage

There are three steps in formulating programs: thematic discussions, programs deliberation, and programs promulgation. Thematic discussions are discussions at the APPCCGOYRD meetings that focus on difficult issues, such as governing high-pollution vehicles and ships to reduce air pollution. Programs deliberation refers to the work arrangements negotiated at the APPCCGOYRD meetings that are transformed into specific work implementation plans by the APPCCGYRD. Programs promulgation refers to through the meeting of the APPCCGYRD, the decision making and release of the work plan made by APPCCGOYRD at the regional level of the Yangtze River Delta.

The programs formulation stage of the ship emission control initiative in the Yangtze River Delta began with a special session of the APPCCGOYRD focused on controlling ship emissions. Subsequently, the fourth meeting of APPCCGYRD examined and reviewed the special work plan for ship pollution control, and then recommended the implementation of a plan for the construction of low-emission control areas for ships. Due to the mobility of ships, the construction of a low-emission control area for ships increased the cost of docking ships, and the plan faced resistance, as mentioned by an interviewee, "Everyone has a consensus on pollution emissions, but once it comes to the port and shipping, there will be a conflict of interest." To ensure a smooth launch, the APPCCGYRD asked the Ministry of Transport to formally encourage the core ports in the Yangtze River

Delta to take the lead in implementing ship emission control areas. This contributed to the successful launch of the ship emission control area in the Yangtze River Delta.

## Policy Implementation:
## Local implementation of regional programs

Policy implementation includes three steps: initiating implementation, local implementation, and supporting improvement. The policy implementation is initiated at implementation meetings held by the APPCCGOYRD and includes the establishment of a special working mechanism. Local implementation occurs when local governments formulate specific implementation plans in accordance with the requirements of the regional program. Finally, supporting measures can be provided by APPCCGOYRD to promote the implementation of the policies.

The ship emission control in the Yangtze River Delta was implemented in accordance with the requirements of the regional program: "take the lead in implementing the ship emission control area initiative." The ship emission control area in the Yangtze River Delta was officially launched on April 1, 2016. Subsequently, the provincial governments in the Yangtze River Delta area issued specific implementation policies, such as plans for the implementation of the ship emission control area at Shanghai port, to jointly promote the policy. At the same time, the Yangtze River Delta region issued the "implementation rules of low sulfur oil subsidy for ship emission control area in the Yangtze River Delta" and other supporting measures.

## Policy Evaluation:
## Carrying out environment and task evaluation

Policy evaluation requires environmental evaluation and task evaluation. Environmental evaluation consists of assessing the specific improvements in regional air quality, which is done by the APPCCGOYRD. The APPCCGOYRD is also responsible for evaluating the implementation of the tasks proposed in the regional program. Environmental evaluation and task evaluation help regional and local governments fulfil their responsibility for air pollution prevention and control, which provides regulatory guarantees for continued evaluation of the effectiveness of air pollution prevention and control.

To evaluate the policies on the ship emission control area in the Yangtze River Delta, the main effect of the use of low-sulfur oil is to reduce the emissions of sulfur compounds, thereby reducing the concentration of sulfur dioxide pollutants in the air, so the environmental air quality is measured before and after the implementation of the ship emission control area. According to the task requirements in the implementation plan of ship emission control, the local governments' task implementation is also investigated, as the interviewees clearly pointed out, "These data are presented in an evaluation report, which is given to provincial leaders and provincial party secretaries, who can let the local supervision departments know whether their task implementation is adequate and offer recommendations for improvements."

## Institutional Logic of the Collaborative Governance Mechanism

According to the ICA framework, transaction costs and cooperation risks in intergovernmental cooperation are the key factors hindering collaborative governance (Feiock, 2009). The analysis shows that the collaborative governance mechanism of air pollution in the Yangtze River Delta region plays its role in reducing transaction costs and cooperation risks through a series of structural and procedural mechanisms, as shown in Table 5.

**Table 5.** Institutional Logic of the Collaborative Governance Mechanism

| Dimension | Type | Mechanism |
|---|---|---|
| Reduce transaction costs | Information/ coordination cost | Structural mechanisms to support the policies such as the AQFFCYRD; collaborative procedural mechanisms of determining agendas and formulating programs with consultation as the core |
| | Negotiation/ division cost | Cooperative projects should be selected prudently, starting with common problems, and different consultation meetings should be held according to the content and stage of the collaboration |
| | Enforcement/ monitoring cost | Special working groups; determining agendas, formulating programs, policy implementation, etc., introduce regional programs, local programs, and unified evaluation |
| Reduce cooperation risks | Coordination risk | Guarantee or decision-making groups, such as the APPCEGYRD; determining agendas and formulating programs; The procedural mechanism of determining agendas with consultation as the core and programs formulation with the characteristics of ministry-province linkage |
| | Division risk | The structural mechanism of APPCCGYRD and APPCCGOYRD. The procedural mechanism of determining agendas and formulating programs with consultation as the core, and policy implementation featuring policy subsidies, fiscal transfer payments, and standard spontaneous sharing |
| | Defection risk | The structural mechanism of APPCCGYRD, APPCCGOYRD and special working group; The procedural mechanism of environment and task evaluation |

## Reducing Transaction Costs

Provincial and municipal governments and related departments in the Yangtze River Delta have given the APPCCGYRD and APPCCGOYRD the authority to coordinate air pollution prevention and control work. As the members of APPCCGYRD and APPCCGOYRD, they directly participate in the consultations and share organizational decisions. Therefore, the agency costs of the collaborative governance of air pollution in the Yangtze River Delta is basically negligible. The collaborative governance mechanism is designed to reduce information/coordination, negotiation/division, and enforcement/monitoring costs.

## Reducing Information/Coordination Costs

The AQFCYRD has a data center for regular or irregular information sharing, thereby solving the problem of incomplete or asymmetric information between the four governments. The information platform uses new technology to realize real-time transmission, which minimizes the time and labor costs of obtaining information from various places. Between 2015 and 2018, the AQFCYRD completed more than 1,000 special reports on air quality forecasts and shared air quality data. Demonstrating the "determine agendas" and "formulate programs" steps of the procedural mechanism, information is exchanged at various consultation meetings, which leads to effective communication and reduces the costs of obtaining information and coordination from all of the participants individually.

## Reducing Negotiation/Division Costs

The reduction of negotiation/division costs is mainly achieved through the procedural mechanism, which specifically includes the following methods. the scientific research conducted by the APPCEGYRD and KLCPCAP provides a scientific basis for the negotiations, which helps to reduce useless negotiation. The possibility of divergence in the determinate agendas stage is minimized through the careful selection of projects. The programs are then formulated according to guidelines at APPCCGYRD meetings, APPCCGOYRD meetings, and the thematic APPCCGOYRD meetings, which reduces the time, labor, property, and other bargaining costs associated with multiple repeated negotiations or divisions. At the same time, the structural mechanisms of AQFCYRD conducts video consultations using its visual business consultation system, which reduces the time, financial, and other costs associated with face-to-face negotiation.

## Reducing Enforcement/Monitoring Costs

The APPCCGOYRD reduces management and regional enforcement costs by establishing special working groups. For example, the Working Group for the Promotion of Ship Emission Control Area in the Yangtze River Delta and the Working Group for the Environmental Protection of High Pollution Vehicles in the Yangtze River Delta are responsible for the implementation of the specific regional tasks. The procedural mechanism, when determining the agenda and formulating the program, ensures that regional work programs or policies respect the wishes of all of the participants, provide specific directions and goals for policy implementation, and standardize the means of enforcement, which helps to reduce enforcement costs. At the same time, the policy implementation process allows the Yangtze River Delta Region authority to introduce specific implementation plans to adapt measures to local conditions, to avoid the "acculturation" of the enforcement of regional policies, which results in enforcement alienation. Finally, supporting the improvement of policy through subsidies provides an impetus for policy implementation, reduces the economic cost of the use of low-sulfur oil for ships, and avoids the phenomenon of "decision without enforcement." In the process of "policy evaluation", regional environmental and work evaluation provide a unified supervision for air pollution prevention and control, to some extent, avoid the cost of multi supervision.

## Reducing Cooperation Risks

The cooperation risk is the possibility that a local government cannot maintain its cooperative behavior or effectively solve the collective dilemma, which affects the transaction costs of collaborative governance and the effectiveness of cooperation mechanisms (Feiock, 2009).

## Reducing Coordination Risk

The lack of coordination risk is high when the tasks are complex and the relationship between cooperative behavior and policy involves many links (Jiang and Yang, 2018). The leader of the APPCCGYRD is the Secretary of the Shanghai Municipal Committee. As a member of the Political Bureau of the Central Committee, the Secretary occupies a higher administrative level and has stronger integration and coordination ability, which to some extent reduces the risk of a lack of coordination in the collaborative governance of air pollution in the Yangtze River Delta. When determining its agenda, the Yangtze River Delta region started by introducing win-win cooperation behaviors, focused on regional commonality issues, thus reduced the risk of a lack of coordination. When formulating the program, the Yangtze River Delta region used the connections between the minister and provinces to obtain high-level policy support to overcome potential lack of coordination. For example, although controlling ship pollution in the Yangtze River Delta was the first policy goal, reaching a consensus on the ship's emission control area was difficult due to the economic interests of the participants. The APPCCGYRD asked the Ministry of Transport for support, and the ministry issued a letter supporting the implementation of the ship emission control area in the core ports, which helped the Yangtze River Delta region take the lead in ship emissions control area. As many interviewees mentioned at the same time, "consensus is formed at the provincial level, and then the central ministries balance the interests of all parties, put forward mandatory requirements, and consciously take the regional action to the country's overall deployment or higher requirements combined, this is typical, this is Ministry-Province linkage."

## Reducing Division Risk

The key to successful collaborative governance is the comprehensive and proper consideration of the relevant interests in the horizontal collaborative process between local governments (Wei and Meng, 2018). How does the collaborative governance mechanism for air pollution in the Yangtze River Delta ensure that benefits are distributed equally? The APPCCGYRD and APPCCGOYRD have representatives from "nine ministries, one city and three provinces", who collectively negotiate methods for preventing and controlling air pollution, which prevents unfair distribution of the benefits. The process for formulating the program allows everyone's interests to be recognized through collective negotiation. The interviewees mentioned that "this process emphasizes communication and respects the willingness of the city to collectively decide on governance tasks and schemes, instead of relying on administrative power, which helps to reduce the risk of unfair distribution." It is worth noting that the level of economic development in Anhui Province is relatively weak and the power of industry is relatively high. If the uniform and compulsory upgrading of emission standards is imposed on the region, Anhui Province would inevitably impose large-scale "close, limit, and stop" directives on the high pollution and high energy consumption industries. Current policies encourage no-mandatory inter-regional financial transfer payments and standard sharing and docking, as the interviewee said, "About the standard, as long as we only need to solicit opinions from enterprises, industry associations and relevant departments in Shanghai, but now we need to solicit opinions from other provinces and cities and share them on the regional platform. In fact, it is a function of informing in advance. If you are willing to follow me, you should take the initiative to follow, but there is no mandatory requirement." These measures are not mandatory, but they encourage cities to learn from and follow each other, balancing costs and benefits as much as possible to reduce the risk of unfair division.

## Reducing Defection Risk

The establishment of the APPCCGYRD, APPCCGOYRD, AQFCYRD, and other institutions is based on national policy requirements. These organizations have introduced their own guidelines, such as the "Work Regulations of APPCCGYRD", and the "Operation Mechanism of APPCCGOYRD", which have created certain institutional constraints that effectively avoid the risk of individual entities withdrawing from collaboration. By sharing the air quality data, the AQFCYRD has created a kind of mutual supervision, while helping local governments to improve their governance enthusiasm and commit to the collaboration. The defection risk is also reduced by formulating local policies, policy subsidies, and other incentives. For example, Shanghai, Zhejiang, Jiangsu, and Anhui provinces have formulated specific implementation plans that respect their local differences and thus reduce defection risk; the "Detailed Implementation Rules for Subsidies for Low-Sulfur Oil for Ships in the Yangtze River Delta's Emission Control Area" have reduced the economic cost of ships using low-sulfur oil, thereby reducing the defection risk. At the same time, the Yangtze River Delta region has mastered the implementation of policies in various places through the evaluation of air quality and work progress, thereby helping to prevent possible risks of abandoning collaboration by all parties.

## Discussions and Conclusion

### Discussions

This study uses the structure-process model to examine the collaborative governance mechanism for air pollution prevention and control in the Yangtze River Delta, describes the structural and procedural mechanisms, and based on the institutional collective action framework, explain the institutional logic of the collaborative governance mechanism for air pollution prevention and control in the Yangtze River Delta from the aspects of transaction costs and cooperation risks.

The Yangtze River Delta region has formed an organizational structure consisting of several core institutions, i.e., the APPCCGYRD, APPCCGOYRD, AQFCYRD, APPCEGYRD, and KLCPCAP. These bodies can be divided into decision-making, executive, and guarantee responsibilities and together provide structural support for regional air pollution prevention and control. This structural mechanism allows ministries and provinces to realize top-down priorities while allowing bottom-up integration of authoritative resources, guaranteed standardization of the governance structure, and improved communication. The procedural mechanism consists of a multi-stage collaborative governance process that determinates agendas, formulates programs, implements policies, and finally evaluates the policies. Among them, the determination of agenda defines the governance tasks for the formulation of programs, and the formulation of programs lays the governance means for the policy implementation. The policy implementation is the premise of the policy evaluation, and the policy evaluation provides guarantee for the policy implementation. The logic of the collaborative governance of air pollution in the Yangtze River Delta is that the structural and procedural mechanisms together reduce the transaction costs and cooperation risks of air pollution prevention and control, including the information/coordination, negotiation/division, and enforcement/monitoring costs, the coordination risk, division risk and defection risk. It also promotes a regional collaborative relationship between local governments.

This study realizes the integration of the respective advantages of the "structure-process" theory of collaborative governance and the theory of institutional collective action. While explaining the overall picture of the collaborative governance mechanism of air pollution in the Yangtze River Delta, it also explains the institutional logic of the collaborative governance mechanism, extends the applicable scenarios of the institutional collective action framework proposed by Feiock (2009, 2013) in understanding the effectiveness of collaborative governance mechanisms. This study responds to the viewpoint that a series of specific mechanisms of the institutional collective action theory in the Western context have differences in the Chinese context (Yi et al., 2018). and sorts out the collaborative governance mechanism of the Chinese context based on the structure and process. On the other hand, this study extends the mechanism selection stage concerned by Cai (2019) to the mechanism realization stage. Based on structural and procedural mechanisms, it analyzes the reduction of transaction costs and cooperation risks, and reveals that transaction costs and cooperation risk factors not only affects the choice of collaborative governance mechanism, and also provides an important explanation for how the collaborative governance mechanism operate well.

## Conclusion

First, a well-designed collaborative governance mechanism for air pollution prevention and control can reduce the transaction costs and cooperation risks of collaborations. The main function of the structural mechanism is to gather the relevant actors and provide a platform for information sharing, consultation, decision-making, implementation, and evaluation. This requires the establishment of a collaborative organization that includes all of the stakeholders, and gives each stakeholder sufficient power to encourage them to actively participate in the negotiation and decision-making process. This is necessary to achieve effective collaboration between horizontal and vertical intergovernmental relationships, which in turn leads to a reduction in transaction costs and cooperation risks. The main function of the procedural mechanism is to determine tasks, formulate specific programs, promote the policy implementation, and ensure the effectiveness of policy. The exertion of effect requires the formulation of clear institutional specifications to achieve fairness and justice in the process of interest expression, benefit integration, and benefit distribution among subjects, thereby reducing transaction costs and cooperation risks, and achieving the effective operation of the collaborative governance mechanism.

Second, the design of a collaborative governance mechanism for air pollution needs to consider both structural and procedural mechanisms. For a period of time, China's relevant policies and regulations mainly require the establishment and improvement of the structural mechanism of air pollution collaborative governance, and the procedural mechanism should also be given high attention. The failure of such structural mechanisms to achieve the desired effect is often due to the absence or mismatch of a procedural mechanism. The process of improving the structural mechanism of collaborative governance of air pollution prevention and control in the Yangtze River Delta included strengthening the procedural mechanism, and ensuring that each organization in the collaboration is supported by a standardized procedural mechanism. The structural mechanism organizes the collaborative governance, and the procedural mechanism puts it into operation. Only when the structure and process are coordinated can the synergy effect be fully exerted.

Third, the full play of the role of the collaborative governance mechanism still needs to take into account the regional cooperation foundation and trust relationships between local governments, which is a long-term process that cannot be created overnight. The establishment of a structural mechanism usually requires policy support or economic resources, and the construction of procedural mechanism requires social resources. The matching of structural and procedural mechanisms is not a straightforward process and needs to be constantly adjusted in practice. The Yangtze River Delta region has managed to form a relatively complete structural and procedural mechanism due to the geographical proximity and affinity of the participants. Since the 1990s, the Yangtze River Delta region has explored and initiated economic development cooperation mechanisms, and has the organizational contacts, regional trust, and negotiation experience to construct collaborative governance mechanisms for air pollution prevention and control. Historical cooperative arrangements or intergovernmental trust can contribute to the quick construction of a new collaborative governance mechanism, otherwise, it will require a certain period of time.

This study focuses on the collaborative governance mechanism for air pollution in the Yangtze River Delta and its institutional logic, but it has some limitations. First, the analysis is focused on the regional (macro) level, and the explanation of causality is relatively weak. Second, the main data source is the in-depth interview for the operators of collaborative governance mechanism in the Yangtze River Delta, which needs to be conducted with the decision-making officials of the mechanism design. Third, this study focuses on a single case and lacks comparison with other regions. In the future, it is necessary to further deepen the field investigation and material accumulation, and focus on the city level, further explore the operation logic of the collaborative governance mechanism in the Yangtze River Delta region, or conduct regional comparative studies to provide suggestions for collaborative governance mechanism of air pollution prevention and control in China.

## References


Ansell C., and Gash A. (2008). Collaborative Governance in Theory and Practice. *Journal of Public Administration Research & Theory*, 18(4), 543-571(29).

Cai Lan. (2019). Research on Collaborative Governance Mechanism in Guangdong-Hong Kong-Macao Greater Bay Area: from the Perspective of Institutional Collective Action. *Academic Research* (In Chinese), (01), 56-63, 177-178.

Emerson K., Nabatchi T., and Balogh S. (2012). An Integrative Framework for Collaborative Governance. *Journal of Public Administration Research & Theory*, 22(1), 1.

Feiock, Richard C. (2007). Rational Choice and Regional Governance. *Journal of Urban Affairs*, 29(1), 47-63.

________. (2013). The institutional collective action framework. *Policy Studies Journal*, 41(3), 397-425.

Feiock, Richard C., Annette Steinacker, and Hyung Jun Park. (2009). Institutional collective action and economic development joint ventures. *Public Administration Review*, 69(2), 256-270.

Guo Shihong, and Qi Ye. (2016). Construction of Collaborative Governance Model for Air Pollution in Beijing-Tianjin-Hebei Region: Based on the Perspective of Intergovernmental Relationship Theory. *Studies on the Socialism with Chinese Characteristics* (In Chinese), (03), 81-85.

Han Zhaozhu, and Lu Bing. (2017). Research on Inter-Government Cooperation Mechanism of Haze Governance in Beijing-Tianjin-Hebei: From the Perspective of Holistic Governance. *Journal of Tianjin Administration Institute* (In Chinese), 19(04), 73-81.

He Wei, Zhang Wenjie, Wang Shulan, Chai Fahe, Li Hui, Zhang Jingqiao, Wang Han, and Hu Jun. (2019). Effects and Improvement Suggestions on Air Pollution Joint Prevention and Control Mechanism in Beijing-Tianjin-Hebei Region. *Research of Environmental Sciences* (In Chinese), 32(10), 1696-1703.

Jiang Liu, and Yang Long. (2018). Theoretical Study of Institutional Collective Action. *Journal of Inner Mongolia University (Philosophy and Social Sciences)* (In Chinese), 50(04), 96-104.

Mao Chunmei, and Cao Xinfu. (2016). Research into Cross-Regional Collaborative Governance of Pollution: Taking the Yangtze River Delta for Example. *Journal of Hohai University (Philosophy and Social Sciences)* (In Chinese), 18(5), 46-51.

OECD. (2000). Government coherence: the role of the centre of government. Budapest, 2000.

Suo Liming. (2018). The Formation and Evolution of Formal and Informal Collaborative Mechanism among Local Government. *Local Governance Research* (In Chinese), (01), 25-39, 79.

Suo Liming, Kan Yanqiu, and Tu Yimei. (2018). From "Interlocal Cooperation" to "Institutional Collective Action": A Literature Review on Collaborative Regional Governance. *Public Administration and Policy Review* (In Chinese), 7(03), 83-96.

Wang Jinna, Lei Yu, and Ning Miao. (2018). Chinese Model for Improving Air Quality: An Assessment of Action Plan of Air Pollution Prevention and Control. *Environmental Protection* (In Chinese), 46(02), 7-11.

Wang Jinnan, Ning Miao, and Sun Yamei. (2012). Study on Theory and Methodology about Joint Prevention and Control of Regional Air Pollution. *Environment and Sustainable Development* (In Chinese), 37(5).

Wei Na, and Meng Qingguo. (2018). Mechanism and Institutional Logic of Cross-regional Collaborative Governance of Air Pollution: Based on the Cooperative Practice of Jing-Jin-Ji Region. *China Soft Science* (In Chinese), (10), 79-92.

Wu Junwei, and Sun Baiying. (2019). Research on Cross-domain Governance in China: Generation Logic, Mechanism and Approaches. *Administrative Forum* (In Chinese), 26(01), 65-72.

Yang Lihua, and Chang Duofen. (2016) The process, characteristics, problems and suggestions of the system changes of air pollution governance in China. *Expanding Horizons* (In Chinese), (01), 94-100.

Yang Yan, and Sun Tao. (2009). Study on the mechanism of local government co-operation in interregional environmental governance. *China Public Administration* (In Chinese), (01), 66-69.

Yi Hongtao et al. (2018). Regional Governance and Institutional Collective Action for Environmental Sustainability. *Public Administration Review*, 78(4), 556-566.

Yu Yizhen. (2017). Improvement of the Haze Joint Prevention and Control Mechanism: Taking the Yangtze River Delta as an Example. *Journal of Environmental Management College of China* (In Chinese), 27(01), 11-13, 28.

Zhao Xinfeng, and Yuan Zongwei. (2019). The Dilemma and the Path Selection for the Collaborative Governance in Beijing-Tianjin-Hebei Regional Air Pollution. *Urban Studies* (In Chinese), 26(05), 94-101.

9

# Cooperation Willingness, Risk and Partner Selection: A Study on Pan Pearl River Delta in China

Liming Suo, Yanqiu Kan, Jie Ma, and Bin Chen

## Introduction

The development of economic globalization and the prominence of regional governance issues have prompted local governments to break through administrative boundaries and shift from competition state to cooperation in various aspects. A number of domestic cooperation zones and urban agglomerations have been established, such as Beijing-Tianjin-Hebei Region, Yangtze River Delta, Pan Pearl River Delta, Chengdu-Chongqing agglomeration, and corresponding cooperation results have been achieved. Meanwhile, there are still many difficulties in regional cooperation which is led by local governments, such as regional information asymmetry and coordination problems caused by different cooperation preferences. Therefore, how to identify the selection tendency of local government cooperation partners in regional cooperation, break the multiple dilemmas of regional cooperation, and promote regional sustainable development is an important research topic at present.

The subjective willingness of actors and the relationship risk in regional cooperation are the main factors affecting the partner selection, the nature of cooperative relationships, and cooperative interaction behaviors. It is an important variable in cracking the formation of self-organizing policy networks in regional cooperation (Berardo & Scholz, 2010, 632-649). Especially under the framework of institutional collective action (ICA), cooperative motivation is the basis for forming cooperative behavior, and cooperative risk is an important variable influencing the choice of cooperative mechanism. Starting from the motivation of cooperation, the early ICA literature pointed out that the cooperative behavior of local governments was the second-generation rational choice behavior, and the cooperative motivation came from the local government's expectation of the net benefits of cooperation. Such expectation constitutes the subjective will of regional cooperation. However, the subjective willingness of a single actor cannot bring about effective institutional collective action, and the ICA literature has developed the risk hypothesis of regional governance. Feiock built a risk model for regional governance from the perspectives of non-coordination, betrayal, and unfair distribution. It provided hypotheses on the possible relationship between the potential net benefits of cooperation mechanisms and the risks of cooperation (Feiock, 2013). Based on this, Feiock and Shrestha, M. established a corresponding relationship between risk types and the network structure of local government cooperation (Feiock & Shrestha, 2016). Jered B. Carr et al. further examined the perception of risk by individual local government officials and its relationship with cooperative action (Carr, 2017). The research progress of regional cooperation risk under the framework of institutional collective action shows that the focus on inter-governmental relations is not only the study on local behaviors of inter-governmental competition, but also not limited to the regional network structure formed by inter-governmental relations. It is an important direction of regional cooperation research to study the subjective factors and behavioral choices of the behavioral subjects in regional governance.

In recent years, with the promotion of regional cooperation practice in China and the introduction of new research methods, domestic studies have begun to pay attention to the development and evolution law of cooperation behavior itself, including the focus on the subjective tendency of cooperation. Existing research points out that the willingness of local governments to cooperate is an important basis for the implementation of cooperative behaviors among local governments, and the decision of local governments will be affected by individual "subjective factors." Therefore, the strength of the willingness to cooperate between local governments directly affects the level of cooperation (Suo, 2014, 25-29). Lu (2018, 202) further points out that the cooperation willingness is based on cognitive consensus, mutual benefit and trust, which is the intention and desire to jointly invest resources for consensus goals. It plays the role of initiating behavior, reducing costs, removing obstacles, and improving effectiveness in cooperative governance. While the willingness to cooperate influences regional cooperation, scholars have also pointed out the risks and possible sources of regional cooperation, including blind imitation, capabilities differences, institutional barriers, pressure from superiors (Li, 2014, 107-110), nature of cooperation problems, composition and institutional background of regional actors, etc (Cai, 2015, 65-69).

It can be found that the influence of the subjective tendency of cooperation in regional cooperation has been noticed by researchers of regional governance, but there is still a certain distance to explore the relationship between the subjective tendency of choosing regional cooperation objects and the actual cooperation behavior. First of all, the generation of cooperation risk and willingness of regional cooperation are two aspects that influence the selection tendency of cooperative objects in regional cooperation. Subjective will is the expectation of potential cooperation, while cooperative risk is the possibility of cooperation failure. If we only talk about willingness but not risk, the possible cooperation behavior will be exaggerated. If only the risk but not willingness is considered, the definition of risk will lack the basis of individual actors. Secondly, if the research on cooperative propensity is only conducted from the perspective of a single actor, the objectivity of the relationship will be ignored. The researchers of inter-governmental agreement point out that in regional cooperation, local governments are in a series of binary relations (Thurmaier & Wood, 2002, 585-598; Suo et al., 2013, 39-43). That is to say, the actors perform a series of cooperative object selection behaviors in regional cooperation. Therefore, the study of pairwise relationships is more conducive to revealing the objectivity of inter-governmental relationships, which requires the research unit to be extended from actors to pairwise relationships. Thirdly, it is difficult to accurately analyze the possible influence of subjective tendency on behavior if only defining the qualitative strength or level of subjective tendency, which makes it necessary to measure the subjective tendency of inter-governmental cooperation. Finally, in the existing research, regional cooperation is often studied as a whole or a state, while the network structure formed by local governments after many times in regional cooperation is often ignored, which has a direct impact on intergovernmental behavior (Feiock & Shrestha, 2016, 2-27). Then the study of cooperation willingness and risk in specific relationship tendencies must consider specific network structures, such as cooperation tendencies under bilateral or multilateral structures.

Therefore, we attempt to establish a tendency model of local government cooperation object selection and explore the relationship between the cooperation willingness dimension and the cooperation risk dimension of the cooperation tendency, such as how they affect the cooperation tendency, and how to influence the cooperation behavior choice. Based on the conceptual model, we measure the willingness to cooperate and the risk of cooperation presented by the "pair" relationship from the perspective of the text to form an analytical model. Then, we research the specific cooperation object selection tendency and cooperation behavior in Pan Pearl River Delta as a case. Finally, suggestions and possible ways to better promote regional cooperation are proposed.

## Bilateral Cooperation Tendency: Willingness and risks

### Bilateral Cooperation

Our research on cooperation tendencies focuses on the emergence of cooperative relationships in pairs, the bilateral structure proposed by the Institutional Collective Action (ICA) framework (Andrew & Carr, 2012, 709-724). The bilateral structure and multilateral structure in the cooperation network have different degrees of complexity (Feiock, 2013, 397-425), which further affects the object selection tendency of local governments. We select the bilateral relationship structure as the research object.

When local governments choose to take actions or make commitments together with other local governments, bilateral and multilateral collaboration also emerges (Suo et al., 2018, 83-96). Figure 1 illustrates the network of bilateral relations in the process of collaborative governance of local governments. There are three collaborative relationships among the three actors, each of which is independent and limited to the participation of both parties (Suo, 2017, 13).

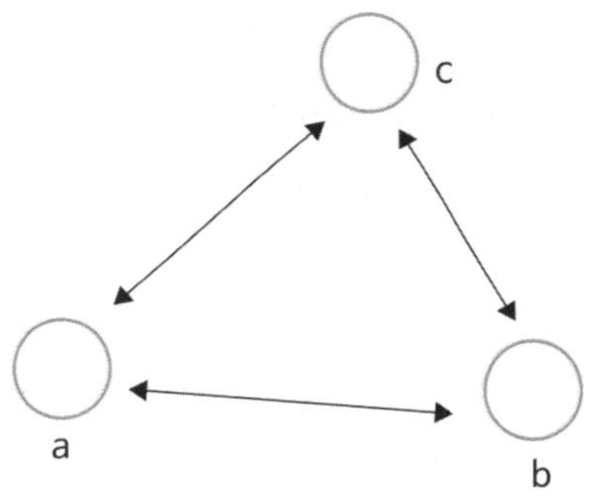


**Figure 1.** Bilateral Network Structure

Source: Created by the author.

After the establishment of bilateral cooperation relationship, based on the principle of reciprocity and minimal cost, the cooperative parties will continuously strengthen this relationship and form a tight binding structure (Suo et al., 2017, 149-172). As a result, the cost of establishing a bilateral relationship is low, but the risk of execution is high. In contrast, bilateral relations can more clearly and directly reflect the tendency to cooperate, because the expression of tendencies will be more directional. From the perspective of bilateral cooperation, which is sensitive to cooperation risks, we make a dynamic analysis on the cooperation tendency logic of local governments in regional cooperation.

## Cooperative Tendency of Local Governments

ICA framework provides a model to explain the mechanism between regional cooperation motivation and cooperative behavior of local governments (Suo et al., 2018, 83-96). The ICA theory holds that as a rational opportunity participant, local governments will have to evaluate the cost benefits of jointly providing public goods or services in regional cooperation. The cooperation benefits of local governments mainly involve collective benefits and selective benefits. Collective Benefit is the benefit of cooperation, including economies of scale, internalized externalities, and spillovers, etc. Selective Benefit includes reputation, trust, status, social capital, etc (Feiock, 2007, 47-63; Feiock, 2013, 397-425). However, the motivation for cooperation is an analysis of a single actor, and the cooperative tendency we put forward on this basis is for a "pair of relationship", which refers to the possibility that a pair of relationship may produce real cooperative behavior or promote cooperative behavior. There are three main characteristics of the tendency of local government cooperation. First, the cooperative tendency is "pairwise." The research is on a pairwise relationship, not the tendency of a single local government, but the relationship between the two. Second, the tendency of cooperation is "directed", which is the nature of the directed relationship of A to B and B to A between A and B. Third, the cooperative tendency is "asymmetric", which means the strength of the directional relationship between A and B is asymmetric, and symmetry is a special case. The tendency to cooperate reflects the possibility of cooperation through the common will and risks of both parties.

## Cooperation Willingness and Risks

In terms of the definition of the cooperation willingness, existing research has emphasized the expected analysis of costs and benefits by actors under the mechanism of cooperation motivation. For example, Bo (2013: 142) points out in her research on China's participation in global climate change governance that the willingness to cooperate is the wish and desire of actors to bear costs and obtain benefits in the process of making or fulfilling international commitments to deal with global problems. According to Wang (2013), willingness to cooperate is the perception of specific cooperative matters and decisions, and cooperative behavior is a choice behavior of cooperative intention. These willingness to cooperate emphasize the unilateral nature of the partners and cannot constitute a relational will for a cooperative relationship. In the relevant literature of ICA, the definition of willingness to cooperate is more specific. The willingness to cooperate refers to the behavioral motivation and decision-making tendency of the collaborators in pursuit of the net benefits of cooperation (Feiock, 2007, 47-63; Feiock, 2009, 356-377; Suo, 2014, 25-29) including whether to cooperate, cooperation objects, and cooperation fields to achieve collective and selective benefits, such as improving the supply efficiency of public goods, realizing the accumulation of social capital and the promotion of influence, and promoting the internalization of externalities. Among them, high willingness means that local governments themselves prefer cooperative development, and have a strong motivation to act as initiator of cooperation. They will actively seek for regional partners. On the contrary, low willingness represents that local governments themselves prefer autonomous development, rather than cooperating with other administrative regions, so there is no strong motivation for them to find potential partners (Suo, 2014, 25-29). We consider that the willingness to cooperate is the strength of willingness of partners to cooperate with each other, which means that the willingness to cooperate is determined by the cooperation motives of both parties in cooperation. In the cooperation tendency, the willingness to cooperate is the dimension of possible positive incentives for cooperation, which can respond to the relative relationship in cooperation.

Factors in the cooperation tendency that may cause non-cooperation or cooperation which cannot continue are risk factors. Coordination risks caused by coordination, distribution and betrayal in regional cooperation are closely related to the selection of bilateral cooperation objects of local governments (Feiock, 2013, 397-425). Specific problems in regional cooperation or the subjective tendency of local governments are crucial in forming solutions to specific ICA problems (Andrew & Kendra, 2012, 514-532; Feiock, 2007, 47-63; Feiock, 2009, 356-377; Maser, 1998, 527-564). Meanwhile, objective factors such as information asymmetry in local government cooperation will lead to an increase in cooperation risks, which exist at all stages of regional cooperation. The cooperation between local governments, from the generation of willingness, taking cooperative actions, to gaining cooperation benefits and continuing to expand, may be interrupted or failed due to risks. High risk means that the cooperation between the two is confronted with the cooperation obstacles caused by excessive transaction costs such as information, negotiation, execution and agency, as well as the cooperation risks caused by poor coordination, abandonment of cooperation and uneven distribution (Feiock, 2009, 356-377), which makes it more difficult to achieve cooperation. Low risk means that there are less obstacles between partners, and there are realistic conditions for establishing cooperation. We still regard the "one pair relationship" as the object to evaluate the cooperation risk, which is also the possibility that the cooperation can not be successful decided by both parties. The two partners may have different cooperation motivations in the cooperation. For example, for both A and B, A is very enthusiastic about establishing a cooperative relationship with B, but B is extremely indifferent to the establishment of the cooperative relationship with A, which brings huge uncertainty to the possible cooperative relationship between the two parties. In terms of assessing the workability of cooperation, this is a negative incentive of cooperation tendency. In other words, the larger the difference of cooperative motivation between a pair of relationships, the greater the risk and the smaller the possibility of cooperation.

Cooperation object selection refers to the measurement of partners based on cooperation risks, costs and benefits. The degree of cooperation risk and the level of transaction cost will also affect the partner's choice of relationship type. Feiock points out that the difficulty of measuring the supply of public goods in cooperation, the degree of geographical proximity and the homogeneity of cooperative objects will all affect the choice of cooperative mechanism by the collaborators. Regardless of the risk, actors tend to choose cooperation mechanisms with high returns and low transaction costs. However, the more cooperative members, the higher the probability of motivation conflict and policy preference inconsistency, which increases the coordination cost and cooperation risk. It can be seen that the consistency of preferences and interest goals is crucial for local

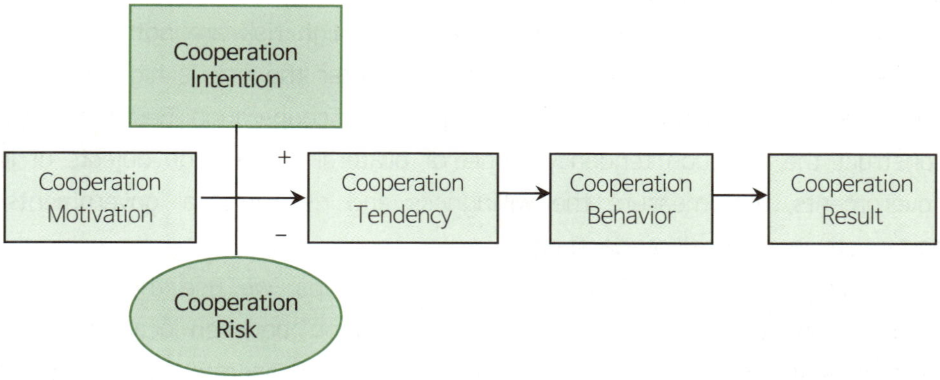


**Figure 2.** Cooperative Tendency Logic based on "Will-risk"

Source: Created by the author.

government cooperation. Therefore, as for the trend of cooperation, local governments can express the cooperation motivation through leaders' speeches, work reports, party congress documents, special documents and other policy texts, and form different degrees of cooperation willingness and risk in the expression of paired cooperation motivation.

## The Cooperation Tendency Model

### Measurement of Cooperation Willingness and Cooperation Risk

Based on our definition of cooperation tendency and the relationship between cooperation willingness and cooperation risk, then the measurement of willingness and risk become the main problem for our study of cooperation tendency. We propose that the greater the gap in the willingness of local governments to cooperate, the higher the risk of cooperation. As a result, it can be inferred that a relationship of high willingness and low risk is more likely to achieve cooperation between local governments and achieve greater results. On the contrary, conditions of low willingness and high risk are not conducive to cooperation between local governments. No matter the risk is high or low, low willingness is not conducive to the development of cooperation. Based on this, we construct the selection tendency model of bilateral cooperation objects of local governments, and measure the willingness and risk of local governments to participate in regional cooperation.

Since we are studying pairwise relationships, we use the sum of the subjective expressions of "motivation for cooperation" between local governments to represent the strength of the willingness to cooperate in a cooperative relationship. However, considering the large number of cooperative relationships among members in a holistic cooperative network, we also need to characterize it, so we define the "high and low" states of cooperation willingness. The formula is as follows:

$$T_{ij} = X_{ij} + X_{ji} - \overline{W}$$

$$\overline{W} = \frac{1}{c_n^2} \Sigma_{ij,\ i \neq j} (X_{ij} + X_{ji})$$

In the formula, $T_{ij}$ represents the willingness to cooperate between each pair of local governments, $X_{ij}$ stands for the number of times that the local government I mentions the local government J. $X_{ji}$ mentions the number of times that the local government J mentions the local government I. But for the sake of standardization and considering the relativity of willingness values, we introduce $\overline{W}$, which is the mean of the sum of the times that local government I and J mention each other. If $T_{ij}$ is more than 0, it indicates that the willingness to cooperate with each other is higher, increasing the possibility of cooperation. In contrast, if $T_{ij}$ is less than 0, it means that i and j are less willing to cooperate with each other, and the possibility of cooperation is also lower.

The "cooperation risk" among local governments is mainly expressed by the difference in the subjective expression times of "cooperation motivation", and also by the qualitative classification of the relative relationship with the mean value, which is expressed as "high and low" risk. The formula is as follows:

$$M_{ij} = |X_{ij} - X_{ji}| - \overline{R}$$

$$\overline{W} = \frac{1}{c_n^2} \Sigma_{ij,\ i \neq j} (X_{ij} - X_{ji})$$

In the formula, $M_{ij}$ represents the cooperation risk between both local governments, $X_{ij}$ stands for the number of times that the local government I mentions the local government J, $X_{ji}$ stands for the number of times that the local government J mentions the local government I. $\overline{R}$ is the mean of the sum of the times that local government I and J mention each other. If $M_{ij}$ is more than 0, it indicates that the cooperation risk between i and j is higher, decreasing the possibility of cooperation. In contrast, if $M_{ij}$ is less than 0, it means that the cooperation risk between i and j is lower, increasing the possibility of cooperation.

## The Model of Local Government Cooperation Tendency

According to the combination of cooperation willingness and risk of local government, we divide regional cooperation into four basic patterns (Figure 3), and construct the cooperative tendency model of local government, including "high willingness and low risk" mode, "high willingness and high risk" mode, "low willingness and low risk" mode, and "low willingness and high risk" mode. These models represent different states of bilateral cooperation between local gov-

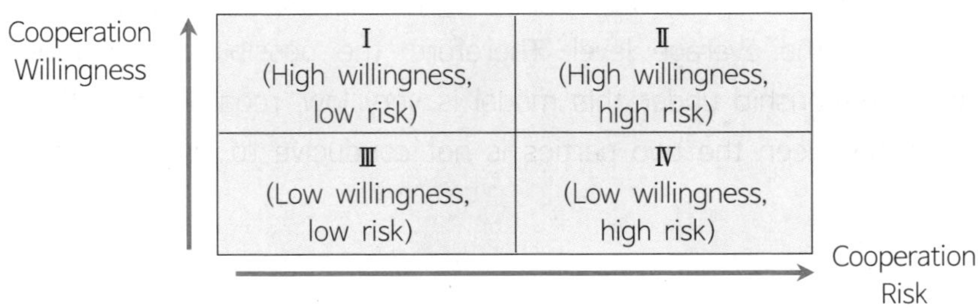


**Figure 3.** Combination Model of Cooperation Willingness and Cooperation Risk

Source: Created by the author.

ernments.

The "high willingness and low risk" mode means that local governments have a strong willingness to cooperate with each other, and the willingness between them is almost the same, which reduces the cooperation risk. Local governments are more inclined to actively seek cooperation, which also reflects the practical needs of establishing cooperative relations between the two sides. In this mode, the probability and efficiency of cooperation between local governments will be greatly improved, thus ensuring the effective implementation of bilateral cooperation projects.

In the mode of "high willingness and high risk", a local government usually has a strong desire to cooperate unilaterally, with a huge gap between the two places. However, the probability of establishing cooperative relationship between the two places is still high due to the active efforts of one side. On the other hand, this mode is less stable than other situations due to the great difference in the willingness of both sides, which is not conducive to the sustainable development of regional cooperation.

Under the mode of "low willingness and low risk", the local governments of the two sides have no strong willingness to cooperate with the same preference and do not have favorable conditions for establishing cooperative relations. However, the degree of political, economic and cultural homogeneity between the two parties will further promote the cooperation.

The "low willingness and high risk" mode mainly refers to that the willingness of local governments of one party to cooperate is significantly higher than that of the other party, but the willingness of both parties to cooperate is still lower than the average level. Therefore, the possibility of establishing a cooperative relationship under this model is very low, regardless of the level of homogeneity between the two parties is not conducive to cooperation.

# Case Study of the Pan Pearl River Delta

## Case Overview and Data Sources

First, the basic situation of Pan Pearl River Delta. In 2003, with the initiative of Guangdong Province and the support of the eight provincial governments of Fujian Province, Jiangxi Province, Hunan Province, Guangxi Province, Hainan Province, Sichuan Province, Guizhou Province, Yunnan Province and the governments of Hong Kong and Macao Special Administrative Regions, the Pan Pearl River Delta regional cooperation was vigorously promoted and achieved results significantly. The Pan Pearl River Delta Regional Cooperation Zone has distinct regional characteristics and is the main representative of China's regional cooperation (Ma et al., 2014, 79-92). Compared with the Yangtze River Delta and Beijing-Tianjin-Hebei, the Pan Pearl River Delta Regional Cooperation Zone is one of the largest economic cooperation zones, with obvious scale characteristics in terms of geographical scope and economic aggregate, accounting for 1/5 of the national area, 1/3 of the population and 1/3 of the national economic aggregate (excluding Hong Kong and Macao) (Table 1). The development of the Pan Pearl River Delta regional cooperation has aroused widespread interest among regional governance scholars, mainly focusing on the areas and methods of Pan Pearl River Delta cooperation (Chen and Liu, 2007, 42-50), the direction of regional governance, the path of innovation (Zhang, 2008, 351-357; Peng, 2008, 102-105), and exploring the regional integration transformation from the construction of the Guangdong-Hong Kong-Macao Greater Bay Area (Zhang, 2018, 58-65).

Second, the data source. We use quantitative research on policy texts. In recent years, quantitative research on policy literature has provided a new analytical approach for studying inter-governmental relations (Huang et al., 2015). Among them, the government work report is an important source of current quantitative research on public policy (Ren et al., 2017). We select the Pan Pearl River Delta as the research area. The mention of other provinces in the government work report of each province reflects its tendency to adopt cooperative behavior. Besides, the cooperation agreement is an important form of regional

**Table 1.** Comparison of Three Major Cooperation Zones (2016)

| Region | Land Area (10 thousand km$^2$) | National Proportion (%) | Population (million) | National Proportion (%) | GDP (100 billion) | National Proportion (%) |
|---|---|---|---|---|---|---|
| Yangtze River Delta | 21.07 | 2.19 | 254.52 | 18.4 | 149.24 | 20.07 |
| Beijing-Tianjin-Hebei Region | 21.8 | 2.27 | 111.58 | 8.06 | 74.61 | 10.03 |
| Pan Pearl River Delta | 192 | 20.00 | 494.31 | 35.75 | 239.21 | 32.2 |
| Nationwide | 960 | 100 | 1,382.7 | 100 | 743.585 | 100 |

Source: Sorted out by the author according to the database of the National Bureau of Statistics.

cooperation and reflects the actual trend of regional cooperation (Zeng, 2015). As for the data on the trend of cooperation, it comes from the number of mentions of the Pan Pearl River Delta Region in the work reports of 11 provincial and regional governments from 2003 to 2015. Among the researches on the co-operation behavior of local governments, we use inter-governmental bilateral agreements, specifically the data of 247 bilateral agreements in the provinces and regions within the Pan Pearl River Region from 2003 to 2015. The data is extracted and sorted out from the official website of "9 + 2" cooperation zone (Pan Pearl River Delta Cooperation Information Network www.pprd.org.cn). On this basis, we have studied the network and domain characteristics of Pan Pearl River Delta inter-governmental agreement (Ma et al., 2014, 79-92; Chen et al., 2015, 1-11).

Third, the description of Pan Pearl River regional cooperation attitude. We can extract the identity and concern of each local government to "Pan Pearl River Delta" from the work reports of governments. According to the government work report, in the early days of the establishment of the Pan Pearl River Delta, the overall regional cooperation tended to be high, and received positive responses from various provinces and regions. The "Pan Pearl River Delta" was also mentioned the highest number of times. While the number of times that "Pan Pearl River Delta" was mentioned in the later period gradually decreased, and the focus shifted to the provinces in the region. Among them, Guangdong Province,

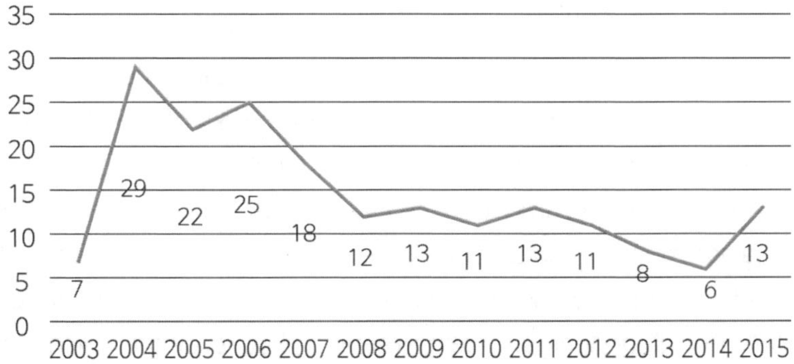


**Figure 4.** Vertical Change in the Number of Times that "Pan Pearl River Delta" is Mentioned

Source: Created by the author on the basis of the data of the Pan Pearl River Delta government work reports from 2003 to 2015.

Guangxi Province, Yunnan Province and other places mentioned "Pan Pearl River Delta" most often.

Guangdong Province leads the start and promotion of Pan Pearl River Delta regional cooperation, and points out in the government work report that: The cooperation and development of Pan Pearl River Delta region has expanded the hinterland of Guangdong's sustainable economic development. While Guangxi Province proposes to actively participate in domestic regional cooperation, and strengthens cooperation between Guangdong Province and Guangxi Province as the focus of participating in the Pan Pearl River Delta regional cooperation. The remaining provinces and autonomous regions have expressed active participation in the Pan Pearl River Delta regional cooperation. On the whole, the Pan Pearl River Delta Region has a strong recognition of "Pan Pearl" as a cooperation zone, which provides a strong realistic support for our subsequent analysis of the cooperation tendency of various provinces.

## Overall Cooperation Tendency of the Pan Pearl River Delta

The provincial government work reports basically reflect their willingness and behavioral tendencies in regional cooperation. First of all, the expression of willingness and the summary of practice in the local government work report are both important. The government work report not only contains the existing cooperation progress and results, but also includes cooperation plans with specific provinces and regions. Local governments often illustrate their cooperation intentions in official annual summary reports. For example, Sichuan Province proposes to "deepen cooperation and development with neighboring provinces and regions such as Guizhou Province and Chongqing City." Guangdong Province proposes to "promote the construction of the Spark Industrial Belt with Guangxi Province, Jiangxi Province, Fujian Province and other regions." In government work reports, most provinces and autonomous regions also mention the willingness and achievements of cooperation in transportation construction, poverty alleviation, and economic and trade relations. It reflects the trend of increasing areas of cooperation in the Pan Pearl River Delta Region and continuing to advance.

Meanwhile, the content of the government work reports also reflects the overlap and nesting of multiple regions. A number of small circle layers have been formed within the Pan Pearl River Delta Region, and various provinces and regions have cooperated to establish multiple economic cooperation zones and industrial belts. Among them, there are urban agglomerations including the Pearl River Delta, the Greater Pearl River Delta, and Chang-zhu-Min, other economic zones, such as the Hengqin Economic Cooperation Zone, Beibu Gulf Economic Zone, Guangfo Zhao (Huaiji) Economic Cooperation Zone, and Jiangxi Marginal Co-operation Experimental Zone. Industrial parks such as the Fujian-Guangdong Central Soviet Area Cooperative Construction Industrial Park are also included. The provinces and regions in the Pan Pearl River Delta have also established close cooperative relations with other regions, such as Hainan Province and Yunnan Province, which have indicated that they will expand cooperation with the Yangtze River Delta, the Bohai Rim, and the Beijing-Tianjin-Hebei region. This results in the cooperation state of size nesting within regions and intersections between regions. Through social network analysis tools, we make a network analysis of the cooperative tendency of the number of times that the provinces and regions of the Pan Pearl River Delta mentioned other provinces from 2003 to 2015. In order to show the mention of provinces and regions more clearly, according to the number of mentions in each province and region, we determine the direction of the connection. In other words, the network connection arrow points from the party with the lowest number of mentions to the party with the highest number of mentions, which means that in a pair of relationships, we use a one-way network to indicate the direction of cooperation. For instance, if Guangxi Province points to Guangdong Province, it means that Guangxi Province mentions Guangdong Province more often than Guangdong Province mentions Guangxi Province, then we consider this pair of relationships as a tendency of Guangxi Province to point to Guangdong Province.

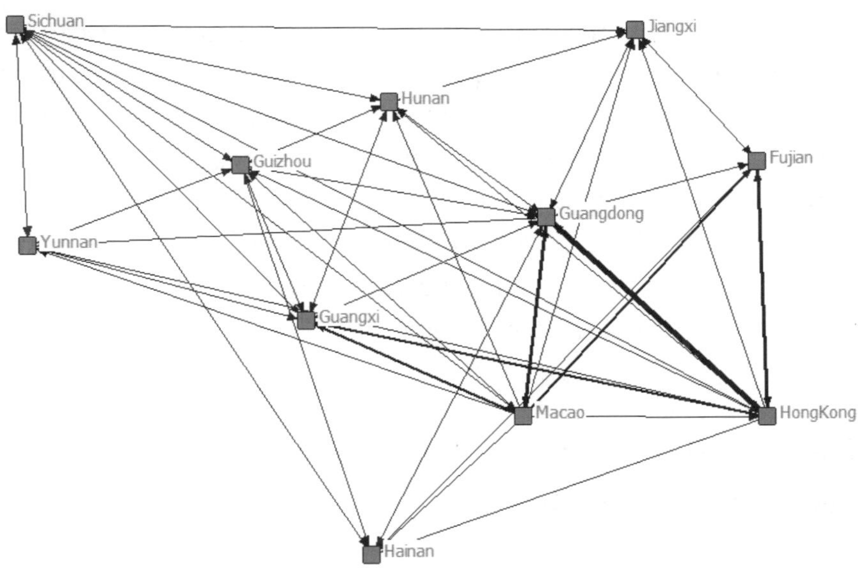


**Figure 5.** The Network Diagram of the Number of Times that Provinces in the Pan Pearl River Delta Region Metion Each Other

Source: Created by the author.

Overall, the mentions of the provinces and regions in the Pan Pearl River Delta Region show an unbalanced state, and the network structure formed by the mentions of each other is not fully connected network (Figure 5). Except for Guangdong Province, Hong Kong, and Macao, the other provinces and regions have not formed a fully connected relationship. Adjacent provinces and regions are more closely connected and mention each other more frequently. It is found that that Hong Kong is mentioned most frequently by other provinces and regions, followed by Macao and Guangdong Province. While Hainan Province is the least mentioned, followed by yunnan.The number of times that Jiangxi Province is mentioned by other province is lower than the number that itself mentions others. Sichuan Province has been mentioned more often because of the earthquake and other natural disasters involving counterpart assistance.

In addition, the government work report cannot exclude the influence of political characteristics and other factors. For instance, the mainland provinces and autonomous regions in the Pan Pearl River Delta Region express their gratitude to Hong Kong and Macao in their annual government work reports. Sichuan Province has received support from other provinces due to natural disasters such as the earthquake, increasing the number of times that Hong Kong, Macao and Sichuan Province are mentioned. To reduce the interference,we exclude the content of thanks in the government work reports. In consequence, although the content of the government work reports on regional cooperation is very limited, the government work reports basically reflect the selection tendency of the cooperation objects of local governments.

## The Regional Distribution of Cooperation Tendency and Inter-governmental Agreement

We analyze the cooperation tendency through the frequency of mutual mentions in the government work reports of the Pan Pearl River Delta Region from 2003 to 2015, and measure the cooperation tendency among provinces and regions according to the above formula. The status of the cooperation tendency includes the following four types (Figure 6, Table 2).

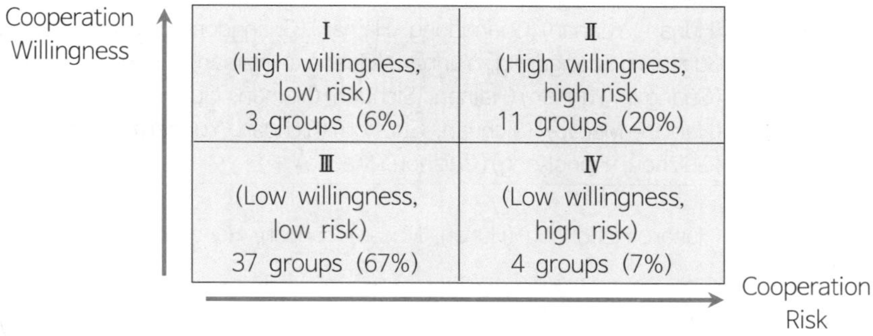


**Figure 6.** Distribution of Bilateral Cooperative Relationship Tendency among Provinces and Regions in Pan Pearl River Delta

Source: Created by the author.

From the distribution of the tendency of bilateral cooperation relations among the provinces and regions in the Pan Pearl River Delta, in all the 55 bilateral directional relationships, the "low will and low risk" combination accounts for 67%, the proportion of "high will and high risk" combination is 20%, the percentage of "low will and high risk" combination is 7%, and the proportion of "high will and low risk" combination is 6%. It can be inferred that the overall tendency of Pan Pearl River Delta regional cooperation reflected in the government work report is low.

**Table 2.** The Combination of Cooperation Willingness and Cooperation Risk of Provinces and Regions in Pan Pearl River Delta

| | |
|---|---|
| I (High willingness, low risk) | (Guangxi, Guangdong) (Guangxi, Guizhou) (HongKong, Macao) |
| Ⅱ (High willingness, high risk) | (Fujian, Jiangxi) (Fujian, HongKong) (Fujian, Macao) (Jiangxi, HongKong) (Guangdong, HongKong) (Guangdong, Macao) (Hainan, HongKong) (Guangxi, HongKong) (Guangxi, Macao) (Sichuan, HongKong) (Sichuan, Macao) |
| Ⅲ (Low willingness, low risk) | (Fujian, Hunan) (Fujian, Guangdong) (Fujian, Guangxi) (Fujian, Hainan) (Fujian, Sichuan) (Fujian, Guizhou) (Fujian, Yunnan) (Jiangxi, Hunan) (Jiangxi, Guangdong) (Jiangxi, Guangxi) (Jiangxi, Hainan) (Jiangxi, Sichuan) (Jiangxi, Guizhou) (Jiangxi, Yunnan) (Jiangxi, Macao) (Hunan, Guangdong) |

| | |
|---|---|
| | (Hunan, Guangxi) (Hunan, Hainan) (Hunan, Sichuan) (Hunan, Guizhou) (Hunan, Yunnan) (Guangdong, Hainan) (Guangdong, Sichuan) (Guangdong, Guizhou) (Guangdong, Yunnan) (Guangxi, Hainan) (Guangxi, Sichuan) (Guangxi, Yunnan) (Hainan, Sichuan) (Hainan, Guizhou) (Hainan, Yunnan) (Hainan, Macao) (Sichuan, Guizhou) (Sichuan, Yunnan) (Guizhou, Yunnan) (Guizhou, HongKong) (Guizhou, Macao) |
| Ⅳ (Low willingness, high risk) | (Hunan, HongKong) (Hunan, Macao) (Yunnan, HongKong) (Yunnan, Macao) |

Source: Created by the author.

There are only three groups of "high willingness and low risk" combination: Guangdong Province and Guangxi Province, Guangxi Province and Guizhou Province, Hong Kong and Macao. From the perspective of specific cooperation practices, from 2003 to 2015, Guangxi Provine and Guangdong Province had the closest cooperation relationship, reaching 35 bilateral and multilateral agreements. Guangxi Provinve has repeatedly mentioned the construction of the "Guangdong-Guangxi Interprovincial Pilot Cooperation Special Zone", while Guangdong Provinve has mainly mentioned the strengthening of economic and trade activities with Guangxi Provinve and its counterpart assistance. The cooperative relationship between Guangdong Province and Guangxi Province is mainly the type of assistance. Guizhou Province and Guangxi Province maintain a relatively close cooperative relationship, with a total of 6 bilateral agreements reached, and the relationship between the two is complementary type. The cooperation content between the two provinces is mainly focused oneconomic and trade exchanges, transportation construction, and planning and construction of cooperative experimental zones. On the other hand, the type of the relationship between Hongkong and Macao is the shared type. They have shown a strong sense of sharing and co-building in the infrastructure construction and the connection of public services, and have reached 7 bilateral agreements.

There are 11 groups of "high willingness and high risk" combinations, most of which include Hong Kong and Macao, typically Hong Kong, Macao, Fujian Province, Hong Kong Province, Macao and Guangxi Province. Mainland provinces and regions have shown a strong willingness to cooperate with Hong Kong and Macao. For example, Fujian Province has repeatedly mentioned strengthening cooperation with Hong Kong and Macao in logistics and finance. Guangxi Provinceand Jiangxi Province attached importance to the economic and trade cooperation with Hong Kong, and Guangdong Province had more extensive cooperation with Hong Kong and Macao. However, Fujian, Guangxi, Guangdong and other inland provinces and regions mentioned Hong Kong and Macao far more frequently than Hong Kong and Macao mentioned these provinces. Even Hong Kong and Macao have never mentioned some inland provinces in the government work reports for more than10 years. As a result, some provinces in the mainland, Hong Kong and Macao showed a high willingness and high risk.

There are 37 groups of "low will and low risk" combinations, all of which are inland provinces, including Guangdong Province, Guangxi Province and other inland provinces such as Hunan Province, Guizhou Province and Sichuan Province. According to the agreement data, Guangdong Province and Guangxi Province had a high degree of centrality in the Pan Pearl River Delta regional cooperation. While in the government work report, because Hong Kong and Macao raised the average of the number of mentioned times, other provinces and autonomous regions in the Mainland, Guangdong Province and Guangxi Province showed a low willingness and low risk. The number of times that Sichuan Province, Yunnan Province, and Guizhou Province mention each other was low, and the cooperation of these provinces was mainly focused on infrastructure construction. Fujian Province and Hunan Province, Hainan Province and Sichuan Province, Jiangxi Province and Macao mentioned each other very few times and did not show a strong willingness to cooperate.

There are 4 groups of "low willingness and high risk" combination: Hunan and Hong Kong and Macao, Yunnan Province and Hong Kong and Macao. Hong Kong and Macao have never mentioned Hunan Province and Yunnan Province. At the same time, Hunan Province and Yunnan Province only mentioned abstractly "strengthening regional cooperation and exchanges with Hong Kong and Macao", which illustrated that Hunan Province, Yunnan Province, Hong Kong and Macao had no positive willingness to cooperate. Hunan Province had 6 bilateral agreements with Hong Kong and Macao, and Yunnan had only 1 bilateral agreement with Hong Kong. Of the 11 provinces and autonomous regions in the Pan Pearl River Delta Region, Hunan Province and Yunnan Province did not appear in the high-will combination, reflecting the low motivation of the two provinces to participate in regional cooperation.

By dividing the number of bilateral agreements in Pan Pearl River Delta with the number of different types of provincial and regional combinations, we can calculate the average number of agreements generated by each pair of relationships. The order of different types of combinations from high to low is: "high willingness and low risk" (16 aggreements), "high willingness and high risk" (11.4 aggreements), "low willingness and low risk" (1.8 aggreements), and "low willingness and high risk" (1.7 aggreements). In regional cooperation, the actor cooperation agreements, and the number of cooperation areas are positively correlated with the willingness to cooperate, and negatively correlated with the risk of cooperation (Andrew and Carr, 2012, 709-724). In other words, the combination of "high willingness and low risk" leads to more cooperation areas and more cooperation agreements. The cooperation area under the combination of "low willingness and high risk" is very limited and cooperation lacks substantive content. From the number of actual cooperation agreements, the number of agreements generated by the combination of "high willingness and high risk" is much larger than that of "low willingness and low risk", indicating that the impact of willingness on the cooperation agreement will be greater than the impact of risk on the agreement. So the establishment of bilateral agreement depends more on the strong desire of both parties, and the sum of the strong desires can make up for the risk of incoordination caused by their differences.

## The Field Distribution of Cooperation Tendency and Inter-governmental Agreement

Do different levels of cooperation tend to have different distribution of cooperation areas, or do certain relationship structures prefer to be formed in certain areas? We divide 247 bilateral agreements into environmental governance, tourism, science, education, culture, labor, transportation, medical care, and economic and trade fields. Then combine the bilateral agreement with the "will and risk" cooperation tendency model to analyze the actual cooperation performance between two provinces and regions with different types of cooperation tendency (Figure 7).

As can be seen from the figure below, first, there is high degree of cooperation in environmental governance, science, education and culture, tourism, economy and trade in the Pan Pearl River Delta Region. Second, in the cooperative relationship of the "high willingness and low risk" combination with the highest tendency of cooperation, environmental governance, tourism and economic trade are the key contents of regional cooperation. Regional public issues such as environmental governance need the active participation of local governments. At the same time, the benefits of tourism and economic and trade fields are higher when the risks are low. Third, in the combination of "low willingness and high risk" with the lowest tendency of cooperation, the number of agreements jointly participated by provinces and regions is very small, and the relative participation in the fields of science, education and culture is relatively high. In the combination of "high willingness and high risk", science, education and culture, economy and trade are the cooperation areas with the highest participation. In the combination of "low willingness and low risk", each province attaches the most importance to tourism, science, education and culture, and labor service, Fourth, in general, regional cooperation among provinces and regions in the two combinations of high willingness covers all fields, while cooperation in tourism, labor service and medical care is excluded in the combination of "low willingness and high risk." There are more cooperation related to science, education and culture in high-risk combinations, mainly due to the participation of Hong Kong, Macao and other regions.

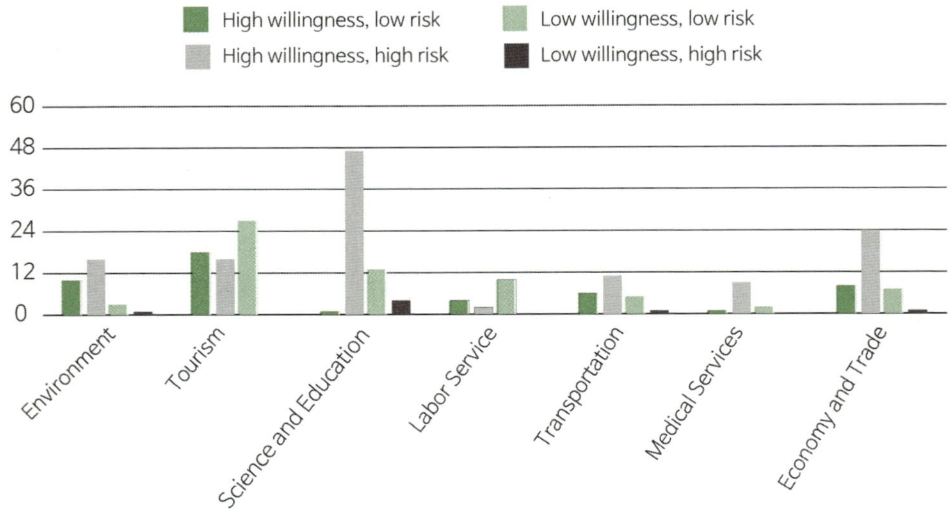


**Figure 7.** The Number of Agreements in Different Fields for the Relationship of Different Cooperation Tendencies

Source: Created by the author based on the number o bilateral agreements from 2003 to 2015.

## Conclusion and Discussion

### Findings

We try to expand the analysis of individual cooperation motivations into two-way cooperation tendencies, constructing a model of local government cooperation tendencies under the combination of "will and risk", and use the practice of bilateral cooperation in the Pan Pearl River Delta as an example. The study found several points as below:

First of all, from the distribution of cooperative tendency combinations, since willingness has a positive effect on cooperative tendency and risk has a negative effect, the combination of "high willingness and low risk" has the most cooperative tendency. Conversely, the combination of "low willingness and high risk" is the most unfavorable to cooperation, with the other two in the middle. From the "Pan Pearl Delta" case, we found that of the four combinations of tendencies, the two combinations with the most cooperative tendencies and the least non-cooperative tendencies are the least in all bilateral relations, with only 3 pairs and 4 pairs, respectively. Most of them are in the middle of the two combinations, of which the combination of "low willingness and low risk" is the largest, accounting for two-thirds of the entire bilateral relationship in Pan Pearl River Delta, indicating that the cooperation tendency formed among members is a risk aversion strategy based on a weak willingness.

Secondly, from the perspective of the actual inter-governmental agreement, although the combination of "high willingness + low risk" is very few in the relationship pair, the amount of agreement output is much higher than other combinations, indicating that the influence of willingness on cooperation is higher than the impact of risk on cooperation. At the same time, judging from the average number of different types of agreements for each group, no matter whether the risk of cooperation is high or low, low willingness is not conducive to cooperation, illustrating that the sum of the overall bilateral cooperation motivations has a greater impact than the difference between them. Therefore, in regional and bilateral cooperation, the key factor for local governments to consider when choosing a partner is the strength of the willingness to cooperate, followed by the risk of cooperation.

Thirdly, from the perspective of the actors characteristics of cooperation tendency combination, in the cooperative relationship of "high willingness and low risk" and "low willingness and low risk", the economic and social development level of the two parties is close to each other, but the geographical proximity is not significant. In other words, the cooperation tendency of low risk will occur between regions with high economic and social development level.On the contrary, in the cooperative relationship tendency of "high willingness + high risk" and "low willingness + high risk", the actors have large differences in regional economic and social characteristics and are not geographically adjacent. In other words, the provinces with large differences in economic and social level are more likely to have unstable cooperation.

Fourthly, from the perspective of advancing the practice of regional cooperation, current domestic regional cooperation has achieved outstanding achievements, but the fluctuation of cooperation risks indicates that there are still many difficulties in regional cooperation, such as poor communication and co-ordination mechanisms, asymmetric information, strong specificity of investment in specific cooperation areas, increasing speculative risks and monitoring costs, obvious regional differentiation characteristics, inconsistent preferences, etc. It is very easy for situations such as low willingness to cooperate and large differences in willingness to cooperate, which is not conducive to substantial progress in regional cooperation. Therefore, to effectively promote the cooperation tendency, on the one hand, the establishment and maintenance of the spatial planning and risk coordination mechanism of the cooperation zone should be emphasized, on the other hand, the optimization and selection of local government cooperation partners should be emphasized, too. For local governments, when establishing a bilateral relationship, more consideration should be given to the possible co-operation motivation of the other party and the cooperation risk of the relationship.

## Research Prospects

The cooperation tendency of local government is an important issue of regional governance. Due to the limitations of research conditions and space, there are still many deficiencies in this article, which can be studied as further research topics in the future.

First, about the research on the interaction between subjective cooperation tendency and objective conditions, institutional collective action gives an analysis framework with transaction costs and risks as the key dimensions. However, we only focus on the risks and the possible tendency caused by the subjective incoordination, and more consideration should be given to the transaction costs and other objective factors affecting the transaction costs, such as the co-operation capacity of local governments, the homogeneity of local economic and social development and policy planning.

Second, about the research on the relationship between multilateral cooperation relations and the tendency to cooperate, we have only focused on the bilateral agreements generated in regional cooperation. In further research, the impact of the tendency to cooperate on the number, distribution, and field of multilateral agreements can be further considered.

Third, about the research on the relationship between the individual characteristics of actors and cooperative behaviors, we only focus on the co-operative relationships of relationship pairs, without considering the performance of actors in multiple two-way relationships, such as being followed by many other local governments but rarely paying attention to the others at the same time. Therefore, it is necessary to define the types of actors and then analyze the cooperative network among different types of actors.

## References

Andrew, S. A., & Carr, J. B. (2012). Mitigating Uncertainty and Risk in Planning for Regional Preparedness: The Role of Bonding and Bridging Relationships. *Urban Studies*, 50(50), 709-724.

Andrew, S. A., & Kendra, J. M. (2012). An Adaptive Governance Approach to Providing Disaster Behavioral Services. *Disasters: The Journal of Disaster Studies*, 36(3), 514-532.

Berardo, R., & Scholz, J. T. (2010). Self-Organizing Policy Networks: Risk, Partner Selection, and Cooperation in Estuaries. *American Journal of Political Science*, 54(3), 632-649.

Bo Yan. (2013). Cooperative Will and Cooperative Capacity: A New Framework for Analyzing China's Participation in Global Climate Governance. *World Economics and Politics*, 1, 135-155.

Cai Lan. (2015). Research on Institutional Collective Action Framework to Solve the Dilemma of Regional Cooperation. *Seeker*, 8, 65-69.

Carr, J. B., Hawkins, C. V., & Westberg, D. E. (2017). An Exploration of Collaboration Risk in Joint Ventures: Perceptions of Risk by Local Economic Development Officials. *Economic Development Quarterly*, 31(3), 210-227.

Chen, B., Suo, L., & Ma, J. (2015). A Network Approach to Interprovincial Agreements: A Study of Pan Pearl River Delta in China. *State & Local Government Review*, 47(3), 1-11.

Chen Ruilian, & Liu Yaping. (2007). Cooperation and Innovation of Pan Pearl River Delta Regional Government. *Academic Research*, 1, 42-50.

Feiock, R. C. (2007). Rational Choice and Regional Governance. *Journal of Urban Affairs*, 29(1), 47-63.

________. (2009). Metropolitan Governance and Institutional Collective Action. *Urban Affair Review*, 44(3), 356-377.

________. (2013). The Institutional Collective Action Framework. *The Policy Studies Journal*, 41(3), 397-425.

Feiock, R. C., & Shrestha, M. (2016). Local Government Networks,The Oxford Handbook of Political Networks. *Oxford University Press*, 8(4), 2-27.

Huang Cui, Ren Tao, & Zhang Jian. (2015). Policy Documents Quantitative Research: A New Direction for Public Policy Study. *Journal of Public Management*, 12(2), 129-137, 158-159.

Li Hui. (2014). The Expectation and Challenge of Cooperation Among Local Governments in Regional Integration: Taking the Synergy Theory as the Analytical Framework. *Social Science Journal*, 1, 107-110.

Lu Wenchao. (2018). Effective Cooperation Willingness of Local Government under Regional Coordinated Fevelopment: A Case Study of Beijing-Tianjin-Hebei Coordinated Development. *Gansu Social Sciences*, 2, 201-208.

Ma Jie, Suo Liming, & Chen Bin. (2014). From Collaborative Zone to Collaborative Network: Structure, Pathway and Evolution: The Analysis 191 Intergovernment Agreements in "9+2" Zone. *China Soft Science*, 12, 79-92.

Maser, S. M. (1998). Constitutions As Relational Contracts: Explaining Procedural Safeguards in Municipal Charters. *Journal of Public Administration Research and Theory*, 8(4), 527-564.

Peng Chunhua. (2008). Review on Regional Cooperation in Pan Pearl River Delta. *Lingnan Journal*, 5, 102-105.

Ren Tao, Huang Cui, & Su Jun. (2017). Approaches and Trends of Public Policy Documents Research. *Chinese Public Administration*, 5, 96-101.

Suo Liming. (2014). Research on Regional Cooperation Model of Local Governments in China: From the Perspective of Institutional Analysis. *Reform of Economic System*, 2, 25-29.

________. (2017). Collaborative Governance Betwork of Local Governments in Urban Agglomeration: Motivation, Constraint and Change. *Research on Local Governance*, 2, 13-26.

Suo Liming, Kan Yanqiu, & Tu Yimei. (2018). From "Interlocal Cooperation" to "Institutional Collective Avtion": A Literature Riview on Collaborative Regional Governance. *Public Administration and Policy Review*, 3, 83-96.

Suo Liming, Ma Jie, & Chen Bin. (2017). Bilateral Cooperation and Multilateral Coordination in Regional Environmental Governance: Based on the Analysis of the Pan Pearl River Delta Agreement from 2003 to 2015. *Fudan Public Administration Review*, 1, 149-172.

Suo Liming, Yang Feng, & Liu Jun. (2013). Policy Networks and Interlocal Collaborative Governance: Local Governments Collaboration Practice in China. *Chinese Public Administration*, 1, 39-43.

Thurmaier, K., & Wood, C. (2002). Interlocal Agreements as Overlapping Social Networks: Picket-Fence Regionalism in Metropolitan Kansas City. *Public Administration Review*, 62(5), 585-598.

Wang Gelin, & Lu Qian. (2013). The Paradox between Willingness and Behavior:

Factors Influencing Farmers' Willingness to Cooperation and Real Payment Behavior on Small-scale Irrigation Facilities in Rural Communities. *Journal of Huazhong University of Science and Technology (Social Science Edition)*, 27(3), 68-75.

Zeng Jingjing. (2015). Policy Textual and Quantitative Research on the Pan Pearl River Delta Regional Cooperation: 2004-2014. *Chinese Public Administration*, 7, 110-116.

Zhang Jingen. (2008). On Regional Cooperation from View of New Regionalism in the Pan Pearl River Delta. *Wuhan University Journal (Philosophy & Social Sciences)*, 61(3), 351-357.

__________. (2018). On the Transformation of Regional Integration of Guangdong-Hong Kong-Macao Greater Bay Area. *Academic Research*, 7, 58-65.

10

# Interagency Relationship within the Collaborative Governance Model in the Prosecution of Corruption in Indonesia

Azwar Abubakar and Eko Prasojo

## Introduction

Corruption is a complex and multidimensional phenomenon (Zhang and Lavena, 2015, xiv). In 2017, Transparency International ranked Indonesia 90th of 176 countries in Corruption Perception Index (Transparency International, 2017). In Indonesia, corruption, collusion, and nepotism have been pervasive in all elements of public administration, including the various levels of bureaucracy, the executive branch, the legislative branch, the judicial branch, the political parties, law enforcement, and the private sector. The significant number of regents, mayors, governors, and ministers involved in corruption cases proves this claim. Members of the House of Representatives (Dewan Perwakilan Rakyat: DPR) and Regional Representatives Council (Dewan Perwakilan Dareah: DPD), Regional House of Representatives (Dewan Perwakilan Rakyat Daerah: DPRD), and Constitutional Court (Mahkamah Konstitusi) are among the government official involved in corruption cases. Additionally, corporations commit bribery to benefit their businesses, and members of the law enforcement officer have committed corruption and punished through the judicial system.

In the context of law in Indonesia, there are several institutions that could be refer to as law enforcement, but this article is limited to law enforcement agencies in prosecuting corruption cases, namely the Corruption Eradication Commission (Komisi Pemberatasan Korupsi: KPK), the Indonesian National Police, and the Attorney General of Indonesia. The investigators on duty at the KPK consist of independent investigators who are recruit directly by the KPK and members of the police and public prosecutors assigned.

The involvement of the law enforcer in criminal acts of corruption has aggravated the current effort towards corruption eradication in Indonesia. Of the three major agencies authorized to prosecute corruption, only the KPK hasn't had any of its members involved in corruption cases. According to KPK's records, since its establishment, 43 individuals from within the environment of its judicial institutions have been proven to have committed corruption. Out of those 43 perpetrators, 15 were judges, 11 were advocates, seven were registrars, seven were prosecutors, and three were of Police background. Nawawi (2012) stated that corruption is a political factor contributing to the decline in the level of trust in the government. Thus, we assert that the corruption in Indonesia, which has resulted in assorted legal problems, increase public distrust in corruption case handling.

Many factors are responsible for the poor execution of corruption eradication in Indonesia: (1) the public's permissive attitude towards criminal acts of corruption; (2) corruption eradication policies that have emphasized the prosecution of corruption over the prevention of corruption; (3) the absence of a government system to provide consistent protection for the public against fraud and a level of transparency that would enable the public to get involved in the supervision of public funds; (4) the dearth of national leaders promoting corruption eradication; (5) the poor functioning of the Government Internal Control System (SPIP); and (6) the absence of synergy and interdepartmental rivalry among agencies or institutions responsible for corruption eradication.

Some instances of conflicts involving law enforcement agencies are evident in conflicts between the KPK and the Police as well as between KPK and the Attorney General. In 2009, the KPK was in conflict with the Police because the

KPK was deemed to have tapped the phone conversations of the Chief of the Indonesian National Police's Criminal Investigation Agency, Susno Duaji. The Police were of the opinion that the tapping was not performed according to the official procedure (Hidayat, 2015). In early 2015, the KPK and the Police were again in conflict when the KPK established the then-Police chief candidate Corm. Gen. Budi Gunawan as a suspect in an alleged gratification case during his office as the Head of the Career Development Bureau. Both cases garnered public interest and were known as the Lizard versus Crocodile cases.

The Law No. 20 of 2001, the Eradication of Criminal Act of Corruption, firmly states that widespread corruption inflicts losses to state finances and constitutes a violation of the social and economic rights of the general public; thus, corruption should be classified as a crime and extraordinary measures must be implemented to eradicate corruption. The current efforts to eradicate corruption rely on multiple related institutions, instead of a single institution, which is in line with the literature; for example, Poochaoren (2014, 15) maintained that collaboration might produce better anticorruption work effectiveness. Collaboration can be effective in efforts to eradicate corruption, that is, through collaboration: (1) anticorruption institutions can share knowledge, expertise, and information pertaining to anticorruption programmes through joint planning, implementation, and evaluation of anticorruption strategies; (2) learning across organisations, sectors, and nations can be accelerated; (3) novel values and definitions can be promoted; and (4) sustainable changes in the political will to combat corruption can be facilitated. Accordingly, to combat the ever-widening spread of corruption across all elements of the public administration, corporations, and the society, corruption eradication should be executed in a collaborative manner. Regarding the prosecution aspect, the collaboration of the involved institutions is expected to create a prosecution system that results in effective deterrent against corruption.

Collaborations should be conducted by all institutions, including institutions previously involved in conflicts and institutions whose members were involved in criminal acts of corruption. Conflicts and involvement in corruption significantly affect the collaborative process. Thus, in this research, we attempted to answer the following question:

How are prosecution agencies related to each other within collaborative governance model and does their relationship affect the corruption eradication in Indonesia?

## Literature Review

### Collaborative Governance

Ansell and Gash (2008) define collaborative governance as a governance arrangement in which one or more government institutions directly involve stakeholders outside the government in formal, agreement-oriented and consultative joint decision-making processes and aims to make or implementing public policies or running public programs or assets. This definition emphasizes six important criteria: (1) Forums are initiated by public agencies or institutions; (2) Participants in the forum include actors outside the government; (3) Participants are directly involved in decision making and not merely consulted by government agents; (4) Forums are officially organized and meet collectively; (5) Forum aims to make decisions by consensus (although consensus is not reached in practice); (6) The focus on collaboration is on public policy and public management.

Emerson et al. (2012) in a broad sense define collaborative governance as he processes and structures of public policy decisions making and management that engage people constructively across the boundaries of public agencies, levels of government, and/or the public, private and civic spheres in order to carry out a public purpose that could not otherwise be accomplished. Emerson's definition provides opportunities for collaborative governance to be use as a broader analytical construction in public administration and allows for differentiation between different applications, classes and scales.

Collaboration is different from coordination and cooperation. The difference lies in the nature of the goals of cooperation and the forms of their dependence.

Coordination and cooperation are the efforts of organizations from different parties to achieve common goals with static goals. Relations between organizations in coordination and cooperation are independent. In collaboration, all parties work together and build consensus to reach a decision that results in benefits for all parties.

According to Peters, in collaborative cooperation, the principal-agent relationship does not apply because the collaboration that occurs is cooperation between participant and participant (Dwiyanto, 2010). In such cooperation, each party involved in the collaboration still has its own autonomy. Collaborating parties are principals and act as agents for themselves. They agreed to work together because they had the same vision and goals to be realized together which might be difficult to achieve when each of them worked alone.

During the process of partnership/collaboration (collaborative process), the collaborating organization can negotiate to combine expectations and build commitment to joint activities. Organizational participation will continue or mutually beneficial commitments if joint activities are carried out reciprocally. Conversely, if there is no mutual collaboration, then participants will reduce their commitment and end the collaboration. Negotiation skills are very important and determine the sustainability of cooperation/partnership programs. If the two collaborating parties have no communication error, then there is no reason for either party to terminate the collaboration.

One critical component of the term collaborative governance is governance. Lynn, Heinrich, and Hill (2000) interpret broadly as "regimes of laws, rules, judicial decisions and administrative practices that limit, determine, and activate the provisions of public support of goods and services publicly." Instead, Stoker (2004) argues; as a basic definition it can be taken that governance refers to the rules and forms that guide collective decision making. Governance is not about making decisions by an individual, but more about groups of individuals, organizations, or systems that make decisions. He also suggested that among various interpretations, there is a basic agreement that "governance" refers to the development of a governance style in which the boundaries between and within the public and private sectors are blurred.

Although many forms of collaboration involve strictly non-governmental actors, the definitions of Ansell and Gash set specific rules for public institutions. By using the terminology "Public Agency", the intention of Ansell and Gash to include public institutions such as bureaucracy, courts, members of parliament and other government institutions both at central and regional levels. By using the term public agency, the aim is to include public institutions, such as bureaucracy, the judiciary, the legislature, and other government bodies at the local, state, and federal levels. Although public institutions are usually observers or initiators of collaborative governance, in the definition of collaborative governance requires participation by non-state stakeholders (Ansell and Gash, 2008). Non-state stakeholders will have real responsibility for the impact of policies so that non-state stakeholders must be directly involved in the entire policy making process.

Smith (1998) argues, "Collaboration includes representatives of all related interests." The term "stakeholder" refers to the participation of citizens as both individuals and groups of organizations. In this definition, the intended stakeholders are public organizations and stakeholders outside the public organization. In addition, this form of government also emphasizes that there are representations of all relevant interests. This definition also emphasizes the opportunity for discussion between stakeholders and in this matter; stakeholders must meet in the deliberation process and be multilateral in nature.

Based on the explanation above, it can be understood that collaborative governance is a process of governance regulation that involves not only government actors, but actors outside the government actively so as to create a division of responsibilities between the factors through official processes and consensus-oriented in the context of implementing public policy.

## Corruption Eradication

Corruption is usually defined as the abuse of public power for personal gain. Personal benefits associated with receiving money or valuable assets, including facilities for family and friends (Lambsdorff, 2007). Public power or authority is exercised by bureaucrats, politicians in various sectors in their positions, such as courts, procurement of public goods and services, business arrangements and licensing, privatization, foreign exchange (including customs, trade licenses and international financial transactions), taxes (including tax returns and excise), police, subsidies, public facilities (water, electricity, telephone, garbage collection) and government services (health and education).

Corruption is a favourite exchange between two actors, agents and clients Agents are given trust with authority from superiors. The leader delegates the task to his subordinates and sets the rules for how this task is fulfilled. Agents should serve clients according to the rules. Bribery, extortion, embezzlement and fraud in the public sector are variations of corrupt habits. In the case of bribery, the client acts as a bribe and makes payments (also called kick back, baksheesh, sweetener, pay off, speed or grease money) to the agent, which is then called the recipient of a bribe. As a reward, clients get benefits such as services or permits that are not entitled to be obtained. Agencies use force, violence or threats in an effort to obtain payment, while embezzlement is a simple theft of public resources. Without client involvement, disobedient agents steal from the leadership. Bribery, extortion, and embezzlement result in rules from betrayed superiors and the interests of hurt leaders (Lambsdorff, 2007).

Corruption-free world is associated with public services that intend to serve the public, have self-motivation in themselves, incentives, threats of punishment, and pressure lurking. Poochaoren (2014) classifies aspects of anti-corruption work into three, namely: punishment or prosecution of corruption, preventing corruption, and encouraging public awareness of corruption. The aspects of punishment or prosecution include responses to complaints, monitoring and investigation by intelligence, gathering evidence, managing cases, recovering assets, and updating laws. Prevention aspects include a code of ethics, a transparent procurement process and financial system, public audits and reporting, asset announcements, protection against whistle blowers, laws on conflicts of interest, and studies. Meanwhile, to encourage public awareness, activities that can be carried out include the provision of public information, education and assistance, official training, knowledge sharing, campaigns through various conventional and social media.

## Methods

The research approach we employed was a qualitative approach. Data was collected using a mix of secondary data collection and in-depth interviews. In the first step, we collected strategic and statistic data from public documents relevant to corruption eradication made available by the government and private agencies. In the second step, we analysed the secondary data and conducted in-depth interviews with several informants, law enforcers, ministry/agency officers, non-governmental organisation officers, and academics to create an outline of the data we obtained regarding corruption eradication, notably in the prosecution stage. Both steps generated data describing factors relevant to interagency relationships. To the ensure validity and reliability of field findings, we used triangulation, peer review, and reference methods.

## Results

In the prosecution of corruption in Indonesia, the factors affecting interagency relationship are consistent with the factors mentioned by Ansell and Gash (2008). We also discovered novel effects of the collaborative process used in the prosecution of corruption in Indonesia, namely, the integrity of the police and attorney, and the leadership style of the law enforcement agencies. These new factors play a part in the relationships among the agencies prosecuting corruption in Indonesia disabled full employment of the collaborative governance model proposed by Ansell and Gash.

According to the relationships we analysed based on the factors mentioned by Ansell and Gash (i.e., starting conditions, institutional design, collaborative process, and outcome) and two ancillary factors (i.e., stakeholder integrity and leadership style), we classified the relationships between agencies prosecuting corruption in Indonesia into five categories: cooperation, competition, conflict, non-use of cooperation opportunity, and the absence of relationship.

Mooi (2007) stated that cooperation is normally characterized by the presence of relational exchange. Relational exchange is the exchange of the expectation of behaviour and covers information exchange, solidarity, and flexibility in a relationship. Information exchange, as a norm, refers to the free provision of information, despite no direct advantage derived by the information providers from such exchanges. Solidarity is a norm for collectively solving individual and public issues. Flexibility, as a norm, refers to the expectation of the parties willing to adapt to condition changes. Cooperation, in combating corruption in Indonesia, refers to inter-organization information exchange with a guarantee that the reputation of the organizations providing the information is not disturbed. Furthermore, information exchange is successful when each party refrains from taking advantage of the information exchanged. Regarding corruption eradication administration, cooperation is established through human resource exchange.

Competition has traditionally occurred in adjacent local units, and information on the performance of all units is readily accessible. Such information leads to comparison, and comparison results in pressure to operate on par with other units that are more efficient (Ostrom et al., 1961). Competition may lead to conflict. Competition for resources and success results in rivalry over a 'win.' Conflicts can be reduced through interest negotiation or by finding a method for collaboration. In the Indonesian context, different corruption eradication institutions compete with each other to demonstrate faster performance and a greater number of case prosecutions in relation to certain culprits.

A conflict is the perception of a network member that her or his goal is hindered by another party (Mooi, 2007). When collaborating, a conflict occurs when the parties involved disagree over goals, expectations, perspectives on strategies and tactics, and efforts to protect or expand partner control of collaboration outcomes (Bryson et al., 2006). Gray (in Bryson, 2006) explained that the preeminent source of conflict is power, which has distinct phases. Furthermore, Gray (1996) observed that power, as the key source of conflict, varies according to phases and circumstances. Bryson et al. (2006) added that differences in two organizations' statuses can worsen their conflict, and these differences included organization size, funding, and reputation. The organization with weaker power requires assurance that its interests will be considered. Therefore, collaborators must provide consideration regarding placing all participants in equal positions by providing education on the concept, information, and tools that facilitate collaboration.

Corruption eradication institutions in the prosecution field may facilitate the exchange of information or human resources between organizations, with a guarantee that the reputation of the organizations providing the information will not face repercussions. In the fifth pattern, absence of relationship, an institution does not establish cooperation, and based on the governing laws and regulations, this institution is not allowed to engage in relationships of any form.

Prosecution is a corruption eradication strategy associated with the downstream side. In Indonesia, three law enforcement institutions are directly involved in prosecution: the KPK, the Indonesian National Police, and the Attorney General of Indonesia. The KPK and the Attorney General of Indonesia have the authority to conduct preliminary investigations, investigations, and prosecutions. Additionally, the KPK has the authority to coordinate and supervise the two other institutions. The dynamics in the relationship among the three law enforcement agencies involve occasional competition and conflicts. In the majority of cases, conflicts occur when the esprit de corps or professional pride of a law enforcement officer is offended, for example, when the KPK manages a corruption case involving another law enforcement officer. In response to such an event, the Police have sometimes taken advantage of their expansive authority and have prosecuted the KPK chief, which increased the intensity of the conflict. Figure 1 presents the interagency relationship pattern in the prosecution of corruption in Indonesia.

The figure above illustrates the pattern of interagency relationships between government institution in term of prosecuting corruption cases. There are 5 patterns that can be mapped based on factual conditions that occur in Indonesia, namely cooperation, competition, conflict, non-use of cooperation opportunity. The first three patterns — cooperation, competition, and conflict — are general patterns and terminology that are often discussed to show the existence of collaborative processes. Meanwhile, the last two patterns are the conditions that exist that were found to show that no collaborative process occurred.

In Figure 1, the dominating pattern of interagency relationship in the

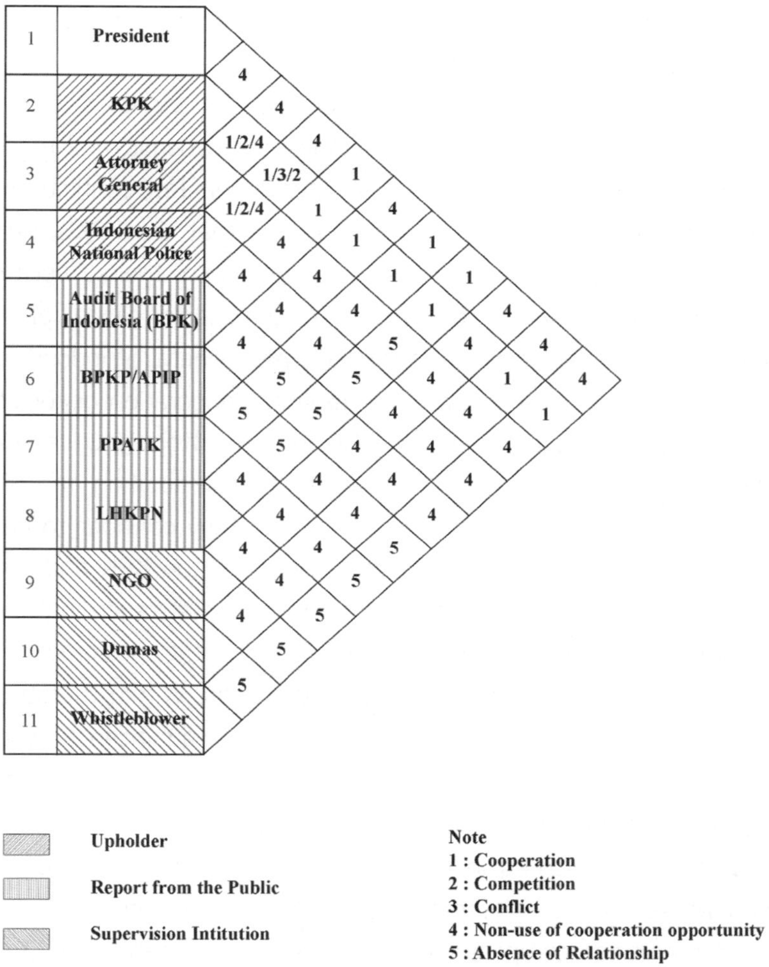


**Figure 1.** Pattern of Interagency Relationship in the Prosecution of Corruption in Indonesia

prosecution of corruption in Indonesia is the fourth pattern: non-use of co-operation opportunity. The KPK, the Indonesian National Police, and the Attorney General of Indonesia share similar authorities: to conduct preliminary investigations and investigations on criminal acts of corruption. The KPK and the Attorney General also have an additional authority, which is to perform prosecution. This similarity in their responsibilities requires cooperation; however, the three institutions are frequently involved in conflicts regarding who receives a case of the criminal act of corruption.

In practice, the relationships between the KPK and the Attorney General of Indonesia and between the KPK and the Police are dynamic, and the KPK and the Attorney General of Indonesia have been involved in few conflicts. However, the Attorney General apparatus has the perspective that the KPK's performance in combating corruption receives more attention than theirs. Furthermore, the Attorney General apparatus believes that the performance of the KPK is incomparable to the performance of the Attorney General of Indonesia because of imbalances in facilities and support. The existing cooperation opportunity is rarely used in the relationship between the KPK and the Attorney General of Indonesia because there is no mutual trust between the two. In addition, the officers of the Attorney General's office have a level of integrity they consider to be inadequate.

The effort to increase cooperation between the KPK and the Police has been made through the use of notification letters regarding investigations; however, this effort has been deemed to exhibit insufficient compatibility, causing the cases reported to be partial instead of thorough. Within the structure of the Police, the division in charge of corruption is of a magnificent size because it is part of an investigation division, namely, the criminal investigation division. Notably, no guarantee has been made that all members of such units have adequate integrity, resulting in the KPK's reluctance to cooperate. This situation has been worsened by an internal issue of the Police, namely, a meagre budget to manage corruption compared with the size of the organisation. The Police also often experience interventions from superiors at the province or regency level. Additionally, the relationship between the Police and the Attorney General in the management of corruption cases is not at its best because the P21 files submitted by the Attorney General to the Police after the investigation process is completed are repeatedly returned because of incompletion. This can hinder cooperation because of the difficulty caused by the Police; thus, a procedure that allows for a clearer process is required.

The Audit Board of Republic of Indonesia (Badan Pemeriksa Keuangan: BPK) as an external auditor and the Finance and Development Supervisory Agency

(Badan Pengawas Keuangan dan Pembanungan: BPKP) and Government Internal Audit Agency (Aparat Pengawasas Intern Pemerintah: APIP) as internal auditor have not provided data for law enforcement officers because they are afraid that the data will be used by parties they perceive to have no integrity. Similarly, the Indonesian Financial Transaction Reports and Analysis Centre (Pusat Pelaporan dan Analisis Transaksi Keuangan: PPATK) has not proactively provided data for law enforcers, except for the KPK. The society and whistle blowers have greater confidence in the KPK than in the other law enforcement agencies.

## Discussion

Relationships between the law enforcement agencies and other supporting agencies involved in the prosecution of criminal acts of corruption have yet to be well-established, and competition and conflicts have occurred in the establishment of the relationships. This situation has led to poor cooperation between the law enforcement agencies and the other agencies. Prosecution has been mostly partial rather than thorough. Additionally, the number of cases exposed and handled is utterly below the potential number of corruption cases occurring in Indonesia. The KPK's practice of hand-catch operations (OTTs) in catching perpetrators has increased the public's trust in the KPK and reduced the public's trust in other state agencies and institutions, earning KPK the strongest trust compared with other state institutions in the effort to combat corruption.

The three law enforcement agencies involved in corruption eradication—KPK, the Indonesian National Police, and the Attorney General of Indonesia—are recurrently involved in competition and conflicts. Such relationships affect the effort to combat corruption and society's trust in state agencies. The results of a survey of public trust conducted by the Polling Center in collaboration with a nongovernmental anticorruption agency, Indonesia Corruption Watch, demonstrated that 86% of respondents considered the KPK to be the most trustworthy agency and most needed agency by Indonesian public today (nasional.tempo.co, 2017). Additionally, the House of Representatives, the private sector, and the political parties have earned the least trust from the public. In the same survey, regarding the factor of trust, political parties earned 35%, the private sector earned 49%, and the House of Representatives earned 51% trust (TEMPO, 2017).

In comparison with the Attorney General of Indonesia and the Indonesian National Police, the KPK the earned the highest public trust. This result is consistent with the results of a survey conducted by Indo Barometer in 2015: the Indonesian National Police earned 56.6% trust, the Attorney General of Indonesia earned 53.5% trust, and KPK earned 82% trust (kompas.com, 2015). According to these results, the KPK is the institution that the public trusts most. This level of trust is related to the corruption eradication strategies of the KPK. The high number of prosecutions conducted by KPK is the main reason for the high level of public trust in KPK.

In Ansell and Gash's model (2008), a leader is a determinant of collaborative governance, acting as a facilitator and mediator. Additionally, in the corruption prosecution collaboration, a facilitative leader is an initiator and role model. A leader in the prosecution of corruption is required to break the deadlock hindering collaboration caused by conflicts and asymmetry. In terms of the stages of collaborative the process, we observe differences between the collaborative governance model proposed by Ansell and Gash and the model implemented in the prosecution of corruption in Indonesia.

Other differences are observed in the variables and sequencing applied in the collaborative process. After the collaboration initiation by the leader, the first step is holding face-to-face dialogues that are modest and about issues of mutual concern. The outcome of the face-to-face dialogues is the Grand Strategy containing the law enforcement agencies improvement strategies and strategies of prosecuting corruption.

After the Grand Strategy is formed, plans to increase trust and law enforcement officer's integrity should be implemented, and the formulation of the prosecution standard operating procedure (SOP) should be conducted. The law enforcement officer's integrity improvement is carried out in the quantity, integrity, competency, and independence aspects, enabling the law enforcement officer to work with other supporting agencies, for instance PPATK, BPK and APIP. The trust building is carried out through the participative formulation of prosecution strategies containing SOP for the handling of corruption cases involving members of law enforcement agencies.

### *Starting Conditions*

The starting conditions of corruption eradication in Indonesia are influenced by asymmetry and conflicts that serve as incentives and constraints to participating in the corruption eradication collaboration. Asymmetry is divided into authority asymmetry, resource asymmetry, and infrastructure asymmetry. Conflicts in corruption eradication are related to stakeholder integrity and the leadership style. Both factors can serve as incentives or constraints in the corruption eradication collaboration.

In essence, the differences in authority, human resources infrastructure, and budget between law enforcement agencies may serve as incentives to participate in the collaboration because they complement each other. The Attorney General has insufficient financial resources and the KPK has insufficient human resources. Thus, the KPK can assist the Attorney General in managing unhandled cases and the Attorney General's human resources can assist with the KPK's case handling duties. The three law enforcement agencies can collaborate, especially in the use of tapping data in the corruption prosecution process. Notably, we observe in the current corruption eradication efforts in Indonesia that rivalry is caused by the asymmetry and each law enforcement agency's confidence that it will be able to eradicate corruption independently is affected. Thus, a leadership style that can realise a collaboration in human resources management, budget allocation, authority, facilities, and infrastructure is required.

In the context of differences in the authority and infrastructure in tapping, the three law enforcement agencies can conduct prosecution collectively with the information gathered from the tapping conducted by the KPK. This step can be used as a strategy for prosecution if the integrity of the three law enforcement agencies is equal. The tapping results can also be used in the prevention of corruption in a given sector. The results of the KPK's tapping can be used to review the budgeting process undertaken by the House of Representatives and the goods and service procurement tender process undertaken by the National Public Procurement Agency (Lembaga Kebijakan Pengadaan Barang Jasa: LKPP).

Such information can be used to improve the goods and service procurement process involving the House of Representatives. Additionally, the Police can use the results of the KPK's tapping to expand the scope of preliminary investigations. With the existing various cooperation opportunities, tapping can be used as a tool of supervision that provides agencies the sense of being supervised and the encouragement to improve.

In the context of human resources asymmetry, the internal allocation of human resources is carried out based on the needs arising in the corruption case handling. The massiveness of corruption cases in Indonesia implies that the corruption eradication in Indonesia requires human resources from law enforcement agencies, including the Indonesian National Police, the Attorney General of Indonesia, and KPK, in a considerable number. To manage the human resources asymmetry, uniform knowledge capacity between the KPK and other law enforcement agencies should be established. The personnel exchange between the KPK and other law enforcement agencies over a given time span should be accompanied by improvements in the compensation system, independence, competency, work arrangement of human resources, supervision, and infrastructure, enabling the maintenance of the integrity of the former the KPK member.

The asymmetry between law enforcement agencies may create collaboration with strengthened coordination and supervision functions for the KPK. The facility that can be built to facilitate such strengthening is an accurate and holistic database of the handling of corruption cases. Moreover, a follow-up must be conducted regarding the report provided by the Police and the Attorney General to provide the two agencies a sense that their case handling is being supervised. The investigators involved in the coordination and supervision functions should be of a certain rank if they are from the Police and of a certain level if they are from the Attorney General to overcome the problem of seniority within the law enforcement agencies.

### *Leader as a Facilitator Role Model*

A facilitative leader is required to serve as an initiator in creating collaboration in the prosecution of corruption in Indonesia. The necessity for a leader in the corruption eradication programme in Indonesia is regarded as crucial because of the massive amount of corruption that involves the law enforcement officer and reducing the law enforcement officer's integrity. A leader is expected to provide facilitation and act as a role model in combating corruption.

Currently, the KPK is regarded as the only agency able to initiate collaboration because the KPK is authorized to conduct supervision and coordination. However, these roles cannot be maximized because the communication strategy applied by the KPK is considered unsuitable. The OTT carried out by KPK against some institutional leaders shows that the potential of interagency communication has yet to be maximized, and this affects some institutions involved in the cooperation to combat corruption. Additionally, the communication style used in handling corruption cases involving the law enforcement officers through media publications may affect image and pride of such agencies. Announcing a corruption case involving the law enforcement officers through mass media may also damage the reputation of, and public trust in, the law enforcement agencies.

A facilitative leader and role model should not be from a law enforcement agency involved in corruption eradication because of the insufficient number of individuals from the internal organ of the law enforcement agencies eligible to be a leader. This situation comes about due to their conflict history, experience, and limited capability to use their authority. Therefore, a facilitative leader in corruption eradication collaboration should be from outside the law enforcement agencies and have the authority to coordinate the law enforcement agencies and other ministries/institutions relevant to the corruption eradication. Thus, the individual eligible to act as a leader is the president. To play this role, the president can delegate authority to the vice president or the ministry in charge of corruption eradication, who has a structurally higher position than law enforcement agencies, to be a facilitative leader.

Corruption is a fundamental topic for Indonesia. Hence, the effort to eradicate corruption cannot be entrusted exclusively to the KPK or another agency. The absence of the president's contribution in corruption eradication may weaken other agencies' intentions to collaborate in the corruption eradication. To be a leader in corruption eradication, the president must make an enduring, continuous commitment.

Corruption eradication has no central head; thus, the president, the head of state and head of government, is necessary to influence the agencies. Other than the president, the only ministry capable of managing corruption eradication in Indonesia is the Coordinating Minister of Political, Legal, and Security Affairs, because this position coordinates the institutions involved in corruption eradication actions.

### *Face-to-Face Dialogues*

Face-to-face dialogues comprise the first stage of establishing collaboration with output in the form of the Grand Strategy for corruption eradication in Indonesia. The dialogues are conducted gradually, starting with dialogues between the facilitative leader and the law enforcement officer, followed by dialogues between the facilitative leader and the law enforcement officer as well as other supporting institutions involved in the prosecution. In this case, the facilitative leaders are from all governmental levels. These face-to-face dialogues are held with the law enforcement officer to build trust, which must start with the stakeholders with a history of conflict so that the law enforcement officer has the confidence to implement the agenda derived from the face-to-face dialogues. This trust increases because through the dialogues, each law enforcement officer acknowledges its obligations and expectations regarding the performance of such obligations.

Overall, these face-to-face dialogues discuss the main tasks and functions, the structured common targets, and the trajectory of the improvement to achieve the structured common targets. These dialogues become vital in the trust-building process because by discussing the main tasks and functions, the agencies involved recognize the obligations of each agency, and by discussing the collectively set targets, they recognize the actions that must be taken and the expectation regarding the performance of each agency. The obligations of each agency are determined based on the National Strategy for Corruption Prevention and Eradication (Stranas PPK) and KPK Strategic Plan. The knowledge regarding the main tasks, functions, and expectation of each agency also encourages coordination between agencies because each agency knows which stakeholders can be invited to cooperate in the exercise of its obligations and in the fulfilment of the president's expectation of the agencies.

Additionally, in formulating the Grand Strategy, the alignment of the values, beliefs, and perspectives of stakeholders is critical to the discussion to obtain foundations and uniform improvement pace. This perspective is related to the understanding of the position of state agencies collectively and affects the perspective of the agency regarding itself and other agencies. The Grand Strategy formulated shall not contradict the relevant legislation; thus, it does not cause hindrances at the operational level and can depict the aspirations of all agencies, creating a consensus and acknowledgement of the roles of each agency. The Grand Strategy also clearly lists the sources of funding for the implementation of the Grand Strategy.

In particular, the face-to-face dialogues between the facilitative leader and the law enforcement officer are held mainly to discuss prosecution matters, including the handling of corruption cases involving members of the law enforcement officer and internal improvement. In case of handling the case that involving members of other law enforcement agencies, these dialogues discuss the standard operating procedures that enabling the prosecution to be carried out accountably and providing a deterrent effect to the aforementioned the law enforcement officer while maintaining the reputations of the agencies. Moreover, these face-to-face dialogues discuss the steps that must be taken to create general synergy between the three law enforcement agencies in the prosecution.

In the context of internal improvement, the discussion focuses on the improvement of the law enforcement officer's integrity because this is a key factor to establishing collaboration between the law enforcement agencies. After the facilitated meetings, informal face-to-face meetings can also be initiated the by KPK or the other law enforcement agencies. Formally, communication can be initiated by the KPK because this agency has the authority to conduct coordination and supervision. These discussions may formulate the collective handling of some cases, enabling a clearer work division in the handling of every case.

The second strategy contained in the Grand Strategy is integrity improvement, including the improvement of human resources integrity and the improvement of institutional integrity, so as to make the institutions more independent from interventions and more agile when collaborating with other law enforcement agencies. The improvement in human resources integrity occurs when law enforcement agency integrity as a whole is on-going, which takes a longer period of time. The group of human resources whose integrity has been improved may work directly with the law enforcement officers from other law enforcement agencies. Thus, the portion of human resources that has completed the improvement process can improve the cooperation without having to wait for the improvement of all law enforcement officer.

The Grand Strategy also contains the Strategy for the Prosecution of Criminal Acts Involving Members of Law Enforcement Agencies. Regarding prosecution, OTT is conducted as a tool of self-improvement for an agency from which a member is arrested, and this is no longer perceived as a corruption eradication achievement. OTT is also used to prosecute criminal acts of corruption that significantly harm the state's financial condition.

### *Trust Building and Commitment Between Agencies*

Three factors can build trust: communication, integrity improvement, role improvement, and the absence of competition. For example, trust is built between the KPK and the Police, between the Police and the Attorney General, and between KPK and the Ministry of Administrative and Bureaucratic Reform as a preventative measure. Collaboration in corruption eradication in Indonesia may be established by building trust. The trust building resulted from the communication in the face-to-face dialogues and from the integrity improvement conducted by stakeholders. Trust can be built through integrity improvement because some inspecting institutions are reluctant to provide the inspection results data to avoid the misuse of opportunities for the interest of certain parties. Thus, only after the integrity is improved and the SOP is formulated can trust be built. The improvement in integrity and the formulation of prosecution SOP are performed based on the Grand Strategy resulting from the face-to-face dialogues.

The Attorney General and the Police have the culture of patronage that inhibits collaboration between law enforcement agencies. Moreover, we observed problems in the independence of the two agencies because of less transparency and less accountable career development. Thus, trust is built through internal improvement. First, the internal improvement encompasses improvements related to integrity, quantity, competency, and independence, enabling cooperation with other law enforcement agencies (KPK, the Indonesian National Police, the Attorney General of Indonesia, PPATK). This improvement emphasized integrity improvement because this factor is a key factor for collaboration in corruption eradication. Internal improvement is formulated in a conceptualized, structured, and systematic manner in the law enforcement agencies. This improvement is made in fields prioritized to handle criminal acts of corruption. Thus, the law enforcement agencies must have adequate integrity and competency, have increased independence, and be provided with sufficient facilities to handle corruption. Consequently, the agencies formed to carry out the internal improvement of the law enforcement officer must fulfil the criteria. The KPK may also use its authority to encourage internal improvements in the law enforcement agencies and in ministries/institutions/regional governments.

Second, to minimize conflicts before the public, the leader encourages the prosecution of criminal acts of corruption in the law enforcement agencies through responsible and accountable cooperation with parent institutions through the formulation of the prosecution SOP. This is conducted by forming a transparent flow of communication between agencies. One implementation we suggest is involving a member working in the law enforcement agency of the perpetrator; thus, the prosecuting law enforcement agency will not prosecute directly. This precaution is necessary to avoid offending the esprits de corps of the agency and to maintain the reputations of the law enforcement agencies in public's eyes; then, the law enforcement agencies' performance could be judged according to the corruption cases occurring within its internal organ and the prosecution of cases in various other fields. Additionally, some law enforcement officer will maintain their spirit and integrity to perform their tasks; thus, through this strategy, public trust to law enforcement agencies could be maintained.

In this context, the KPK can implement a technocratic approach by contacting the chief of the law enforcement agency concerned with punishing the perpetrator. Otherwise, the KPK may report to the president, and the president will instruct the chief of the law enforcement agency aforementioned to prosecute the case. The implementation of this approach will not disrupt the stability of the human resources of law enforcement agencies in question institutionally. If no response is received, the KPK may announce the case to the public. This strategy will offend the esprits de corps of the law enforcement agency handled by the KPK less. Stakeholders' commitment can be formed through trust building. Building trust and commitment takes considerable time because integrity improvement is conducted in a gradual manner. After intermediate outcomes are produced, trust and commitment increase in strength.

### *Cooperation in the Prosecution of Criminal Acts*

Stranas PPK can serve as a reference for encouraging the improvement of law enforcement agencies' human resources as a first step in implementing collaborative governance in corruption prosecution. The president, the head of state and government, directs the management of human resources and budget as well as the prosecution strategies without interfering through case-by-case basis and allowing the chiefs of law enforcement agencies to act as co-leaders in collaborative governance.

To improve the collaborative governance effectiveness, improvements in judges' handling of criminal acts of corruption are also critical. To have an accountable, competent and incorruptible judges, the president, the Supreme Court, and the Judicial Commission should collaborate. Sources of corruption evidence that can be used to streamline prosecutions can be obtained from the APIP, Report of State Officials Wealth (Laporan Harta Kekayaan Pejabat Negara: LHKPN), and Financial Transaction Reports and Analysis Centre (Pusat Pelaporan Analisis Transaksi Keuangan: PPATK). The KPK can promote development programs for human resources, especially the young ones, by providing acknowledgement for and appreciation to programs able to instil anticorruption values.

Figure 2 is the scheme of the relationship between the president as the facilitative leader and the chiefs of the three law enforcement agencies.

According to Figure 2, it is possible for the facilitative leader to intervene

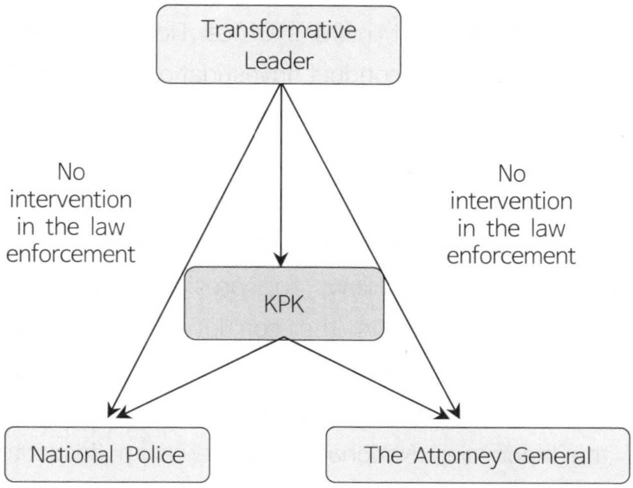


**Figure 2.** Relationship Between the Transformative Leader of Three Law Enforcement Agencies

in the three law enforcement agencies' budget processes and resources management, but it is not possible for the facilitative leader to intervene in the three law enforcement agencies' implementation of law enforcement. In terms of law enforcement, the three agencies may establish a cooperative or collaborative arrangement that accelerates the speed of case settlement. To this end, dialogues between the law enforcement agencies that facilitate creating a common understanding of corruption eradication are necessary. For that purpose, the facilitative leader should focus the Stranas PPK by determining the targets to be achieved.

Administratively, the KPK, Indonesian National Police, and the Attorney General of Indonesia have the position below the president. This position enables the facilitative leader control arising conflicts while remedying or minimising causes of conflicts, namely, human resources, authority, and infrastructure asymmetry. If the KPK has insufficient human resources, it will be backed up by the Attorney General and the Police. Additionally, the facilitative leader has the ability to promote faster human resources development South Korea and Singapore are satisfactory examples of two countries with anticorruption agencies strengthened by their presidents. Singapore has the Corrupt Practices Investigation (CPIB) under the Prime Minister's Office. Despite being under the Prime Minister's Office, the CPIB can conduct investigations into political leaders and state officials (Quah, 2010, 9). Similarly, South Korea has the Anti-Corruption and Civil Rights Commission (ACRC), established in 2002, under the Prime Minister's Office. The ACRC can manage public complaints, improve the quality of the administrative system, and prevent and prosecute criminal acts of corruption (Arsema Tamyalew, 2017). This allows the president to involve other anticorruption agencies to collaborate in the corruption eradication, which can be performed as long as the president is compliant with the law and rules.

Institutionally, the internal supervisory bodies of the Attorney General of Indonesia and the Indonesian National Police [Itwasum (Inspectorate General of the National Police) and Divpropam (Profession and Security Division)] must also be reinforced through internal improvement and enhancement of their roles in performing corruption prevention functions within the environment of the Attorney General of Indonesia and the Indonesian National Police. For internal improvement, the Police and the Attorney General may further capacitate their human resources to ensure they obtain adequate levels of competencies, commitment, and integrity to eradicate corruption. Figure 3 presents the human resources refinement scheme.

In Figure 3, the human resources of the KPK and the human resources of the Indonesian National Police and the Attorney General of Indonesia have an identical level of integrity, competencies, commitment, and systems. Human resources refinement can be performed in the following three strategic steps: (1) deploy the law enforcement officer of the two agencies who have the necessary integrity, commitment, and performance to support the corruption eradication in one group; (2) recruit law enforcement officer to support the corruption eradication; (3) improve the quality of the existing members by using the appropriate punishment according to transparent and accountable performance assessments and provide adequate compensation. Compensation can be increased through nontax state revenue. Thus, the law enforcement agencies may cooperate with the Ministry of Finance to create a government regulation governing remuneration and nontax state revenue.

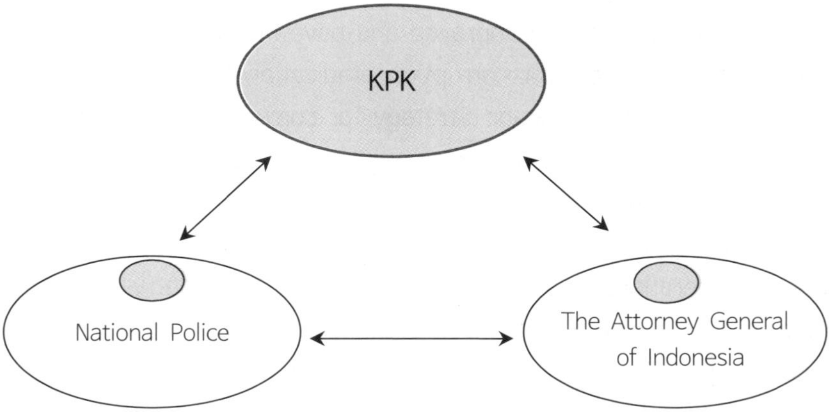


**Figure 3.** Human Resources Refinement Scheme of the Attorney General and the Indonesian National Police

Human resources improvement can also be conducted through the corruption court. In the context of the corruption court, the Judicial Commission supervisory system must also be strengthened. A system that can improve the transparency and accountability of court decisions must be established as well. Regarding human resources management, the selection of judges must be based on publicly available records. In other words, selected judges must have the experience and knowledge concerning corruption eradication. This improvement can be implemented by re-establishing the requirements for becoming a judge for criminal acts of corruption.

To promote cooperation among the law enforcement agencies, improvement in governance and business process is necessary to enhance the compatibility between the agencies conducting prevention and prosecution, thereby reducing differences in understanding and friction between law enforcement agencies. The human resources with comparable qualities in the three agencies should be grouped together in the Police and the Attorney General. In the Police, organization development for corruption handling are conducted through a dedicated institution to reduce the control range, placing it directly below the Chief of the Police. This enables the institution to be faster, more agile, and more independent in its corruption eradication cooperation. Additionally, the task forces under the Attorney General are improved and have increased in number, allowing for more effective and efficient corruption eradication by the Attorney General.

In the context of the Grand Strategy for corruption eradication, the KPK's role in the trigger mechanism can be maximized. Through the refinement of law enforcement officer, the KPK can provide information to and provide cooperation coaching for other law enforcement agencies for the purpose of corruption case prosecution cooperation. This action will close the asymmetry of facilities and infrastructure. This asymmetry can also be managed by using the management of resources belonging to the law enforcement agencies. Additionally, the authority asymmetry between the Attorney General and the Police in handling cases can be aligned with the Government Agency Performance Accountability System.

To handle cases involving members of the Police and the Attorney General, the KPK can employ a technocratic approach. First, the KPK chairman can coordinate with the chiefs of the other law enforcement agencies. Second, the KPK supervises the handling of cases that have been responded to by the other law enforcement agencies. Third, if there is an absence of satisfactory response in the case handling, the KPK takes over the cases. The warrant of commencement for investigator is used as a means to improve the relationship between the Attorney General, the Police, and KPK in the case handling. The warrant of commencement for investigator reported by the Attorney General and the Police should be responded to by the KPK for the two agencies to improve the prosecution they are conducting. Hence, the supervision function can be performed. To strengthen the supervision function, the KPK requires human resources reinforcement in the quantity aspect.

To support the prosecution, the resources management of the law enforcement agencies must also be improved. The refined agencies must have their independence maintained while still conducting coordination with the top leader of each of the other law enforcement agencies. This goal can be achieved by elucidating the system through an SOP of corruption case prosecutions free from intervention. This system also specifies that the law enforcement officer must not be intervened case-by-case by specific individuals and provides special indicators of cases that must be followed up on immediately by the law enforcement officer, enabling the law enforcement officer to determine strategic cases with a level of handling urgency. This system can cover the agencies' limited human resources and financial resources and improve the effectiveness of the corruption eradication.

The systems of control range and human resources management of the Police and the Attorney General should be set in a centralized manner so they will not be vulnerable to intervention when prosecuting corruption, especially at local levels. The patterns of relationships between the Police and the Attorney General can be improved using technology to increase transparency. Members of the Police and the Attorney General with integrity are grouped together, and this group also has the same compensation system, supervision, structure, and interaction patterns as the KPK, which will increase the effectiveness of the corruption prosecution.

To increase the effectiveness of the prosecution, some institutions may collaborate and establish fair, effective, and efficient prosecution. Figure 4 is the scheme of the relationship between such institutions.

In Figure 4, the president, as the head of state, can also collaborate with the Supreme Court and the Judicial Commission to establish an accountable, fair, and transparent anti-corruption court. This establishment necessitates that the judges of the court have adequate competencies and integrity. To this end, the court judge recruitment system must be improved, to ensure that corruption court judges can reach a verdict on a case from an accountable and fair foundation. The Judicial Commission also supports the supervision of the corruption court judges. To improve the effectiveness and efficiency of the prosecution, the BPK, PPATK, BPKP, and KPK through the LHKPN can be prosecution information sources.

To maximize the effectiveness of the corruption prosecution, the selection of the chief of law enforcement must also consider the candidate's record from the beginning of her or his career. After assuming the chief of law enforcement, statutes of limitation must be established as cross-checking against mistakes becomes a crucial factor in the effectiveness and efficiency of corruption eradication in Indonesia.

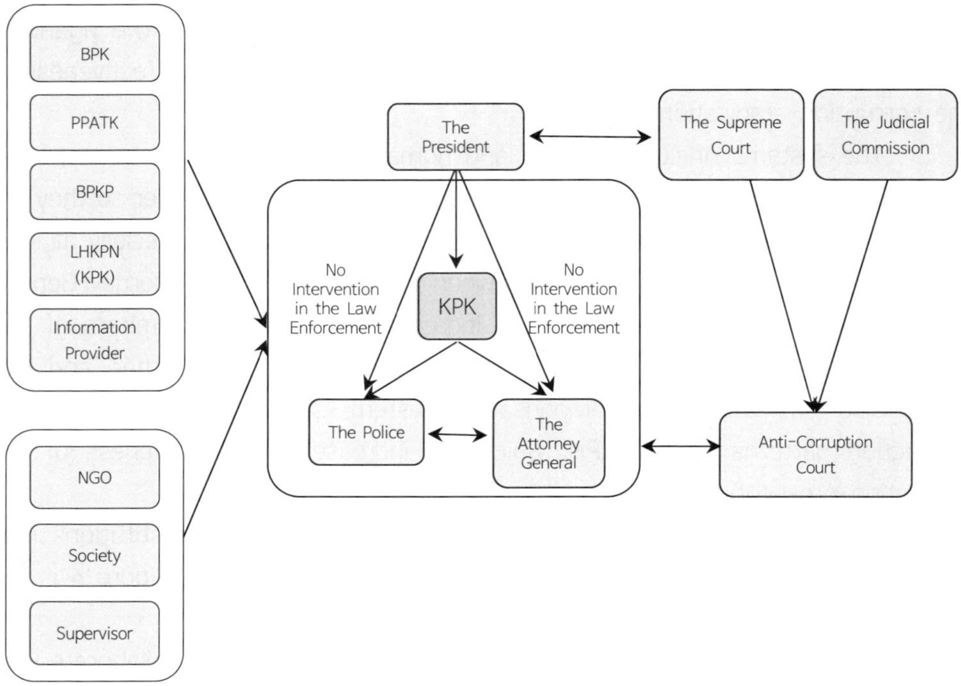


**Figure 4.** Scheme of Interagency Relationship in the Prosecution of Corruption

***Intermediate Outcomes, Collaboration, and Evaluation in Corruption Eradication***

The commitment of all enforcement agencies that is the impetus for the coordination and cooperation in the early stages produces intermediate outcomes that can be enjoyed, satisfies the entities involved, and enables the entities involved to earn appreciation and acknowledgement worldwide. This phenomenon pushes the cooperation to a more comprehensive level, namely, collaboration. The outcomes of this interagency cooperation are intermediate outcomes in the form of small wins. These small wins lead to the establishment of collaboration because they serve as a proof of commitment and trust, as aforementioned. This increases the level of trust and strengthens the collaboration. These intermediate outcomes encourage the improvement of commitment and trust, leading to collaboration. The collaboration, once established, can bring all the entities together to engage in corruption eradication actions.

Afterwards, stakeholders conduct an evaluation by assessing the performance of the cooperation based on the existing field data, and this information is the basis for the implementation of face-to-face dialogues. The evaluation is carried out in accordance with the primary targets formulated in the Grand Strategy. The evaluation is carried out in an accountable and measured manner, yielding feedback for the betterment of the Grand Strategy; thus, the accountability of the actions in the Grand Strategy is administrative in nature and provides improvements and information regarding the performance of corruption eradication in Indonesia in the prosecution field.

The aspects to be assessed are as follows: (1) the cooperation aspect, interagency relationships in the corruption eradication actions, and (2) the system improvement aspect. Both aspects are on the higher level through the development of relevant personnel and implementation of prevention programmes, and both aspects are on the downstream side through evaluation against the prosecution and the implementation of the prosecution SOP for cases involving law enforcement officer. The results of this assessment are used as a basis for the Grand Design at hand. The results of the evaluation are used as a basis for the realisation of actions under the Grand Strategy that has been formulated.

### *Organizational Culture and Institutional Design*

Organizational culture also influences the ability of an organization to eradicate corruption. The organization being in a comfort zone makes making improvements difficult. Hence, bureaucratic reform can be used for corruption prevention. By creating a corruption-free area, serving public information openness, establishing e-government, and planning a performance-based budget, a government that is clean, competent, serving, will able to push bureaucracy into a competitive zone can be created. This effort must be led by a strong institutional leader who can act as a role model for her or his subordinates. For this reason, an external pressure is necessary for improvement.

One factor that can influence collaboration is institutional design. One of the institutional designs governing collaboration is the rule underlying the Grand

Strategy. This rule refers to the Stranas PPK. This rule contains the basis for the collective realization of the strategy for corruption eradication with measured targets, interagency relationship in corruption eradication, tasks and roles of each institution, and minimum institutional or structural requirements for each institution involved under this Stranas PPK. This rule also delineates a clear allocation of roles based on the prevailing laws and regulations. Moreover, the allocation of roles for the Grand Strategy's realization purpose is performed without violating the ordinate laws and regulations, providing clarity in the organizational and operational stage. All agencies are subject to the Grand Strategy, and the KPK is not an exception because its independence is limited to law enforcement. The KPK remains a part of the government outside the law enforcement substance; thus, the president can control its office's human resources and financial governance.

The institutional design of each law enforcement agencies must also be built to ensure that they is not vulnerable to intervention. In this context, the Police and the Attorney General both require a party capable of being a protector for the lowest-level organizations to make them invulnerable to intervention. This goal can be realized through a centralized career development system. All Chiefs of Regional Police and Chiefs of Departmental Police have no authority in employee career development; thus, in case of intervention, they cannot use their authority to transfer employees on the grounds of noncompliance with leaders' directions. Centralized career development is also conducted to align the values of human resources across levels within the body of the Police. Additionally, leaders' ranks must also be established to ensure their invulnerability to intervention.

Structurally, the Police are only tasked with prosecution. The Police are not responsible for prevention because this aspect remains in the process of integrity and independence improvement. This phenomenon is especially true for local areas. The improvement of control range must be performed to change the institutional design of the Police. The arrangement of the control range of the law enforcement agencies, especially the Police, increases supervision over the Police and reduces the chance of corruption within the Police. Before a significant improvement is performed, the prevention function cannot be granted to the Police. Hence, the prevention function allocated to the Police is only internal.

The internal supervision function in the Attorney General's office must also be strengthened to ensure that the Attorney General and the Police can collaborate with the KPK. For example, the KPK can cooperate in prosecutions. Additionally, the reinforcement of the internal prevention of the Police and the Attorney General also increases cooperation with supervisory institutions because the internal supervision function convinces the supervisory institutions that their information will be followed up on in accordance with the criminal law. The public will also have greater confidence to complain to the two law enforcement agencies, which eventually leads to the law enforcement officer having increased capacity and potential.

In addition, the KPK strengthens the coordination and supervision function by formulating cooperative tasks to do for law enforcement. The KPK can create a dedicated department that coordinates supervision for prevention and prosecution purposes; then, the two corruption eradication approaches can be implemented.

## Conclusion

The dominating interagency relationship pattern in the prosecution of corruption in Indonesia is the non-use of cooperation opportunities, followed by competition and conflicts. This pattern is due to interagency distrust and a leadership style that offend the esprit de corps or professional pride in the handling of law enforcement officers committing criminal acts of corruption. This relationship pattern prevents the prosecution effort from maximizing the potential of the agencies that have been granted substantial authority to eradicate or combat criminal acts of corruption in Indonesia.

## References

Ansell, C., & Gash, A. (2008). Collaborative Governance in theory and Practice. *Journal of Public Administration Research and Theory*, 18, 543-571.

Bryson, J, M., Crosby, B. C., and Stone, M. M. (2006). The Design and Implementation of Cross-Sector Collaboration: Propositions from the Literature. *Public Administration Review*, 66, 44-55.

Dwiyanto, Agus. (2010). *Manajemen Pelayanan Publik: Peduli, Inklusif dan Kolaboratif* (Public Service Management: Care, Inclusive and Collaboirative). Yogyakarta: Gadjah Mada University Press.

Hidayat, Qur'anul. (2015). Menengok Kembali Panasnya Perseteruan 'Cicak Versus Buaya'. Diunduh pada 27, December 2016. http://news.okezone.com/read/2015/01/15/337/1092467/menengok-kembali-panasnya-perseteruan-cicak-versus-buaya

In Zhang, Y., & In Lavena, C. (2015). *Government Anti-corruption Strategies: A Cross-cultural Perspective.*

Kirk Emerson, Tina Nabatchi, & Stephen Balogh. (2012). An Integrative Framework for Collaborative Governance. *Journal of Public Administration Research and Theory*, 22(1), January, 1–29. https://doi.org/10.1093/jopart/mur011

Lambsdorff, Johan Graf. (2007). *The Institutional Economics of Corruption and Reform. Theory, Evidence and Policy.* Cambridge: Cambridge University Press.

Lynn, Jr., Laurence, Heinrich, Carolyn & Hill, Carolyn. (2000). Studying Governance and Public Management: Challenges and Prospects. *Journal of Public Administration Research and Theory*, 10. DOI: 10.1093/oxfordjournals.jpart.a024269

Mooi, E. A. (2007). *Inter-organizational Cooperation, Conflict, and Change.* Amsterdam: Tinbergen Institute.

Nawawi, Juanda. (2012). Membangun Kepercayaan dalam Mewujudkan Good Governance. *Journal Ilmu Pemerintahan,* 1(3), 19-29.

Ostrom, V., Tiebout, C., & Warren, R. (1961). The Organization of Government in Metropolitan Areas: A Theoretical Inquiry. *American Political Science Review*, 55(4), 831-842.

Poochaoren, O. (2014). Collaboration in anti-corruption work: who to work with and how? *Working Paper No. LKYSPP 14-12. Lee Kuan Yew School of Public Policy.* National University of Singapore, Singapore.

Smith, Susan. (1998). Collaborative approaches to Pacific Northwest fisheries management: The salmon experience. *Willamette Journal of International Law and Dispute Resolution*, 6, 29.

Stoker, G. (1998). Governance as theory: five propositions. *International Social Science Journal*, 50, 17-28. DOI: 10.1111/1468-2451.00106

# List of Abbreviations

| ABBREVIATION | BAHASA | ENGLISH |
|---|---|---|
| APIP | Aparat Pengawasan Intern Pemerintah | Government Internal Audit Agency |
| BPK | Badan Pemeriksa Keuangan | Audit Board of Republic of Indonesia |
| BPKP | Badan Pengawas Keuangan dan Pembanungan | Finance and Development Supervisory Agency |
| DUMAS | Pengaduan Masyarakat | Public Complaints Officer |
| DPD | Dewan Perwakilan Daerah | Regional Representatives Council |
| DPR | Dewan Perwakilan Rakyat | House of Representatives |
| DPRD | Dewan Perwakilan Dareah | Regional House of Representatives |
| KPK | Komisi Pemberatasan Korupsi | Corruption Eradication Commission |
| LHKPN | Laporan Harta Kekayaan Pejabat Negara | Report of State Officials Wealth |
| MK | Mahkamah Konstitusi | Constitutional Court |
| PPATK | Pusat Pelaporan dan Analisis Transaksi Keuangan | Indonesian Financial Transaction Reports and Analysis Centre |
| SOP | Prosedur Operasional Baku | Standard Operating Procedure |
| SPIP | Sistem Pengawasan Internal Pemerintah | Government Internal Control System |
| Stranas PPK | Strategi Nasional Pencegahan dan Penanggulangan Korupsi | National Strategy for Corruption Prevention and Eradication |

11

# Collaborative Disaster Risk Governance in Thailand

Tavida Kamolvej and Wasan Luangprapat

In the manner of governance, we expect to see collaboration within and between agencies across departments and areas. This is due to the dynamics of public problems and developments which require multi-dimensional solutions and integrated implementation. Governance, as we know, emphasizes the importance of shared goals, resource exchange, regular interaction and communication, and trust among relevant agencies. However, public agencies are designed to perform their functions within their mission-directed budgets rather than coordinate and cooperate to work towards mutual goals or shared visions. This is actually typical around the world for public agencies, especially within bureaucratic systems.

From a management point of view, collaborative governance should not need much structural redesign or formal re-engineering. Collaborative governance is underlined by network management encouraging public agencies to work together with mutual goals, shared resources, frequent communication, and the value of mutual trust. However, network management is more likely to work better within the atmosphere of profit-oriented multi-organizational operations. On the one hand, "profit-oriented" speaks for itself as a mutual goal. It is easy to convince and obtain collaboration when there are concrete benefits that all organizations involved will gain or share. On the other hand, lack of capacity drives network initiative. It is usually initiated because one agency lacks the competency to achieve a new level of service quality.

Recent occurrences of hazardous public events and disaster risks have increased awareness of the need for effective risk management of such extreme events. Disasters are normally compounded, making them complex and difficult. Disaster risk reduction, therefore, requires multi-disciplinary knowledge and understanding in order to prevent and mitigate their impact on society. Following prevention and mitigation, lack of understanding and systematic information about the risks to which communities are exposed results in an unprepared response to sudden threats and changed conditions. Such events lead to devastation and unpredictable impacts, spread widely across communities, and result in sudden damage to infrastructure, transportation, communications, and property, along with losses of life, health, and livelihoods. In addition, states of emergency require multiple agencies to perform different tasks simultaneously to return the situation to normal. Unorganized and inexperienced responses can delay disaster assistance and recovery processes. Increasing manpower alone as a network of multi-agency operations will be neither effective in facilitating a coordinated response nor will it assist in systematically integrating the functions of each agency.

Intergovernmental management raises the question of what roles and authority should be assigned to participating agencies individually and co-operatively. Radin et al. (1996) argue that multi-organizational arrangements are solutions for inter-organizational problems that cannot be achieved by a single organization working alone. States of emergency need to take into account the adaptive capacity of individual units and the effective coordination of multilevel governmental agencies. Kettl (2002) and Salamon (2002) argue that new governance moves its focus to networks rather than hierarchy in organizational forms. Under states of emergency, public managers have the obligation and responsibility to make decisions regarding life and death. Their training may have focused on command and control as a traditional means of disaster management. Public executives may believe that strictly top-down decision making and a single operational unit will result in more efficient disaster management.

Nevertheless, there are many arguments that situate intergovernmental relations in a narrower perspective within governmental networks although Rhodes (1997) has identified, in the latter, non-governmental organizations, the private sector, and communities as being within the network of government. Therefore, collaborative governance is a more appropriate lens through which to explain operations of multiple agencies that involve simultaneously collaboration. Ansell and Gash (2012) define collaborative governance as "A governing arrangement where one or more public agencies directly engage non-state stakeholders in a collective decision-making process that is formal, consensus-oriented, and deliberative and that aims to make or implement public policy or manage public programs or assets." This definition can clearly explain Thailand's disaster risk governance, whether collaborative or not.

However, both the impacts and countermeasures of disaster risks are transnationalized. Managing disaster risks across jurisdictions has given rise to more complications and difficulties in intergovernmental relations and governance. After prevention, mitigation, and preparedness, risk identification and warnings are the key elements to saving lives. All nations that share the same geographic risks automatically coordinate risk data and analyses as well as response and relief operations. Disasters, by definition, are a state of overwhelming threat and devastation that requires a capacity from other jurisdictions nearby. Mobilizing resources to be utilized in other jurisdictions forces confrontation with accountability issues both domestically and internationally. Ostrom (1990) then introduces that collective action or governance of the commons requires an institutional perspective for a polycentric governance system. It requires codes of conduct among multi-agencies regarding laws, regulations, and rules of the game as a pattern for interoperability.

In 2004, a combination of low awareness of the risk of tsunamis and a lack of experience in disaster risk governance led agencies to misunderstand the level of risk they faced and resulted in an unorganized and inadequate response. Due to this lack of understanding, Thai national, provincial, and local governments struggled to work collaboratively to provide assistance to communities damaged by the tsunami, which wreaked massive devastation across six coastal provinces.

Similarly, during the floods of 2011, even though flooding is one of the most frequent and recurrent disasters in Thailand, the Thai government was unable to coordinate, let alone collaborate, at any level to manage the disaster effectively and efficiently. This time, the level of flood risk was misinterpreted not because of a lack of awareness, but rather owing to bad management and a failure to prepare. In addition, political conflict between the government and the opposition interfered in the response, disrupting the shared vision and making a unified approach to handling the flood impossible. Now, as the government faces the COVID-19 pandemic, the national government is once again unable to efficiently coordinate multiple agencies and find a unified command thanks to a lack of understanding of the country's incident command system.

This chapter examines and assesses the existence of collaborative governance over disaster risks in Thailand through three cases: the 2004 tsunami, the 2011 floods, and the COVID-19 pandemic of 2020. These three cases all offer different insights into how the government handles different types of disaster risks. Tsunamis are rare and emerge suddenly, while floods are recurrent and slow to emerge and COVID-19 is a new disaster that is aggressively contagious and difficult to contain. The tsunami and flood cases are examined using previous research, while we look at the government response to COVID-19 using a preliminary analysis of participatory observations and secondary data from agency reports. This chapter seeks to identify gaps in Thailand's disaster risk governance and offer recommendations for how agencies and institutions can collaborate more effectively and efficiently in the future.

## Conceptualizing Collaborative Governance in Disaster and Emergency Management

Collaboration on disaster risk governance is a process that is neither easy nor linear. Disaster risks are dynamic, uncertain, chaotic, and political. Disaster risk governance is both specific and technical as well as interrelated and administrative. To find out whether Thailand has improved its disaster risk governance toward risk reduction, this chapter reviews interagency relations, intergovernmental relations, network management, and governance through institutional analysis. We seek to understand the country's disaster risk governance structure and explain how all levels of government — national, provincial, and local — collaborate to achieve the goal of becoming a disaster-resilient nation.

Pfeffer (1992) suggests that the exercise of control, influence and authority that relies on the existence of recognized hierarchies is now rarer. Such changes have undermined hierarchies and made collaboration and cooperation more useful management tools than the old methods of top-down command and control. In less hierarchical organizations, the most effective managers are those who take the time to persuade others to their way of thinking — campaigning rather than coercing. This also tends to produce wiser decisions. He suggests that there are three ways of getting things done: (1) through hierarchical authority, which is badly out of fashion; (2) by developing a strongly shared vision or organizational culture, which is very time and resource consuming; and (3) through the use of power and influence. He focuses his attention on this third way, stating that it emphasizes method rather than structure. However, disaster risk governance research argues in favor of an incident-command-system rather a single directive command with a multi-agency coordination network where collective actions are executed.

Provan and Milward (2001) comment that the delivery of public service at multiple levels requires the integration and coordination of a variety of organizations into service delivery, while Meyers et al. (2001) assert that the devolution appears to have moved the boundaries of program authority and responsibility both downward and outward. Getting agencies to work together does not merely require individual readiness. Putnam (1993) supports that networks of civic engagement facilitate coordination and communication, and amplify information about the trustworthiness of other individuals. Local communities have knowledge about their areas and the people in them. This familiarity with location and resources becomes crucial when the authorities and participating agencies need to access this potential.

Bardach (1998) proposes that many institutional features of our policy making system suggest that unexploited opportunities to create value in this way are abundant. The process of trying to exploit such opportunities involves leveraging personnel and financial resources for collaborative purposes, designing and managing an effective operating system, reaching and maintaining consensus on basic goals and on tradeoffs among relevant sub-goals, creating an effective culture or ethos of interpersonal working relationships, and securing the implicit or explicit consent of elected officials. It is a complex developmental process that unfolds over a long time period which requires the government to shift its administration from one of hierarchy to one of networks.

For organizations to function well, Graber (2003) suggests that they must have structures that are appropriate to organizational goals, stating "Structures refer to the patterns of information flow inherent in formal organization charts and reflected in work manuals." These official structures provide a restricted, standardized communication environment that enhances the stability and predictability of organizational behavior (J. March and H. Simon also note the importance of structures). She explains that the chief goal of networking is "to establish communication links with significant others to share information about mutually relevant situations," while that of network analysis is "to explain the communication roles played by organization members and the consequences for the performance of the organization."

Effective collaborative governance cannot function without the strong link created by effective information technology and communications systems. Decision-making, under the pressure of time constraints and threats to life, needs sufficient information to support participating agencies in making more accurate decisions. Knowledge, data, and information need to be integrated into a systematic database shared among all participating agencies and the public when necessary. The best information cannot serve organizations at the highest capacity without a good communications system and management. A communications system is crucial in facilitating the information flow among participating agencies and the public to keep all operations connected.

## Arguments on Thailand's Collaborative Disaster Risk Governance

This chapter debates (1) whether hierarchy is needed and, if so, to what extent, as well as which design should be used to shift to a network rather than command-and-control system; (2) whether relying on multi-agency integration and coordination results in a lack of direct collective action; (3) whether civic engagement amplifies trustworthiness or chaos; (4) whether rules and regulations can be leveraged for collaborative purposes; (5) whether collaboration can emerge by adopting shared goals and facing common threats; (6) to what extent values are shared and codes of conduct are adhered to; and (7) whether the design of information flow and frequent communication about risk governance is advantageous to tasks and operations overall.

## Thai Governance: Structures, systems, and mechanisms

In Thailand, public policy is generally implemented through administrative organizations in five clusters, namely, the central administration, the provincial administration, the local administration, state enterprises, and public organizations. However, state enterprises and public organizations are under the supervision of the central administration. Therefore, Thailand's bureaucratic system is centered on the three major structures of the central, provincial, and local administrations.

### Central Administration

Under the direct command of the Cabinet, Thailand's central administration is the main public administration organ (national government). It has a direct role in strategy and policy, academics, and support, as well as in policy implementation. The central administration follows the principles of centralization with affiliated administrative agencies including:

- The Office of the Prime Minister (equivalent to the ministerial level)
- Ministerial-level agencies help guide implementation by compiling the work for departmental-level agencies.
- Department level roles include formulating strategies, policies, and measures in addition to supporting academic work and other ministerial work, and implementing ministerial missions
- Administrative agencies (equivalent to the department level) are not affiliated with the Office of the Prime Minister, ministries, or bureaus and are under the direct command of the Prime Minister. Moreover, Thailand's administrative agencies serve as key operational or policy implementation agencies and have expanded their office locations throughout the nation.

## Provincial Administration

The provincial administration is the key to sub-national governance as a representative of the central government, implementing law and policies at the local level. Thailand's provincial administration is characterized as a local state government which plays a role in implementing policies at the local community level nationwide (devolution) with the help of government officials and agencies from the central level. Provincial administrations, which are headed by provincial governors, have an important mechanism for operations, namely, the provincial committees represented by heads of administrative offices under ministries, bureaus, and departments with offices located in each province. The provincial administration has the roles of (1) maintaining peace and order in the area; (2) formulating provincial development policies and plans, and providing public services to solve local problems and respond to local needs; (3) supervising local administrations and the operations of other administrative offices; and (4) implementing or enforcing strategic plans, strategies, policies, and matters of law in the area.

Over the past several decades, the provincial administration has faced numerous changes in terms of local-level problems and needs, as well as institutional changes in the structures and operational roles of various public sector agencies. The changes in economic, social, and political conditions have resulted in the provincial administration's main role becoming less significant, while its roles in development and strategy have increased in importance as area-based-governance. However, these new roles overlap to some extent with those of the central administration, which has expanded and established offices in the provincial areas.

## Local Administration

The role and authority of Thailand's local administration was limited in the past. After "Black May of 1992", a political reform process which focused on decentralization provided power to local administrations. After the promulgation of the 1997 Constitution and the enactment of the *Determining Plans and Process of Decentralization to Local Government Organization Act* (1999), various organizations were placed under the local administration in Thailand, including:

- Local Administrative Organizations (LAOs), including:
  - Provincial Administrative Organizations (PAOs), established as upper-tier units or large-scale LAOs focused on providing public services generally for the whole province or clusters beyond the capacity of small-scale LAOs
  - Municipality and Sub-district (Tambol) Administrative Organizations (SAOs), established as lower-tier units or LAOs near local communities that play a role in providing basic public services based on the problems and needs within their own jurisdiction
- Special Local Administrative Organizations, including:
  - Bangkok Metropolis
  - Pattaya City

The result of decentralization allowed Thailand's LAOs to grow significantly, expanding their roles and authority, and to start moving towards institutionalization as a key mechanism in public administration with public recognition. However, the consequence of having the central, provincial, and local administrations all together in the same area complicates local governance.

## Thailand Disaster Risk Governance: Structures, systems, and mechanisms

Before 2002, disaster governance in Thailand did not have a clear identification, and there were no specific policies or strategies that directly served the purpose of disaster risk governance. Responsibilities for disaster-related tasks were shared between agencies with roles involving central-provincial-local administration. Policies became clearer after the establishment of the Department of Disaster Prevention and Mitigation (DDPM) under the Ministry of Interior in 2002. Missions and operations to respond to disasters were combined. Manpower and managerial resources were transferred from the Department of Rural Development, the Civil Defense Division of Department of Provincial Administration, the Accident Prevention Committee under the Office of the Permanent Secretary for the Prime Minister's Office, the Victim Assistance Division of the Department of Public Welfare, and the Basic Skills Services Agency of the Department of Community Development. However, frontline agencies to respond to disasters were still comprised of local authorities and volunteers.

The structure and operational systems started to become clearer and more systematic after the promulgation of the *Disaster Prevention and Mitigation Act* (DPM) of 2002, which replaced previous related Acts such as the *Civil Defense Act of 1979 and the Fire Defense Act* of 1999. In other words, the aforementioned 2007 Act officially certified disaster risk governance related tasks as public policies while also establishing work systems and mechanisms for handling disasters. Under the aforementioned law, the National Disaster Prevention and Mitigation Committee (NDPMC) was created as a mechanism to link relevant administrative agencies together. Since 2007 until the present day, the government has periodically constructed and created mechanisms for the implementation of core functions through the determination and improvement of strategies, work plans, and work systems. The 2007 Act also more clearly identifies and designates the DDPM as a national collaborator which drives the implementation of National Disaster Prevention and Mitigation Plans through disaster risk related multi-agency missions.

The primary function of disaster governance falls under the DDPM, which is the core coordinating agency in disaster governance. The main structure is separated into the following three parts: (1) the central agency (DDPM) which includes internal administrative agencies that are responsible for making disaster risk governance policy, sharing knowledge with its agencies and partners, and performing other secretarial work for the department; (2) regional agencies, namely Disaster Prevention and Mitigation Regional Centers 1-18, which are scattered around the country according to geographical disaster risk similarities and which have the responsibility to provide instruments and training to prepare for disaster governance; and (3) provincial agencies, namely the Provincial Disaster Prevention and Mitigation Office under the governor, which is responsible for coordinating emergency response and relief.

Disaster risk governance in Thailand is designed to consider the variables of scale, severity, complications, and jurisdiction in deciding who the commander-in-chief is. There are four levels of disaster management. Level 1 denotes disasters that occur within the jurisdiction of a local administration or city, and in this case the mayor or sheriff will be the commander-in-chief respectively. Level 2 disasters are those which exceed the capacity and jurisdiction of a local administration or city, and in this case the provincial governor will be commander-in-chief. Level 3 disasters occur outside the capacity and jurisdiction of the provincial government, and the Minister of Interior becomes the commander-in-chief, and level 4 disasters are those which are national or which exceed the capacity and jurisdiction of many provinces. Level 4 disasters may require international assistance, and in such cases the prime minister or designated deputy prime minister takes over as commander-in-chief. Under the *Disaster Prevention and Mitigation Act* of 2007, when the commander-in-chief declares a state of disaster, all agencies within their jurisdiction fall directly under the purview of the commander's singular command system. The Incident Command

System (ICS) clearly states how multi-agency coordination operates through collaborative governance; however, ICS is not mandated by law.

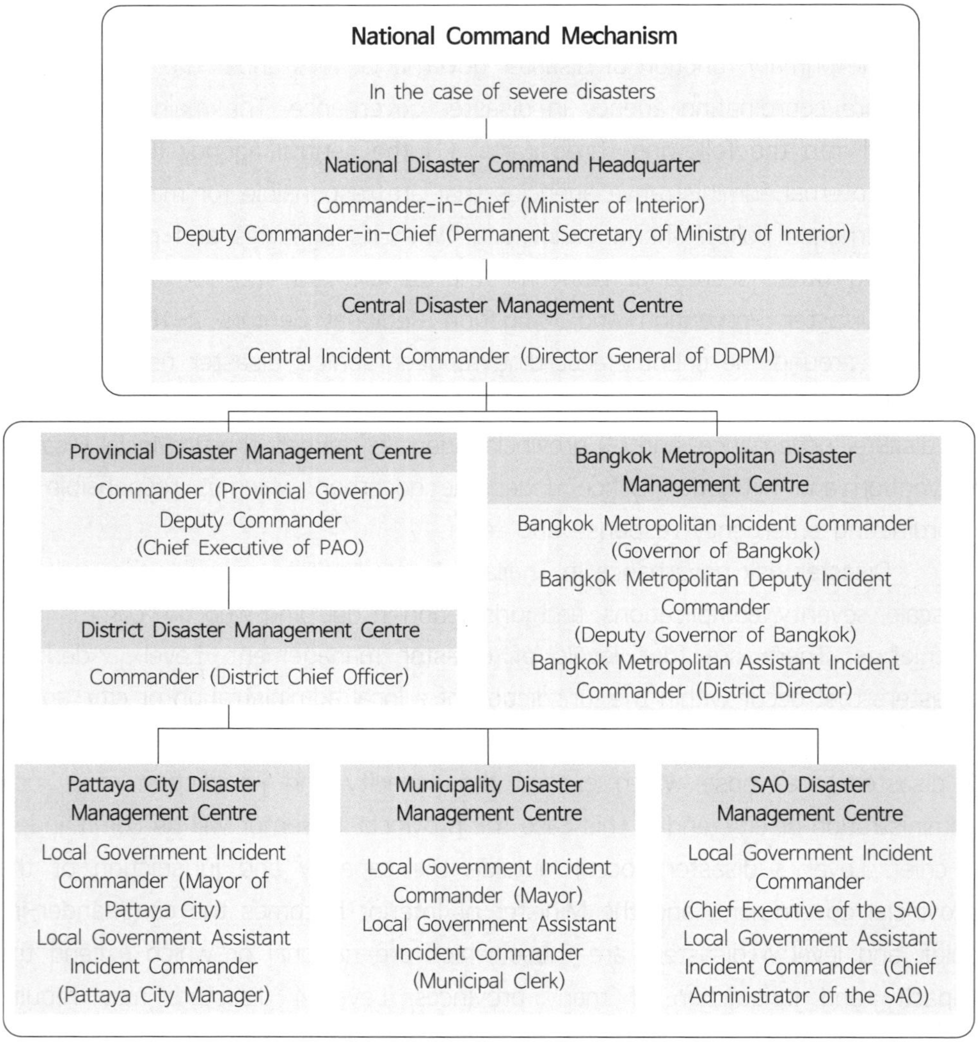


**Figure 1.** Area Level Control Mechanism

## Mechanisms for Disaster Policy Implementation and Control[1)]

Thailand's public administration follows a systemic operational structure with a clear distribution and arrangement of responsibility both by function and geographic area. The government of Thailand's policy implementation process faces several challenges, including redundancy and overlaps in roles and authority; lack of good coordination and collaboration and fragmented use of managerial resources; lack of appropriate and clear distribution of roles and authority between central, provincial and local administrations; and lack of clearly and systemically-established relationship both internally and among central, provincial and local administrations.

The main issue in Thailand's policy implementation at the area level is the result of a structural problem within the country's public administration. The legal authority to carry out various missions remains clustered in the central administration at the department level. At the same time, the central departments with such authority do not usually have an effective way to "decentralize" or "devolve" their power to provincial and local administrations (including administration at the sub-district and village levels, which are considered an extension of the provincial administration). Central departments usually establish offices or field service agencies without having to depend on the provincial administration. Yet, these offices report directly to the central departments, further centralizing public administration. Departments have legal authority to carry out government activities and utilize managerial resources to implement public policies. Government agencies within these departments try to spin off from the governing department and transform themselves into new departments with their own resources, authority, budgets, and the freedom to determine their own positions and capacity. This eventually leads to each administrative agency creating its own independent territory.

1) Report on Disaster Risk Management Public Expenditure and Institutional Reviews (DRM-PEIR) in Thailand from Fiscal Years 2012-2015, United Nations Development Program under the support of the National Economic and Social Development Bureau, Bureau of the Budget — Office of the Prime Minister, and the Department of Disaster Prevention and Mitigation — Ministry of Interior.

Moreover, each agency has legal restrictions in how they may carry out their duties and responsibilities, especially the central departments. They are forced to find solutions within their limitations based on their existing authority and resources. This results in ad hoc activities in the form of small-scale projects that do not require excessive time and resources, such as advocacy campaigns, seasonal activities, or offering periodic area services. Carrying out such ad hoc activities prevents the overall implementation of policies and strategies from creating a real policy outcome/impact and may lead to wasted resources. Moreover, such ad hoc activities are neither consistent nor permanent. They are only undertaken periodically depending on available inputs, namely, the amount allocated from the annual budget. In addition, the Thai government has launched an "integrated budget" category in the hopes that disaster risk reduction agencies would allocate and utilize this budget with purpose. However, the more frequent outcome is that each agency later asks to shift the integrated budget towards other direct mission-oriented purposes which fall outside disaster risk reduction.

As the designated focal agency in disaster risk governance (DRG), the DDPM is, therefore, an attempt to create an efficient mechanism to build linkage among DRG missions towards a common direction. DDPM was established as the national focal point under the 2015 National Disaster Prevention and Mitigation Plan to integrate the core functions of various agencies and create a common understanding of DRG as a multi-disciplinary issue that requires cross-sectoral collaboration at all levels. This, however, means that the DDPM must be equipped with technical DRG knowledge, including both physical engineering measures and non-engineering measures, to be able to provide advisory services and serve as the central agency linking strategic goals across DRG-related agencies. Unfortunately, the relevant agencies have a relatively low level of understanding and capacity regarding disaster risk governance, making it difficult for them to collaborate in mainstreaming DRG missions into their core functions. As a result, trust between the DDPM as a professional DRG unit and disaster risk reduction-related agencies is lacking. With this lack of trust and failure of capacity, the ability of the DDPM to engage in collaborative governance with its relevant agencies is questionable.

Each agency must also prioritize and align its action plans, projects, and activities with DRG objectives as set forth in the National Disaster Prevention and Mitigation Plan. This is to ensure consistency with the national DRG strategy included in the National Disaster Prevention and Mitigation Plan. Additionally, the DDPM should have the mandate to implement policies and set indicators for policy implementation apart from shared monitoring and evaluating processes. This would allow the DDPM to communicate, monitor and govern the direction of DRG mainstreaming into various plans and strategic objectives, leading to more systematic results. However, the role of the focal agency, i.e., the DDPM, in facilitating this National Plan does not include oversight and monitoring of the progress or results of policy implementation in accordance with the National Plan and plans of related agencies.

The Disaster Risk Reduction Multi-Agency Focal Point (also known as the DRR Focal Point) was established under the National Disaster Prevention and Mitigation Planning Sub-committee to communicate, disseminate, and build linkage with the goals of the 2015 national policy and plan in line with the Sendai Framework for Disaster Risk Reduction (SFDRR). It is critical to appoint members to the working group who specialize in a specific aspect of DRG. Such personnel will allow for the fruitful translation of policy into action that reflects an understanding of and the inter-linkages between the core functions of each agency and DRG. Moreover, the working group serves as an important mechanism for the overall evaluation of DRG resource utilization, in turn contributing to the development of a safer society.

## Thailand's Disaster Risk Governance Policy

The "National Preparedness Policy" provides direction for setting strategies, guidelines, measures, and action plans to maximize effectiveness in emergency management. All sectors must collaborate during normal times by preparing appropriate systems for the prevention, mitigation, and suppression of security threats as well as plans for post-crisis recovery. This collaboration must also take into account two key auxiliary plans — the 2010-2014 National Disaster Prevention and Mitigation Plan, which supports disaster management with the DDPM under the Ministry of Interior as the focal agency and is supported by the 2017 Ministerial Level Integrated Action Plan on Disaster Prevention and Mitigation, and the National Defense Plan, which was created by the Ministry of Defense to strengthen Thailand's national defense capabilities.

There are two mechanisms for determining and implementing all strategies and operational plans related to disaster management, including the incident command system in times of disaster. Firstly, policy frameworks play a role in the establishment of strategies and operational plans to mainstream disaster management into the national agenda. As the DRM-PEIR 2017 lays out, "At the policy level, a 'joint committee' is established to facilitate integration and collaboration between the agencies involved. The 'NDPMC' is an operational mechanism established under the DPM Act that aims to integrate the agencies involved together under the national agenda on disaster risk management. For that reason, the committee's composition reflects the direct involvement of administrative agencies. The NDPMC reflects the effort to integrate joint operations among all agencies involved into a network by appointing representatives as different members and specifying their roles and responsibilities under the plans and activities performed" (DRM-PEIR, 2017).

Secondly, in policy implementation, operational plans play a practical role and have two important phases: (1) the pre-disaster phase, which means in normal times, all relevant agencies assure that the assessment of risks and establishment of prevention and mitigation measures are in place, and disaster preparedness is enhanced in risk-prone areas to be consistent with national strategies, policies and plans; and (2) the disaster phase, during which operations are divided among the national, provincial, and local government levels. While local and provincial agencies assure that incident response plans are accurately executed, national agencies are to administer and support local operations if the scale, severity, and complexity of the disaster exceed the capacity of local command-and-control in the affected area. As amended in the DPM Act of 2007, level 1 and 2 disasters are under the command and management of local/municipal and provincial administrations, respectively. Thus, during level 3 disasters the Minister of Interior or the deputy prime minister assigned takes on the position of commander-in-chief, and the prime minister becomes the national commander at time of national crisis, or level 4 disasters (DPM National Plan, 2010-2014).

Policy implementation at the area level lacks policy integration and ongoing, permanent operations. This is the rolling consequence of a structural-institutional problem, namely, the lack of integration of policies and resources for strategic cooperation. This causes implementation at the area level to be scattered across different agencies based on their authority and existing resources at the central, provincial, and local levels, which in turn limits the expected results to within the authority and resources of each agency operating independently. Each agency is therefore unable to perform any large-scale activities or create significant policy impacts. As a result, activities tend to be performed on a small scale, following the limitations of the authority and resources that each agency possesses. The heart of DRG is the agencies located in disaster-affected areas. These local agencies have the information, familiarity, and experience with risky situations in affected areas, which is closely linked to an understanding of the required levels of preparedness of the community and the public, readiness of local management systems in responding to disaster risks, and capacity to manage adverse impacts and recovery. Additionally, local agencies can mobilize resources, are familiar with changing circumstances in the area, and can easily recognize risks. Centralization is not effective when applied to the local operations that are more likely to be efficient in their disaster response.

DRG policies, strategies, plans and activities in Thailand have progressed in the same direction as international principles and with significant improvement in the linkage between policies and plans as observed from written documents. However, the complete development and translation of policies into action relies on more than the lessons learned from past disasters or political drive and support. Those who make decisions regarding policy and resource allocation must have the determination and commitment to DRG objectives to build a safe society and raise awareness on adaptive capacity development. The results from these commitments will serve as a key foundation to sustainable development. Later on, we will discuss the need for mutual understanding in disaster risk reduction

(DRR), which is the ultimate goal.

## The Journey from the 2004 Tsunami to the 2011 Flood and COVID-19 Pandemic: Has Thailand improved its disaster risk management?[2)]

After a devastating tsunami hit Thailand in December of 2004, education and capacity building programs were spread out to assure that at-risk communities and nation's public at large learned about the tsunami threat and its consequences. An end-to-end tsunami early warning system was activated in tsunami risk-prone areas and later expanded to become a multi-hazard early warning system. International and regional collaborative networks on tsunami practices have exchanged knowledge and lessons learned to create resilient communities. The revision and redesign of the Disaster Act in 2007 has contributed to making the structure of authorized disaster agencies, incident command and multi-agency coordination, and emergency operational plans clearer and more flexible. All such agencies have been trained in multi-hazard risk countermeasures and disaster management. In addition, scholars have researched both lessons learned and ways to improve the nation's resilience to tsunami risks. Unfortunately, only survivors and affected communities have maintained the momentum that built immediately after the disaster of 2004 and continued to learn and improve. The major lessons from the tsunami have centered around the building of knowledge and infrastructure, and ensuring that the public is well aware of the risk of another tsunami and well prepared to respond. However, after the flood of attention focusing on tsunamis subsided and a new system was established, the nation turned its attention back to other public issues and focused on preparing for other, rarer disaster risks. Ultimately, the tsunami of

2) See also Kamolvej, Tavida. "Has Thailand Disaster Management Improved From the 2004 Tsunami to the 2011 Flood?" *Journal of Politics*, Politics and Government College, Mahasarakram University, Volume 2, September 2013-February 2014.

2004 left behind a painful experience of traumatic loss among the locals who were affected.

In 2011, another large-scale disaster hit Thailand. The flooding which occurred in 2011 was beyond the nation's expectations and experience. The water quickly surpassed the capacity of the country's water sheds, dikes, and reservoirs. It did not take an engineer or scientist to see that the threat was tremendous at the time, or to see that the Thai agencies were confused and failed to predict the amount, direction, and impact of this flood. The level of deployment of technical infrastructure was surprisingly low due to the inability of these agencies to assess and manage the flooding, even though floods are a relatively frequent occurrence in Thailand. As mentioned in the previous section, the lessons learned from the tsunami led the Thai government and relevant agencies to review and revise laws, regulations, policies, plans, and operations to be more coherent. These changes intended to create greater organization flexibility and a way for national, provincial, and local authorities and agencies to systematically coordinate their responses. However, political conflict at the national level found a way to intervene in the decision making process when it came to managing the situation. In the end, despite thorough research, the analysis still could not conclude that the overall performance would be more effective and efficient if the government activated the flood disaster operation center under the Disaster Act rather than the Administrative Act. Moreover, Thai culture had a strange impact on the efficiency of the government's disaster management, including the tendency to underestimate risks, tendency to ignore alarms, and a lack of discipline to maintain social order. Evacuation centers outside of Bangkok never reached full capacity due to the fact that evacuees preferred to stay at temporary shelters closer to home even though these shelters were also located in a risk-prone area. This illustrates the lack of communication and coordination between agencies and communities on the details of how to go about the process of evacuation and what should happen afterward.

Between 2011 and March 2020, which marks the end of the National Disaster Prevention and Mitigation Plan 2015, Thailand has deepened its commitment to the ultimate goal of disaster risk reduction (DRR) as one of foundations of the UN's Sustainable Development Goals. Throughout these nine years, Thailand has confronted several types of disaster risk, namely the earthquake which occurred in the North, Pabuk Typhoon, and severe flooding in the southern and northeastern parts of the country. The earthquake, which was minor, caused only one death and a few injuries with some damages, and did not result in any major changes to disaster risk management by either the government or the public. Pabuk Typhoon reduced her speed and precipitation and by the time it made landfall, the damage and devastation was not very severe. This time, with the memory of the 1995 Gay Typhoon which caused a high number of deaths and damage, local and provincial administrations worked together closely, and the locals were well-prepared and took the warning seriously. However, the flooding that occurred in the southern and northeastern parts of the country posed a difficult and seemingly unending problem for every level of government. Following the 2011 flood, all levels of government became more focused on protecting the central part of the country where major cities and businesses are located. However, trying to protect one particular part of a country definitely results in large-scale devastation to other areas. The inability to perceive the shared risk has given rise to a lack of trust between the central government and provincial and local governments. We can also see this reflected in the Thai government's response to COVID-19.

Although disaster risk management in Thailand only began to gain attention in 2005 after the Indian Ocean tsunami, over the past 15 years, Thailand has taken significant steps to develop the country's capabilities to deal with and manage disaster risks. The numerous disasters that the country has faced since then provided many lessons to the government, the private sector, and the public, who have all gained a better understanding of the basics of disaster risk governance and the developmental gaps that need to be addressed. Thailand has moved forward, although slowly and incrementally, from emergency response and relief to disaster risk reduction. The government, over the years, has put a lot of effort into initiating, planning, implementing, and enhancing the capacities of all levels of administration on disaster risk analysis and activities. The country's overall prevention, mitigation, and preparedness have improved. Although Thailand continues to face familiar problems, the disasters which have occurred since 2005, including the ChiengRai Earthquake, BangSapan-ChaUad and

UbolRatchathani floods, and Pabuk Strom over NakornSriThammarat province caused less damage. It seems as though the national and local administrations have been able to reinstate their agency-based disaster risk related functions.

It was not until the second week of January 2020 that Thailand began to take the novel coronavirus (COVID-19) as seriously as it should have. The central government issued the *Disease Control Act* in 2015 using the twin structure of medical networks through the Ministry of Public Health and provincial and local networks under the governor and municipalities. This act gave the provincial governors absolute power to act as commander-in-chief and make the decisions necessary to execute all operations within their jurisdiction by consulting with the provincial disease control committee. Through the national disease control committee, the Prime Minister can legitimately bind provincial governors to follow the guidance from the Disease Control Department (DCD). However, the decision not to ban inbound travelers from risk-prone countries and have the port authority conduct efficient screening and quarantine procedures meant that ultimately, the level of risk exposure was still high. Moreover, later on during mid-March of 2020, the Bangkok Metropolitan Authority and the governors of provinces in the vicinity instituted a lockdown of several private enterprises, causing risk mobility. Migrant workers from other provinces around the country had to return to their homes outside of Bangkok. As a result, Thailand declared a state of emergency using the Emergency Decree that focuses on enforcing stricter social distancing around the country as well as concentrating all of the decision making power to allow the use of a single command point throughout each province. At the time of this writing, the number of infected patients continues to climb exponentially. The decree has not yet fully implemented the highest possible level of restriction. The provincial governments are reluctant to make such a decision due to the lack of directive guidelines and pandemic experience. Unfortunately, the dynamism of the pandemic has rapidly complicated the situation.

Management of the COVID-19 pandemic reflects six classic problems of Thai governance, which are (1) a lack of legally binding authority to be deployed with a comprehensive understanding of the flexibility to integrate all relevant agencies as well as official entities to engage in service operations; (2) fragmentation or departmentalization meaning the relevant agencies do not automatically collaborate and efficiently communicate about their related tasks; (3) all relevant agencies have never understood the cross-boundary-tasks let along perceived disaster risk reduction as a mutual goal instead of focusing on their own directive mission-oriented responsibility; (4) a lack of trust among every level of government as well as in every relevant agency as strategic partner in delivering integrated goal services such as disaster risk reduction and emergency management; (5) resources are restricted by the jurisdiction and function of each agency rather than being shared, which makes it difficult to create a foundational budget and for effective disaster risk governance work; and (6) lack of integrated big-data systems and high quality information to support strategic decision making processes for any level of commander-in-chief. In addition, data collection and application systems are not standardized throughout national, provincial, and local operations. These pull-back factors have both delayed comprehensive strategic decisions and resulted in the first implementation of social distancing in the country being relatively ineffective. At the time of revision of this writing, three months have passed since the first case was identified, and the number of infected cases is still exponentially climbing although the national government has declared a state of emergency. The Emergency Decree gives absolute power to the prime minister with the delegation of power to the provincial governors. The argument is whether the decree should enforce stricter social distancing measures or whether it should collectively make different levels of government work together.

## Challenges: Ways forward for Thailand toward efficient disaster risk governance

The Thai government has grown more aware of the severe problems that are likely to increase in frequency and severity and which create the need for various sectors to raise public knowledge, awareness, and understanding and to be able and prepared so that they can respond to emergencies and return to normalcy as soon as possible. This also corresponds to the objective of disaster risk reduction in the DPM National Plan 2015, which commits to the implementation of the SFDRR. However, relevant agencies in various sectors, particularly the government, are still searching for clear rationale and mission-oriented design in dedicating resources to risk reduction. Thailand's disaster risk governance policies have previously failed at building understanding about the correct focus and content of DRG in addition to serving only as a policy framework that neither assigns nor translates the objectives of DRG in a unified manner. Translating this policy framework into core policies, strategies, work plans, tactics, projects, and activities is done based on each ministry "mandatory functions", not on disaster risk reduction as shared goal. This means that such translation is done according to the interpretation of each department and agency rather than focusing on program implementation to create real DRG results.

Disaster risk governance is viewed as an administrative operation performed by core agencies rather than technical work that relies upon multi-agency coordination of information, the sourcing of information from qualified technical experts, increasing understanding of the characteristics of each risk and raising awareness within communities in risky areas, and skill training for relevant personnel and the public. To ensure all relevant agencies understand and perceive disaster risks in one coherent direction, significance should be placed on the designation and development of technical standards in all agencies, for every administrative function and every community. This is necessary so that projects and activities under the overall risk reduction strategy in the future can be distributed to facilitate preparedness and response, and give greater priority to non-structural measures over structural measures alone.

Throughout most of the past decade, the situations and disasters that have occurred illustrate how policies for disaster risk governance and reduction have been unsuccessful in preventing or mitigating negative impacts. The areas frequently affected by disasters such as flooding and mudslides continue to lack concrete protective measures and other measures to reduce the severity of such disasters. Basically, disaster risk governance policies are area-based policies. Therefore, integration for the purpose of implementing work needs to happen in risk-prone areas under provincial and local administrations. There are difficulties in collaborating in area-based cross-jurisdictional operations and among different administrative agencies. The joint committees at the provincial level are not as functional as the committee on the national level. These committees cannot pool resources for collaboration since most of the budget allocated for area-level operations is function-based for the provincial offices that represent central departments at the area level with pre-determined activities and expenditure lists. This portion of the aforementioned area-based budgets is earmarked for overall provincial development and other economic problems rather than disaster risk governance.

During states of emergency, response operations are multi-agency based. All relevant agencies, although trained by various experts and practitioners for the past 10 years, are still unclear about how to coordinate an emergency response effectively. The conceptualization and implementation of many international standard operating procedures, such as incident command systems (ICS), emergency operation center management (EOC), emergency support functions (ESF), and incident management assistance teams (IMAT) are not coherent or well executed. Due to the bureaucratic nature of Thailand's departmentalization, relevant agencies operate within their own core networks, with their own resources, and under their own Disaster-related Acts, which obstruct the integrated collaboration of the taskforces of multiple agencies. Besides, politicians at all levels are more likely to intervene in decision making processes regarding alternatives to counter-measures against disaster risks, preventing timely execution. This intervention obstructs the use of data, knowledge, and methodologies from technical personnel and local authorities who are more familiar with the context of individual areas to make informed decisions. The Thai government must turn its attention and make a strong effort to design and develop official Standard Operating Procedures (SOPs) for all tasks and operations needed for all relevant agencies so that the multi-agency coordination tasks are systematized and need less intervention.

On the one hand, collaborative disaster risk governance relies significantly on effective and efficient collective action as well as the presence of a directive single command. Incident Command Systems and Multi-Agency Coordination are the two integrated operation systems that form the foundation of disaster response. On the other hand, integrated big data systems of shared risk information for strategic decision support must be built into ICS and MAC operations. Thailand lacks both integrated systems and the data quality necessary for risk assessment and disaster risk governance, regardless of collective risk prevention and mitigation. Therefore, Thailand also has an urgent need to establish joint risk information integrated systems to be utilized to make such strategic and informed decisions.

Lastly, regarding Thailand's safety culture, although Thai agencies have learned to work together and explore new solutions, the mandatory functions of each agency still means they generally work alone. Besides, political conflict also leads to less acceptance of collaborative networks of operations and shared information. At the same time, communities at all levels need to change the way disaster risks are perceived as well as how they mitigate and reduce disaster risks as situations change. With a strong commitment to use risk-driven perception and communicate frequently about shared operations, preparedness through early warning systems, evacuation exercises, and training can be executed effectively. A cohesive network of well-trained and capable agencies and communities help facilitate and manage disasters effectively and efficiently.

## References

Ansell, C., and Gash, A. (2012). Collaborative Governance: Theory and Practice. Published by Oxford University Press on behalf of the *Journal of Public Administration Research and Theory*, Inc.

Axelrod, R., & Cohen, M. D. (1999). *Harnessing Complexity: Organizational Implications of a Scientific Frontier*. New York: The Free Press.

Bardach, E. (1998). *Getting Agencies to Work Together: The Practice and Theory of Managerial Craftsmanship*. Washington, D.C.: Brookings Institution.

Boin, Comfort and Demchack. (2010). *Designing Resilience*. Pittsburgh, University of Pittsburgh Press.

________. (2010). *Strategic National Action Plan for Disaster Risk Reduction* (2010–2019). Bangkok, Government of Thailand.

________. (2014). *Glossary of Terms in Disaster Risk Management*. Bangkok, Government of Thailand.

________. (2015). *National Disaster Prevention and Mitigation Plan 2015*. Bangkok, Government of Thailand.

Graber, D. A. (2003). *The Gower of Communication: Managing Information in Public Organizations*. Washington, D.C.: CQ Press.

Kamolvej, Tavida. (2010). Public Policy in the Context of Governance. In Public Governance: *Public Administration in the 21st Century*, Amporn Tamronglak (Ed.). Bangkok, Textbooks and Printed Materials Project, Faculty of Political Science, Thammasat University, 62-84.

________. (2013). Look for an Incident Action Plan through Thailand's Provincial Action Plans for Disaster Management. *Journal of Political Science*, 34(2), May-August 2013. Bangkok, Politics and Government College, Mahasarakram University.

________. (2014). How has Thailand Disaster Management Improved from the 2004 Tsunami to the Flood of 2011? *Journal of Politics*, Vol. 2, October 2013-February 2014. Bangkok, Politics and Government College, Mahasarakram University.

________. (2014). Or is the Centre for flood Relief meaningless in managing the 2011 floods? *Journal of Political Science*, 35(2), May-August 2014. Bangkok, Politics and Government College, Mahasarakram University.

________. (2015). Earthquake in Nepal and Thailand's Medical and Public Health Assistance. *Political Science*, 1(2), July-December 2015. Bangkok, Politics and

Government College, Mahasarakram University.

Kettl, D. F. (2002). *The Transformation of Governance: Public Administration for the Twenty-first Century America*. Baltimore, MD: Johns Hopkins University Press.

Luangprapat, Wasan. (2010). Public Governance and Intergovernmental Relation. *Public Governance: Public Administration in the 21st Century*, Amporn Tamronglak (Ed.). Bangkok, Textbooks and Printed Materials Project, Faculty of Political Science, Thammasat University, 62-84.

_________. (2013). Public Sector Reform in Thailand: 15 Years of Changes within Thai Politico-Administrative Institutions, 1992-2006. *Journal of Political Science*, 34(2), 175-249. Bangkok, Thammasat University.

March, James G., and Johan P. Olsen. (1989). *Rediscovering Institutions: The Organizational Basis of Politics*. New York, Free Press.

Mektrairat, Nakharin, Wasan Luangprapat, and Panrat Nimtalung. (2010). The Modification of Institutional Mechanisms for Strengthening Capabilities in Child-related Works of Local Administrative Organisations. Bangkok, UNICEF, 2010.

Pfeffer, J. (1992). *Managing with Power: Politics and influence in organizations*. Boston, MA: Harvard Business School Press.

Provan, K. G., & Milward, H. B. (2001). Do networks really work? A framework for evaluating public sector organizational networks. *Public Administration Review*, 61(4), 414-423.

Radin, et al. (1996). *New Governance for Rural America: Creating Intergovernmental Partnership*. Lawrence, KS: University Press of Kansas.

Salamon, L. M. (Ed.). (2002). *The Tools of Government: A Guide to the New Governance*. New York: Oxford University Press.

Samudavanija, Chai-Anan. (2002). *Thailand: State-Building, Democracy and Globalization*, Bangkok, IPPS.

Sylves, Richard. (2008). *Disaster Policy and Politics*. Washington, D.C.: CQ Press.

Tamronglak, Amporn (Ed.). (2010). *Administration in the 21st Century*. Bangkok, Textbooks and Printed Materials Project, Faculty of Political Science, Thammasat University, 62-84.

United Nations. (2005). Hyogo Framework for Action (HFA) 2005-2015. Kobe, World Conference on Disaster Risk Reduction.

United Nations for Disaster Risk Reduction (UNISDR). (2015). Expert Session Report on Sendai Framework for Disaster Risk Reduction: Terminology and Indicators. Geneva.

# Index

# Biography

### Sook Jong Lee

Sook Jong Lee is Professor of Graduate School of Governance at Sungkyunkwan University and directs the East Asia Collaboration Center. She created the Asian Democracy Research Network in 2015 for the collaborative studies on Asian democracy. Her research interests include global governance, democracy, NGOs, and citizen participation. In addition to numerous articles, her recent book publications include Populism in Asian Democracies (eds. forthcoming 2020), *Transforming Global Governance with Middle Power Diplomacy* (ed. 2016), *Keys to Successful Presidency in South Korea* (ed. 2013 and 2016), *Public Diplomacy and Soft Power in East Asia* (eds. 2011). Dr. Lee received her Ph.D. in sociology from Harvard University.

### Rosa Minhyo Cho

Rosa Minhyo Cho is Professor of the Graduate School of Governance at Sungkyunkwan University and has served as the Director of Secretariat of the Asian Association for Public Administration since 2018. Before coming to SKKU, she was an assistant professor at Brown University in the Department of Education and Public Policy between 2006 and 2012. Her recent research interests include evaluating the various effects of social welfare policy, education policy, immigrant policy, and labor policy using large-scale quantitative datasets. Dr. Cho received her Ph.D. in the Harris School of Public Policy from the University of Chicago in 2006.

### Hyung Jun Park

Hyung Jun Park is Professor of department of public administration and graduate school of governance at Sungkunkwan University in Korea and directs 'Governance and Policy Evaluation Institution.' He is General Director of Asia Group of Public Administration and Asia Pacific Public Policy Network. He received best academic paper award from ASPA in 2009. His research on policy analysis, policy network, collaborative governance, government innovation, local governance, regulatory policies, disaster management and other many PA as well public policy topics have been published in many SSCI International journals including *Public Administration Review* and Korean journals. He received his Ph.D. in Askew school from the Florida State University.

### Sung Min Park

Sung Min Park is Professor in the Department of Public Administration and Graduate School of Governance at Sungkyunkwan University, as well as is currently serving as an adjunct professor at the National Human Resource Development Institute, Seoul, Korea. He received Ph.D. in public administration from School of Public and International Affairs at the University of Georgia. He has held academic appointments as an assistant professor at the Greenspun School of Environmental and Public Affairs, University of Nevada, Las Vegas. He has also served as a managing editor of the *International Review of Public Administration* and a reviewer to various SSCI/SCOPUS journals on public administration, management, and governance.

### Azwar Abubakar

Azwar Abubakar is former Minister of Administrative Reform Republic Indonesia (2011~2014). He passionately involved in conducting policy on public sector reform, in particular the issues of corruption eradication in public sector. The law that was successfully passed during His tenure are Law on Civil Service and Law on Government Administration. His research interest includes corruption eradication, civil service management and performance management. He received doctoral degree in Public Administration from Universitas Indonesia.

### Alex B. Brillantes Jr.

Alex B. Brillantes Jr. is Professor and former Dean of the University of the Philippines National College of Public Administration, and is President of the Asian Association for Public Administration. He was Executive Director of the Local Government Academy of the Department of Interior and Local Government, and Commissioner (Deputy Minister) of the Commission on Higher Education. He has published in local and international journals and has written three books, *Dictatorship and Martial Law, The Philippine Presidency* and *Innovations and Excellence in Local Governance*. Dr. Brillantes received his Ph.D. in Political Science from the University of Hawaii.

### Bin Chen

Bin Chen is Associate Professor in the Austin W. Marxe School of Public and International Affairs at Baruch College, a doctoral faculty at Graduate Center, The City University of New York and a research fellow with China Institute for Urban Governance, Shanghai Jiaotong University. He studies cross-sectoral and interorganizational collaboration, government-nonprofit relations, regional networked governance, and comparative public administration and policy. His research methods include social network analysis (SNA) and qualitative comparative analysis (QCA).

### Zitao Chen

Zitao Chen is a Ph.D. student of School of International and Public Affairs at Shanghai Jiao Tong University. His research interests include public policy analysis and government performance management.

### Minhyuk Cho

Minhyuk Cho is a Ph.D. candidate of Graduate School of Governance at Sungkyunkwan University and Research fellow of institute of Governance & Policy Evaluation. His research interests include policy evaluation, local governance, risk perception, public relations. His recent publications include *Grounded Theory Approach to Limitation of Public-private Partnership: Focused on Immigrant Support Policy* (2019), *The Role of Non-governmental Organizations in Refugee and Immigrant Integration: A Qualitative Exploratory Study of Seoul, South Korea* (2019).

### Tavida Kamolvej

Tavida Kamolvej is currently Dean of School of Political Science, Thammasat University, Thailand. Her academic expertise and research interests emphasize Disaster Management, Social Network Analysis, Research Methodology and Public Policy. In her field of expertise, Dr. Tavida also serves as disaster management advisor to the Department of Disaster Prevention and Mitigation, Ministry of Interior, and the strategic advisor to the Bangkok Metropolitan Authority (BMA), Thailand. At the international level, Dr. Tavida used to be communication and coordination instructor for the US State Department Senior Crisis Management Seminar Program in collaboration with American University, Washington, D.C. USA. She also served as Disaster Management Consultant to the Pacific Disaster Center, Hawaii, USA, and to UNESCO/IOC in Community Resilience and Education for Disaster and Risk Management Program.

### Yanqiu Kan

Yanqiu Kan received her master's degree from University of Electronic Science and Technology of China. She is a doctoral student majoring in urban development and management in Zhouenlai School of government, Nankai University. Her main research areas include urban governance and planning, regional cooperation and development. In recent years, she has published articles on regional cooperation and urban governance in some Chinese journals, such as *Journal of Public Administration*, *Public Administration and Policy Review*, *Journal of Gansu Administration Institute*, *Journal of Beijing Administration Institute* and *Fudan Public Administration Review*.

### Masao Kikuchi

Masao Kikuchi is Professor of Public Policy and Management in Department of Public Management, School of Business Administration, at Meiji University in Tokyo, Japan. His research interests include comparative local governance and crisis management in Asian region. He has published articles in *Public Administration Review*, *Environment Policy and Governance*, and others. He also contributed chapters in *Handbook of Public Administration in East Asia*, *International Handbook on Civil Service Systems*, *Global Encyclopedia of Public Administration, Public Policy and Governance*, and others. Dr. Kikuchi received his Ph.D. in political science from Meiji University.

### Bomi Kim

Bomi Kim is manager of Loan & Deposit Planning Dept. at Korea Development Bank. She assesses and manages environmental and social risk in projects. Her research interests include public policy and civil society with an emphasis on citizen participation, conflict and participation systems. Previously, she was a researcher at Gyeonggi Research Institute, Korea Environment Institute, East Asia Institute and East Asia Collaboration Center at Sungkyunkwan University. Her recent publications include "*Deliberative Democracy, Collaborative Governance, Conflict Management, Social Problems, Inclusive Policies Case Studies*" (2019), "*Social Responsibility, Social Corporation*" (2015). Dr. Kim received her Ph.D. in public administration from Sungkyunkwan University.

### Youhyun Lee

Youhyun Lee is Assistant Professor at Hannam University. Her research interest includes energy, environment, data and comparative analysis. Prior to the current role, she was legislative researcher at National Assembly of Korea, researcher at East Asia Collaboration Center in Sungkyunkwan University. She holds a Ph.D. degree in Legal Science from the University of Paris 1 Panthéon-Sorbonne (Paris, France).

**Jessica Yu-Wen Lin**

Jessica Yu-Wen Lin is Adjunct Assistant Professor in the Department of Public Policy and Administration, National Chi Nan University, Taiwan and received her Ph.D. in public administration in the same department in 2015. Her research interests include Public Service Motivation, intergovernmental relations, metropolitan governance, and public management.

**Qianqian Liu**

Qianqian Liu is Research Associate at researcher Center for Reform, Innovation, and Governance at Shanghai Jiao Tong University. She received her master's degree from School of International and Public Affairs at Shanghai Jiao Tong University. Her research interests include collaborative governance and government performance management.

**Wasan Luangprapat**

Wasan Luangprapat is currently the Director of Sanya Dharmasakti Institute for Democracy and Assistant Professor at School of Political Sciences, Thammasat University, Thaiand. He received his Doctor of Political Science from Graduate School of International Cooperation Studies (GSICS), Kobe University, Japan. His academic expertise and research interest focus on Bureaucratic Reform, Local Governance, Decentralization, and Collaborative Governance. In his field of expertise, Dr. Wasan also serves as the director of Promotion and Coordination of Research Projects for Local Self-Government Center (PCRP), Thailand Research Fund, to both distributing fund to research on strengthening decentralization and local governance and also creating and initiating a network of local researchers around Thailand.

**Jie Ma**

Jie Ma is Associate Professor in the School of Management and Economics, University of Electronic Science and Technology of China. Her research and teaching interests are regional economics and policy analysis, water resources governance, and network governance. She has been a principal investigator on two National Science Foundation of China research grants as well as grant awards from local governments. Her work appears in the *Journal of Public Management* and *Fudan Public Administration Review*.

### Windy Thi-Ngoc-Minh Phan

Windy Thi-Ngoc-Minh Phan is a Ph.D. Student in the Department of Public Policy and Administration, National Chi Nan University, Taiwan. Her research interests include public service motivation, public administration development, and the applications of Q methodology in politics.

### Eko Prasojo

Eko Prasojo is Professor of Public Administration and Dean of Faculty of Administrative Science Universitas Indonesia. He was vice Minister of Administrative Reform Republic of Indonesia (2011~2014). He is currently the President of Asian Group for Public Administration and the Vice President of Asian Association for Public Administration. His areas of expertise are administrative reform, public policy, comparative public administration, decentralization and civil service management. Among his recent publications are "Intergovernmental Strategies Advancing Performance Management Use (https://doi.org/10.1080/15309576.2020.1736588) and "The Challenge of Reforming big bureaucracy in Indonesia" (https://doi.org/10.1080/01442872.2019.1708301). He received the Braibant Award 2019 from International Institute of Administrative Sciences.

### Zhao Qin

Zhao Qin is a Ph.D. candidate of School of International and Public Affairs at Shanghai Jiao Tong University. His research interests include collaborative governance.

### Karl Emmanuel V. Ruiz

Karl Emmanuel V. Ruiz graduated with a degree of Bachelor of Library and Information Science (BLIS) in the University of Santo Tomas in 2015 (Manila, Philippines), with distinction as a Benavides Outstanding Achievement awardee. He garnered the top 1 rank in the national licensure examination for librarians in the Philippines in 2016. He is a librarian at the University of the Philippines National College of Public Administration and Governance and currently taking up Master of Library and Information Science in the School of Library and Information Studies, University of the Philippines.

### Milan Tung-Wen Sun

Milan Tung-Wen Sun is Distinguished Professor in the Department of Public Policy and Administration, National Chi Nan University, Taiwan. His research interests include intergovernmental relations, local and metropolitan governance, and the applications of Q methodology. In addition to numerous articles, he has published *From Authoritarian Gov-*

*ernment to Democratic Governance* (2003, in Chinese); co-edited *Trust and Governance Institutions: Asian Experiences* (2012), *GIS and Public Administration* (2007, in Chinese), and *Intergovernmental Relations* (2001 and 2004, in Chinese). Dr. Sun received his Ph.D. in political science from Kent State University, Ohio, USA.

### Liming Suo

Liming Suo is Professor at Zhou Enlai School of Government and Joint Research Center of Chinese Government and Policy, Nankai University, China. His research and teaching interests are interlocal collaboration, network governance, cyberspace governance and local sustainable development. He has been a principal investigator on two National Science Foundation research grants as well as grant awards from local governments. His work appears in *Public Administration Review, State and Local Government Review.*

### Reginald G. Ugaddan

Reginald G. Ugaddan is Assistant Professor, College Secretary and Director of the Center for Public Administration and Governance Education at the National College of Public Administration and Governance of the University of the Philippines Diliman. He teaches courses in research methods, organization studies, and local government and urban affairs. His specializations include human resource management in the public sector, public management, public sector leadership, organizational behavior, disaster management, e-Government, international and local governance, and democracy. Dr. Ugaddan received his Ph.D. in public administration from Sungkyunkwan University, Seoul, Korea.

### Jiannan Wu

Jiannan Wu is Distinguished Professor, Executive Vice Director of China Institute for Urban Governance, and Director of Center for Reform, Innovation, and Governance at Shanghai Jiao Tong University. His research interests include urban governance and environmental policy. He has served as General Secretary of Asian Association of Public Administration since 2018.

### Na Gyeom Yang

Na Gyeom Yang is a master's student of Graduate School of Governance at Sungkyunkwan University. She worked as a researcher at the East Asia Center for Collaboration (EACC) and the Research Center for Public Human Resource Development (RCPHRD) from 2018, conducting significant research projects probing and analyzing the patterns of social conflicts and conflict resolution mechanisms among six Asian countries.

Her research interests include behavioral public administration, e.g., a way of understanding how such factors as gender and social status affect people's preferences for policy topics.

### Jeong Ho Yoo

Jeong Ho Yoo is a Ph.D. candidate of the Graduate School of Governance and a researcher of the Institute of Governance and Policy Evaluation at Sungkyunkwan University. And he has served as the executive secretary of the Asian Association for Public Administration since 2018. His recent research interests include evaluating the various effects of social welfare policy, education policy as well as citizen participation, training of public officials. Mr. Yoo received his master's degree in the Graduate School of Governance from Sungkyunkwan University in 2015.